Basic
Speech

Jon Eisenson

San Francisco State University

Paul H. Boase

Ohio University

Basic Speech

Third Edition

Macmillan Publishing Co., Inc.

New York

Collier Macmillan Publishers

London

Macmillan Publishing Co., Inc.
866 Third Avenue
New York, New York 10022

Collier-Macmillan Canada, Ltd.

Library of Congress Cataloging in Publication Data

Eisenson, Jon, (date)
  Basic speech.

  Includes bibliographies and index.
  1. Speech. 2. Public speaking. 3. English
language—Phonetics. I. Boase, Paul H., joint author.
II. Title.
PN4121.E4   1975   808.5   74-6631
ISBN 0-02-331870-8

Printing: 1 2 3 4 5 6 7 8   Year: 5 6 7 8 9 0

Preface

Everybody talks about communication. Some understand the theories and the process. Only a few manage to master the speech skills, those essential ingredients in every effective communication experience. Like those in the classic Negro spiritual who may "talk" about Heaven, but "ain't goin' there," many who talk about communication, who even understand the fundamental principles, may fail to reach that Promised Land. We hope through this revised edition of *Basic Speech* to help students, faced with daily communication problems, to join in an on-going and continuous quest for excellence in speaking and listening. As an intellectually curious adult, the student will want to learn as much as possible about communication through speech—those skills and characteristics that set the human race apart from all other living beings.

The primary objective—effective communication

Although this book has many objectives, our primary aim is to assist and to challenge the student to improve proficiency in speech communication, both in speaking and in listening. Communication begins within the individual who generates through visible and/or vocal signs and symbols the ideas, concepts, and feelings that may in turn excite an appropriate response from a receiver. The listener may be only one person, a small formal or informal group, or an audience of two hundred or two hundred million sitting in front of radios or television sets. We shall study the speech symbols intensively, examining the scientific, physical, and psychological bases of the speech components—thought, language, action, and voice. Particular attention will focus on the means of improving vocal quality and of achieving an acceptable standard of pronunciation. This approach will include a study of voice production, a rather detailed consideration of the sounds of American-English speech, and the correlation of theory with practice materials in both voice and articulation.

Communication theory

Throughout the text, a discussion of *communication theory*, as free as possible from technical terminology, provides a foundation to assist students in developing the necessary speech skills, whether in the one-to-one exchange, the small group encounter, the public speaking situation, or for radio and television. Wherever possible, a body of information is presented to the student to provide a basis of knowledge for a mode of communicative behavior. Thus, theoretical concepts and practical experience are freely intermixed, enabling the student to learn the *what* and *why* as well as the *how* of the many forms of speech communication, i.e., public speaking, interpersonal communication, discussion, debate, and oral reading.

Ethical responsibilities and free expression

In our treatment of speech communication as a practical art, we have not lost sight of the ethical and moral responsibilities we all share alike as speakers and listeners. Private and public speech, discussion and debate, are more than mere verbal persuasion; they are the tools that determine the nature and destiny of a free society. The ultimate objective of this book is to assist the student in becoming not only an adequate speaker but also an adequate personality with a heightened ability to make intelligent, moral choices. With this in mind the relationships between speech and personality and the way in which a well-adjusted person deals with ideas, meanings, and meaningful relationships provide a basic philosophy for the text.

Flexibility

Because of the variety of topics treated, *Basic Speech* offers the student and the instructor widely different avenues for the study of communication. With its scientific orientation toward speech improvement, the text also lends itself to the public speaking course, the small group, the interpersonal communication approach, or the more eclectic fundamentals of a speech program. The abundance of exercise materials in voice and diction and the selections for oral reading provide additional stimulation for use in listening laboratories and for radio and television studios.

The many adjustments in the new edition reflect the authors' reliance on the advice and assistance of our colleagues and students and for their willingness to share their insights and ideas with us. Particular thanks are due to Professors Raymond C. Beaty, Ted J. Foster, John H. Timmis, Ray E. Wagner, Carl H. Weaver, and Richard F. Whitman. The responsibility for the sins of omission and commission is, of course, ours.

J. E.
P. H. B.

Contents

Illustrations

Chapter 1

Speech: Nature & Functions

WHAT IS SPEECH?

Speech is a form of behavior capable of evoking responses from somebody. The somebody may include oneself or another person. The nature of the meaningful response may vary from the broad and crude to the precise and highly specific. To get meaningful responses through speech, linguistic symbols (words) are usually employed. Spoken words may be *audible* or *visible*. Ordinarily we have audible symbols in mind when we say that we speak. Audible words are produced by the actions of the lips, the tongue, the teeth, the palate, and the vocal mechanism. We also produce *visible symbols*, which are in many ways equivalent to words, through the actions of the face, hands, arms, shoulders, and occasionally other parts of the body. These actions, if readily identified, constitute visible symbols known as *gestures*.

To sum up, speech is a method of getting meaningful responses through the use of audible words and gestures produced by the activity of the human body. Words and/or gestures are known as *speech symbols*.

If we were to stop with this definition, our concept of speech would be limited. The significance of speech cannot be appreciated unless we know something about speakers and listeners *as persons*. If we have such understanding and appreciation, we can broaden our concept so that we may look upon speech as a complex function that is at once a manifestation of attitude, purpose, feelings, and thoughts. This manifestation is presented in a symbol (language) code and in a manner that is culturally determined yet individually formulated and expressed. Thus, we speak a variety of English, but the specific way we cast our thoughts, formulate our sentences, and utter our words are individualized, so that we can often be identified by how we say what we think and feel. We do not have to be linguistic detectives to recognize the prominent statesmen, politicians, entertainers, or other public figures. The brothers Kennedy, though remarkably alike in some aspects of their diction and voice, were nevertheless significantly different and readily identifiable. They shared a common dialect, and perhaps some special family characteristics in manner of speaking, yet each had his own style, his own way of turning a phrase and giving emphasis to a point. So, to coin a word, each had

1

his own "individuolect." Through the individuolect, each of us speaks for, of, and about himself.

Speech is the way of life for man. What we are, what we do, and what we decide to do are accomplished through speech. Through the medium of speech we form and reveal our attitudes, our personalities, and our purposes in life; we learn how others feel and think and we indicate our own thoughts and feelings. Through speech, or indirectly through written language which records speech, we gain and give meaning to our existence. Through these devices we are able, in some measure, to modify and control our environment.

SPEECH SYMBOLS AND SPEECH PURPOSES

The symbols we use in speech and the manner in which we use them depends pretty much on the particular purpose we have in speaking. The purpose of our speaking may be determined by the response we seek. If we want an intellectual response, if we want to know how our listener is thinking, symbol use must be precise. We must then choose our words with care and make certain that our words not only convey our own thoughts, but are of the kind that are likely to induce and evoke thinking rather than feeling in others. By manner of speaking as well as by choice of words, thinking should be elicited. On the other hand, if we want a reaction of a nonintellectual nature, the precise choice of words may not be so important as the manner in which the words are presented. This point will become clear in our consideration of the various purposes of speech.

Expression

When speech is used merely as emotional expression, the words themselves have little significance. In fact, it is possible to get along without words and still be engaged in emotional expression. A sigh may be expressive beyond words, and crying requires only sobbed sounds. What matters in emotional expressions is the tone and manner in which the sounds are produced. Swearing, for example, isn't a matter of what you say but rather of how you say it. The tone is far more important than the words. Mark Twain was aware of this point; his wife, it seems, was not. Once, according to the story, the wife determined to cure her author-husband of his habit of swearing. The habit was firmly established and went back to the days when Mark Twain piloted a steamboat on the Mississippi. Mrs. Mark Twain, as an object lesson in the horrors of swearing, rebuked her husband with a selection of his favorite swear words. When she was finished, Mark Twain regarded his wife with sympathetic understanding, and then calmly informed her, "Woman, you know the words, but you don't know the music."

Expressive speech is not limited to emotional outbursts. Some of us talk for the sake of hearing ourselves make sounds. Small children talk to themselves even though other persons are near them. Adults sometimes talk to themselves when alone. A self-conscious adult may prefer talking to an animal pet who is incapable of responding to anything but the voice of the speaker. Grown women as well as children talk to stuffed dolls; full-grown men who think that talking to stuffed dolls or to animal pets is perfectly silly sometimes make queer sounds at uncomprehending infants. We speak to people who don't understand us, and we indulge in nonsense talk with children and adults whose understanding of us includes tolerant acceptance of our shortcomings. Occasionally we may even go on a talking jag and become almost intoxicated with the exhilarating effect of our verbal effusions. Because of social pressures, we usually pretend to be talking to somebody. Actually we are talking in the physical presence of somebody rather than to somebody. In most of these situations we talk for the sheer pleasure of the activity. Producing a mouthful of sounds can be fun. If the sounds are set to music, the pleasure may be heightened. How else can we account for many of the words and most of the refrains of our old English ballads and madrigals. For example, a madrigal by Thomas Nashe (1567–1601) called "Spring, the Sweet Spring" ends with:

> Cuckoo, jug-jug, pu-wee, to-witta-woo!
> Spring, the sweet spring.

Shakespeare ends his *Twelfth Night* with a song that includes a once uttered and four times repeated line:

> With hey, ho, the wind and the rain.

Lewis Carroll used even fewer recognizable word forms for his "Jabberwocky," which opens with the telling lines:

> 'Twas brillig, and the slithy toves
> Did gyre and gimble in the wabe;
> All mimsy were the borogoves
> And the mome raths outgrabe.

However much some of us may disparage our contemporary writers of popular songs, we should appreciate that Shakespeare, the writers of sea chanties, and the writers of songs for adolescents may be kindred in respect to the motives for "creating" a line such as, "With a hey nonny-nonny and a ha-cha-cha."[1]

[1] It is likely that apparent verbal nonsense may always have had denotative meaning for persons who are members of an in-group or a special culture. So, song lyrics that were popular in the late 1960s and early 1970s had considerably more specific (denotative) meanings for persons identified as hippies and for those in the so-called

Many alleged conversations fall in the category of expressive speech engaged in for the pleasure of talking. The tête-à-têtes of cocktail parties or tea parties are really monologues with one speaker waiting for an opportune moment to break in when a pause stops the verbal flow of the other. The pause may have been generated by the need to stop for breath or to quench thirst with whatever thirst quencher that was appropriate for the occasion. Whatever the cause, the second speaker seizes upon the opportunity and begins another monologue. In time, an arising need may permit the tables to be turned and the first of the interrupted monologues may again be resumed or a new one undertaken.

Social gesture

When speech is used for the purpose of social gesture, individual words are not greatly significant. In fact, it is not even important that all the words we use should be precisely understood. It is only important that in a given social situation we say something that sounds right for the situation. Occasionally the words may be quite inappropriate, except that there is little likelihood that anyone will pay much attention to them. The wag who went through a long receiving line and who mumbled at each of the notables to whom he was introduced, "I've just murdered my wife, and I'm glad to meet you," created no stir. It was assumed that he said something appropriate, something along the lines of "How do you do, I'm very happy to know you." That something very different was said went entirely unnoticed because the manner of speaking, if not the actual speech content, was appropriate to the social situation.

Most greetings between persons who are acquainted with one another fall in the category of social-gesture speech. Here, for example, we have an item of conversation between two men who have known each other for many years.

> BILL: Hi, Joe, what you been doing?
> JOE: Good to see you Bill, what do you know?
> BILL: Nothing much. Just kicking around.
> JOE: How's the wife and kids?
> BILL: Just fine, Joe. Just fine. Yours?
> JOE: No complaints.
> BILL: See you around. Give my best to Mary.
> JOE: Thanks, fellah. Keep it going.
> BILL: Right on, Joe. Right on.

Now, what does such an interchange mean? Most likely not what any literal interpretation of the utterances might imply. Joe was not really

---

drug culture. We venture that many nonsense verses had comparable semantic histories at the time and for the persons for whom they were intended.

expected to tell Bill what he was doing at any unspecified time. Nor was Bill expected to give any detailed account of what he knew. Neither is there any suggestion that Bill offended Joe by ignoring his question and responding instead by a statement that he was "kicking around." Just what Joe wanted to have Bill "keep going" will remain a mystery, as will Bill's apparent direction for Joe to go "Right on."

When speech is employed as social gesture, the individual words and even isolated sentences have little specific intellectual significance. Taken together, the words and the sentences assume a vague significance. In the conversation cited above, the speakers felt that the situation required more than a simple "Hello," or a smile, or a nod of the head. The elaboration of the greeting was an indication that something more needed to be said. Beyond the significance of "Hello" (the "Hi, Joe"), all the rest was talk. But it is the kind of talk out of which the amenities of civilized society are made. Social-gesture speech may be meaningless if we expect that each spoken word be weighted with significance. But social speech seldom makes such demands. What is demanded is a pattern of words accompanied by a voice that sounds amiable. If the reaction to the pattern is friendly, the purpose of social-gesture speech is served. People who know one another expect to converse when they meet. What is said, in terms of the literal significance of words, is usually of little or no importance. So, at best, we are either oblivious, or at worst, only marginally aware of the number of times a speaker may say "you know" or "I mean" or any other term used as substitutes for commas or pauses in a verbal interchange.

Speech to allay fear

We often talk when we feel afraid in the hope that we can talk ourselves out of being afraid. Such talk may be equated to "whistling in the dark." The superstition of whistling as one goes by a graveyard at night probably has its origin in the unconcious hope that the graveyard spirits will interpret whistling as unconcern and not molest the whistler who, by the very act of his whistling, is supposedly presenting audible evidence of his bravery. Some of us pretend to be talking to someone else when entering a dark house or a dark room of the house. Such talk has a dual function. It is expressive in that it is a manifestation of fear. At the same time the talk is supposed to impress a possible lurker in the dark with the idea that the speaker is not alone and that more than one person will have to be contended with in the event of trouble.

We sometimes use speech in a social situation in order to prevent or allay hostility. This is exemplified in our behavior when we approach or are approached by an ominous-looking stranger. We talk to him—what we say is of little moment—"to show him that we are not afraid." The stranger may answer us for the very same reason. Speech may be very useful in talking ourselves out of fear.

Specific responses

Speech reaches its highest level of capability when we use it to convey a specific idea in order to get a specific response. The ability to differentiate his ideas and to distinguish between concepts of objects nearly alike belongs to man alone. This ability is employed usually for obtaining satisfaction of wants and needs, for getting what we like, and putting off what we don't like or don't want. We may use this ability to convey our thoughts or to conceal them by communicating ideas we wish the listener to have, even though we may not hold them ourselves.

Our thoughts as well as our tastes can be presented through carefully chosen words. Most of us, however, are not nearly so certain about what we think as we are about what we want in the way of indulging our tastes. That is why we are much more expert in ordering our meals than we are in putting our thoughts in order. How to do something about making our ideas specific and clear will be considered in a later chapter.

Speech responses

When we speak we get responses from one or more persons. One of these persons is always the speaker himself. We listen to our own words as we talk. If they sound satisfactory, we continue in our intended way. If we find ourselves not saying what we had in mind, we change our words and our thoughts, or expand them, or present the same words with a different emphasis. Usually the responses we obtain from our listener or listeners give us added information about the adequacy of our speech.

Audience responses

When we address a group of persons who constitute an audience we do not usually get the same kind of response as when we talk to a few people or to one person in a conversation. In a conversation we get an almost immediate reaction, even if it is only a dead silence. By what is said or not said, we are able to judge the effectiveness of our speech. If we try to induce someone into a way of thinking, we try to get some response that tells us how successful we are in our purpose. When we talk to a large group, no such immediate verbal judgment is possible. Except when the group escapes our control, or when its members become unsocial enough to boo or walk out, it takes some time to get a verbal reaction to a speech. In fact, unless individual persons of the group can be questioned, the speaker may never know precisely how his listeners reacted.

There are, of course, other significant responses a speaker gets from his listeners. Failure to elicit anticipated smiles or laughter and physical movements indicating tension, boredom, or annoyance are evidence of unfavorable response when these are not desired by the speaker. On the other hand, activity such as laughter or applause in the "proper places" and postures and facial expressions reflective of attentive listening give the speaker important information about how the listeners are going along with him.

Thinking

Much, probably most, of our speaking takes place with only ourselves as significant reactors. Such a situation exists whenever we talk for the pleasure of talking. More important, however, is the talking that goes on with ourselves when we engage in thinking. We think in symbols, and often in verbal or word symbols. Usually thinking is inner speech. When we are alone we may think by speaking aloud. Even those of us who think in silent speech may not be so silent as is usually supposed. Even for the "silent" thinker, thinking is frequently accompanied by lip movements that fall just short of being suppressed. In fact, a sensitive electrical instrument attached to the throat just below the "Adam's apple" reveals that sounds often are made that are not loud enough to be heard. Frequently thinking is accompanied by subvocal speaking.

SOME BARRIERS TO COMMUNICATION

Although communication is one of the most important of speech purposes, we are not always in a position to be able to communicate the thoughts or feelings in our minds. There are many instances in which it becomes socially necessary to avoid presenting the content of our minds and to offer instead some socially acceptable content. We consider such a response acceptable and not hypocritical, provided that what is said is not intentionally misleading or untruthful.

Social appropriateness

The bachelor by choice who is asked by a fond mother, "Now, what do you think of my baby?" may be forgiven if he answers, with appropriate tone and inflection, "Well, this is a baby." Husbands by the score have learned that it takes courage bordering on foolhardiness to answer with truth the wives' question, "Tell me, what do you *really* think of my new dress?"

There is another kind of situation, more serious in its implications, in which it becomes difficult to communicate what we are actually thinking or feeling. The situation might be typified by the scene of the irate mother confronting her small son with the pieces of a broken picture frame and demanding to know, "Why did you break Aunt Susan's picture?" It would do the small boy little good to explain that he doesn't like Aunt Susan because she's mean and stingy and a little bit on the ugly side and that he was tired of seeing Aunt Susan leer at him every time he entered the living room. Such an explanation, despite its close adherence to the truth, is less likely to be accepted than another the small boy may offer. The boy may have learned that it is socially more acceptable to explain, "I'm sorry; it was an accident. I promise I won't do it again."

Truth, if it is painful to offer and painful to accept, may become a barrier to the communication of our thoughts. As children we learn that frequently our listeners do not want to know how we really think or feel. We learn that it is sometimes socially desirable to reveal only that part of the content of our minds which our listeners are willing to accept. We learn that there are barriers to communication, and that sometimes the desire for comunicative speech must give way to social-gesture speech.

Personal objectives and ulterior motives

There is another barrier to communication less innocent than the desire to be safe rather than courageous, or socially proper rather than completely truthful. The barrier is the desire a speaker may have to persuade his listeners that he believes something he really does not believe. Political speakers may make inconsistent statements, directly or by implication, to different groups of listeners. A political speaker may wish one audience to be left with the impression that he advocates a sharp cut in the cost of living. Another political speaker may favor a high tariff or a low tariff or have no opinion on the question of tariff. He may, however, speak as if he had a definite opinion and appear to have a different opinion according to his particular group of listeners.

Personal and ulterior objectives may become barriers to the communication of our thoughts. Political speakers, however, are not the only ones who, because of personal objectives, encourage listeners to think as they may not themselves really think. Political speakers possibly do so in public situations more often than other speakers. All of us, however, may do so both in our private conversations and in our public pronouncements.

Ambivalence

Not all issues are clear-cut. Sometimes we are asked to take a position on an issue or in regard to a person when we are still ambivalent or undecided or need more time to weigh values and come to a conclusion or to state an opinion. Occasionally we find ourselves in conflict between our feelings and wishes and our intellectual considerations. If we permit ourselves to be forced to a conclusion and express an opinion or an attitude when we are still essentially ambivalent, we do justice to no one. We may in fact feel resentment for, if not actually hostile to, the participant in a discussion or conversation whom we hold responsible for urging us out of a state of indecision. Consciously or unconsciously we have become involved in creating a barrier to communication, at least insofar as these participants are concerned.

Meaning

There is still another barrier to communication for which the speaker has less responsibility. It is the barrier of meaning. Our communication conventionally takes place through word symbols. Unfortunately the symbols do not have precisely the same meaning for all speakers and for all listeners. Differences in meanings result in misunderstanding, and constitute what is probably the most important unintentional barrier to communication. How to overcome this barrier will be considered in Chapter 9, "Speech, Language, and Meaning." Some of the historical and cultural bases for differences in verbal meanings are considered in Chapter 5, "Our Changing Speech Patterns."

Deviant speech

Speech, if deviant, may disturb or interfere with communication. The speech sounds we produce and the way we produce them, the voice and the gestures that accompany the speech sounds, may get in the way of our meanings. Speech sounds that are difficult to identify or that are produced in an atypical manner attract attention to themselves and thus distract from what they are intended to mean. A deficient voice, one that is either not loud enough or too loud, a voice of such quality that it fails to reflect changes in feelings or thought, is likely to become a barrier to communication. Inappropriate intonation may give a foreign flavor to a speaker's utterance, and thus distract from or interfere with ready communication of meaning. Often the effects of the communicative barrier are temporary and last only as long as it takes to permit a listener to "tune in" on the speaker. However, if the speaker's message is brief, the communicative effort may be over before the "tuning in" period and so, unfortunately, the deviance in speech constitutes an effective barrier to communication.

Other barriers

This discussion of barriers to communication is intended to be suggestive rather than conclusive. Other barriers may exist which may deserve no less, or perhaps even more, attention than those briefly mentioned in this limited space. For example, the personal prejudices and special interests of listeners may cause them to read many of their biases into what the speaker is telling them, so that they cannot really understand what is being said. It is also possible that a speaker, becoming aware of the listeners' personal prejudices and interests, may not say what he would really like to say.

Although we cannot control all factors that may interfere with communication, some are definitely subject to modification. These will be considered in greater detail in other parts of this book.

SUMMARY

Speech is a distinctly human accomplishment. Man was able to achieve speech because of his possession of (1) a set of organs capable of being modified and adapted for the function of speech, and (2) a nervous mechanism including a highly developed brain. Through the nervous mechanism man is able to integrate and translate his sensory impressions and experiences into spoken words. Speech may be defined as a method of getting meaningful responses from one or more persons through the use of audible and visible symbols. Spoken words and gestures are speech symbols.

Speech is used effectively when the speaker is readily able to share with and convey to another person or persons his thoughts and his feelings. The effective speaker is one who knows how to modify the manner and content of his speech in keeping with the needs of the speech situation, human and physical-environmental.

The use we make of speech symbols depends on the purpose of our speech according to the individual speaking situation. Speech may be used for the following general purposes: (1) to express feelings and emotions; (2) as social gestures; (3) to prevent or allay hostility; (4) to convey or communicate specific ideas in order to get specific responses. Speech responses come from the speaker himself as well as from the person or persons addressed. When we speak to a single person or a small group of persons in informal situations, responses are almost immediate. Through the evoked responses we are able to evaluate the success of our purpose in speaking. When speaking to large groups in formal situations, verbalized responses are usually delayed, or are not forthcoming, and an evaluation of the success of speech purpose is not immediately possible. In a general way, the nonverbal conventions of audience behavior—applause or lack of it, movement, and evidence of attention or inattention —do inform us of the overall success of our speech purpose. However, unless a question and discussion period follows an address, how successful we are with regard to specific purposes may never be known.

Thinking often is a modified form of speaking in which the speaker and responder is the same person. Thinking is usually accompanied by inner, silent speaking.

We are not always able to communicate the thoughts and feelings we entertain. Barriers to communication include (1) social appropriateness (or inappropriateness), (2) personal and ulterior objectives, (3) failure of words to have the same meaning for speaker and listener, (4) defective speech or voice, and (5) listener prejudices and special interests.

Much of this book will be concerned with the improvement of speech so that (1) barriers to communication of meanings will be minimized, and (2) maximum responsiveness consistent with our legitimate purposes as speakers may be achieved.

QUESTIONS AND EXERCISES

1. (a) What is speech? (b) What is meant by the statement "Speech is behavior reduced to symbols"? (c) What is a speech symbol?

2. (a) Can you think of any purposes of speech not indicated in the text? (b) What is the relationship between our speech purpose and the way in which we use speech symbols?

3. Analyze two or three brief conversations. How much of the speech employed was for the purpose of communicating or obtaining specific information? How much of the speech content was essentially self-expressive?

4. Does speech serve the same purposes for a three-year-old child as it does for a child of thirteen? For you?

5. Are there any significant differences between adult men and women today in their content or purposes of social speaking?

6. What is the first thing you remember saying this morning? What was the speech purpose of what you said?

7. Analyze your speech activities for a full day. What speech purposes did you satisfy? How much of the time were you interested in communicating specific ideas?

8. (a) How can you determine the effectiveness of your speaking? (b) How does the situation differ when talking to one person and when talking to a large group of listeners?

9. In what way may thinking be considered talking? How does thinking differ from talking to another person?

10. Tape-record several conversations in the student center. What speech purposes were served by the conversations? How much of the time was devoted to interchange of information? How much for expression of feelings? For social gesture? For any other purpose?

11. Plan a model situation that you think is conducive to a truly communicative interchange for which you have a specific speech purpose. Was the purpose achieved? If not, what happened to change it? Were there any other purpose or purposes served?

12. What are some barriers to communication? Are all of them surmountable? Are there any you can think of not mentioned in this text?

13. Conjecture what our civilization might be like if the tape recorder had been invented before the printing press.

14. Do you speak as you think and think as you speak? If not, what are the differences?

RECOMMENDED READINGS

CARROLL, J. B. In J. B. CARROLL, and R. O. FREEDLE (eds.). *Language Comprehension and the Acquisition of Knowledge.* New York: John Wiley & Sons, Inc., 1972, chap. 14.

EISENSON, J., J. J. AUER, and J. V. IRWIN. *The Psychology of Communication.* New York: Appleton-Century-Crofts, 1963, chap. 1.

VETTER, J. *Language Behavior and Psychopathology.* Skokie, Ill.: Rand McNally & Co., 1969, chaps. 1 and 2.

WHATMOUGH, J. *Language.* New York: St. Martin's Press, Inc., 1956.

Chapter 2

The Speech Mechanism

ESSENTIALS FOR SOUND PRODUCTION

For the production of sound, three requisites must be satisfied. The first requisite is a body capable of vibration (the vibrator), the second is a force that may be applied to the vibrator, and the third is a medium for transmitting the results of vibration. These requisites are contained in the breathing, or respiratory, mechanism of the human body. The first two will be considered in some detail. Normally the medium for transmission of sound is air.

The vibrator (vocal bands)

The vibrators that satisfy the first essential are the vocal bands.[1] (See Figure 2-1.) These are two very small bands, or folds, of connective tendinous tissue situated in the larynx, or voice box. The larynx is located in the neck between the root of the tongue and the trachea, or windpipe. The outer and largest part of the larynx in the shieldlike cartilage known as the thyroid cartilage. (Actually the thyroid cartilage consists of two catilaginous shields fused together along an anterior line.) We can locate the thyroid cartilage, and so the larynx, by feeling for the "Adam's apple." The "Adam's apple" is at the front apex of the larynx. After locating the "Adam's apple," we can determine the location of the vocal folds by running the index finger and thumb down toward the chest on a straight line from the "Adam's apple" while vocalizing a long *ah*. Vibration should be felt all along the line, but should be greatest about halfway down the line of the thyroid cartilage. That is the place of attachment of the vocal bands to the thyroid cartilage within the larynx. This fact will become clear from an examination of the diagram of the larynx.

The vocal bands are attached to the curved walls of the thyroid cartilage at either side (Figures 2-1 and 2-4). In the midline, they are attached to the angle formed by the fusion of the two halves (shields) of the thyroid cartilage. At the back of the larynx, each of the vocal bands is attached to a pyramidal-shaped cartilage known as the arytenoid. The arytenoids, because of their shape and muscular connections, can be made

---

[1] The terms *vocal bands, vocal folds,* and *vocal cords* will be used synonymously. Other synonymous terms include *vocal lips,* and *laryngeal folds.*

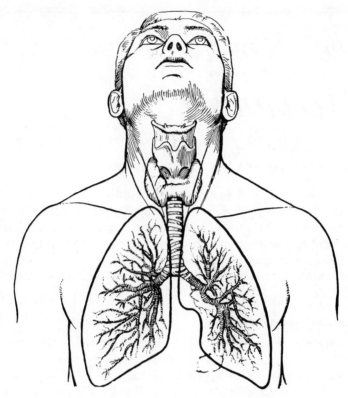

FIGURE 2–1. The larynx, trachea, and lungs.

to move in several ways. They can pivot or rotate, tilt backward, and slide backward and sidewise. Through these movements of the arytenoids, the vocal bands can be brought together or pulled apart. When the vocal bands are brought together, vocalization becomes possible. When the vocal bands are separated, the wide opening between them permits ordinary quiet breathing rather than vocalization. It might be pointed out that for normal vocalization the vocal bands are brought together (approximated, or adducted) so that they are close and parallel (see Figures 2–2 and 2–3).

Voice production

Normal vocalization (phonation) results when the stream of breath under pressure meets the approximated vocal bands and forces them to be "blown" apart. As a consequence the stream of air flowing with relatively high velocity escapes through the glottis (the opening between the vocal bands). The vocal bands, of course, continue to be held together (approximated) at both ends. Vocalization is maintained as a result of a combination of several factors: (1) reduction of pressure beneath the

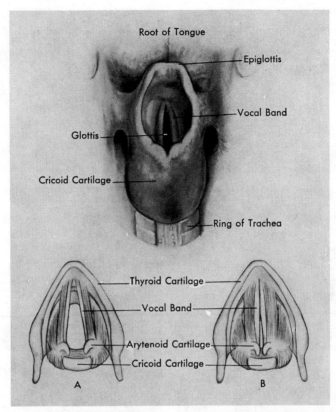

FIGURE 2–2. Diagrammatic representations of the larynx and the vocal bands showing attachments to cartilages of the larynx.
Upper diagram: The larynx seen from above and behind; posterior (dorsal) aspect. *A:* Vocal bands in position for quiet breathing. *B:* Vocal bands in position for vocalization.

bands, (2) reduction of pressure along the sides of the high velocity air stream, (3) the action of the bands themselves in terms of their elasticity. Together, these factors bring about recurrent closures after outward movements of the bands. The effect is maintained vocalization. When the activity or the position of the vocal bands fails to produce a "complete" though momentary interruption in the flow of air, we get a quality of voice that is identified as breathy or hoarse.

The *vocal bands,* as we have indicated, are comparatively small, tough strips of connective tissue,[2] continuous with folds of muscle tissue. As seen from above, the vocal bands appear to be flat folds of muscle that

[2] *The larynx* is lined by *mucous membrane.* On each side of the larynx, the mucous membrane is thrown into two transverse folds that constitute the vocal bands. The upper pair of transverse folds form the false vocal bands. The lower pair form the true vocal bands.

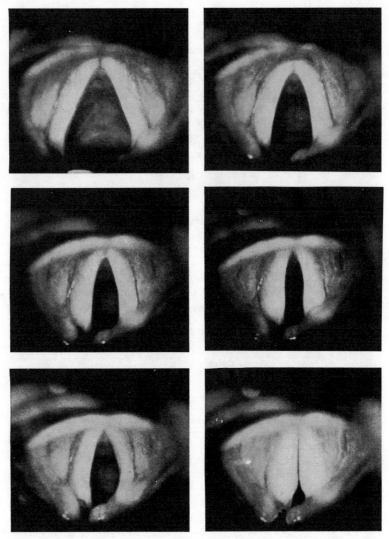

FIGURE 2–3. High-speed photos showing changes in position of the
vocal bands from quiet breathing to voicing. (Courtesy Bell
Telephone Co. Laboratories, N.Y.)

have inner edges of connective tissue. In adult males the vocal bands
range from about ⅞ inch to 1¼ inches in length. In adult females the
length ranges from less than ½ inch to about ⅝ inch. Later we shall consider the relationship between length of vocal folds and pitch of voice.

It might be pointed out that the vocal bands assist in a very vital
function not related to speech. This function is to keep foreign matter out
of the breathing mechanism. This becomes clear when we recall the
coughing that takes place when saliva or a bit of food is "inhaled" when

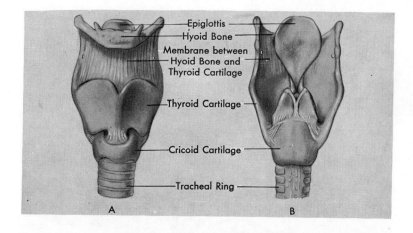

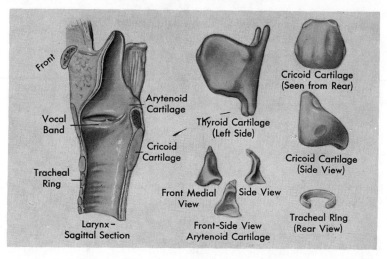

FIGURE 2–4. *Upper diagram:* The larynx and trachea. *A:* Anterior view. *B:* Posterior view. *Lower diagram:* The cartilages of the larynx.

we try to talk and swallow at the same time. The vocal folds are sensitive to the presence of foreign matter. If any foreign matter touches the vocal folds, reflexive activity will occur. This activity produces the sudden expulsion of air that we recognize as coughing. The action serves to clear the foreign matter from the trachea.

Loudness and reinforcement

The loudness of vocal tones is determined mostly by the vigor with which air is forced from the lungs through the larynx. Fortunately, however, we are able to "build up," or reinforce, vocal tones without resorting to constant energetic use of air pressure. This reinforcement takes place

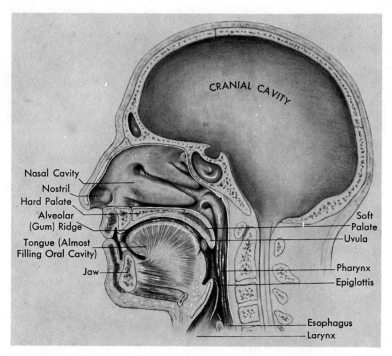

FIGURE 2–5. Section of head showing articulatory organs and principal resonators.

in the resonating cavities of the human speech mechanism (Figure 2–5). These important resonators are the cavities of (1) the larynx itself, (2) the throat (pharynx), (3) the mouth (oral cavity), and (4) the nose (the cavity above the roof of the mouth). To a lesser degree, the trachea —the part of the windpipe below the larynx—also acts as a resonator.

The chest cavity (motor mechanism)

The thoracic, or chest, cavity consists of a framework of bones and cartilage which include the collar bone, the shoulder blades, the ribs, the sternum, and the backbone. The *diaphragm* is the floor of the thoracic cavity as well as the roof of the abdominal cavity. Above the diaphragm are, among other organs, the lungs and trachea. Below, in the abdominal cavity, are the digestive organs including the stomach, the intestines, and the liver (Figure 2–6).

The lungs

The lungs consist of a mass of tiny air sacs supplied by a multitude of air tubes and blood vessels. The lungs contain much elastic tissue. They play a passive role in respiration. They expand or contract only because of differences in pressure brought about as a result of the activity of the

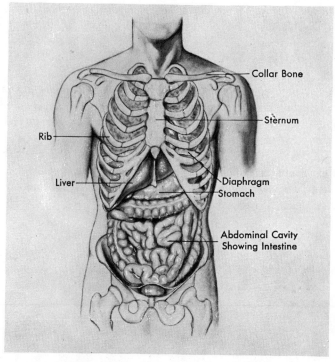

FIGURE 2–6. The chest and abdominal cavities.

rib and abdominal muscles that expand and contract the thoracic cavity. The lungs, having no muscle tissue, can neither expand nor contract directly. Air is forced into the lungs as a result of outside air pressure when the expanded chest cavity provides increased space for the air. Air is forced out of the lungs when, as will soon be described, the chest cavity decreases in size and the pressure of the enclosed air is increased.

Diaphragmatic action

Air enters the lungs by way of the mouth or nose, the throat, and the trachea when the volume of the chest cavity is increased. Such an increase may be produced by the downward movement of the diaphragm, by the outward movement of the lower ribs, or by a combination of both activities. In inhalation, the contraction of the diaphragm is an active process. In exhalation, the diaphragm merely relaxes. The diaphragm returns to its former position because of the pressure of the abdominal contents upon it. In controlled muscular activity necessary for speech, the muscles of the front and sides of the abdominal wall contract and press inward on the liver, stomach, and intestines. These organs exert an upward pressure on the undersurface of the diaphragm, which in turn exerts pressure against the lungs and so cause air to be expelled. Throughout the respirator cycle the diaphragm remains roughly dome-shaped (actually, double dome-shaped), but the height of the dome is greater after exhalation than after inhalation (see Figure 2–7).

Although the diaphragm is muscularly active only in the process of inhalation, it nevertheless serves a highly important function in exhalation. The diaphragm maintains some degree of muscle tension at all times. In relaxing as a result of pressures of the abdominal contents upon it, it does so slowly and gradually as the breath is expired. If the diaphragm were to lose all muscle tone at once and to relax suddenly and completely, the air from the lungs would be expelled with a sudden rush. Such an expulsion of air would be useless for speech purposes. By maintaining some degree of muscle tonus, a steady stream of breath is provided which can be used for speech purposes.

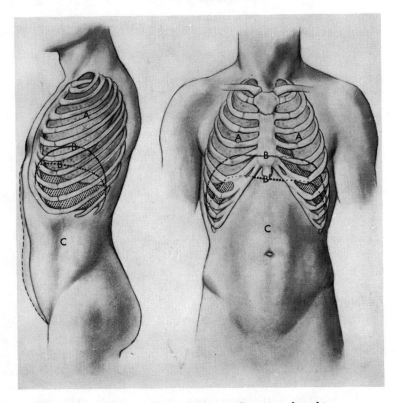

FIGURE 2–7. Diaphragmatic and abdominal action in breathing. A: The thorax or chest cavity. B: The diaphragm "relaxed" as at the completion of exhalation. B': The diaphragm contracted as in deep inhalation. C: The abdominal cavity. Note the forward displacement of the abdominal wall which accompanies the downward movement of the diaphragm during inhalation. The cross-hatched portion of the lung represents the additional volume of the expanded lung as in deep inhalation.

The respiratory cycle

In *normal breathing* that does not involve speech, only a small part of the air in our lungs is moved or exchanged. Each respiratory cycle probably involves no more, on the average, than an interchange of about a pint (500 cc) of air. Vigorous speaking or shouting may require more air. Many persons, however, use no more breath for speaking loudly than they do for conversational speech. In any event we seldom use more than a small amount, perhaps 10 to 20 percent, of the volume of air we are capable of holding in our lungs. The amount of air we are capable of inhaling has little significance for voice production. Of greater significance are control of the breath and use of the resonators to reinforce vocal tones.

The contraction and relaxation of the diaphragm and the abdominal muscles produce the cycles of inhalation and exhalation in the process of breathing. Under normal circumstances, when vocalization and speech are not involved, changes in the physiological conditions of the parts of the breathing mechanism determine the manner of our breathing. Usually these changes take place without conscious effort and with little or no awareness of what is going on. It is only when something unusual happens that we become aware that we are breathing. Running up several flights of stairs, for example, is generally enough to make us conscious that we are breathing more rapidly than normally. After running, we need to breathe more rapidly to restore the oxygen supply that has been used up because of our energetic action.

Breathing for speech usually calls for a modification of the respiratory cycle. In silent (nonspeech) breathing, the periods of inhalation and exhalation are about equal. In speech, the period of exhalation exceeds the length of the period of inhalation. That means that normally, in speaking, we inhale quickly and, while speaking, exhale slowly. The necessary modification of the respiratory cycle creates the need for voluntary, or conscious, control that is not required for automatic breathing.

Articulated sound

Voice, as we know, is but one component of speech. Combinations of articulated sounds presented in conventional patterns constitute spoken words. Speech sounds are produced when the stream of breath coming up from the lungs by way of the windpipe and larynx is modified in the mouth before it (the breath) is permitted to leave the body. The breath is modified in the mouth by the action of the tongue, the teeth, the lips, and the parts of the roof of the mouth (the palate). Most sounds in English speech are emitted through the mouth. The exceptions are the sounds *m* and *n* and the consonant sound usually represented by the letters *ng*. These three are nasal sounds—that is, they are routed through the nasal cavity (the area above the roof of the mouth) and the nose (the nostrils) before they are emitted.

Flexibility of human voice

The human sound-producing mechanism has a wide range of variability and can produce different kinds of sounds because it is so highly modifiable. Voice can be varied in pitch by changes in the tension of the vocal bands. At will, we can stop or continue the flow of breath that produces sound. The shape and to some extent the size of our resonators can be modified through muscular contraction and relaxation. Within limits, the openings of our sound mechanisms can be small or large and of various shapes according to what we do with our jaws and lips. Through these modifications, both pitch and tone quality can be changed.

A mechanism so highly modifiable must necessarily be fairly complex in its functioning. And the human speech mechanism is a most complicated apparatus! Fortunately the superior nervous system man possesses makes it possible for him to modify and control the delicate mechanisms involved in the production of speech. The nature of this control will be considered later in the chapter.

VOICE AND THE PHYSICS OF SOUND

In this section we shall consider briefly the production of voice from the point of view of the science of physics. Although voice is not produced directly as a result of vibratory action, the determinants of vocal pitch nevertheless pertain to human vocal production.

Breathing

If a cavity having a single opening is increased in size, the pressure of the surrounding atmosphere will cause air to come in by way of the opening. When, on the other hand, the size of the cavity is decreased, air will be forced out. As we have noticed, air enters the lungs (we inhale) when the size of the chest cavity is increased, and air is forced out of the lungs (we exhale) when the chest cavity is reduced in size. In controlled exhalation, air is forced out gradually so that it may serve the function of speech.

Pitch

The pitch of a sound is determined by three characteristics of the vibrating body. These are length, mass or thickness, and tension. Short vibrators produce higher-pitched sounds than long ones; thin vibrators (small mass) produce higher-pitched sounds than thick vibrating bodies of equal length; vibrators that are taut or tense produce higher-pitched sounds than less taut vibrators of equal length and mass. In brief, the pitch of a sound-producing body varies directly with the degree of tension and inversely as the length and mass of the body.

The basic reason for the higher-pitched voices of women is apparent. Both the length and mass of women's vocal folds are less than those of men's. We have considerable control over the degree of tension of our vocal folds and so can voluntarily control the pitch of our voices. Involuntary pitch changes, however, do take place when muscle tensions change. The tension of the vocal folds tends to vary as other muscles voluntarily or involuntarily become tense. We might test this point by producing the sound *ah* continuously while gradually clenching our fists. It will be noted that as our fists become tightly closed, the pitch of the voice becomes higher. It is likely also that the voice under states of heightened emotion become higher in pitch because heightened emotion brings with it increased muscle tension.

Pitch perceptually (subjectively) is what the auditory system responds to or perceives when it is exposed to a body that is vibrating within the listener's range. Most young persons with normal hearing can respond to sounds within the range of 20 to 20,000 vibrations (cycles) per second.[3] Older persons usually lose hearing in the upper pitches.

The average fundamental or basic frequency for male voices is 128 Hz. The average is about twice as high, between 200 and 256 Hz, for female voices. Ordinarily we do not think of vocal pitch in terms of number of vibrations per second. Instead, we use such terms as bass and baritone and tenor for male voices and alto, mezzo-soprano, and soprano for female voices.

Cavity resonance and quality

The reinforcing or resonating function of the larynx, throat, mouth, and nose may be explained in terms of cavity resonance. We know that sounds are "built up" when a hollow form or cavity is close to the source of the sound. The body of a musical instrument serves this function. In the violin, for example, the sounds produced by the vibrating strings are reinforced by the hollow shape of the form below the strings. In a wind instrument, the hollow horn reinforces the sounds resulting from the vibration of the reed in the mouthpiece. A given sound may be reinforced by a number of possible resonating cavities, but of the number, one cavity will produce better results (reinforce the sound) than the others. When a cavity is especially built to reinforce a particular sound or range of sounds, optimum reinforcement is obtained. We might test this through a very simple experiment. Arrange five or six glass tumblers in a row and fill each tumbler with a different amount of water. Strike a metal bar or

[3] The abbreviation Hz (Hertz) is now commonly used to designate pitch so that 250 Hz would be translated to 250 cycles per second (cps).

a fork (if available, use a tuning fork) and hold it over each tumbler. The unfilled parts of the tumblers are resonating cavities. Each cavity, being different in size and shape from the others, will reinforce the sound produced differently. One tumbler cavity will do the job better than the others.

In the human sound mechanism the resonating cavities of the head and throat (speech mechanism) reinforce the sounds produced in the larynx. Because we can modify the size and shape of our resonating cavities,[4] we can get different qualities of sound. We can also reinforce sounds more widely than a musician can who is handling a musical instrument. For example, the vowels we produce in our speech are essentially different qualities of sound resulting from the variations in the size and shape of the mouth. A little vowel exercise in front of a mirror will make this point visibly apparent. Try producing the vowel in the words *he, hit, hay, hen, hat, who, ho, ha, her,* and *hum.* Note the position of the jaw and the shape of the lips, and that the tongue position will vary somewhat for each of the vowels.

We attain optimum resonance in speaking when, as a result of adjustments of our resonating cavities, we are able to produce easily audible sounds with the least expenditure of effort. We characterize vocal sounds by the resonating cavity most concerned in their production. Thus, we talk of a throaty tone or a nasal tone. An important difference between a trained singer and someone who just sings is that the trained singer uses his resonating cavities to optimum advantage. He does not use a "bull fiddle"-shaped mouth for a violin-string tone. The same point might be made in comparing trained speakers with persons who just talk. Most of us who have never learned to do the job well enough to talk without strain or to talk with a fairly pleasant voice need help in making the proper adjustment for attaining optimum resonance. (See Chapter 7 for suggested exercises for this purpose.)

HEARING AND SPEAKING

Hearing

Without hearing few of us could learn to speak. Speaking, for most persons, is learned through seeing and hearing.[5] As children we learn to speak by unconsciously imitating the sounds and voice patterns we hear. Through seeing we learn how speech sounds look. Through hearing we

---

[4] The mouth is the most modifiable of our resonating cavities; the nasal cavity the least.

[5] Some children with severe hearing losses can be taught to speak orally through the use of other combinations of sensory avenues, such as seeing and feeling. Usually, the speech of such persons is not of as good a quality as the speech of persons without hearing loss.

are able to check on our speech so that we know whether the sounds we produce are like those we are trying to imitate. Listening to ourselves enables us to check on our voices as well as on our articulation.[6] In short, through hearing we discover whether we are using the appropriate sounds to form the words we mean to say.

The process of hearing involves three integrated functions: (1) the reception of sounds; (2) the transmission of sounds and the transformation into nerve impulses; and (3) the interpretation or translation of sounds for their meaning. Sound reception and transmission are made possible by the structure known as the ear. Interpretation or translation of sound into meaning is achieved through the operation of special nerve fibers and the cortex of the brain. (See pages 29–31 for a discussion of the functions of the brain cortex.)

The ear

There are three parts to the ear (see Figure 2–8): (1) the outer ear, (2) the middle ear, and (3) the inner ear. *The outer ear* consists of a shell-like structure known as the *pinna,* and a short canal or auditory *meatus* which carries sounds to the eardrum, or *tympanic membrane.* The auditory meatus is approximately one inch in length. The eardrum consists of a somewhat dome-shaped and taut connective tissue membrane.

The middle ear begins on the inner side of the eardrum. In its cavity

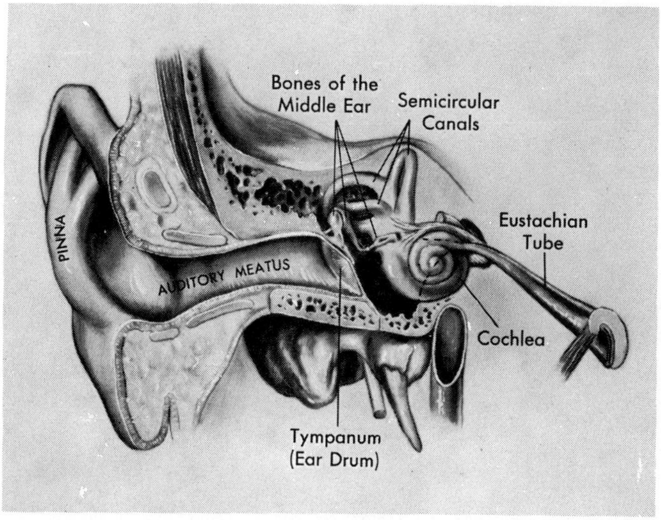

FIGURE 2–8. A sectional view of the ear.

[6] It is known that persons who develop hearing losses after they have learned to speak tend to have faulty articulation and poorly modulated voices.

are three very small connecting bones that extend from the eardrum to the inner ear. Functionally the middle ear transmits sound (vibrations) from the outer ear to the inner ear. A short passageway, the *Eustachian tube,* connects the middle ear cavity with the upper part of the throat cavity. The Eustachian tube plays no part in assisting us to hear. Frequently, in fact, the Eustachian tube interferes with hearing because of infections that begin there and spread to the middle ear.

The inner ear is a complicated structure. It consists of a series of passageways, or canals, that extend from the middle ear deep into the temporal bone. Part of the inner ear—*the semicircular canals*—is concerned with the function of balance rather than of hearing.

The passageways of the inner ear are filled with fluid. The vibrations of the middle ear bones are transmitted to the fluid of the inner ear. Part of the inner ear, the *cochlea,* contains tiny cells with hairlike projections that are sensitive to these vibrations. These hair cells are connected to the fibers of the auditory nerve which relay the translated sound waves to the brain. (See Figures 2–8 and 2–9.)

In brief, we hear in the following way: Sound vibrations stimulate the eardrum. The vibrations are transmitted by the bones of the middle ear to the fluid lying within the inner ear. The inner ear contains nerve endings that transmit to the brain the nerve impulses produced by the vibrator. In the cortex of the brain the nerve impulses are interpreted for their symbolic significance. To appreciate how the transmission and interpretation by nerve impulses is accomplished, we now turn to a study of the nervous mechanism.

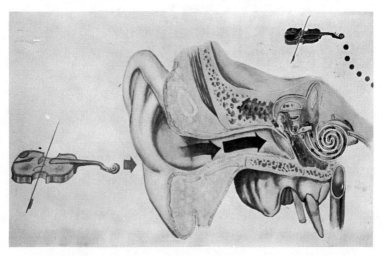

FIGURE 2–9. View of the ear, indicating schematically how sound is transmitted to and interpreted by the brain.

THE NERVOUS SYSTEM

The speech mechanism exists in man alone because only he has a neurological system capable of transforming what were originally unconsciously produced grunts and wheezes into articulated sounds and voice. The sounds of speech are produced, as we have learned, by organs concerned for the most part with the vital processes of breathing and eating. Many animals have mechanisms capable of producing vocal sounds. The ape comes closest to producing sounds in an almost human way. But only man can start with a sneeze and end with an articulated apology for having sneezed. Man's capacity to talk lies in his ability to integrate organs of respiration and digestion for an additional purpose. In this special integration there is also an ability to inhibit the actions of the organs in their original biological purpose. But even beyond this, man's capacity to talk must be explained by his *ability to learn and to remember what he has learned.* Vocal occurrences that happen to the child as incidents of play can be recalled and used again as words. Human beings can take greater advantage of "accidental" experiences than can any other form of life. With superior insight the human being can seize upon an incidental occurrence and have it stand out and acquire a new significance. This essentially explains the how and the why of our learning language and speech.

To understand the "unregulated miracle" of speech, we must learn something about the nervous system. More especially, we must learn something about the brain of man because therein lies man's superiority over animals.

The division of the nervous system which is especially concerned with speech is part of the so-called *central nervous system* (CNS). This division includes the brain itself and the spinal cord. (See Figure 2–10.) Associated with the central nervous system is a series of nerves that extend from the lower part of the brain and the spinal column to the muscles of the body that are under conscious or voluntary control.

Except for the cerebrum of the brain (the cerebral hemispheres), the nervous system of a man is pretty much like that of a dog and almost identical with that of an ape. The cerebrum, however, is significantly different. To begin with, there is a lot more of it than even the ape possesses. We can see the difference in the high expanse of the forehead that covers the frontal bulge of the brain. In man, this brain area pushes farther forward and is considerably larger than is the case with any other animal. Though our scientific knowledge of the brain is still limited, this much we know: injury to this part of the nervous mechanism brings about important changes in the individual's personality, in his thinking, and in his speaking.

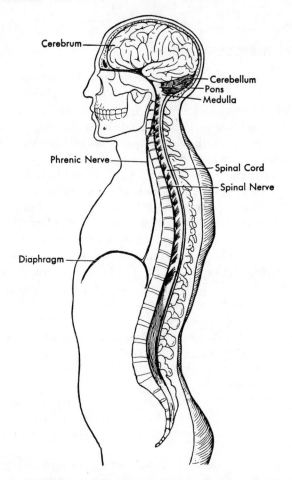

Cerebrum

Cerebellum
Pons
Medulla

Phrenic Nerve

Spinal Cord

Spinal Nerve

Diaphragm

FIGURE 2–10. The central nervous system in relation to speech. The Cerebrum: normal meaningful speech is dependent upon the integrative activity of the parts of the cerebrum. The Cerebellum "sorts and arranges" muscular impulses that come to it from higher brain centers. Impulses are here correlated so that precise muscular activity such as is needed for speech becomes possible. The Pons is a bridge of nerve fibers between the cerebral cortex and the medulla. The Medulla contains the respiratory and other reflex centers. The Spinal Cord and its nerves control the respiratory muscles. The Phrenic Nerve emerges from the spinal cord in the neck region and extends to the diaphragm. It supplies the impulses which cause the diaphragm to contract in breathing.

The nerves are the message carriers. Nerve fibers, much like telephone wires, carry messages to the brain from the skin, the hands, the eyes, the ears, the tongue, the lips, and the other organs of the body. In addition, they carry the impulses the brain initiates to the muscles and glands.

These impulses induce the movements of muscles involved in speaking, writing, and reading.

The brain cortex

The brain itself is a great coordinator and integrator of activity. In the brain, impulses set up by sounds and movements received through the ear and eye and other sense organs are translated into words and images that have significance and meaning.

"Brain power" may best be considered as a form of chemicoelectrical energy. All the impulses that course throughout our nervous systems and carry and convey the messages that result in thoughts and actions are, in effect, minute bursts of electrical energy. These bursts of energy are produced within billions of individual nerve cells that comprise our nervous system.

The brain is divided into areas according to a division-of-labor arrangement. Most of this can be seen in the diagram of the cortex (outer covering of gray matter) of the brain (see Figure 2–11). We may notice

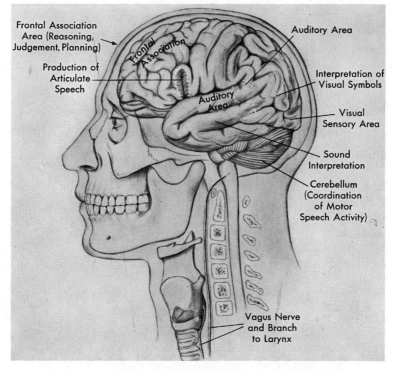

FIGURE 2–11. Localization of brain function in relation to speech (the left cerebral cortex).

that among the marked areas are those for "hearing," "seeing," "movement," and "motor speech." The significance of these areas lies in their capacity to analyze and synthesize, to evaluate specialized experience for the brain as a whole. For example, the region in the back part (occipital lobe) of the cortex functions especially in the evaluation and interpretation of impulses coming from the eyes. Without that area we might see an object such as a tree but fail to understand that the combinations of brown trunk, branches, and leaves together constitute a tree, or that a particular combination of glass and brick and wood means a house. In fact, even color or shape or size could not be appreciated without the visual brain area. Similarly the auditory area interprets and evaluates experiences brought to it by way of the ear.

Most of what we know becomes known to us through more than one sensory avenue. A peach is something we taste and smell, see and feel. It is juicy and sweet and round and fuzzy and smells "peachy." The combination means a peach. As perceived merely by the sense of taste, a peach or a steak, soup or coffee, mean little. Take away the nose and the eyes and you have merely one-dimensional objects. Smell and see, as well as taste, and you have full-bodied dishes. The added meaning is a result of interinterpretations of sensory values which is made possible for us by the many billions of cells in our brain cortex. The interconnections among these cells make it almost literally possible to "see sounds" and "feel noises" and "taste" the cold and the warmth. In this way the ocean gets meaning, and winter and summer mean more than changes in the time of the year.

Cortical differentiation

As indicated in Figure 2–11 the cerebral cortical areas have specialized functions. There are also different, though broadly related functions served by the two cerebral hemispheres. These differences are especially important for higher human functions—hearing, speaking, and thinking. Specifically the perception of speech events is normally a function of the left temporal lobe (designated in Figure 2–11 as the auditory area). The perception of auditory nonspeech events—such as environmental sounds, music, and animal and mechanical noises—are normally perceived and processed (identified) in the temporal lobe of the right cerebral hemisphere.[7]

From the point of view of speaking rather than of understanding, the motor speech area of the brain is of special interest. In this and the immediately surrounding areas occurs an integration of impulses received and evaluated by other parts of the brain. In addition, impulses originating here are transmitted eventually to the tongue and the lips and the

[7] See J. Eisenson, "The Left Brain Is for Talking," *Acta Symbolica,* 2:1 (1971), 33–36, for further discussion of brain differentiation related to speech.

other parts of the so-called speech mechanism, enabling us to articulate sounds and give voice to them in the activity called speech.

Effects of brain damage

It is fairly evident that unless the brain is intact we cannot get the maximum meaning out of our experiences. We cannot, because meanings are impaired if the brain is damaged. That is why children born with brain injuries are slow in beginning to talk and often seem retarded compared with most children born without such handicaps. Damage to the brain after we have learned what things mean frequently results in a disturbance of their meanings, as shown by defective understanding and speaking, and sometimes in impairments in the parallel functions of reading and writing.

We may suffer a permanent injury to the brain as a result of a blow, exposure to explosives, or the effects of disease. Temporary injury may be caused by shock, excessive fatigue, or overindulgence in alcohol. The effects on speech and language, except for the matter of time, are similar. Strong emotion such as fear and anger may also serve to make us behave as if we had no cerebral integration and control and render us temporarily unable to produce speech on a normal, voluntary level.

THE ENDOCRINE SYSTEM

The endocrine system is another part of the bodily mechanism which enables us to correlate activities and make adjustments to the environment.[8] The important difference between the two systems—nervous and endocrine—is to be found in the kind of correlation of activity that each helps to accomplish. Through the functioning of the nervous mechanism, and especially of the central nervous system, immediate, rapid, and specific responses to situations are made. For example, we look at an object and call it by its name; we engage in conversation and respond with particular words to what is said to us.

The endocrine system influences the manner, rather than the content of the response. The endocrine system exerts an influence over general and long-term reaction patterns toward situational changes in the environment. For instance, the sitting hen's urge to "sit" is largely determined by endocrine changes within her. Having the urge, the hen looks for something on which to sit. If she has no eggs of her own, the hen will use another chicken's eggs. If no egges are available, she may sit on objects resembling eggs. The point is that when a hen is so inclined, she appears bound and determined to "sit" on something. The human being having a "set," or attitude, is more discriminating and is not likely to

---

[8] The nervous mechanism has its own endocrine system which makes it possible for impulses to be mediated through its circuits.

confuse golf balls with eggs. But the internal condition of the organism makes one kind of behavior—behavior consistent with the set—more likely to take place than another in regard to general or cyclic changes in the environment.

The products of the endocrine system are known as *hormones.* Hormones go directly from the glands which produce them into the bloodstream. By means of the circulating blood, hormones are quickly diffused throughout the entire body. This ready diffusion makes it possible for an overall bodily response to take place as a result of endocrine system action.

Our consideration of the endocrine system will necessarily be brief and limited to those glands and their products that have some close or direct relationship to voice and speech production. The location of each of the glands can readily be seen by referring to Figure 2–12.

The pituitary gland is located in a small, bony pocket in the center of the skull directly underneath the brain. Through the several hormones produced by the pituitary, the gland serves many and diverse functions. It has a master function of serving as a regulator or controller of most of the other endocrine glands. The growth-promoting hormone of the pituitary has a definite influence on voice and speech. This influence can best be observed when the gland fails to function normally in regard to its hormone production. Overactivity results in an abnormal enlargement of the muscles, bones, and cartilages of the head and throat. Specifically the tongue, the vocal folds, the larynx, and the lower jaw become enlarged. The effects on speech frequently include a hoarse and husky voice and blurred, thick articulation. In the event of underactivity of the growth-promoting hormone, voice and articulation are likely to be weak and to sound "infantile."

The pituitary exercises an indirect effect over voice and speech by way of its regulatory action on the sex glands. The changes in speech, and more especially in voice pitch, associated with adolescence and physical maturity are under the indirect influence of the pituitary.

The thyroid gland is located at the base of the neck, lying in front of the windpipe. In its functioning, the thyroid gland is intimately associated with the pituitary. The hormone *thyroxin* is produced by the thyroid. The effect of thyroxin hormone is to speed up metabolic activity of the body cells and to increase *tonus* of the muscles of the body. An overactive thyroid gland tends to make the individual highstrung, irritable, and restless. This condition may reflect itself in speech by a rapid rate of articulation or a high-pitched, unpleasant voice. An underactive thyroid gland is likely to have opposite effects. These include general muscular sluggishness, slow and indistinct articulation, and a hoarse, poorly modulated voice. Intellectual sluggishness to a degree of mental deficiency may accompany severe underactive thyroid gland activity. This is especially significant in small children, where insufficient thyroxin may result

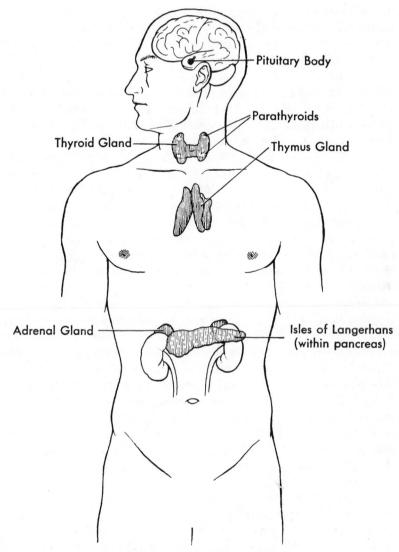

FIGURE 2–12. The endocrine glands.

in a failure of physical and mental development. In extreme form this developmental failure is called *cretinism*. The speech of a cretin is consistent with his mental and physical deficiencies. Not much is spoken by the cretin because he entertains few ideas and so has little to say. What he does say is spoken slowly, articulated poorly, and accompanied by a colorless and immature voice.

The parathyroids are tiny glands that lie close to the thyroid gland. The hormone of the parathyroids regulates the concentration of calcium in the bloodstream. The responsiveness of the nervous and muscular system is determined by the calcium content of the blood. Persons with parathyroid hormone deficiency tend to be high-strung, irritable, and "nervous." The speech of such persons will frequently be rapid and arhythmic, and unpleasant to hear.

The adrenal glands are found in the abdominal cavity just above the kidney. Different hormones are produced by the inner and outer portions of the adrenal glands. The inner portion of the adrenals produces the hormone known as adrenalin. The effect of adrenalin is to prepare the individual for quick and energetic emergency action. The entire body becomes toned up and ready for physical struggle. Adrenalin brings about a more rapid heartbeat, so that the blood circulates more quickly, the blood pressure is raised, and added sugar is released from the liver into the blood. The bodily changes we recognize as part of the picture of violent emotional states such as fear and anger and rage are brought about by the action of adrenalin in the bloodstream. The speaker who is excited and the speaker suffering from stage fright may attribute many of the physical changes that take place within him to the effects of adrenalin.

The sex glands, in addition to producing sex cells necessary for reproduction, are also producers of hormones. The hormones of the sex glands help to bring about the physiological and behavioral changes that are necessary in reproduction. In addition, secondary sex characteristics such as bodily contour, hair distribution, and vocal changes are effected. The last-mentioned characteristics, especially noticeable in the adolescent male, results from the rather sudden enlargement of the larynx that takes place at puberty.

There are several other endocrine glands that we need not consider here because no intimate relationship to voice or speech can be demonstrated. These include the adrenal cortex, the pancreas, the thymus, and the pineal gland.

The endocrine system is intra- and interrelated—with respect to the activities of the individual glands and in the correlated functioning of the system as a whole with the nervous system. Probably the best way to think of both systems is as coordinators of behavior. The more complex the behavior, the finer the coordination required. There is little question that speech represents the most complex act of all human behavior. In respect to spoken and written language, the central nervous system of man is more complex than the nervous systems of all other animals, including the subhuman primates.

SUMMARY

Speech production is accomplished through the adapted use of organs of respiration and digestion.

In producing vocal tones, the vocal folds act as pulsators. They are set into action by air coming from the lungs. The voiced sound is reinforced by the resonating cavities of the body. The chief resonators are the cavities of the larynx, pharynx, mouth, and nose.

Articulated (speech) sounds result from a modification of the breath by the organs of articulation. The articulators include the lips, teeth, gum ridge, tongue, and palate.

The essentials for sound and speech production are summarized in Table 2–1.

Hearing enables most persons to learn to speak. The process of hearing includes three highly integrated functions: (1) sound reception, (2) sound transmission, and (3) sound interpretation. Sound reception takes place in the outer and the middle ear. Transmission of sound in the form of nerve impulses is the function of special parts of the inner ear and the auditory nerve. Interpretation of sound is accomplished in the cortex of the brain. The left cerebral cortex normally processes speech (linguistic) events. The right cerebral cortex normally processes nonlinguistic auditory events.

The high degree of complexity of the nervous mechanism of man has made it possible for him to achieve speech. The presence of a well-developed cerebral cortex most clearly distinguishes man's nervous system and speech mechanism from those of "higher animals" such as the ape.

The endocrine system supplements the functioning of the nervous mechanism. The glands of the endocrine system produce hormones. These are chemical products that affect the overall activity of the living individual. The thyroid and pituitary glands have the most direct influence over speech activities.

Table 2–1   Sound Production

Requisites for sound	Musical instruments	Human sound (voice)-producing mechanism
1. Body capable of vibration	Reeds, plates, skins, strings, air column	Paired vocal bands and pulsations of air
2. Energy applied to body (1)	Air, percussion, friction	Air (breath)
3. Medium for transmission	Air, wires, water, solid masses, etc.	Air
4. Reinforcers of sound (an aid but not a requisite)	Resonating cavities, sounding boards, pipes, etc.	Cavities of the larynx (voice box), pharynx (throat), mouth, and nose

QUESTIONS AND EXERCISES

1. Compare a wind instrument with the human voice-producing mechanism with respect to (a) the vibrators, (b) the force applied to the vibrators, (c) the manner in which pitch changes are brought about.

2. Why do most women have higher-pitched voices than most men? Do you identify the sex of a speaker by attributes other than pitch?

3. Why is the pitch range of a cello lower than that of a violin?

4. What is the relationship between sound quality and resonance?

5. Why is accurate speech difficult to produce when one is tired?

6. Why is the pitch of the voice raised in excitement?

7. Why are persons with defective hearing likely to have some defect in speech? Can you suggest how normal voice quality may be retained despite defective hearing?

8. Indicate briefly the function of each part of the hearing mechanism.

9. Why does brain damage often result in impaired speech?

10. Discuss the implications of the observation that "normally the left brain is for linguistic listening, and so for speaking."

RECOMMENDED READINGS

ANDERSON, V. A. *Training the Speaking Voice*. New York: Oxford University Press, 1961, chaps. 2–4.

DENES, P. E., and E. N. PINSON. *The Speech Chain*. Baltimore: Williams and Wilkins, 1963, chaps. 3–4.

EISENSON, J. *Voice and Diction: A Program for Improvement*. New York: Macmillan Publishing Co., Inc., 1974, chap. 2.

EISENSON, J. "The Left Brain Is for Talking." *Acta Symbolica*, 2:1 (1971), 33–36.

PALMER, J. M., and D. A. LaRUSSO. *Anatomy for Speech and Hearing*. New York: Harper & Row, Publishers, Inc., 1965, chap. 8.

VAN RIPER, C., and J. V. IRWIN. *Voice and Articulation*. Englewood Cliffs, N.J.: Prentice-Hall, Inc., 1958, chaps. 7–10 and 13.

Chapter 3

The Components
of Speech

Words, Voice, and Action

Almost all audible speech, including most emotional expression, may be thought of as words set to impromptu "music" with some accompanying action. We are more likely to be aware of the words we speak than we are of our vocal tones or of our actions. Words usually inform the listener about our thoughts. Voice, though capable of communicating intellectual content,[1] is more frequently used to express how we feel about our thoughts. Actions (gestures) help us to get our ideas across. This effect is accomplished in two ways. Directly, actions (accompanying gestures) help us to underscore and to reinforce ideas. Occasionally actions may succeed in communicating our thoughts when words are not found or are not wholly adequate for our purpose. Indirectly, actions are helpful because their use frees us from or reduces physical tension and so makes thinking and communicating easier. Most of us use gestures almost as much to help ourselves in speaking as we do to make our speech intelligible to others. That is why we gesticulate even when our listeners cannot see us, as we do when talking over the telephone, making a recording, or talking into a microphone.

The three components of speech—words, voice, and action—usually tell a consistent story. When the musical underscoring provided by the voice is not too strong, we are likely, as listeners, to accept the words for their intellectual significance. When the vocal tones predominate, what we feel rather than what we think becomes emphasized. At such times the music drowns out the words, and we react to the essential feelings expressed, rather than to the words that assume only an incidental significance.

---

[1] The "music"—the prosody or melody that accompanies our articulatory movements —is, of course, produced according to the rules or conventions of the particular oral linguistic system. Every natural language has its own prosodic or intonational system. The prosody or intonation of American English will be considered later in this chapter. We shall also consider how vocal changes per se are capable of expressing intellectual content.

WORDS, MORPHEMES, AND PHONEMES

Words, the lexical units of an utterance, consist of morphemes. A *morpheme* is defined as a minimal grammatical unit of a language that constitutes either an entire word or a meaningful part of a word. Thus *books* consists of two morphemes, *book* and *s*. If *books* is used as a noun, the *s* designates plural; if *books* is used as a verb, the *s* designates present tense. The word *return* is composed of the morphemes *re* and *turn*.

Morphemes consist of individual and differentiated sounds or phonemes that permit us to distinguish word and morphemic meanings.[2] Thus, the words *mad* and *bad* are phonemically different (sound different and have different meaning) by virtue of the first phoneme in each of the words. In the words *bid* and *bad* the meaning is changed by the second phoneme. In the words *bat* and *bad* the morphemic difference is a result of the third phoneme.

Considerable intellectual as well as emotional content can be communicated by single morpheme words such as *yes, no, good, bad, stop, go, me, you, I, help,* etc. However, we usually speak in larger units than single word-morpheme sentences. In a later chapter we shall consider other aspects of word and sentence meaning.

To speak a language—any language—we must acquire the habits and learn the rules for the formation of words and sentences. Linguists refer to the rules of a language as grammars. Thus we have phonemic grammars—sounds that do or do not occur in sequence within a syllable, or those that occur in one part of a word but not in another. In English we have many sequences of *sp* (spoon, spot, gasp, respite) and *st* (stun, past, aster) and *tr* (tree, astride) and *shr* (shrimp, shriek), but we do not have the combination or blend *sr*. The blend *kl*, usually spelled *cl* in English, occurs in *clean, incline,* and *sickle.* However, the blend *tl* does not occur at the beginning of a word but is found at the end, as in *settle.* The blend *dv* is reserved for foreign names, as in *Dvořak.* The single nasal phoneme spelled *ng* occurs either medially or finally, as in *ringer* and *going,* but does not occur initially in our language. The *ng* is a frequently occurring initial sound in several African languages.

We are probably more aware of the grammar of a sentence—the rules for arranging a string of words to form phrases and sentences—than we are or were of phonemic grammar. The grammar for word strings is referred to as *syntax.*

Linguist V. A. Fromkin sums up the various knowledges we acquire as we learn to speak a language, as follows:

---

[2] In chapter 6, "An Introduction to Phonetics," we shall discuss the phonemic system in considerable detail.

Knowledge of a language must therefore include rules for the formation of words and sentences. In order to account for a speaker's ability to form a potentially infinite set of sentences and for his linguistic judgments concerning the well-formedness of words and sentences, linguistic theorists posit that what is learned in language acquisition is a grammar that includes a finite set of basic elements and a finite set of rules for their combination, including a recursive element to allow the formation of sentences of unlimited length. Furthermore, there must be a hierarchy of such elements: discrete elements of sound (phonemes) combine in restricted ways to form syllables, which combine to form meaningful units (morphemes or words), which are combined to form phrases, which are combined into sentences.[3]

VOICE AND STATES OF FEELING

We can express feelings without using words. We could regularly make vocal noises, as infants and animals do, and so express our feelings. Training and the pressures of convention, however, work against our using a mere snarl to express anger or distaste, or a purr to express satisfaction. Convention permits laughter, and on special occasions weeping, as emotional expression. Usually, however, we use words or phonemic patterns or combination (word forms) that closely resemble words in sound if not in meaning.

Voice, when not consciously controlled, reflects our feelings readily and involuntarily because the production of voice is a muscular activity, and muscle tonicity is tied up with the emotional state of the organism. The role of the adrenal glands on muscular action was explained in the discussion of the endocrine system. Under strong emotion the entire body becomes tense. The vocal bands, because of their tension, produce tones of a higher pitch. The increase in sugar in the bloodstream permits more energetic activity. As a result, voice becomes louder. Because of these involuntary muscular changes, heightened emotion in a speaker is reflected in a louder, higher-pitched voice than is characteristic of relatively unemotional speech.

Depressed states are associated with muscular relaxation. When we feel "let down," our muscles tend to go flabby. Technically our muscles lack adequate tone. Vocal bands that are relatively overrelaxed, or hypotonic, produce low-pitched tones of comparatively weak intensity. When

[3] V. A. Fromkin, "Slips of the Tongue," *Scientific American,* **229**:6 (December 1973), 110–117.

we are depressed, our voices are on the dull, soft, low-pitched end of the scale.

When we speak with relatively neutral feeling, our voices tend to be moderate in pitch and loudness. That is, the vocal tones will fall somewhere within the middle part of our pitch range. Changes in pitch and loudness occur, but they are not of the marked variety associated with the extremes of emotion. Figure 3–1 presents graphically the relationship between voice and emotional states.

Our use of words to accompany the voice gives us a definite advantage over animals. We can express shades of feeling and subtleties of meaning. By a vocal tone we can make a single oral word express the equivalent of a written paragraph. We can make words say what they don't ordinarily mean or reveal feelings without being held responsible for any real meaning. Thus, a bachelor, if asked his opinion about an infant, may respond with "That's quite a baby." A young man may say of a girl of about his own age "That chick's my old woman," without the listener demanding proof of age, species, or relationship. Similarly the young woman may refer to her peer-age companion as "My old man" and enjoy the same semantic immunities as her male friend.

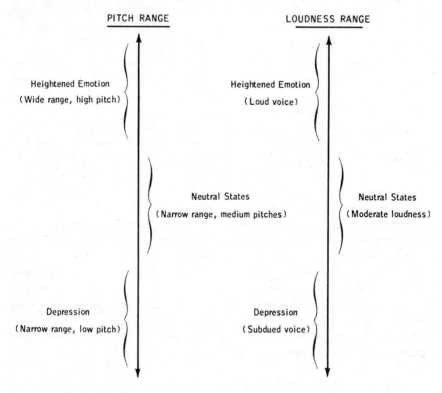

FIGURE 3–1. The relationship between changes in pitch, loudness, and states of feeling.

NONINFORMATIVE WORDS

It becomes apparent, then, that words may not always be used to inform. Sometimes they are no more than vehicles to carry tones, used to express feeling rather than to provide information.

Almost any word may be uttered in such a way that only the vocalization retains significance. But some English words, notably those of Anglo-Saxon derivation, seem better suited for snarling than others.[4] The names of some animals are frequently snarled when applied by one to another human being. Skunks, hounds, curs, snakes, and rats are a few examples. We also purr animal names for very different effects. Bunny, kitten, and honey bear are among the more favored animals.

It is clear that words used for their vocal effects serve an expressive rather than an informative function. They help to tell how the speaker feels much more clearly than to tell how he thinks. In fact, words that are "not words" probably tell us that the speaker has stopped thinking and has given way almost entirely to feeling. Probably only the residual influences of social pressure and the desire to hold on to some degree of human dignity prevent the person from going completely animalistic under the stress of emotion. If we were not concerned with what our friends and neighbors might say, it is possible that some of us, like the animal, might use nonverbal vocalizations to indicate our strong feelings about others, or to express our own internal disturbances associated with hunger, love, fear, or hate.

INFLECTIONAL CHANGES

Although changes in vocal tones normally are produced involuntarily as a by-product of muscular change, we are capable of voluntary control of vocal tones. Intentionally produced changes in vocal tone are revealed in the inflections of our speech. Because these changes are intentional and voluntarily produced, they are associated essentially with the intellectual rather than the emotional aspect of speech.

Vocal variation is inherent in almost all spoken languages. In some languages the changes in vocal tones are relatively slight. In English speech vocal tone changes, especially those of pitch, are outstanding characteristics of the spoken language. Through changes in pitch, emphasis and intellectual significance are given to particular words within groups of words. In some instances the literal, or denotative, meanings of words are modified by pitch changes, so that a group of words is given an interpretation that would not obtain from an understanding of any one

---

[4] It may, of course, be possible that we are just better able to snarl the short Anglo-Saxon words because we have practiced on them more frequently and regularly than the more complimentary terms of Romantic origin.

of the words, or the usual meaning of the words taken together. (Examples of this situation will be given later.)

Through pitch change, on intonation, the speaker reveals his attitude about what he is saying or toward the person to whom he is speaking. Through pitch change, there are made temporary modifications of or additions to the basic or stable meanings of the word or words that are derived from a particular combination of sounds. The basic meanings of written language can be found in a dictionary.[5] The meanings of spoken words go considerably beyond these denotative meanings, or definitions. The infinity of shades and subtleties to which we respond when we hear spoken language goes beyond the recording possibility of any dictionary.

INTONATION

A change in pitch on an individual sound is technically known as *inflection*. A combination, or pattern, of pitch changes on a meaningfully related group of sounds is known as *intonation*. Each spoken language has its own intonation pattern. We speak with a *foreign intonation* when a pattern native to one language is carried over to another language. In essence, a foreign intonation means that we are mixing the words of one language with the tune or melody native to another language. It is something the English-speaking person may do when he learns the words, but not the melody pattern, of French. The Frenchman is using a foreign intonation when he intones English words with his native French melody.

American-English intonation patterns are characterized by the use of downward inflections to indicate complete or emphatic statements and upward inflections to indicate doubt or uncertainty.[6] For example, a representative intonation pattern demonstrating the use of the falling inflection at the conclusion of a unit of thought would be:

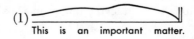

(1) This is an important matter.

This pattern may be contrasted with one in which the (first phrase) of the thought unit includes the use of a rising inflection:

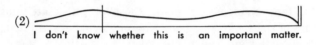

(2) I don't know whether this is an important matter.

[5] The meaning of any statement is, of course, determined by context and the relationship of the words to and within the linguistic situation.

[6] This is admittedly a simplification—perhaps an oversimplification—of the complex subject of American intonation. For a detailed and advanced consideration of the subject, see Kenneth Pike's *The Intonation of American English* (Ann Arbor, Mich.: University of Michigan Press, 1946). For an alternate way of presenting intonation contours, see A. J. Bronstein and B. F. Jacoby, *Your Speech and Voice* (New York: Random House, 1967), chap. 4.

Other more or less representative intonation patterns are illustrated in the following sentences:

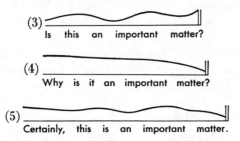

(3) Is this an important matter?

(4) Why is it an important matter?

(5) Certainly, this is an important matter.

It must be emphasized that these are pattern types. They do not actually present the speech of any one person. Each speaker varies in his pitch pattern according to the occasion and specific intent of his speech. An actual graphic representation will not be nearly so smooth as the curves here illustrated. For example, the statement "This is an important matter" might specifically be spoken as

This is an important matter.

rather than as in example (1) above.

The following graphic representation is that of a somewhat more complex sentence than most of those above.

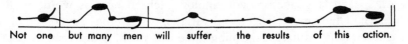

Not one but many men will suffer the results of this action.

With these reservations in mind, we might arrive at the following generalizations relative to the use of pitch changes and intonation patterns in American speech:

(a) A *falling inflection* is used when we make positive assertions (5) and when we wish to indicate the completion of a thought (1). A falling inflection is also used on the final word of questions that begin with an interrogative word (4).

(b) A *rising inflection* is used to indicate incomplete, or dependent, thoughts and to express doubt or uncertainty (2). The rising inflection is also used in questions that may logically be answered by the word "Yes" or "No" (3).

(c) *The pitch level* of the most important word within a thought unit is likely to be higher than the other words of the phrase.

(d) *The stressed syllable* of a word is usually spoken on a higher-pitch level than the unstressed syllable or syllables of the word.

(e) *A circumflex inflection* is used when the speaker's intended meaning is not consistent with the literal meaning of the word or thought unit.

(f) An inverted circumflex or a wedge [\\⌄↗] inflection is used to indicate a change of thought on a specific word to suggest a sudden change of mind.[7]

Pitch in speaking and singing

In speaking, pitch changes are continuous within a spoken phrase, or unit of thought. This contrasts with the pitch changes in singing, which are generally characterized by the holding of each note (sung syllable) on a relatively constant level. Changes in pitch while singing usually occur in relatively distinct steps between syllables of the words of the song.

Another important distinction between pitch changes in speech and in song is related to the matter of meaning. In spoken utterance the general tendency is for the more important words to be on a higher-pitch level than the less important words. In singing, however, changes in pitch are related to the overall melody of the song, often without regard to the intellectual significance of the particular word or syllable on which the pitch change occurs. These differences may be brought out by first singing and then speaking the words of a familiar song.

Pitch changes in other languages

All spoken languages do not employ pitch changes as we do in English. The Chinese use inflectional variation to give one sound combination several very different meanings. We can see how different the word meanings can be from the single example of the Mandarin (North Chinese) sound combination *shih.* When *shih* is pronounced with an even, or level, tone, it has a dictionary meaning of "corpse"; with a rising inflection, it means "ten"; with a falling inflection, it becomes the English equivalent of "scholar"; and with a falling-rising inflection, it means "arrow."

It is apparent, then, that pitch changes in Chinese are an integral rather than an incidental aspect of the spoken language. It is more closely associated with the intellectual content of speech than is pitch as used in English. Whereas we use pitch to reveal our subjective reaction to what we are thinking and saying, the Chinese use pitch to distinguish different meanings for what is essentially a basic sound combination. In

---

[7] Dramatic speech, such as may be employed in the theater, may use other inflectional patterns as well as combinations of patterns. For our present purposes, the inflectional patterns we have indicated above are sufficient.

Chinese, pitch changes are as much a part of a word as are the vowels and consonants of the word.[8]

We recognize, of course, that there are differences among the dialects of Chinese. Spoken Mandarin employs four different tones. Other spoken Chinese dialects use as many as thirteen different tonal patterns.

The use of pitch change to give words intellectual significance is not restricted to the Chinese. The African Sudan language make a comparable use of pitch. In fact, in African Sudan different vowel-consonant combinations with the same pitch tones may constitute words having the same dictionary, or denotative, meaning. Persons speaking different dialects of African Sudanese will understand one another if the same pitch levels are used in speaking, even though they are intoned on otherwise different sound combinations.

We need not go to China or to the African Sudan to find languages in which the melody is an integral part and intellectual aspect of the spoken language. Norwegian, Swedish, and Lithuanian, to name but a few, are languages which, compared with English, have relatively fixed intonation. English pitch variation is relatively free.[9] There is melody in English speech, but it is a melody determined in part by the mood of the speaker and in part by the conventions of sentence formation. In Chinese and in many other languages, pitch melody is more closely related to the semantic or intellectual significance of the particular words within the sentence.

FORCE

Another type of vocal change, that of variation of energy, or *force* (stress), is a strong feature of English speech. Syllable stress in English is used to distinguish words that are otherwise the same. Its value therefore is intellectual rather than emotional. For example, *digest* has two basic meanings. If the first syllable is stressed, we have a noun; if the second syllable is stressed, we have a verb. We may also notice that the shift in stress results in a change in the pronunciation of the vowels of both syllables of the word. Other examples of this type of vocal change include *re*bel *and* re*bel;* con*duct and con*duct; *per*mit and per*mit.*

Along this line of vocal change, a syllable that is ordinarily unstressed may occasionally be stressed to clarify the meaning of a sentence. For example, the word *undo* is ordinarily spoken with a second-syllable stress. If, however, the sentence, "I want you to undo it," were to be spoken in answer to the question, "Shall I do it?" the word *undo* would receive a first-syllable stress and so be pronounced *un*do.

[8] The Chinese speaker *must* use the proper tone in order to identify all but a very small number of relatively unimportant words such as the negative particle "bu." In Chinese, intonation is denotative; in English, intonation is normally connotative.

[9] German and Dutch share this characteristic with English.

Whole-word or even whole-phrase stress is used in English for the purpose of emphasis. In general, words spoken with greater force are made more prominent in relationship to the total speech context. Prominence and emphasis go together. Because of this, increased energy of vocalization is essentially an intellectual rather than an emotional aspect of speech. Stress is usually used to clarify the speaker's meanings rather than to reveal the speaker's feelings about what he is saying.

DURATION

Duration is another aspect through which vocalization is given variety and meaning. Changes in duration, as in pitch, may be used for communicating either intellectual or emotional implications of speech content.

Duration and Significance

On the emotional side, a slow rate of utterance is associated with depressed states; a rapid rate with happier states. We behave slowly when depressed, in speaking as well as in our general conduct. Our behavior when happy is characterized by more rapid movement, and in speech by relatively rapid articulation. When we are in a high state of elation our articulatory activity may become so rapid as to be indistinct.

On the intellectual side, speech content articulated at a slow rate is considered more important than content spoken at a rapid rate. The reason for this can be readily explained on a psychological basis. If we are listening to what is spoken, we necessarily listen longer to content that is spoken slowly. Having given the content more time and more attention, we assume it to be more important. The assumption of importance is usually not consciously formed. We cannot help but remember better that which we have attended to longer. Other things being equal, words spoken slowly become more significant than words spoken quickly.

Changes in duration are achieved either through variations in rate of articulation or through the use of pauses between groups of articulated sounds. Either device may be used to make a word or a phrase stand out and so become important. Frequently lengthened duration is accompanied by increased intensity so that two factors make for the added intellectual significance given the stressed word or phrase.

Vowels and vowel-like consonants such as *l, r, m,* and *n* lend themselves by nature of their manner of production to modifications in rate of articulation. Words having many vowels and vowel-like sounds take longer to be articulated than do words with a smaller proportion of vowels and a larger proportion of consonants. We would have to make a special effort to say lines such as:

> Alone, alone, all, all alone,
> Alone on a wide, wide sea!

in anything but a slow manner. On the other hand, lines such as:

> Come, and trip it as you go,
> On the light fantastic toe

lend themselves to a rapid rate of articulation.

A comparison of the two verses above brings out the differences in emotional value between slowly articulated and rapidly articulated utterance. The effect of the first two lines of verse from Coleridge's *The Rhyme of the Ancient Mariner* is a depressing one. The second verse, from Milton's *L'Allegro*, is obviously in a gayer mood.

SUMMARY

The components of speech are words, action, and voice. Generally, words reveal what we think, and voice reveals how we feel about what we think. Gestures usually reinforce thoughts. Gestures are also used in place of words that are not adequate to convey our thoughts. Words are sometimes used to reveal nonintellectual content. Voice, on the other hand, may be used to convey subtleties of intellectual content.

Words are composed of *morphemes*, minimal semantic units that may constitute an entire word or a meaningful part thereof.

Some vocal variation is inherent in the pattern of almost all spoken languages. In English speech, pitch changes are especially important. Through pitch changes, English-speaking persons give emphasis and intellectual significance to words within phrases.

Inflection is a pitch change that occurs in the production of a sound. Patterns of inflectional changes constitute *intonation*. A foreign intonation is a pattern of pitch change that is native to one spoken language and applied to another language.

American-English speech uses three basic kinds of inflectional changes. (1) The falling inflection generally indicates emphasis or finality. (2) The rising inflection implies indefiniteness, uncertainty, or incompletion. (3) The circumflex inflection is used when the literal meanings of the speaker's words are inconsistent with his intended meaning, or to indicate a change of thought.

In tonal languages such as Chinese, inflectional changes are an integral rather than an incidental aspect of the spoken language. The Chinese use pitch changes to distinguish different meanings for a particular combination of sounds constituting a word.

Besides pitch variation, American-English speech employs changes in *force* and *duration*. Syllable stress obtained through changes in force usually has intellectual significance. Changes in duration may be used for either intellectual or emotional significance. When used in an intentional, controlled manner, changes in duration are associated with intellectual content. When the rate of speech is not intentionally controlled, duration becomes associated with feelings and emotions. As such, a slow rate is related to a depressed state of mind, and a fast rate is associated with heightened feelings and emotions.

QUESTIONS AND EXERCISES

1. (a) What are the components of speech? (b) What function does each serve in conveying meaning? (c) When a speaker's voice and words are in apparent conflict, which do you accept and respond to as revealing the speaker's true state of thinking and feeling? (d) What is meant by the statement "Actions speak louder than words"? (e) Under what circumstances may a speaker use voice without words to convey meaning? (f) When may he use gesture without words?

2. What is the general relationship between (a) pitch changes and feeling? (b) pitch changes and meaning?

3. Words are not always used to inform. (a) How else may words be used? (b) Under what circumstances? (c) What are "purr words" and "snarl words"? Give examples of each. (d) What are your favorite words for approval and disapproval

4. (a) What are the three basic types of pitch change? (b) What is the intellectual significance of each? (c) What is the relationship between irony, sarcasm, and innuendo to pitch? (d) Demonstrate each in the words "I sure do like him."

5. (a) What is intonation? (b) When does a speaker use a foreign intonation? (c) Compare two foreign-born speakers of different national origin in respect to their American-English speech. What differences do you note?

6. (a) What is the relationship between force and meaning? (b) In the sentence "I want to go soon" what different meanings are indicated by changing the stressed word from *I* to *want* to *soon*?

7. (a) What is the relationship between duration and meaning? How are changes in duration achieved? (c) How is the use of *pause* related to meaning?

8. Listen to three or four friends or acquaintances engaged in a lively discussion. Note the type or types of vocal change used by each discussant. What conjectures can you make about the personality of each speaker and the vocal device used to highlight or emphasize a point?

9. Determine which form of emphasis (pitch, force, or duration) or which combination you would use for the italicized word in the following sentences.

(a) Come here *now!*
(b) I feel just *bored.*
(c) Well, *that* idea would *never* occur to me.
(d) It's *no* use your asking again. The *answer* is a definite *maybe.*
(e) What *she* had to say was of *very* little interest to *me.*

RECOMMENDED READINGS

ANDERSON, V. A. *Training the Speaking Voice.* 2nd ed. New York: Oxford University Press, 1958, chap. 5.

BRONSTEIN, A. J., and B. F. JACOBY. *Your Speech and Voice.* New York: Random House, Inc., 1967, chap. 4.

BROWN, R. *Words and Things.* New York: The Free Press, 1958, chaps. 1 and 4.

EISENSON, J., J. J. AUER, and J. V. IRWIN. *The Psychology of Communication.* New York: Appleton-Century-Crofts, 1963, chaps. 1–3.

PIKE, K. *The Intonation of American English.* Ann Arbor, Mich.: University of Michigan Press, 1946.

Chapter 4

Nonverbal Communication

Speaking Without Words

> Every man is the builder of a temple,
> called his body.
>
> HENRY DAVID THOREAU

During the Watergate hearings in 1973–1974 a central controversy raged around the recording of conversations that occurred in the Oval Office of the White House between President Nixon and his staff and visitors. Many were convinced that listening to the tape recordings would reveal conclusively the guilt or innocence of the parties involved in the alleged Watergate coverup. But this would not be the complete truth. Without the nonverbal cues—the speaking that was never recorded—the audio tapes themselves could never be conclusive. The sly wink, the raised eyebrow, or a subtle gesture could easily reverse completely the meaning of any audible statement. One frequent visitor at the White House, when informed of the electronic eavesdropping, said, with obvious relief, that during his "conversations" with the President he merely "nodded."[1]

In the 1950s and 1960s the student of speech communication could find little published research on this fascinating study of nonverbal communication. During the 1970s a new and expanding interest in what Edward Hall called *The Silent Language* prompted scholars in many disciplines—including psychology, sociology, anthropology, and speech communication—to explore all aspects of the messages we transmit without words. Using controlled scientific experiments, researchers have attempted to determine the significance of the signals we transmit to others through body position, facial expression, hand and arm gesture, and even in our selection of the space between ourselves and others (proxemics) when we meet and react with one person or many.

[1] *Time*, July 30, 1973, p. 11.

Several popular paperbacks now promise their readers an insight into the "personal secrets" of others through a study of body language that knows not "how to lie." We are frankly skeptical of any infallible claims to certainty in this highly complex, contradictory area where individual and cultural differences in both the transmitter and the receiver play so marked a role. Yet we also need to recognize the fundamental importance of the signals we send and receive with or without accompanying words and phrases. Experience and research do tend to confirm the concept that when the verbal message contradicts the nonverbal, the visible action is more likely to reflect the true feeling of the sender. Your parents and grandparents, for example, danced the Lindy Hop as they sang "Your lips tell me no no, but there's yes yes in your eyes."

As a student of basic speech you will want to devote close attention to the relationships of visible action to the total process of message transmission. Although controlled research is relatively recent, a study of the language of visible action is ancient. Greek and Roman rhetoricians and the elocutionists of the eighteenth and nineteenth centuries studied and wrote extensively on the management of the body. Indeed, the elocutionary school's preoccupation with the teaching of delivery to the neglect of the verbal idea led in part to its downfall. In 1872 Charles Darwin published his classic work *The Expression of Emotions in Man and Animals,* reissued in 1965. David Efron's work *Gesture and Environment,* published in 1941, was reissued in 1972 as one of the pioneer studies in the relationships between cultures and gesture patterns.[2]

In this chapter we will deal largely with relatively formalized gestures and their implications in communication. Some considerations will also be given to individualized, expressive movements and their significance for the speaker and the listener. In subsequent chapters devoted to the preparation and delivery of the message, we will offer specific suggestions for public speaking, debate, discussion, and oral reading.[3]

NONVERBAL ORIGINS OF SPEECH

Whenever we communicate, we engage in overt (visible) as well as covert activity. The words and the melody of speech are impossible without accompanying action. A considerable amount of that action is not readily seen, but the results are heard in the production of voice and articulated sounds. One possible theory suggests that conventionalized actions—gestures—formed the basis for human speech. The essence of this theory might be summed up as follows: Human speech arose out of unconsciously produced actions, or gestures, made initially by the hands,

---

[2] *Journal of Communication,* **22** (1972), 462. The entire issue of the journal is devoted to nonverbal communication.

[3] See Chapter 15, pages 333–338; and Chapter 16, pages 356–360.

arms, and the body as a whole, including the tongue and the lips. When the hands were occupied with tools, the gesture movements were confined to the tongue and lips, and resulted in the production of conventionalized sound symbols or words that corresponded directly to the gestures. The hearer in turn recognized the sound symbols because he had unconsciously reproduced the original gesture or sequence of gestures that accompanied the production of the sound patterns (words).[4] The linguist Mario Pei states his position and that of many students who are concerned with the origin of language with the observation: ". . . gestural language is commonly conceded to have preceded oral speech, some say by at least one million years. It is further estimated that some seven hundred thousand distinct elementary gestures can be produced by facial expressions, postures, movements of the arms, wrists, fingers, etc., and their combinations. This imposing array of gestural symbols would be sufficient to provide the equivalent of a full-blown modern language."[5]

In our discussion of language it was pointed out that language is capable of being specific and intellectual, but that language is not always used for such purposes. A similar point might be made for gestures. On their highest level of capability, gestures may be used to enhance or clarify the meanings of the sound symbols with which they are usually accompanied in speech. Gestures may even be used a step beyond this. When words fail us, we may resort to gesturing in a final attempt to communicate our meanings. If we fail in our attempts at communication, but persist in our efforts to try to say something, thought is likely to give way to feeling, and feeling to emotion. Gestures, like words, may lose their intellectual significance and become movements expressive of emotion. Comprehension of such gesticulation is possible because the actions excite sympathetic movements in the observer, who then begins to respond approximately as he himself feels when the movements are self-initiated.

TYPES OF NONVERBAL ACTIVITY

If we wish, we may classify nonverbal activity into two broad types of gesture. The first, *articulatory gestures,* carry symbolic or intellectual value. Articulatory gestures represent oral sound equivalents. The second type, *expressive* or nonsymbolic gestures, call forth feelings or arouse emotions, but do not have significant intellectual value. Postures that reveal emotional states and facial grimaces such as sneering and smiling are examples of expressive nonsymbolic gestures.

[4] This is one brief theoretic explanation of the origin of speech. Many other explanations have been offered. Some of these are reviewed in G. W. Gray and C. M. Wise, *The Bases of Speech,* 3rd ed. (New York: Harper & Row, 1959), chap. 8.

[5] M. Pei, *The Story of Language* (Philadelphia: Lippincott, 1949), p. 13.

Articulatory gestures may be subclassified along four functional lines, namely *graphic, plastic, denotative,* and *symbolic.* Gestures considered as graphic are those which, through suggestion of an outline, stand for a particular object. For example, if we turn our hand, index finger extended, in a series of loops, we are using a graphic gesture to describe a spiral-shaped object. In using *plastic* gestures we picture the shape of an object or a person through executing molding movements of the hands. We can suggest the shape of a box or an "hour-glass figure" with such a gesture.[6]

On a higher symbolic level, we may use *denotative gestures.* This type of gesture involves the selection and suggestion of a striking characteristic of an object to stand for the object. For example, the sign language used by many deaf-mute persons employs a gesture suggesting the removal of a hat to stand for the idea of a man. On a still higher level of abstraction, we have the *symbolic gesture.* This type of gesture is probably closest to abstract language usage. The meaning is dependent on an association of idea and symbol. In the sign language of the American Indian, for example, cupped hands stand for *drinking* rather than for an object for drinking. If cupped hands were to stand for an object, we should have an example of a *plastic* gesture. But when cupped hands stand for an act rather than an object, a higher level of abstraction is attained, and we have a *symbolic* gesture.

Articulatory gestures probably began as involved and elaborate movements. In time, both the complexity and amount of movement were reduced. With the reduction in the nature and amount of movement came an increase in the intellectual significance of the movements. As we think of articulatory gestures today, we may characterize them as intentionally produced, meaningful acts that have gradually been reduced to a few relatively simple movements for convenience in presenting ideas and in obtaining intellectual responses.

GESTURE AS AN INTERNATIONAL LANGUAGE

Articulatory gestures are as close as we have ever come to an interternational language. Persons who have no common audible language and who must communicate with one another are likely to resort to the use of gesture. Usually a modicum of communication is possible even for those who have made no special study of the language of gesture. For those who have made this study, a considerable amount of communication is possible.

The American Indian was aware of the advantages of gesture language. The intelligent American Indian spoke in two ways. One was the

---

[6] For further classification of gestures into many subcategories, see P. Ekman and W. V. Friesen, "Hand Movements," *Journal of Communication,* **22** (1972), 353–374.

audible language of his tribe or nation, in which oral words were reinforced by gestures; the second was the use of a gesture language for purposes of intertribal communication.

Probably the most completely standardized international gesture language is that which has been evolved by deaf-mute persons.[7] In many of the signs employed, the gesture language of the deaf-mute bears a striking resemblance to the intertribal sign language of the American Indian. The Trappist monks, whose members take a vow of perpetual silence, have evolved a system of gestures that also strikingly resembles that used by deaf-mutes. The reason for the many resemblances among gesture languages, regardless of place of origin, should be fairly apparent. Gesture words are for the most part limited to the immediate experiences of the speaker which frequently include the observer. When not so limited, the many descriptive "words" of gesture language recall concretely the basic element for idea association. Much of the vocabulary of gesture language consists of concepts that have objective attributes, or states of being.

Organized gesture languages, such as are used by deaf-mute persons, have conventions of sentence structure and syntax. For example, in the sign language of deaf-mutes, the subject of the sentence comes first, and the object of the sentence generally precedes the verb; adjectives precede the modified noun. A fundamental rule of gesture language is to present signs or words in the same order as we are likely to see and respond to them visually.

The language of gesture is devoid of prepositions, conjunctions, and abstract words. The convention of order of presentation makes it possible for the gesture speaker to dispense with prepositions and conjunctions. Abstract verbs are replaced by specific concepts that permit the essential meaning to be communicated.

NONVERBAL REINFORCEMENT OF AUDIBLE SPEECH

Those who can hear and have learned to use oral speech have little or no opportunity for using highly organized gesture language. In ordinary circumstances we use gestures to reinforce, or emphasize, our audible part. We use gestures unconsciously and become aware of their use only when, for some reason, we are physically or socially restrained from gesturing. What would happen if we agreed to eliminate gestures completely from our speech? This was done in an experiment, with highly significant results. In the first place, there was a considerable reduction in the fluency of the oral speech. Second, the speaker's articulation was not as

---

[7] Specific sign languages employed by the deaf, e.g., The American Sign Language of the Deaf, are closely identified in syntax and lexicon (vocabulary) with the spoken language of the culture or country. In this way the sign language of a French-speaking deaf person is significantly different from that of an English-speaking deaf person.

clean-cut and precise as was usually the case. Finally, the size of the speaker's effective vocabulary was appreciably reduced. In brief, the speaker who is accustomed to using gestures but who is restrained from doing so has difficulty in speaking and in being understood. It would appear, then, that in conversational situations we not only are dependent on gestures to make ourselves understood, but also are accustomed to respond to gestures in order to comprehend the speech of others.

Many of us have had an experience in which we found that our manner of speaking somehow failed to support the assertions we wanted others to accept. We did not succeed in sounding persuasive. Our vocal tones, even if they were not quivering, did not suggest security and self-conviction. In such situations it is highly likely that our actions, as well as our voices, betrayed us. The "betrayal" was a result of a lack of control of our visible movements as well as those that produce words and voice.

AFFECTIVE INFLUENCES ON NONVERBAL BEHAVIOR

Earlier we saw what happens to oral language when the controls are relaxed or broken down. Comparable changes take place in nonverbal behavior—the visible aspect of speech. When our hands tremble, when we feel uncomfortable standing and fidget when sitting, when our muscles twitch and our knees "turn to water," we are revealing through unconscious but expressive movements that we are no longer in complete control of the intellectual situation and are giving way to emotion. Some of us have seen the wild and disorganized activity of a hysterical person. In one form of insanity, bizarre postures, which a mentally normal person could not maintain for more than a few moments, are assumed and maintained by the hour. A morbidly depressed individual scarcely moves. An emotionally excited individual is likely to engage in disorganized and exaggerated movement.

The gestures of emotion in which we are most interested are those most of us produce without awareness and without apparent cause. Such gestures include licking our lips when they are not dry, closing our eyes when we are not sleepy, adjusting our clothes when they are in perfectly good order, and smoothing our hair when it is in no need of further attention. These are examples of movements or gestures that are not intended for the response of another person. They are self-directed gestures that represent instead an unconscious aspect of the response of the performer.

Support for the unconscious aspect of these self-expressive movements comes from Wolff, who found that under experimental conditions subjects failed to recognize movements of their hands and face and their own gait.[8]

---

[8] W. Wolff, "Involuntary Self-Expression in Gait and Other Movements," *Character and Personality*, 3 (1935), 327–344. See Albert E. Scheflen, *Body Language and Social Order: Communication as Behavioral Control* (Englewood Cliffs, N.J.: Prentice-Hall, Inc., 1972), chap. 5.

According to the findings of one investigator,[9] self-directed gestures are supposed to have a definite relationship to personality type. The clothes-adjuster may be an insecure individual; the hair-smoother, a vain but not altogether adequate personality; the pouter, a dependent, infantile person.

SELF-DIRECTED GESTURES

Self-directed gestures may arise as a result of inner conflict and may be indicative of personal frustration, or unresolved conflict. The frustration may be momentary, as may the feeling of tension which accompanies unresolved conflict. Tension may be lessened by the execution of such a gesture as snapping the fingers or scratching the head. We recognize that when we get into a "tight spot" most of us engage in self-directed gestures. We may suddenly feel an itchy nose, or find that our ears require scratching. Sometimes these acts might actually create an element of danger. The ear-scratching or eye-blinking that begins to take place while we drive a car under difficult road conditions would increase the difficulty of driving, except that the gestures serve to reduce physical tension.

Some self-directed gestures occur often enough in different persons to have acquired symbolic significance. For example, a sudden tightening of the jaw may very well stand for aggression. The gesture of passing the hand over the face, eyes shut, may stand for a wish to evade or get rid of an unpleasant situation. According to one student of unconscious gesture movements, this gesture constitutes an escape from the world of reality, an escape in which the actor, momentarily at least, removes himself from a situation he cannot physically leave.

THE NONVERBAL IN ART AND RELIGION

Although gesture is possibly the basis of human speech and serves as a component of spoken language, the nonverbal aspects of communication continue to enjoy an independent existence. They have an almost completely intellectual function in organized sign languages. The nonverbal components of communication also have artistic as well as intellectual inclinations. In the drama, gesture is seen in pantomime, a play employing action without words. Interpretative dancing is gesture that suggests artistic mood as well as meaning.

The language of gesture has always assumed a significant place in man's religious behavior. Worshipers in churches perform certain move-

[9] M. H. Krout, "Autistic Gestures: An Experimental Study in Symbolic Movement," *Psychological Monographs*, 46, No. 208 (1935). See also his later studies in *Journal of General Psychology*, 51 (1954), 121–152; 296–308.

ments that have significance only as the actions pertain to the ceremony of religion. In some churches, priests perform elaborate ritualistic gestures as a part of the religious ceremony. Ritualistic gesture is part of the religion of ancient as well as contemporary cultures. It was and still is employed in Oriental as well as Western civilization. The American Indian appealed to his tribal gods through pantomime and dance. The North American white man does not ordinarily appeal to God through the dance, although some modern churches use it on special occasions and have in no sense abandoned the pantomime.

CULTURAL AND INDIVIDUAL DIFFERENCES

Authorities differ in their conclusions about the universality of gesture language across all cultures. An increasing number of studies seem to substantiate the similarity of facial expression in certain basic emotional states such as fear, anger, happiness, sadness, and others.[10] Although gesture languages are characteristically more striking for their similarities than for their differences in meanings, differences do exist. For example, in Western cultures hand clapping means approval or applause; in Eastern cultures hand clapping is usually used to summon an inferior or menial person. In some European countries, military personnel may, upon ceremonial occasions, bestow kisses on one another's cheeks. American military persons being honored by their European counterparts accept this gesture. They do not, however, include the kiss-on-cheek as part of their own awarding of military honors. The embrace and the kiss of greeting among women have their counterpart in a handshake or slap on the back among men. Specific gestures occasionally assume a local significance which may constitute a source of danger among the uninformed or unwary. Thumbs in ears and waving fingers may be silly or amusing as a gesture among Americans in most parts of the United States; the use of the same gesture may be foolhardy or dangerous in some parts of the United States inhabited by recent immigrants or first-generation Americans.

Cultural differences become apparent when we contrast the frequent and generous use of gestures by the Southern Europeans with the more restrained use of gestures by the Northern Europeans. The French, the Italians, and the Spanish people as a group are much freer in their use of gesture than are the inhabitants of the Scandinavian countries. The differences are more likely cultural than racial. This is suggested by the results of a study among American immigrants. It was found that first- and second-generation Americans tend to use gestures in keeping with the

[10] P. Ekman and W. V. Friesen, "Constants Across Cultures in the Face and Emotion," *Journal of Personality and Social Psychology,* **17** (1971), 124–129.

prevalent custom of their new environment, rather than with the custom of their racial group. For example, the Italian immigrants who lived among other Italians continued to use gestures much as they did in their native land. The children of Italian immigrants, on the contrary, were less disposed to the gestures of Italy and more inclined to the use of those prevalent among Americans in their part of the United States. It is reasonable to assume that persons of Nordic origin living in South Europe or among persons of Latin derivation anywhere might begin to take their hands out of their pockets and become more mobile in their speech.

Whatever the initial reason for cultural variations in use of gesture, there is no good reason for believing the variations to be biologically inherited. We learn to use visible movements much as we learn to use oral vocabulary. If gestures are a customary part of the manner of speech, gestures will be incorporated into our speaking. If immobility and physical restraint characterize the speakers of our community, most of us will learn to speak with a minimum use of gesture. Gestures, like oral words, are learned through imitation of persons in our environment. The imitation, however, still permits considerable room for individual variability. Our actions, as well as our words, continue to be our own because of the manner in which we use them. Persons with large vocabularies and relatively fluent speech may have less need for gesture than persons with more limited vocabularies and less fluent speech. Voluble persons usually talk with an abundance of gesture as well as an abundance of audible words. Gestures appropriate to some public speakers may be most inappropriate to others. A medium-sized man on a public platform might emphasize a point by banging his fist on the speaker's stand. The same gesture by a short person might seem ludicrous. For a tall, heavy-set person to bang on a speaker's stand might constitute a threat.

SUMMARY

Nonverbal communication—the "words" of action—is an integral part of speech. Indeed, we interpret meaning through an integration of the audible and the visible. The process is unitary. As used by the individual, gestures may signify specific thoughts, imply attitudes or moods, or be expressive of thoughts or feelings. Although cultural differences exist, many gestures tend to be alike the world over. Because of their similarity of meaning, the language of gesture comes close to being an international medium of communication. An independent art form, gesture also plays an important role in the rituals of religion. Properly employed and controlled, the nonverbal may serve as an adequate substitute for oral words. When not controlled, gestures are equivalent to the use of vocal noise without words. Unconsciously produced, self-directed gestures may reveal conflicts of personality. The effective communicator strives to coordinate the verbal and nonverbal in a way that reflects the intended message.

QUESTIONS AND EXERCISES

1. Do foreign-born persons of your acquaintance vary in their use of gesture? What about their children?

2. Prepare a short speech in which you demonstrate two types of articulatory gestures. Use as many examples as you can.

3. Develop a two- to three-minute dramatic pantomime in which the story is told entirely through action, facial expression, and gesture. Members of the class will jot down their impressions as the skit unfolds.

4. If possible, watch a video tape of yourself in a discussion group or in a speech presentation. Analyze each nonverbal clue you used. Write a short critique indicating what your nonverbal actions said to you as a viewer.

5. During a television talk show, turn off the sound and attempt to read the message solely through sight and your interpretation of the gestures and facial expressions.

RECOMMENDED READINGS

BIRDWHISTELL, RAY L. *Kinesics and Context.* Philadelphia: University of Philadelphia Press, 1970.

BOSMAJIAN, H. A., ed. *The Rhetoric of Nonverbal Communication.* Glenview, Ill.: Scott, Foresman and Company, 1971.

CRITCHLEY, M. *The Language of Gesture.* London: Edwin Arnold & Co., 1939.

EFRON, DAVID. *Gesture and Environment.* New York: King's Crown, 1941. Republished: *Gesture, Races, and Culture.* The Hague: Mouton, 1972.

EISENSON, J., J. J. AUER, and J. V. IRWIN. *The Psychology of Communication.* New York: Appleton-Century-Crofts, 1963, chap. 2.

HARRISON, RANDALL P. *Beyond Words: An Introduction to Nonverbal Communication.* Englewood Cliffs, N.J.: Prentice-Hall, Inc., 1974.

KELTNER, JOHN W. *Interpersonal Speech Communication.* Belmont, Calif.: Wadsworth Publishing Co., Inc., 1970, chap. 6.

KNAPP, MARK L. *Nonverbal Communication in Human Interaction.* New York: Holt, Rinehart and Winston, Inc., 1972.

MEHRABIAN, ALBERT. *Nonverbal Communication.* Chicago: Aldine-Atherton, 1972.

MORTENSEN, C. DAVID. *Communication: The Study of Human Interaction.* New York: McGraw-Hill Book Company, 1972, chap. 6.

Chapter 5

Our Changing Speech Patterns

Although we do not have to accept literally George Bernard Shaw's observation that "England and America are two countries separated by the same language," there is little doubt that from the time of the American Revolution to World War II, American English emerged as a language with enough divergence in pronunciation and word usage to require us to think of the differences despite the basic similarities. Interestingly, since World War II, the influences of improved communication, radio, television, and film have worked in the opposite direction.

American English is in a process of change because it is a living language. Classical Latin and Greek have become stabilized because they are "dead" and no longer spoken by persons engaged in social or economic intercourse. As Whatmough observes, "If language could not change, it would be incapable of coping with new demands, new concepts, new inventions. . . ."[1]

In this chapter we shall consider some of the factors and historical influences that resulted in English becoming the language of the United States, features that characterize American English and its dialectal variations, and some psychosocial forces that are currently and dynamically influencing the sounds, the lexicon, and even the syntax of our language.

ENGLISH HISTORICAL BACKGROUNDS

From the time of ancient Romans until the eleventh century the land masses known as the British Isles were successively conquered and occupied by peoples of many nations. Each of the conquering peoples left traces of influence on a language whose basic forms and structure were not to be determined until the sixteenth century.

The Romans under Caesar came to Britain in 55 B.C. and did not finally leave until about A.D. 400. The inhabitants who remained behind, other than the Romans, spoke a Celtic dialect but retained the use of Roman names for roads and many geographic locations (place names).

In the middle of the fifth century Angles, Saxons, and Jutes began to invade Britain and drove the Celts westward into Wales and Cornwall

[1] J. Whatmough, *Language* (New York: St. Martin's Press, 1956), p. 174.

and northward toward what is now Scotland. The term *English* is used for the Germanic speech of these groups of invaders and their descendants. It is important to appreciate, however, that the earlier inhabitants of Britain did not suddenly change their speech habits, and those who stayed behind and were not pushed to the west or to the north continued to speak a language much as they had spoken, except that new linguistic forms—those of their conquerors—were incorporated and modified into their previous linguistic habits. Essentially, despite military conquests, the language of the conquered assimilated that of the conquerors.

Christianity came to Saxon England during the first half of the seventh century. With the advent of Christianity, Latin was introduced as the spoken and written language for religious and learned purposes. This influence on the common man, however, was not significantly reflected in his everyday speech.

Between the eighth and eleventh centuries Scandinavians in increasing numbers came to Britain, and with it Scandinavian influences on what was to become English. The Scandinavians, for the most part Danes, also invaded and conquered the northeastern parts of France and ultimately became the ruling aristocracy of Normandy. During this period of achievement the Scandinavians assumed Gallic ways, including French as a language, and their own Germanic speech was lost.

In the historically critical year 1066 the descendants of the Scandinavians, who now were Normans and who had become essentially French in culture and in their linguistic habits, invaded England under William the Conqueror, and became the established power in England. Though French then became the language of the ruling class in England, the masses continued to speak a Germanic language. In time the language of the Norman conquerors was reduced in influence, and all but disappeared, at least as far as the speech of the common man was concerned.

The English most people in England speak today, and the American English most Americans speak, are both derived from the speech of the inhabitants of the London area from the time of William the Conqueror through the Elizabethan period. But England throughout its history has never been free of divergent dialects. The Germanic groups—the Angles, Saxons, and Jutes—came from different parts of the continental lowlands. The groups spoke different dialects, settled in different parts of England, and left their linguistic influences where they settled. One important result is that the dialectical differences among the inhabitants of England today are greater and more divergent than are the regional-dialect differences in the United States.

It does not require an expert ear to discern differences between American and British speech, even assuming that the comparison is made between an educated Englishman who has lived most of his life in or near London and an educated American who has lived most of his life in or around Boston and is a Harvard graduate. These representative speakers are selected because, though the differences between American English and upper-class London English are comparatively few, yet differences exist. They exist in idiom and in specific words to denote situations and events as well as in word pronunciation and stress and in manner of articulation. Differences are also found in speech melody. The Londoner and the Bostonian are not likely to express their enthusiasms or their irritations with the same choice of words or the same manner of vocal melody. *A bloody American mess* has different connotations from *a bloody English mess.* The Bostonian gets about in streetcars or subway trains while his London cousin gets about in trams and by way of the underground. The Bostonian who does not own his own home lives in an apartment; his London counterpart lives in a flat. The Bostonian leaves his car in a ga*rage* rather than in a *garage*. He watches *TV* rather than *"telly."* The Bostonian law enforcer is a *policeman,* or a *cop,* rather than a *bobby;* the Bostonian is entertained at the *movies* rather than at the *cinema.* The melody pattern of the Londoner, whether his utterance is intellectual or emotional, is likely to be characterized by wider inflectional changes than is that of the Bostonian. Articulatory differences may also be heard. The sound *t* in an unstressed syllable, as in *pity,* is likely to be more clearly and more lightly articulated by our English representative than it is by the American. Neither speaker is likely to pronounce an *r* when it is in a final position in a word, as in *dear* or *hear,* but the *r* would be articulated differently in words such as *very.* Our English representative pronounces the word *very* in a manner which phoneticians describe as a single flapped sound. Americans may think of it as approximating the pronunciation *veddy* as in "veddy nice," which of course it is not, except possibly to the prejudiced and motivated ear of an American comic strip artist trying to get across a notion of English pronunciation to an American comic strip reader.

STANDARD ENGLISH SPEECH?

If an American living in the first quarter of this century were to judge English speech by what he heard from Englishmen who were visiting in the United States, he might well have concluded that Englishmen speak pretty much alike. Had he read Shaw's *Pygmalion,* he would have been puzzled by Professor Higgins' complaints. Yet both the American's and Professor Higgins' observations were correct. It is likely that the American, unless he happened to have traveled widely in England, would have been exposed only to the speech of British stage personalities, British political personages, members of the royal family, and well-to-do and well-educated Englishmen with public (really private) secondary school and Oxford or Cambridge backgrounds. Their speech is almost standard.

The speech of these groups is characterized by English phoneticians as *Received Pronunciation;* by *received* is meant "accepted in approved circles." This speech is described by the English phonetician Daniel Jones in his *An Outline of English Phonetics.*[2] Individual recommended pronunciations may be found in Jones' *Pronunciation of English.*[3]

Though "Received speech" was the one that Professor Higgins spoke as a matter of course and that Eliza Doolittle learned to speak after much rigorous training, but which broke down under emotional stress, it is not the standard for the speech of all Englishmen—not even for those with moderate amounts of education who live in or near the City of London. Members of the English Parliament, including those who represent the Conservatives, are today more likely to speak with the accents and pronunciations of the British Broadcasting Company than those identified with Eton and Oxford. A Labor member of Parliament is not likely to assume Tory accents, or even a Tory vocabulary, when he is aware that he may be on the air and his words heard by his constituents in the evening news broadcast. In brief, the forces of democracy in England, as well as the forces of the mass media of communicating, have worked in directions away from Received Pronunciation. Despite Professor Higgins, the English will go on being themselves and listening, so that they can appreciate British Broadcasting Company diction, American movies, and American television programs.

There are, of course, variances within the London area that are wide enough to require "translation" for many British as well as American citizens. McCabe, an American journalist, presents the following as an example of the Cockney dialect:

> "A lorry pranged the banger in the boot and I hadn't the readies to get it out of the ricky, so do you fancy taking the tube to the cinema or slipping around to the pub for a pint."

This translates to:

> "A truck smashed into the trunk of my car and I didn't have the money to fix it, so do you want to take the subway to the movies or go to the neighborhood bar for a beer?"[4]

Despite variations in dialects "within cultures" we may conjecture with popular linguist Mario Pei, who in 1949 predicted:

[2] Daniel Jones, *An Outline of English Phonetics* (8th ed.: Cambridge, Eng.: W. Hefner and Sons, 1956).

[3] Daniel Jones, *The Pronunciation of English* (3rd ed.: Cambridge, Eng.: W. Hefner and Sons, 1950).

[4] Charles McCabe, "The Fearless Spectator," *San Francisco Chronicle,* March 21, 1972.

Granted a continuation of present historical conditions, the English language of two hundred years hence will be likely to represent a merger of British and American phonetic habits, with comparatively little in the way of morphological or syntactical innovations, but with a turn-over in vocabulary and semantics that would make it difficult, not to say incomprehensible, to the English speaker of today.[5]

AMERICAN BEGINNINGS

When, may we say, did American speech become sufficiently different from the English to give us the beginning of American English? What were the influences that produced and nurtured these differences? In what ways were they peculiarly a result of a new culture and new forces related to this culture? What forces, regardless of culture, continue to exert their effects on our ever-changing speech patterns?

At the opening of the nineteenth century the United States had its critics and deplorers who raised the hue and cry, "What is happening to our language?" They were referring to English, and were warning Americans about the need to keep their language pure and free from new vulgarisms. John Witherspoon, a Scottish clergyman who came to the United States to become the president of Princeton, suffered considerable anguish at the thought of the development of an American language. Mencken, in *The American Language*, cites Witherspoon as being pained by what he heard in "public and solemn discourses." Said Witherspoon:

> I have heard in this country, in the senate, at the bar, and from the pulpit, and see daily in dissertations from the press, errors in grammar, improprieties and vulgarisms which hardly any person of the same class in point of rank and literature would have fallen into in Great Britain.[6]

But persons such as Witherspoon, however great their prestige, were opposed by such Americans as John Adams and Thomas Jefferson. Perhaps more realistically, as Mencken notes on the same page, Jefferson declared:

> The new circumstances under which we are placed call for new words, new phrases, and for the transfer of old words to new objects. An American dialect will therefore be formed.

[5] M. Pei, *The Story of Language* (Philadelphia: Lippincott, 1949), p. 303.
[6] H. L. Mencken, *The American Language* (New York: Knopf, 1946), p. 5.

While the dispute between Americans for English English and those for American English was going on, Noah Webster was busily at work on his *Grammatical Institute of the English Language* and, perhaps more important, on his *American Dictionary of the English Language.* Certainly, with the publication of the latter in 1828, American English achieved status and recognition, and became established as a major variant of the English language.

Even a cursory review of the forces that established American English as an independent variant of the English language would reveal the following: The American geography and physiography presented new features, new creatures, new ways of working for a livelihood, and with them the need for new words. Many of the words came from the Indians and had no competition from the mother tongue. Thus, words such as *skunk, hickory, moose, opossum, persimmon,* and *squash* came into our language. Place names, Mencken points out,[7] also came from the Indians. So did such names for articles of clothing and frequently used objects as *tomahawk, wigwam, toboggan,* and *mackinaw.*

It would, however, be erroneous to conclude that the spirit of rebellion and the influence of the Indians were the only forces that shaped American English. The early colonists, from the very outset, had linguistic influences as a result of accretions from the languages of other colonizations. From the French came words such as *cache, portage,* and *voyageur,* as well as *prairie, bureau,* and *gopher.* From the Dutch in New Amsterdam, Mencken tells us, came such words as *cruller, cole-slaw, cookey, scow, patroon,* as well as *boss* and *Santa Claus.*[8] Many place names in the Hudson area containing *dorp, kill,* and *hook* are also directly from the Dutch. The word *Yankee,* according to Mencken (p. 110), is possibly the most notable of all contributions of Knickerbocker Dutch to the American language.

Spanish influences came later, at a time when American English had become well established as a variant of British English. Texas, the Southwest, and California had been colonized by the Spanish and were developed by Mexico when it won independence from Spain. Spanish and Mexican contributions to American English are readily recognizable in place names, architecture, agriculture, and animal husbandry. Some of the characteristic geographical features of the Southwest are known by the Mexican-Spanish names such as *Mesas, canyons,* and *arroyos.* The American, for the most part of Anglo-Saxon origin, who took over the Southwest not only learned how to construct buildings of mud and straw bricks but learned to call them *adobes.*

Many of the words we associate with cattle-raising are also of Spanish origin. These include *ranch, lasso,* and *riata.* The chaps worn by cowboys

---

[7] H. L. Mencken, op. cit., p. 105.

[8] H. L. Mencken, op. cit., p. 108.

to protect their legs are an abbreviation of *chaparajos*. The word *rodeo* has its English translation as "round-up." Now it is used as well to refer to an exhibition and competition in the skills cowboys were and to some degree are still expected to perform in cattle-raising. The word *ranch* has been extended to refer as a noun to an agricultural establishment and as a verb to farming activities.

The American colonists were ready borrowers of words from other languages, but they were also ready creators of words and phrases that were "coined in English metal" (Mencken, p. 113). Some of these words were a product of the new circumstances and conditions in which the colonists found themselves, but others reveal an underlying way people— any uninhibited and resourceful people—have with words. For a variety of reasons words were invented. One of the reasons is that inventing words is fun. It is a kind of pleasure in which we indulged ourselves as very young children and again as adolescents. Word-inventing can be a sheer delight, and our American colonists needed to be delighted. Mencken reminds us that "the American, even in the seventeenth century, already showed many of the characteristics that were to set him off from the Englishman later on—his bold and somewhat grotesque imagination, his contempt for dignified authority, his lack of aesthetic sensitiveness, his extravagant humor" (pp. 113–114). Not restrained by grammatical awareness or a knowledge of the structure of their language, and largely illiterate, our uncouth and headstrong early colonists added words as the needs of the occasions demanded. So nouns such as *cowhide* and *logroll*, and adjectives and adverbs such as *no-account, no-how,* and *lickity-split* became terms to reckon with and by in the utterances of our seventeenth-century Americans. These speakers also introduced such compound words as *bullfrog, hogwallow,* and *hoecake*. All of these are useful terms for persons who are busy working with or against the creatures and forces of nature in a new environment.

A living language shows the effects of a busy people. Early in our history the word *cent,* a verbal invention of Gouverneur Morris, was sub-stituted for the two-syllable English word *penny. Dime* was a Jeffersonian invention derived from the French word *dixième*.

Later we shall consider, in some detail, other examples of abbreviatory processes that have us riding in autos or cars rather than in automobiles, or watching TV rather than television.

ONGOING FORCES FOR CHANGE

Thus far we have traced the influences that created an American English and some of the differences in linguistic forms between British English and American English. Now we shall consider some of the forces that make any living language a changing language, constantly though slowly yielding to human inclinations and to changing verbal habits. To begin with, we should appreciate the effects of our contemporary ability for speed of movement and our general mobility as a nation of people on wheels or on wings. Washington and Julius Caesar traveled on state occasions in much the same kind of vehicles. Except for slight differences in styling and the addition of springs, similar vehicles were used by our Presidents up to McKinley, though out of choice rather than of necessity, to ride to their inaugurations. Recent Presidents are no longer earthbound. They may now move about with supersonic speed. What influence future Presidents or future English-speaking citizens—American or British, or from other parts of the English-speaking world—will have on American speech, or English speech, is a matter of conjecture.

Despite the efforts of some of our nineteenth- and early twentieth-century teachers of elocution and diction who considered British English a more genteel standard than the emerging American differences, the people of the United States do not observe or aspire to a single standard of what constitutes *good American speech*. Differences, however, at least among educated speakers, are relatively small. The members of Congress, regardless of the states they represent, have no difficulty in understanding one another because of differences in pronunciation or idiom. Nevertheless, as McDavid points out, ". . . every speaker of American English knows that other varieties exist, different from the one he speaks, empirically he has learned to distinguish several of these varieties. . . ."[9] In 1958, C. K. Thomas identified ten major regional dialects in the United States.[10] The dialectical features, for the most part in pronunciation, enabled Thomas to "map" the United States into the following major areas (see Figure 5-1):

> Eastern New England, New York City, Middle Atlantic, the South, Southern Mountain States, the North Central Area, the Central Midland, the Northwest, the Southwest Coastal Area, and Western Pennsylvania.[11]

Regional differences

In continental United States, differences in pronunciation are most striking along the Atlantic Coast. As we move inland and westward, the differences, C. K. Thomas observes, ". . . become blurred. Over large areas, from the Connecticut valley to the Oregon Coast, for instance, differences are so slight that casual listeners rarely notice them at all." Al-

---

[9] R. McDavid, in W. N. Francis, *The Structure of American English* (New York: Ronald Press, 1958), p. 482.

[10] By dialect we mean a variety of language with features of pronunciation, grammar, or vocabulary that distinguish it from other varieties (dialects) of the same language.

[11] C. K. Thomas, *An Introduction to the Phonetics of American English* (2nd ed.; New York: Ronald Press, 1958), p. 232.

FIGURE 5–1. Map showing the major regional speech areas: *A:*
Eastern New England; *B:* New York City; *C:* Middle Atlantic; *D:*
Southern; *E:* Western Pennsylvania; *F:* Southern Mountain; *G:*
Central Midland; *H:* Northwest; *I:* Southwest; *J:* North Central.

though differences are greatest along the Atlantic Coast, the merchant
from Maine has no anxiety that he will not be readily understood if he
speaks by telephone to a merchant from New York, or Maryland, or
Florida.

Most students of American dialects agree with Thomas that "the most
striking differences between the various regional pronunciations, and the
difference around which the most lively, though inconclusive, arguments
have resolved, is the nature of the sounds which correspond to the letter *r.*"[12]

Figure 5–2 is another dialect map of the United States. We may note
that the western part of the country is still "unmapped."

Table 5–1 indicates differences in word usage in some parts of the
Northern, Midland, and Southern dialect areas within the United States.
The reader may compare his own usage for the identified items with
those of his friends or associates.

DIALECTS AND SOCIAL CLASS

Not all dialectical differences are limited to geographic regions. Within
some regions there are dialectical differences related to social class and
socioeconomic status. McDavid observes that "Social differences in lan-

[12] C. K. Thomas, op. cit., p. 195.

FIGURE 5–2. Some of the dialect areas in the United States. (From R. W. Shuy, *Discovering American Dialects*, National Council of Teachers of English, Champaign, Illinois, 1967.)

Table 5–1   Dialect Area

Item	Northern	Midland	Southern
Paper container	bag	sack	sack
Type of cheese (cottage cheese)	dutch cheese pot cheese	smear-case	clabber cheese
Bread	johnny cake corn bread	corn bread	corn bread corn pone
Valve mechanism over a sink	faucet	spigot spicket	spigot spicket
Small, striped, bushy tailed animal	skunk	skunk polecat woodpussy	polecat
Cherry seed	pit stone	seed stone	seed stone
Container	pail	bucket	bucket

Source: Adapted from R. W. Shuy, *Discovering American Dialects,* National Council of Teachers of English, Champaign, Illinois, 1967, pp. 26–27.

guage are usually more apparent in morphology and syntax. But in some communities, particularly in the South, they manifest themselves in pronunciation as well."[13] Many speakers, perhaps more so in the South than elsewhere in the United States, are bidialectal for both social and economic reasons. Certainly many politicians—Huey Long and Eugene Talmadge may be cited as examples—are able to accommodate themselves to the dialect of their constituents or to the standards ordinarily observed in Congress without, of course, ever giving up the southern "flavor" of their speech.

Black English

Unlike dialects "confined" to regions or characteristics of social classes within regions, contemporary Black English has no geographic boundaries. Black English is spoken or understood by a majority of persons in the United States who identify themselves as Blacks.[14] Despite its early origins and development in the southern colonies and states, Black English is now heard in most "inner cities" throughout the United States. In Chapter 8 we will present some of the phonemic, morphemic, and syntactical features that have established Black English as a variant or dialect of "Standard" American English. Our concern in this chapter will be to highlight some of the contributions of Black English to post–World War II American English, and some of the dynamics behind these contributions.

In recent years much American slang has been taken directly from Black English. The phrase "right on" may have achieved respectability beyond its usage as slang. It is heard in political speeches and in radio and television commercials. "Rip off" is a phrase with multiple meanings. When a friend has been "ripped off" you have cause to worry whether he has been robbed, cheated, overcharged, arrested, or murdered. "Rap" is to talk or to argue. So, many of us held "rap sessions."

There is considerable poetry in the vocabulary of Black English in that words carry values and associations beyond their immediate meanings. For example, the substitution of "fox" for "woman" implies either an evaluation of women or a description of behavior. "Stone" is a "heavy" adjective, and a "stone fox" is "something else." A "dude" is the successor of the *hip cat* of the 1950s.

There are a number of speculations on why Black English slang is entering and, temporarily at least, becoming part of contemporary American English. One possibility could be found in the identification or sympathy of a number of socially alienated white young people with the

[13] R. McDavid, op. cit., p. 536.

[14] J. L. Dillard, in his *Black English: Its History and Usage in the United States* (New York: Random House, 1973), claims that 80 per cent of American Blacks speak Black English.

conditions and alienation of Blacks. Both white student activists and the late "hippy community" formed something of a counterculture, which adopted some Black terminology if not the syntax or phonology of Black English as its own. Within this counterculture, skill at using Black English carried prestige. Both components of this counterculture received considerable coverage in the mass media in the late 1960s. Thus, elements of Black English were literally broadcast and became current verbal coin.

It should be noted that most of these lexical contributions come from poor and working-class Blacks. A few exceptions are those made by Blacks who have been successful in the entertainment industry, where the use of Black English can be a professional asset. It is also generally assumed that the dialect of comparatively wealthy Blacks, the "respected speakers in the community," in the parlance of this book, is a variety of Standard English. It is possible to raise the question of whether there is a "Black Standard English," and if so, who are its users. The Black clergy and some Black political figures have an oratorical style different from both white Standard English and the Black English of the poor and working classes. Much of the Black clergy was trained at all-Black seminaries. There were similarities in the diction and oratory of the late Dr. Martin Luther King, Jr., and the late union organizer A. Philip Randolph. King's diction differed from that of his contemporary, the late Bishop James Pike, and Randolph's style of speech was different from that of his contemporary, the late Walter Reuther. There may well be a Black Standard English, or at least a "Standard English" as used by Blacks.

Who determines standards of usage? The dictionaries

Now, having briefly sketched some of the forces and influences that have given us American-English speech and its dialectical variations, historical and contemporary, we will return to Standard American English. Who determines when new words become respectable, and older words acceptable in regard to meanings they have assumed through usage? Who determines what are "proper" pronunciations? When does a slang term cease to be slang and become a "respectable" standard term? One answer is "when the educated, respected members of a culture use the terms." But the task still remains for terms and pronunciations to be recorded, and for decisions for what is to be recorded. Because we have no equivalent of a French Academy, whose members have stated meetings to make decisions and "fix the language," the responsibility inevitably falls on the editors of dictionaries. Fortunately, even Samuel Johnson noted in the preface to his famous Dictionary, published in 1755, that "words are the daughters of earth." Johnson opposed the notion of an Academy with authority to determine what is correct and acceptable. Despite this, Johnson admits personal bias in his lexical selection. For example, he included words he recognized as obsolete "when they are found in authors not obsolete, or when they have any force or beauty that may deserve revival." Johnson's authorities were the English writers he respected. He recognized that "no dictionary of a living tongue ever can be perfect, since while it is hastening to publication, some words are budding, and some falling away."

Noah Webster published his *Compendious Dictionary of the English Language* in 1806. Webster's dictionary acknowledged that current usage rather than prescription should determine lexical entries, and their definitions and pronunciations. The title page of his *Compendious Dictionary* indicates that five thousand words were added "to the number found in the Best English Compends," and that definitions of many words were "amended and improved."

Contemporary dictionary editors are usually insistent that they record what is established and current, and are reluctant to accept the responsibility for establishing standards by virtue of printed and widely distributed publications. Harrison Platt, Jr., presents what we consider a fair view of the degree of responsibility and authority the editors of a respected dictionary cannot avoid. In an Appendix to *The American College Dictionary*, Platt says:

> What . . . is the rôle of a dictionary in settling questions of pronunciation or meaning or grammar? It is not a legislating authority on good English. It attempts to record what usage at any time actually is. Insofar as possible, it points out divided usage. It indicates regional variations of pronunciation or meaning wherever practical. It points out meanings and uses peculiar to a trade, profession, or special activity. It suggests the levels on which certain words or usages are appropriate. A dictionary . . . based on a realistic sampling of usage, furnishes the information necessary for a sound judgment of what is good English in a given situation. To this extent the dictionary is an authority, and beyond this authority should not go.[15]

In the light of the above, we may reassess the significance of the entry on *ain't* in *Webster's Third New International Dictionary*. *Ain't*, according to the entry on page 45, is a contraction of *are not, is not, am not,* or *have not*. Further, we are told, *ain't* ". . . though disapproved by many, and more common in less educated speech [is] used orally in most parts of the U.S. by many cultivated speakers esp. in the phrase *ain't I*." Some critics of this dictionary have pointedly asked what is meant by "less educated speech" and imply that somewhere and somehow a comparison seems to be missing. On page 209, we learn that the entry *between* is no

[15] Harrison Platt, Jr., "Appendix," *The American College Dictionary* (New York: Random House, 1964), p. 1425.

longer limited to an implication of two but may be used to suggest division or participation by two or more. The entry cites such usage by *Time Magazine* and by eminent scholars, including a linguist from Harvard University.

One of the supporters of the changes accepted, and so presumably given authority in Webster's Third Edition, is Bergen Evans, recognized as a lexicographer, a language specialist, as well as the coauthor of *A Dictionary of Contemporary American Usage*. Professor Evans, in an informative and amusing article,[16] opens with the suggestion to "Mind your language, friend: words are changing their meaning all the time, some moving up the ladder of social acceptability and others down." In response to critics who accuse dictionary editors of condoning corruptions and "low usage," Evans says: "Alas, the tendencies they deplore have been evident for as long as we have any record of language and are as indifferent to indignation or approval as the tides." As examples of changes in word meaning, Evans points out that the word *resentment* once could mean "gratitude"; in Samuel Johnson's time, it came to mean "a species of revenge" and now means "indignation." The word *censure* once meant simply "to pass judgment"; *censure* now implies "a judgment with negative criticism." The word *uncouth* once meant "unknown" (*couth* itself meant "known") without any contemporary implications of "a lack of polish or 'good' (approved) manners." Few of us are aware that *wench* could once (as late as 1200) be used to refer to "a child of either sex" or that *counterfeit* once had no implication of illegal reproduction but meant "to imitate" or "to model," even after a worthy ideal.

Sumner Ives, in an article reviewing as well as anticipating the controversy that followed the publication of *Webster's Third New International Dictionary*,[17] makes a number of points relative to diction and grammatical usage that are decidedly worthy of our consideration. We shall summarize several of these points:

1. English has changed more during the past fifty years than during any similar period in the past.
2. "Language, any language, is a system of human conventions rather than a system of natural laws. . . ."
3. A dictionary is reliable only insofar as it comprehensively and accurately describes current practices in a language, including community opinion as to the social and regional associations of each practice described.
4. ". . . 'good' English is that which most effectively accomplishes the purpose of the author (or speaker) without drawing irrelevant at-

---

[16] Bergen Evans, "Couth to Uncouth and Vice Versa," *New York Times Magazine*, November 10, 1963, pp. 22ff.

[17] Sumner Ives, "A Review of Webster's Third New International Dictionary," *Word Study* (December 1961).

tention from the purpose to the words or constructions by which this purpose is accomplished. Thus, for ordinary purposes, 'good' English is that which is customary and familiar in a given context and in the pursuit of a given objective."

5. Words may have more than one pronunciation. "Standards" of pronunciation must make allowances for regional variations and for differences related to specific contexts. *Webster's Third New International Dictionary* represents "the normal pronunciation of English as it is spoken by cultured persons in each major section of the country—the 'language of well-bred ease,' culturally determined."

Slang and argot

Argot is the special vocabulary and idiom of a particular profession or social group. Historically argot is identified with the vocabulary of underworld characters, devised for "private" or in-group communication and identification. Thus, we are informed by *The Random House Dictionary of the English Language* that the "Beggar's Opera is rich in thieves' argot." The *Random House Dictionary* defines *slang* as "very informal usage in vocabulary and idiom that is characteristically more metaphorical, playful, elliptical, vivid, and ephemeral than ordinary language."

McDavid, in his discussion of Usage, Dialects, and Functional Varieties in the preface to the *Random House Dictionary* (page xxii), makes the following observation about slang and argot:

> *Slang* was once a synonym for argot, the ingroup language used by those who participate in a particular activity, especially a criminal one. In fact, much slang still derives from small, specialized groups, some of it nursed along tenderly by press agents. Popular musicians have originated many slang expressions now in general use. The word *jazz* itself is a good example: a Southern term meaning to copulate, it was used by the musicians who entertained in New Orleans brothels to describe their kinds of musical improvisations and soon came into general use despite the horror of Southerners who had previously known the word as a taboo verb. Today much slang originates with narcotic addicts, spreads to popular musicians, and then gains vogue among the young while falling into disuse among its inventors. Other argot, however, is restricted to the practitioners of a particular field: *boff*, meaning variously "a humorous line," "a belly laugh," or "a box office hit," seems restricted in its use to theatrical circles; *snow*, as it means "cocaine or heroin," is a common term only among drug addicts.

The fate of slang and argot terms is unpredictable.

Most of them disappear rapidly, some win their way into standard use, and still others remain what they were to begin with. *Mob,* deplored by Swift and other purists of 1700, would never be questioned today, but *moll,* meaning "a prostitute" or "the mistress of a gangster" has been in use since the early 1600's, and is still slang.

Technical terms arise because it is necessary for those who share a scientific or technical interest to have a basis for discussion. The difference between scientific and popular usage may be seen most strikingly in the biological sciences. A Latin term like *Panthera Leo* (lion) has a specific reference, while *cougar* may refer to any large wild American feline predator, or *partridge* may designate the bob-white quail, a kind of grouse, or some other game bird, according to local usage. Common words may be used with specific reference in a given field: *fusion* denotes one thing in politics, another in nuclear physics. As a field of inquiry becomes a matter of general interest, its technical terms will be picked up and used with less precision. Because of popular interest in Freudian psychology, such terms as *complex, fixation,* and *transference* are bandied about in senses Freud would never have sanctioned.

There is little question today that most of us employ slang and argot in both formal and informal speaking without awareness of the origin of the terms or the semantic intentions of the originators. From contemporary learning theorists and *behavior shapers* we have such terms as *conditioning reinforcement,* and *discriminative responses* as well as the abbreviated S→R. In our discussion of Black English we included some terms that are used by persons identified with the *counterculture* as well as by Blacks. It is too early to make any predictions about how many of these terms will become part of the everyday terminology of speakers of English, or whether some terms will, because of frequency and wide distribution of usage, become entries in the dictionaries of the 1970s and 1980s.

Some idea as to the rapidity of change in slang comes to us from the special glossary prepared by the United States Air Force for the American Prisoners of War (POWs) who were released following the conclusion of our active participation in the Vietnamese conflict. The introduction to this glossary notes: "We hesitate whether or not to call this language progress, but facts are facts. This is part of the slang being used by your sons and daughters." So, to help our returning POWs adjust, or at least to prepare them for what they were likely soon to hear, they were provided with a glossary that included the following entries:

Acid—Refers to the hallucinogenic drug Lysergic Acid Diethylamide LSD.

Acid rock—Psychedelic music; emphasizes electronic sounds, has a prominent beat and repeated sounds, very loud.

Bad scene—Unpleasant experience, place or event; a disappointment.

Bag—Person's way of life, now generally replaced by the term "trip" Example: "He's into a jazz trip."

Be-in—Gathering of people for spontaneous and hopefully creative activities.

Blow your mind—Be totally overcome by an idea, place, thing, or person.

Bread—Money

Bummer—Unpleasant experience, especially with drugs. It is also an exclamation of disgust or sympathy for another's bad experience.

Burn—Hurt emotionally, being taken.

Bust, Busted—Arrested, arrest.

Commune—Community where nothing is privately owned, usually associated with hippies. Social structures and values vary considerably.

Cool—Self-assured, knowledgeable. One who is aware of the times.

Cop out—Refuse to face issue or responsibility, usually a social one.

Dig—Enjoy, comprehend to fullest extent possible.

Do your own thing—Follow your own interest and activities. Usage has decreased in frequency.

Down—Unhappy, depressed. No longer under the influence of a drug.

Drag—Boring, a tedious experience.

Far out—All-purpose expression of approval often for an unusual experience. Used as exclamation. Now often used sarcastically to indicate disgust or boredom.

Gas, It's a—Cool, great. Refers to an event.

Get it together—To get organized.

Hang up—(1) Dislike, a mental block. (2) Reoccurring problem, source or irritation or disappointment with no apparent solution.

Hassle—(1) Problem: troublesome or irritating situation or event, conflict situation. (2) To disagree, argue or bother.

Heavy—Deep, complicated, meaningful. Bad or disgusting.

Hip—Aware. Connotes understanding and familiarity with drug scene and/or the radical view of political reality.

No way—Impossible.

Out of sight—Wonderful or terrific.

Pad—Place where one lives. Room or residence.

Split—Go. Leave or depart.

Tell it like it is—To be open and honest. Withholding nothing about what one believes and feels.

Uptight—In a state of tension. Worried, upset, or inhibited.

Vibes—Vibrations. Nonverbal expressions of thoughts or feelings.

Where it's at—The core of a situation or event.

Zap—Emphasize in an unforgettable manner.

Psychological determinants

In concluding our discussion of changing speech patterns, we shall review a few psychological factors that determine choice of words and the effects of such choice on our patterns of verbal behavior. By and large the words we use are selected according to our needs as speakers. The words we select to be impressive depend on the situation and the person or persons we wish to impress. Not infrequently this person may be the speaker himself, rather than the listener. As speakers, we may have occasional need for a large mouthful of sounds and so speak polysyllabically and at length in a manner that would make Freudian listeners click their tongues and nod their heads with weighty surmises. More frequently, however, other factors determine the words we select. One such factor is *ease of pronunciation*. With few exceptions short words are easier to pronounce than long words, and so, other things being equal, short words are likely to be chosen over long ones if they can be used effectively in communicating our thoughts and feelings. It is no accident that the most frequently used words in our language are shorter than the words less frequently used. George K. Zipf demonstrated that frequency of word usage is related to length (shortness) of words and that *words become shorter as spoken words* with increased frequency of usage. Zipf wrote, "There are copious examples of a decrease in magnitude of a word which results so far as one can judge solely from an increase in the relative frequency of its occurrence, as estimated either from the speech of an individual, in which the shortening may occur, or in the language of a minor group, or of the major speech group."[18]

We shorten words by processes of *assimilation,* by *truncation,* and by *abbreviatory substitution.* All three processes, incidentally, also result in

---

[18] *Psycho-Biology of Language* (Boston: Houghton Mifflin, 1935), p. 29.

ease of pronunciation. As examples of assimilation, we have dropped *p* from *cupboard* and most of us drop the *d* from *handkerchief*. Even short phrases are made shorter. For example, the modification of *goodbye* to *gdby,* or just *gby*.

Truncation can be exemplified by the change from *amperes* to *amps, elevator* to *el, telephone* to *phone* either as a verb or a noun, and *automobile* to *auto*. In the San Francisco area the Municipal Transportation System is briefly referred to as the *Muni. TV* for *television* is an example of truncation by abbreviation.

Abbreviatory substitutions are exemplified by *car* for *automobile, juice* for *electric current,* and *prexy* for *president*. The last two terms, to be sure, are usages within special groups, but the groups are large and influential. The word *cop* for *policeman* exemplifies the process of truncation and abbreviation: from *copper* to *cop* as truncation, and *cop* for *policeman* as abbreviatory substitution. The processes of word-shortening and the substitution of abbreviations exemplify Zipf's "principle of least effort."[19] According to Zipf, the changes that are associated with word-frequency usage are expressions of a general principle of human behavior that indicates that over time we tend to minimize or reduce our average rate of work expenditure to accomplish an objective.

There are, however, counterforces that exert influence in preventing overfrequent use of the same words and with it the process of word-shortening. The most potent of these forces is the human drive for variety of experience, including our experience with the words at our command. To avoid monotony we use synonyms that may be less precise in meaning than would be reiterations of the same word. Early in our school careers our teachers encouraged us to avoid the repeated use of a word merely because repetition is considered undesirable. Partly because of the authority of our teachers and partly because of our drive for variety, we go out of our way to use several different words to communicate an idea that might well be semantically more precise had a previous used word been used (employed).

Until recently verbal taboos and superstitions were cultural forces that worked against the use of some words, mostly of Anglo-Saxon origin, as expletives, adjectives, and verbs. Of late our daily metropolitan newspapers and our magazines use rather than abbreviate "four-letter" words. Except for some senior citizens, these words have lost their shock value and are no longer taboo. We find also that there is less difference in the productive vocabularies between adolescent boys and girls and between young men and women in social situations. However, grandparents—if not parents of the emancipated generation—continue to use circumlocutions and euphemisms to suggest, rather than forcibly say, what they

[19] G. K. Zipf, *Human Behavior and the Principle of Least Effort* (Reading, Mass.: Addison-Wesley, 1949).

mean or intend. Thus, there are still some children who are *born out of wedlock* and so are *illegitimate*. People still *pass away* or *pass on*[20] because speakers do not like to have them *die*. Undertakers are *morticians* whose establishments are *mortuaries*. Verbal habits and defensive attitudes persist, for at least part of the population, in maintaining and even increasing the use of terms that another part of the population may aggressively avoid.

These, briefly, are some of the forces and counterforces that have molded our language, influenced our verbal habits, and continue to modify our slow but ever-changing speech patterns. A living language is a growing language and one that changes forms, adds words and drops others, and modifies pronunciations. Some of the forces are global; others are rather peculiarly American.

RECOMMENDED READINGS

DILLARD, J. L. *Black English: Its History and Usage in the United States.* New York: Random House, Inc., 1973.

FRANCIS, W. N. *The Structure of American English.* New York: The Ronald Press Company, 1958.

LABOV, W. *Language in the Inner City.* Philadelphia: University of Pennsylvania Press, 1972.

MENCKEN, H. L. *The American Language.* New York: Alfred Knopf, Inc., 1946.

SHUY, R. W. *Discovering American Dialects.* Urbana, Ill.: National Council of Teachers of English, 1967.

[20] *Pass on* may be used by persons who believe in an afterlife.

Chapter 6

An Introduction to Phonetics

The Study of American-English Speech Sounds

If an individual produces a speech sound, or a combination of sounds, in an atypical manner, he gets in the way of the purpose of his speaking. An atypical manner is one that varies significantly from the accepted manner of most members of the speaker's community. Speech that sounds different attracts attention to itself rather than to the meanings of the speech symbols. Whenever the person attracts attention directly to his manner of speaking, he detracts, however briefly, from what he means or intends to communicate. Such detraction may result from the use of an unusual speech melody or from unusual or unacceptable ways of producing particular sounds or combinations of sounds.

Our interest in studying the sounds of American speech is twofold. The first purpose is in keeping with the general thesis of this text. It is to present a body of knowledge that will make us better informed and therefore more intelligent about the tools of speaking. Oral speech is sound production. It is important that we know not only how sounds are produced, but something about the character of the sounds we intend to produce.

The second purpose in studying phonetics develops from the first. Sound production that falls within acceptable standards will enhance the communication of meaning. If listeners must divide their efforts between trying to identify the symbols and trying to interpret them, understanding is impaired. Speech that falls within acceptable standards, however these may vary, is easy to listen to and easy to understand.

SOUND REPRESENTATION

English spelling inconsistent in sound representation

There is only a rough correspondence between the sounds of English speech and the 26 letters of our alphabet that are used to represent the sounds. As small children we learned that the frequently occurring combinations of the letters *ough* had many different pronunciations. Some of these are represented in the words *bough, enough, through, thorough,* and *cough.* We also learned that the same sounds were frequently represented by different alphabetic letters, and that this was true for both consonants and vowels. Spelling became something of a chore when we had to remember that the sound usually spelled *sh* in some words had spelling as variable as *ci, delicious; ch, machine; ss, assure; s, sugar; ti, patience.* The vowel sound usually represented by the double *e* as in *see* could also be represented, we had to learn, by such different spellings as *ea, mean; eo, people; i, machine; ei, receive; ie, believe.*

When we grew up, some of us had an opportunity to learn that there usually was a reason for the inconsistency between English spelling and pronunciation. We may have been informed that the spelling of most of our words represented their pronunciation at some former period in English history. This knowledge may have consoled us for the difficulties we had, and may still have, in spelling and pronunciation. In any event our spelling today provides us at best with about a 50 per cent correspondence between word pronunciation and spelling (phonemic-graphemic correspondence).[1] Thus, an approach other than spelling is needed for the study of pronunciation. We believe that the approach of choice is the study of phonetics and the use of the phonetic symbols of the International Phonetic Alphabet.

Questions and exercises

1. (a) How many different pronunciations do you know for the letters *ough?* (b) for the letter *c?* (c) for the letters *th?* (d) for the letter *s?* (e) for the letter *z?*

2. (a) How many pronunciations do you know for the letter *a?* (b) for the letters *ea?* (c) for the combination *oo?*

3. Do all educated speakers pronounce words the same way in your community? If not, what are some differences?

4. List ten words that have two or more acceptable but different pronunciations. Is there any consistent feature of the word—stress, vowel, consonant—that makes for the difference?

THE SOUNDS OF AMERICAN ENGLISH

The phoneme

Our study of phonetics will be approached through a consideration of the basic sound unit, or the *phoneme.* Phonemes are distinctive phonetic

---

[1] P. Hanna et al. investigated the correspondence between American-English spellings and word pronunciation. They concluded: "About half (49+ percent) of all the words in the 17,000+ corpus can be spelled correctly on phonological bases alone. To the extent that the corpus is a representative sample of the entire lexicon, this statement can be generalized to hold for the entire lexicon of American English." (Hanna et al., 1966, p. 122)

elements of a word. Distinctive sounds are those that enable us to distinguish between words. For example, the words *hip* and *hid* are distinguished by their last sounds; the words *dime* and *time* are differentiated by their first sounds; *bag* and *bug* are phonetically different because of their second sounds. *Distinctive significance* is one aspect of the phoneme concept.

A second aspect of the phoneme concept is the recognition of variation. Speech sounds vary in production according to context. The vowel in *hit* is somewhat different from the "same" vowel in the word *ink*. The vowel in *cat* is essentially the same but not identical with the vowel of *cad*. The production of the *t* in *lets* differs somewhat from the *t* of *tin* and the *t* of *later*. The first sound of *can* is not identical with the first sound of *car*. The *r* in *tree* differs from the *r* in *very* and the *r* in *run*. All of these variations are relatively minor. They do not represent distinctive differences in the basic sound unit.

There is also considerable variation from person to person relative to the production of speech sounds. Nationwide, we are not as one in the way we pronounce the vowel of the word *hat*. Rarely, however, despite possible modifications in the length or quality of the vowel, is the variation so significant that we fail to recognize what word was intended. Individually we may even consider the other person's pronunciation a bit unusual and be aware that it is unlike our own. If, despite differences, there is no question in the mind of the listener of what is meant, if meaning is not disturbed, then we are dealing with a nondistinctive variation of the sound.

A phoneme, then, may be defined as the smallest distinctive group or class of sounds in a language. Each phoneme includes a variety of closely related sounds (*allophones*) that differ somewhat in production and in acoustic result because of context or conditions of speech. In American speech there are approximately forty-four distinctive groups of sounds or phonemes. The number of allophones is theoretically infinite.

The International Phonetic Alphabet

Our approach to the study of pronunciation will be simplified through the use of a system of sound symbols free of the historical whimsies of our spelling. We shall use the symbols of the International Phonetic Alphabet (the IPA). In general, we may accept the principle that in the IPA system only one symbol is used for each distinctively different sound or phoneme. The same phoneme, including all its variants (allophones), is always represented by the same symbol. Sounds and the symbols that represent them are consistent.

The different sounds of American-English speech and their phonetic symbols are listed in Table 6–1.

In learning the phonetic symbols, it may be of some help to know that sixteen of them are taken from the orthographic alphabet. These sixteen

Table 6–1 Consonant and Vowel Sounds

Key word	Phonetic symbol for italicized letter or letters	Key word	Phonetic symbol for italicized letter or letters
1. *p*et	/p/	23. *h*e	/h/
2. *b*e	/b/	24. *w*e	/w/
3. *t*en	/t/	25. *wh*at[a]	/ʍ/ or /hw/
4. *d*ime	/d/	26. fr*ee*	/i/
5. *c*ake	/k/	27. *i*t	/ɪ/
6. *g*ot	/g/	28. c*a*ke	/e/
7. *f*un	/f/	29. l*e*t	/ɛ/
8. *v*ote	/v/	30. h*a*t	/æ/
9. *th*ing	/θ/	31. *a*sk[b]	/a/
10. *th*an	/ð/	32. c*a*lm	/ɑ/
11. *s*ee	/s/	33. h*o*t[c]	/ɒ/
12. *z*ero	/z/	34. s*aw*	/ɔ/
13. *sh*all	/ʃ/	35. el*o*pe	/o/
14. mea*s*ure	/ʒ/	36. f*u*ll	/ʊ/
15. *ch*urch	/tʃ/	37. s*oo*n	/u/
16. *j*udge	/dʒ/	38. c*u*t	/ʌ/
17. *m*ay	/m/	39. *a*bove[d]	/ə/
18. know*n*	/n/	40. supp*er*	/ɚ/
19. ri*ng*	/ŋ/	(General American	
20. *l*ay	/l/	Pronunciation)	
21. *r*an	/r/	41. b*ir*d[e]	/ɜ/ or /ɝ/
22. *y*es	/j/		

DIPHTHONGS[f]

b*y*	/aɪ/		
p*oise*	/ɔɪ/	*go*	/ou/
h*ow*	/aʊ/ or /aʊ/	f*use*	/ɪu/
m*ay*	/eɪ/	*u*sing	/ju/

[a] Many Americans do not distinguish between the /hw/ in *what* and the /w/ in *watt*, but pronounce both as *watt*.

[b] Most Americans do not use this sound except as part of the diphthong sound in the words *I, aisle, mine*. The vowel of *ask* is most frequently pronounced with the vowel of *hat* and occasionally with the vowel of *calm*.

[c] Most Americans use the same vowel in *hot* as they do in *calm*.

[d] This sound, as a pure vowel, is used only in unstressed syllables.

[e] Persons who habitually pronounce their *r*'s whenever the letter appears in the spelling of a word are likely to use the vowel /ɝ/ which has definite *r* coloring in words such as *bird, heard, girl*, and *spurn*.

[f] It should be noted that not all vowels in immediate sequence are diphthongs. For example, the words *drawing* and *sawing* have the sequence of vowels /ɔ/ and /ɪ/ rather than the diphthong /ɔɪ/.

The diphthongs /aɪ/, /ɔɪ/ and /au/ are phonemic. The others are not. /eɪ/ and /ou/ are nondistinctive diphthong variants of /e/ and /o/.

Table 6–1   (continued)

OTHER SYMBOLS USED IN PHONETIC TRANSCRIPTION

ˌ   Placed below a symbol, a syllabic sign

~   Indicates nasalization

:   Lengthening sign

ˈ   Placed above and before the beginning of a syllable to indicate primary stress

ˌ   Placed below and before the beginning of a syllable to indicate secondary stress

/ʔ/   Indicates a glottal or laryngeal "stop."

are: /p/, /b/, /t/, /d/, /k/, /g/, /f/, /v/, /s/, /z/, /m/, /n/, /l/, /r/, /h/, and /w/.

STANDARDS OF PRONUNCIATION[2]

A person doing much traveling in the United States and who is inclined to believe that those who are unlike him are odd might soon come to the conclusion that many, perhaps most, people are odd. A more tolerant traveler might form another opinion. He might, even if he were only a moderately good listener, conclude that people spoke somewhat differently in various sections of the United States. For the most part, however, though he might note shades of differences, he would have little or no difficulty in understanding American speech wherever he might be. If the American traveler had the additional advantage of having been in England, the thought might also occur to him that despite the geographic smallness of England proper, the variations in speech in England are much greater than those in his own, larger country.

Speech areas

Any attempt to divide the United States into speech areas must necessarily be in terms of broad approximations. We shall follow the approximations of C. K. Thomas (1958), who recognized ten speech areas in the United States. These comprise (1) Eastern New England; (2) the Middle Atlantic area: (3) the South; (4) New York City, a rather anomalous region in its resemblances to both the Middle Atlantic and Southern speech areas; (5) the North Central area; (6) Western Pennsylvania; (7) the Southern Mountain Area (most of the mountain settlements of the southern states); (8) the Central Midland; (9) the Northwest; and (10) the Southwest Coastal area.

---

[2] Standards of pronunciation and dialectical differences in pronunciation are considered in some detail in Chapter 5, "Our Changing Speech Patterns."

The geographic distribution of these major speech areas is indicated in Figure 6–1.

It is important to remember that no hard-and-fast lines divide the speech regions, and that all the regions are much more alike than they are different in their speech. Even the special characteristics of a given region are shared, in part, by other regions. For example, New York City speech shows some characteristics of Southern speech and many of the Middle Atlantic areas. It must, above all, be emphasized that no educated person of any speech region would have any difficulty in understanding the normal speech of an educated person in any other of the American speech regions. It might also be noted that, by and large, differences in speech among better educated persons are not usually as wide as among persons who have had fewer educational advantages. Geographically and numerically the General American dialect (Central Midland) is most widely represented throughout the country. A second map of dialect areas is shown in Figure 6–2. (These maps are also considered in Chapter 5, Figures 5–1 and 5–2.)

Variations in sound production in the main speech areas

CONSONANTS. Except for the sound /r/, there is little difference in consonant production on a purely regional basis. All the major speech areas follow the same practice for the articulation of words beginning with the letter *r* (*right, run, real,* etc.) and in words in which the letter *r* is pre-

FIGURE 6–1. Map showing the major regional speech areas: *A:* Eastern New England; *B:* New York City; *C:* Middle Atlantic; *D:* Southern; *E:* Western Pennsylvania; *F:* Southern Mountain; *G:* Central Midland; *H:* Northwest; *I:* Southwest; *J:* North Central.

FIGURE 6–2. Some of the dialect areas in the United States. (From
R. W. Shuy, *Discovering American Dialects*, National Council of
Teachers of English, Champaign, Illinois, 1967.)

ceded by a consonant and followed by a vowel (*great, proud, three,* etc.).
Except for parts of the South, the /r/ is also regularly articulated when
it is preceded as well as followed by a vowel as in *very*. Practices differ,
however, relative to words such as *carpet, sharp,* and *sword,* in which
there is a medial *r* followed by a consonant. There is also wide variation
of practice in words such as *bar, star, fear,* and *door,* in which the letter
r is final.

The regional tendencies for the articulation of the *r* may be summed
up as follows:

1. In all regions, the letter *r* is pronounced as /r/ whenever it occurs
   initially in the word.
2. In general, *r* is pronounced as /r/ whenever the letter *r* is immediately followed by a vowel in the same word. Exception to this will
   be found in some parts of the South.
3. In the South, eastern New England, and usually in New York City
   the /r/ is likely to be omitted in the pronunciation of words in which:
   (a) the letter *r* is followed by a consonant as in *sharp, fearful,* and
       carpet, and
   (b) whenever the letter *r* is final in the spelling of a word as in
       fear, door, bear, and *lower* and is *not* immediately followed by
       another word beginning with a vowel in the same phrase.
4. When the letter *r* occurs at the end of the word and is followed by
   a word beginning with a vowel in the same phrase (*far along, pour
   out, roar of a lion*), the /r/ sound or a vowel with /r/ coloring /ɚ/

is pronounced by most speakers in eastern New England and New York City.

5. In General American speech, the /r/ sound or a close equivalent is usually pronounced whenever the spelling of the word includes the letter *r*.

VOWELS. Differences in practice relative to the pronunciation of vowels are fairly wide among the major speech regions. Space limitations of this text will not permit detailed discussion of the varied and acceptable pronunciations of the vowel sounds. Brief mention will be made of the differences in the pronunciation of the vowel in words such as *class, path, laugh, last, branch,* and *dance.* In eastern New England, many speakers regularly use the vowel /a/ or /ɑ/ in these words, though /æ/ may also be heard. In New York City, most speakers are likely to use the vowel /æ/, but the vowels /a/ and /ɑ/ are also heard. Throughout the remainder of the United States, including the General American area, the vowel /æ/ as in *hat* is likely to be heard fairly uniformly and consistently.

In our later consideration of the vowel sounds, individual variations will be taken up in somewhat greater detail.

Dictionaries and pronunciation

Many of us regard dictionaries as authorities for the pronunciation of the words we speak. We may fail to appreciate that if a particular dictionary has any authority, it is authority democratically arrived at through the process of recording the most frequent pronunciations of the listed words. A dictionary does not determine word pronunciation or word usage. The editors of dictionaries record the current pronunciation and usage of words. If a given dictionary is revised so that it continues to be current, if the indicated pronunciations (and definitions) are revised periodically so that contemporary speech is reflected, the dictionary may be considered authoritative. An outdated, unrevised dictionary becomes a historical document rather than a guide for determining how speakers should pronounce words in current use.

Most dictionaries indicate more than one pronunciation for many of their listed words. The order of listing is usually decided on the basis of frequency of usage. The authority of a dictionary, in respect to meaning and pronunciation, is also considered in Chapter 5, "Our Changing Speech Patterns."

STYLES OF SPEECH

Informal and formal speech

Our speech-minded traveler pondering the question "Which is the correct way to say a word?" would arrive at no adequate answer unless he modified his question. If his modified question were to take the form of "Under a given set of circumstances, and for a specific occasion, how should a particular word in context be pronounced?" an attempt at an adequate explanation might be made.

Speech—in manner as well as in content—is appropriate or inappropriate, "correct" or "incorrect," according to circumstances and occasion. Whether the speaker is educated or uneducated, his manner of speaking will vary according to time, place, and speech situation. The minister at home, speaking to members of his family, is not likely to address them as he would members of his church when delivering a sermon. The lecturer speaking to a large audience on a formal occasion will use more "elevated" language than the same lecturer talking to his friend on a fishing trip.

Speech may be "correct" and highly informal if it is appropriate to the occasion. In general, when we speak informally we use more contractions than on formal occasions. (This, incidentally, though to a lesser degree, is also true of informal writing.) When we speak conversationally to intimate friends, *he's, won't, don't, I'm,* and *wanna* are likely to be used instead of the more formal *he is, will not,* etc. In conversations held with persons who are in some relationship superior to us, we are not so likely to make use of contractions.

Public addresses, in general, are likely to be delivered in a more formal style than most conversations. Important exceptions are the humorous after-dinner speeches and broadcasts of athletic events. Sports announcers do not hesitate to use contractions and unusual grammatical constructions in their description of sports events. In fact, American audiences would consider it strange if an announcer at a football game were to tell his listeners, "Brown is trying to make his way through the line. He does not appear to be successful. In fact, he has been thrown off his feet. He may not be able to arise, unsupported. No, I am in error. Brown regained his feet. Courageous fellow." The audience is more likely to hear. "Brown is hitting the line. He's getting nowhere. Brown's off his feet. I don't think he'll make it up. No, I'm wrong, he's up again. What a man!"

Substandard speech

Does the acceptance of differences between formal and informal speech imply that no form of speech is substandard? We think not. Pronunciations, word selection, and syntactical usage *with allowances made for dialectical variations* are appropriate, and in that sense "standard" if they are consistent with the objectives of the speaker and the expectancies of the listener or listeners relative to a given situation. Speech is off-standard if not substandard if expectancies are not met and the judgments and tastes of the listeners are disturbed or are violated. We are likely to feel such violation if a lecturer on nuclear physics, a philosopher, a statesman, or a historian were to address us in a lecture hall setting in the manner of a sports announcer.

Pronunciations as well as word selection and syntax may be considered substandard if they are not identifiable with a recognized dialect and are not currently used by any persons whose backgrounds and reputations make their judgments of speech usage worthy of respect. Personally, we also prefer that bidialectal speakers should employ a dialect consistent with situation and audience expectancy. Such preference might even permit the word *ask* to be pronounced *aks* in some situations, but probably not *ast* in any. Similarly we believe that *picture* should not be pronounced as a homonym of *pitcher*.

Questions and exercises

1. What is a phoneme? What factors determine phonemic differences in sounds?

2. How does the International Phonetic Alphabet differ from the alphabet used in the spelling of American-English words? From diacritical symbols?

3. Which word in each of these groups (reading across) has a vowel sound distinctly different from the vowels of the other words of the group?

hack	hat	harm	hang
rail	cake	pain	aisle
rule	should	through	sue
arms	alms	scalp	heart

4. What is the practice relative to the pronunciation of the letter *r* of persons living in your speech area?

5. In what major speech region do you live? Are you aware of whether your own speech pattern conforms to the general characteristics of most speakers in your region? Is there any way in which your own speech appears to be different? Can you account for the difference?

6. Indicate phonetically the vowel you would use in the stressed syllable of each of the following words: *drama, hand, ask, class, path, market*.

7. List five words that might be pronounced differently by speakers in the eastern New England region and persons in the General American region. What is your own practice in regard to the pronunciation of these words?

8. Listen to your local radio or television news announcer. Compare his speech on a local program with that of an announcer on a nationwide hookup. What basic differences in pronunciation or word usage do you hear?

9. Read the discussion on American-English pronunciation in *Webster's Third New International Dictionary* (G. & C. Merriam Company, 1961) and *The Random House Dictionary of the English Language,* Unabridged

Edition (Random House, 1967). Is a single standard of pronunciation recommended in either of these dictionaries? What is your own point of view?

10. When is the pronunciation of a word substandard? Indicate phonetically substandard pronunciations you may have heard for any of the following words: *ask, burst, column, February, chimney.*

11. You know many words with more than one acceptable pronunciation. Such words might include the following: *abdomen, caisson, catchup, guard, length, penalize, roof, Tuesday, neither,* and *aunt.* What would determine your own choice of pronunciation of these words?

12. How can the choice of the pronunciation of a word affect ready understanding of speech?

13. *Webster's Third New International Dictionary* has been subject to considerable criticism because of its listings of words, usages, and pronunciations previously considered substandard. What is your position relative to the criticism and controversy? Has the same kind of criticism been directed to any more recently published dictionary?

14. What are the most current and frequent meanings of the following terms: *right on, straight, tight, square, split, neat, acid, sauce?* How many of these meanings are listed in the dictionary you most frequently use? How often do you use the terms according to the dictionary meanings (definitions) compared with your own current one? Has the most frequent meaning for any of the terms changed for you during the last year or two?

ANALYSIS OF SOUND PRODUCTION

Distinctive features of speech sounds

Sounds of speech have features that enable phoneticians and linguists and others to whom it is a matter of concern to distinguish one phoneme from another. Thus, a phoneme may be defined as a "bundle" of distinctive features. The sound features or characteristics are products of the place of articulation (locus of the articulatory mechanism where contact or near contact is made to produce the sound), manner of production, and the presence or absence of a vocal component during the act of articulation.

Phoneticians and linguists are not at all unanimous in considering which features are so distinctive that they must be included in a full and differential description of a sound. Perhaps the most detailed, and also the most "theoretic," feature systems are those of Jakobson, Fant, and Halle (1965) and of Chomsky and Halle (1968). For our purposes, however, we can do with fewer features relative to place, manner, nasality, and voicing. Manner (aspects of the articulatory process) covers or subsumes many of the feature details that are considered important and distinctive in the systems cited above.

Miller and Nicely (1955) developed a consonant classification system that employed the features of voicing, nasality, affrication (amount of fricativeness), duration, and place of articulation. The classification system that we shall use is quite close to that of Miller and Nicely. The reader who is interested in reviewing and comparing distinctive feature systems relevant to English speech may consult the references cited above and/or in addition Winitz (1969, pages 79–96).

A perceptual test of the "psychological weight" of distinctive features may be found in asking ourselves the basic questions: "Are there any sounds that we respond to as being close to one another and others that we consider (respond to) as being further apart? What is the perceptual psychological distance between the sounds *p, t, k, g, b,* and *d* or the syllables *pa, ta, ka, ga, ba,* and *da*?" A study that answered these questions was done by Greenberg and Jenkins (1964) with college students as subjects. These investigators found that (1) sounds that were alike in all but one feature were consistently judged as closer to one another than sounds differing by two features; (2) distances between points of articulation were ranked as follows: labial (lip), alveolar (upper gum ridge), alveolar-velar (palate), labial-velar. An examination of figures indicates that these perceptual distances conform to actual articulatory facts.

The student may test himself to see how closely his perceptual responses agree with the Greenberg-Jenkins (1964) observations by asking himself whether he perceives the psychological distance between the stop sounds *p, b, t, d, k, g* as they are represented in the schematic representation adapted from the cited study (see Figure 6–3).

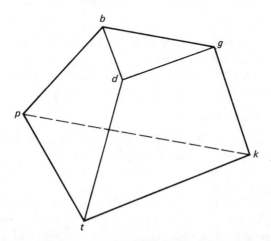

FIGURE 6–3. Schematic representation of the psychological distance for *p, t, k, b, d, g*. [Adapted from J. H. Greenberg and J. J. Jenkins, "Studies in the Psychological Correlates of the Sound System of American English," *Word,* 20:2 (1964), 157–177.]

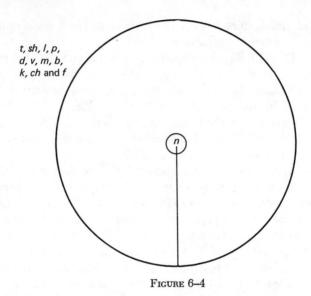

t, sh, l, p,
d, v, m, b,
k, ch and f

FIGURE 6–4

Exercises for distinctive features

1. To emphasize the differences and psychological perceptual space between some of the consonant sounds of our language, arrange the indicated sounds according to the distances between each and the sound *n*. Use *n* as the "bull's-eye" and place the individual sounds on the radius.

2. Compare your perceptual judgments with those of a friend. Is there any principle you can generate from the results?

3. Now arrange the same sounds on the radii according to your responses with respect to distance between the sounds as well as the distance from *n*.

4. Try the same procedure with the sound *m* as the bull's-eye and the sounds *w, r, ng*. Is there any tendency in your placements different from those in the first and second arrangements? Can you tentatively arrive at any principle that determined your perceptual responses?

Classification of speech sounds

We shall follow a modified distinctive feature approach in our classification and description of speech sounds. Before we do so, however, we shall provide some broad classifications and definitions for the phonemes of our language system.

Articulation refers to the action of the organs of the mouth and the breathing mechanism that result in a modification of the breath stream to produce the sounds of speech. Later in the chapter and in succeeding chapters we will analyze the movements and contacts made by the organs of articulation—the lips, gum ridge, teeth, tongue, and palate—in the production of the sounds of American-English speech.

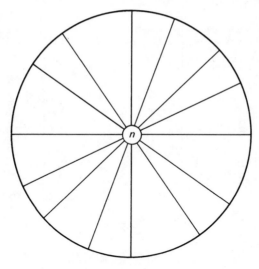

FIGURE 6–5

Sounds of speech are generally classified into three groups: consonants, vowels, and diphthongs. Each of these will be defined.

Consonants are speech sounds produced with some degree of obstruction of or interference with the breath stream by the organs of articulation.

Vowels are produced by a modification in the size and shape of the mouth and position of the tongue without obstruction of or interference with the breath stream.

Diphthongs are voice glides uttered in a single breath impulse. Some diphthongs are blends of two vowels. Most, however, represent an instability or "breakdown" of what was originally one vowel.

Speech sound classification: consonants

Earlier we indicated that we will present a classification system for consonants that will include features relative to place of articulation, manner of articulation, vocalization, and nasality. These features are summed up in Table 6–2. We shall highlight these features in the discussion that follows related to these broad phonetic features.

If we produce the following pairs of words slowly and carefully, paying especial attention to the initial sounds, we will be able to arrive at the bases for the classification of consonant sounds.

car	and	*tar*
sue	and	*zoo*
me	and	*be*
sum	and	*gum*

The acoustic difference between *car* and *tar* is a result of the different place of contact made by the tongue and the palate in the production of

Table 6–2 Production of Consonants in American-English Speech

ARTICULATORS USED

MANNER OF ARTICULATION	Lips (bilabial)	Lip-teeth (labio-dental)	Tongue-teeth (lingua-dental)	Tongue point gum (lingua-alveolar)	Tongue and hard or soft palate (palatal)	Vocal folds (glottal)
Voiceless stops	p			t	k	
Voiced stops	b			d	g	
Voiceless fricatives	hw /ʍ/	f	θ (th)	s, ʃ (sh)		h
Voiced fricatives		v	ð (th)	z, /ʒ/ (zh)†		
Nasals (all voiced)	m			n	ŋ (ng)	
Glides (vowel-like consonants; voiced)	w			r*	j (y), r‡	
Lateral				l		

* The tongue tip in many instances is curled away from the gum ridge toward the center of the hard palate.

† Two additional consonant blends should be noted. These are the affricates /tʃ/ and /dʒ/, the first a voiceless and the second a voiced blend. Because of the second component, they are actually produced with the tongue in a post-alveolar position.

‡ In combinations such as k or g followed by r, the r sound may be produced in this position.

Source: From Eisenson and Ogilvie, *Speech Correction in the Schools*, 3rd ed. (New York: Macmillan, 1971).

the initial sounds. The /k/ sound of *car* is produced by contact between the back of the tongue and the soft palate; the /t/ of *tar* is produced by contact between the tip of the tongue and the upper gum ridge. For both /k/ and /t/ the stream of breath is completely obstructed and then suddenly released with a puff or "explosion."

In the words *sue* and *zoo*, the distinguishing element in the production of the first sounds is that of voice rather than place or manner of articulation. The /s/ is voiceless; and /z/ is produced with vocal fold vibration.

The initial sounds of the words *me* and *be* are different because of their manner rather than place of articulation. Both the /m/ and the /b/ are produced by action of the lips. The /b/ is emitted through the mouth when the lips are suddenly separated. The /m/ sound is emitted through the nose while the lips are closed.

In the words *sum* and *gum* three kinds of differences characterize the production of the initial sounds. The /s/ is produced with the tip of the tongue close to but not quite touching the upper gum ridge. The sound emerges "fricatively" through a narrow opening between the teeth. It is unvoiced. The /g/ is produced with the middle or back of the tongue in contact with the soft palate. As with the /t/ and /d/, the stream of air is completely cut off and then suddenly released. The sound /g/ is voiced. Other feature differences will be found if we compare words such as *late* and *date*, *yet* and *wet*, *chum* and *from*, *thigh* and *thy*, and *dame* and *name*. If we were to analyze carefully what our articulators and vocal folds do in the production of the initial and final consonants for the word pairs, we would arrive at a classification that includes the broad headings and divisions in Table 6–2. The table provides detailed descriptive and prescriptive information for the consonants of American-English speech. With practice we should be able to identify and produce each of the sounds in isolation on the bases of the feature-directions implied in the descriptions. First, however, some of the more specialized terms used in the table and later in sound descriptions will be explained.

Stops are produced by a stopping and sudden releasing of the stream of breath. The plosive sounds are /p/, /b/, /t/, /d/, /k/, /g/. When a voiceless stop is the first sound of a stressed syllable and is immediately followed by a vowel, the release of air is accompanied by a puff of breath (aspiration). This may be observed in the pronunciation of words such as *pen, atone,* and *comely.*

Fricatives are produced by a partial closure of the articulators. This partial closure results in the creation of a constricted passage through which the stream of breath must be "forced." This may take place as a result of a grooving of the tongue, or by having other organs of articulation come close together. In the production of the /s/ *and* /z/, both may take place. The fricative sounds of American speech are /f/, /v/, /θ/, /ð/, /s/, /z/, /ʃ/, /ʒ/, and /h/. The /r/, as in *tree*, may also be included as a fricative consonant.

Nasal sounds are reinforced and emitted through the nose rather than the mouth. All three nasal sounds, /m/, /n/, /ŋ/, are produced with accompanying vocalization.

Affricates are blends of two sounds, one a fricative and the other a plosive. Of the affricates in American speech, /tʃ/, as in *chum,* is produced without vocalization; /dʒ/, as in *jam,* is produced with accompanying vocalization.

There is one *lateral consonant* /l/ in American speech. The /l/ is produced by having air emitted at both sides of the tongue while the tip of the tongue is in contact with the gum ridge.

A *glide* consonant is characterized by continuous movement of an articulator or articulators while the sound is being produced. The glide consonants include /w/, /j/, and /r/ in some contexts. The sound /w/ results from simultaneous activity of the lips and the back of the tongue. (Note its double placement on the consonant chart.)

The /r/ sound results from either the activity of the tongue tip or mid-tongue. When /r/ is immediately preceded by the sounds /t/, /d/, or /θ/ in the same syllable, it is likely to be produced as a fricative sound.

The sound /hw/ is sometimes produced as a fricative-glide and so may also be included among the glide consonants. It is more frequently produced as a pure fricative, as indicated by its position on the consonant chart.

The sound /j/ is produced by activity of the front of the tongue raised toward the hard palate.

The glides, as may be noted from Table 6–2, are included among the *semivowels.* The articulation of consonants is characterized by contact or narrowing of the organs of articulation. Vowels are characterized by changes in resonance associated with modification in the shape of the oral cavity. The glides share some of the characteristics of the consonants, as well as the resonant quality of the vowels. For this reason they are included among the semivowels.

At this point it should not be difficult to figure out why the consonant /b/ is described as a voiced bilabial stop or why /s/ is described as a voiceless, lingua-alveolar fricative. The student can test his ability to follow directions as well as his knowledge of the specialized vocabulary of phonetics by producing the sounds according to each of the following prescriptive descriptions, in this fashion: *The labio-dental voiced fricative.* (Lower lip in contact with upper teeth; breath forced through constricted passage between lip and teeth; vocal folds in vibration. The sound /v/ is produced.)

By way of practice, the following might be tried:

1. bilabial nasal
2. lingua-dental voiceless fricative
3. lingua-velar voiced stop

4. lingua-alveolar voiceless stop
5. labio-dental voiceless fricative
6. bilabial voiced glide.

Exercises for sound classification

1. What is the common difference between the word pairs *pin* and *bin, ten* and *den, fan* and *van, seal* and *zeal?*

2. The sound /r/ and /l/ are referred to as liquids. (Check with the Chomsky and Halle or the Jakobson and Fant references at the end of the chapter.) Why is this an appropriate term for /l/ and /r/?

3. Say the word pairs *right* and *light, rice* and *lice, rip* and *lip*. Repeat, producing the pairs silently. Can you arrive at an explanation of the confusion some speakers of Oriental languages have with these sounds?

4. How do the Miller and Nicely (1955) sound classification features differ from those we have used?

5. What difference makes for the difference in meaning in the sentence pairs (a) Then Buddhism was the rage, (b) Zen Buddhism was the rage.

6. Write two sentence pairs such as the ones in exercise (5) that have significant difference in meaning on the basis of a single sound feature of one word.

AMERICAN VOWELS AND DIPHTHONGS

Vowels

PRODUCTION. When we studied the production of consonants we were able to conclude that these sounds differed from one another according to (1) place of articulation, (2) manner of articulation, (3) the elements of voice and nasality. If we produce a few of the vowels of American speech listed in our phonetic alphabet (Table 6–1) we will see that the criteria for differentiation among consonants do not hold for vowels. Vowels, we will notice, have these characteristics in common: (1) All are voiced sounds; (2) all are articulated in essentially the same manner; that is, all vowels are continuant sounds produced without interruption and without restriction of the stream of breath; (3) though lip activity is involved, tongue activity characterizes the production of all vowels.

VOWEL CLASSIFICATION. Although the entire tongue necessarily participates in the production of all vowels, vowels may be classified according to the part of the tongue *most actively involved* for each of the sounds (see Table 6–3).

If we concentrate on the vowel sound of the words *sea* and *soon*—/i/ and /u/—we should be able to note that the blade of the tongue moves forward toward the hard palate for *sea*. In the word *soon,* the back of the

Table 6–3 Vowels of American-English Speech

FRONT VOWELS

	Phonetic symbol	Dictionary symbol
meet	[i]	ē
milk	[ɪ]	ĭ
may	[e]	ā
men	[ɛ]	ĕ
mat	[æ]	ă
ask*	[a]	a

CENTRAL VOWELS

	Phonetic symbol	Dictionary symbol
mirth	[ɜ] or [ɝ]	ûr
about	[ə]	ə
upper	[ɚ]	ɚr
mud	[ʌ]	ŭ

BACK VOWELS

	Phonetic symbol	Dictionary symbol
boon	[u]	ōō
book	[ʊ]	ŏŏ
boat	[o]	ō
ball	[ɔ]	ô
bog	[ɒ]	ŏ
balm	[ɑ]	ä

* When the speaker compromises between the vowels of *mat* and of *balm*. This vowel is intermediate in placement as well as in sound between [æ] and [ɑ].

tongue moves toward the soft palate for the articulation of the vowel. Now let us contrast the vowels in *set* and *saw*—/ɛ/ and /ɔ/. In *set* as in *see*, the vowel sound is produced with the blade of the tongue most active in front of the mouth. The tongue, however, is not so high up for /ɛ/ as it is for /i/. (Compare *see* and *set*.) For the vowel of *saw*, the back of the tongue is most active in the back of the mouth, but the tongue is lower for /ɔ/ than it is for /ʊ/. (Compare *soon* and *saw*.) On the basis of the production of the four vowels considered above, a twofold classification is possible.

1. Vowels differ in production with respect to *place of articulation*.[3] They may be produced either in the front or in the back of the mouth, with the blade or back of the tongue most active. If we attend to the production of the vowel sounds in the words *burn*, *butter* (second vowel), and *sun*, we will note that the *midtongue* is most actively involved.
2. Vowels differ with respect to the height of the tongue position. Some vowels such as /i/ and /u/ are produced with a high tongue position. The vowels /ɛ/ and /ɔ/ have a lower tongue position. The vowels of the words *hat* /æ/ and *calm* /ɑ/ are still lower with respect to tongue position.

If we trace the tongue position for the vowels in the words *be, bit, bath, bet, bat*, it will be noted that the blade of the tongue and the lower jaw are lowered from a relatively high position in *be* to a low position in *bat*. Those of us who use a different vowel for *bath* /a/ than for *bat* /æ/ should be able to notice an even lower tongue position for the vowel /a/. In terms of tongue position we might outline the tongue roof of mouth relationship for the front vowels as shown in Figure 6–6.

It might be noted that the tip of the tongue is placed behind the lower gum ridge in the production of all the front vowels. This tip-of-tongue position holds for the articulation of all vowels, whether front, mid, or back. For back vowels, however, the tongue tip is pulled back a little along the floor of the mouth.

If we continue this analysis for midvowels, our outline of tongue position changes would now approximate those in Figure 6–7.

Similarly the back vowel outline might be presented as in Figure 6–8.

Now, if we combine all three vowel diagrams into one figure and replace the tongue outlines by dots to indicate the *high point* of the tongue, our diagram would approximate Figure 6–9.

Muscle tension provides a third basis for the classification of vowels. If we compare the vowel of *peek* with that of *pick*, we should be able to feel that the tongue is tense for the vowel of *peek* and relaxed for the vowel

---

[3] In regard to vowels, *place* refers to the part of the tongue most actively and differentially involved in the production of the individual vowel sound.

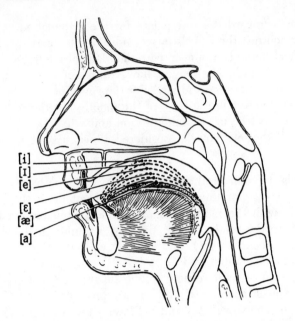

FIGURE 6–6. Representative tongue positions for front vowels.

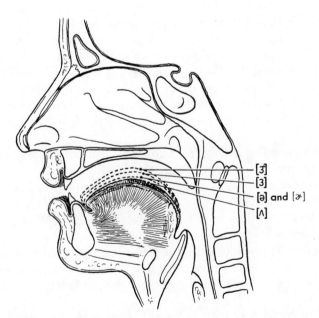

FIGURE 6–7. Representative tongue positions for central vowels.

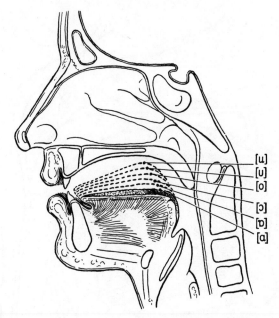

FIGURE 6–8. Representative tongue positions for back vowels.

of *pick*. Similarly the vowel of *shoot* is produced with a tense tongue in contrast with the vowel of *should,* which is produced with a lax tongue. Differences in tension are not confined to the muscles in the tongue. The muscles under the chin also show characteristic differences. In addition, the apex of the larynx—the "Adam's apple"—rises more for the tense vowels than it does for the lax vowels. These distinctions in muscle tension may be observed if you look at the mirror while producing the vowels of *peek* and *pick* or *shoot* and *should.* You should be able to note the following: (1) for the vowels of *peek* and *shoot,* a tense tongue, upward movement of the apex of the larynx, and bunching of the muscles under the chin; (2) for vowels of *pick* and *should,* a relaxed tongue, no muscle bulge under the chin, and little or no upward movement of the apex of the larynx.

LIP-ROUNDING. If we produce each of the vowels as isolated sounds according to their position on the vowel diagrams, a fourth basis for vowel classification becomes apparent. The back vowels, especially the high back vowels /u/ and /ʊ/ and the mid-high back vowel /o/, are produced with the lips in a *rounded position.* The degree of "roundness" varies and decreases from /u/ to /ɒ/. The low back vowel /ɑ/ is "unrounded."

The matter of lip-rounding is not a distinctive feature of vowel production in American speech. Emphasis on lip-rounding in vowel articulation may be of some importance to speakers who distinguish between the

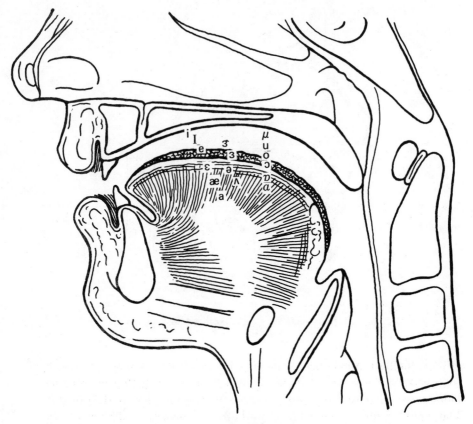

FIGURE 6–9. Representative tongue positions for the vowels of
American English speech. In actual speech there is considerable
variation from these positions from person to person, and
according to speech context, for each person.

vowel in words such as *cot, hot, doll* and the vowel in *palm, farm, harm.*
For speakers interested in making the distinction, one way of doing so
is to make a point of rounding the lips for the vowel in *cot, hot,* and *doll*
as we would for the vowel in *pall,* while assuming the lowered tongue
position as we would for the vowel in *alms.*

SUMMARY OF VOWEL CLASSIFICATION

Now, by way of summary, we may list the fourfold bases for vowel
classification. Vowels differ in articulation according to:

1. Place of articulation (front, mid, or back of the mouth in relationship to the palate).
2. Height of the tongue. (Tongue is arched high, midway, or low.)
3. Degree of muscle tension.
4. Lip-rounding. (Back vowels with the exception of /ɑ/ may be

rounded. Front vowels and central vowels are not rounded. Lip-rounding, however, is not a distinctive feature of vowel articulation.)

SOUNDS IN CONNECTED SPEECH

Strong and weak forms

If we say the words *butter, mother, brother* while concentrating on the articulation of the vowels, we should be able to observe the difference between *strong* and *weak* vowels. Two vowels are used in each of the words *butter, mother,* and *brother* /ʌ/ and /ə/ or /ɚ/. The vowels sound very much alike. On the basis of their articulation, they are very much alike. The significant difference between them is that in each word the first vowel is *stressed* and *strong*, while the second vowel is *unstressed* and therefore *weak*.

Weak vowels

As mentioned earlier, an outstanding characteristic of American-English speech is the general use of weak vowels in unstressed syllables of polysyllabic words. This may really be noted in such words as *about, woman, today, conclude.* In each of these words the vowel of the unstressed syllable is approximately the same as the unstressed vowel /ə/ in the word *about.*

The vowel /ə/, though the most frequently used vowel in unstressed syllables, is not the only vowel so used. Perhaps next in frequency is the vowel /ɪ/ which we find in the unstressed syllables of the word *added, noses, hurting* and as alternatives for /ə/ in such words as *obligate, exist, certain,* and *satisfy.* It may be of some interest to note that though the vowel /ə/ as a pure vowel is used only in unstressed syllables, the vowel /ɪ/ may be used in either stressed or unstressed syllables. In the words *sinful, tin, filter,* the vowel /ɪ/ is stressed. In the words *purify, beautiful, infer,* the vowel /ɪ/ is unstressed. It should be noted, however, that /ə/ might also be used as the unstressed vowel instead of /ɪ/. In the words *singing, vindicate, instill,* the vowel /ɪ/ appears in both the stressed and unstressed syllables.

Weakening of vowels is a frequent occurrence in so-called "connecting words" of English. Pronouns, prepositions, auxiliaries, articles, and conjunctions—unless they are stressed for a special reason—are generally used in their weak forms. For example, the most frequent pronunciation of the article *the* is /ðə/.[4] Ordinarily a sentence such as "The book is green" would be transcribed "[ðə bʊk ɪz grin]." If, however, a particular book were being talked about, which had special significance for both speaker and listener, the sentence might then become "[ði bʊk ɪz grin]." A study of the words listed below will reveal some of the differences in vowel usage in stressed and unstressed syllables.

[4] Before a vowel, however, as in "The old man" the article is likely to be pronounced as /ðɪ/.

Vowel when *stressed*	Vowel when *unstressed*
/ɛ/ rebel (noun)	/ɪ/ or /ə/ rebel (verb)
[ˈrɛbɪl] or [ˈrɛbəl]⁵	[rɪˈbɛl]
	[rəˈbɛl]

/ʊ/ full	[fʊl]	/ə/ pitiful	[ˈpɪtifəl]
/æ/ man	[mæn]	/ɪ/or/ə/ woman	[ˈwʊmin] or [ˈwʊmən]
/i/ scene	[sin]	/ɪ/or/ə/ scenario	[sɪˈnæriou]
			[səˈnæriou]

The following list presents some of the more common words that are usually spoken in their weak forms.

Written word	*Strong form or forms*	*Weak form or forms*
a	[eɪ] (rarely used)	[ə]
an	[æn] (before a vowel)	[ən], [n]
and	[ænd], [æn]	[ənd], [ən], [nd], [n]
at	[æt]	[ət]
could	[kʊd]	[kəd]
do	[du]	[də]
for	[fɔ], [fɔr]	[fə], [fər]
from	[frɑm], [frɒm]	[frəm]
have	[hæv]	[həv], [v]
he	[hi]	[hɪ], [ɪ]
her	[hɜ] or [hɜ˞]	[hə], [hə˞], [ə]
must	[mʌst]	[məst], [məs]
of	[ɑv], [ɒv]	[əv]
shall	[ʃæl]	[ʃəl], [l]
she	[ʃi]	[ʃɪ]
that	[ðæt]	[ðət]
the	[ði]	[ðə], [ðɪ] (before a vowel)
them	[ðɛm]	[ðəm], [əm], [m]
to	[tu]	[tə], [tʊ] (before a vowel)
was	[wɑz], [wɒz]	[wəz]
were	[wɜ], [wɜ˞]	[wə], [wə˞]
will	[wɪl]	[wəl], [l] (as a contraction)
you	[ju]	[jə]
your	[jʊə], [jʊər]	[jʊ], [jə]
	[jɔə], [jɔr]	[jʊr], [jər]

⁵ The stress mark (ˈ) in phonetic transcription appears *before* the stressed syllable.

ASSIMILATION

The person who indicates his intention to buy some new clothes for the winter by telling us [aɪm gɔnə baɪ səm nu klouz ðɪs wɪnə] may be thought of as a careless speaker. A phonetician or student of language, however, might view with greater understanding such pronunciations of [gɔnə] for *going to* and [wɪnə] for *winter*. These pronunciations might well be viewed as illustrations of economy of effort in speech. They would exemplify the general tendency to simplify the movements of the articulatory mechanism in producing speech sounds. To the student of language these pronunciations, though they would be characterized as substandard, would nevertheless represent the same kind of changes that have produced the accepted pronunciations of [hæŋkətʃɪf] for *handkerchief* and [tɪʃu] for *tissue*. The name given to this kind of phonetic change is *assimilation*.

Assimilation in speech refers to the phonetic changes that take place when one sound is modified as a result of the influence of a neighboring sound. A detailed analysis of assimilation is beyond the scope of this book. We might, however, briefly consider a few types of assimilative changes.

Anticipatory changes

Most assimilations reveal the influence of anticipatory changes. That is, the articulators, in anticipation of a sound that is to follow, modify a preceding sound. The change will be such as to simplify or facilitate articulation. For example, in *congress* the letter *n* is sounded as /ŋ/ in anticipation of the sound /g/ that follows. It is easier to articulate the combination /ŋg/ than /ng/ simply because both the /ŋ/ and the /g/ are produced with the same parts of the tongue and palate. Similarly it is easier to say [hɔ(r)ʃʃu] than [hɔ(r)sʃu] for *horseshoe*; [ðɪʃʃou] for *this show*; and [ɪŋkəm tæks] for *income tax*.

Voicing

This type of assimilative change is perhaps best exemplified in the matter of voicing or unvoicing of final *d* or *s*. In words such as *aped, leaped, raked, guessed,* and *hoped* the next to the last sound is a voiceless consonant. (The letter *e*, in each case, is silent.) As a result, the final sound is /t/ despite the spelling of *d*. Similarly the letter *s* is sounded as /s/ in words such as *ropes, lifts,* and *takes*.

In words such as *passes, wishes, ledges,* and *stitches,* the final *s* is pronounced as /z/ under the influence of the preceding sound. (The letter *e* is sounded as a weak vowel.) In words such as *tags, kegs, teams,* and *reams,* the final *s* is pronounced /z/ because of the influence of the preceding voiced consonant.

Other assimilations

Some assimilations result in the complete loss of one or more sounds replaced by a third sound. This happens in the assimilated pronunciations of *nature, lecture,* and *feature.* An extreme form of such assimilation is exemplified by the pronunciation of the English proper name of Cholomondeley as [tʃʌmli].

In the pronunciation of [klovz] for *clothes,* the *th* /ð/ is dropped because of the difficulty in pronuncing this sound before a /z/.

Assimilation, it should be noted, frequently takes place within a phrase because of the influence of sounds in adjacent words. For example, *miss you* and *meet you* may be assimilated in conversational speech to [mɪʃu] and [mitʃu]. The individual words *miss, meet,* and *you,* if spoken in isolation, would not show any such phonetic modification.

Assimilations and speech standards

Although it is easy to understand the general nature of assimilation and the influence of the process in speech, not all assimilative changes are acceptable. Persons who would use the word *lazy* where we use the phrase *economy of effort in articulation* would be inclined to resist recognized changes in speech sounds. Such persons might, for example, object to the pronunciation of *income* as [ɪŋkʌm] and insist that the prefix *in* maintain its identity in the more careful pronunciation of [ɪnkʌm]. A similar argument might be presented for the maintenance of the pronunciation of *congress* as [kɑngrɪs] rather than [kɑŋgrɪs].

Some assimilative influences are not considered desirable because quality of tone is affected. For example, if the words *nice, nail,* and *my* are produced with no effort to raise the soft palate after the articulation of the nasal consonant, in each instance the entire word tends to become nasalized.

In any event, regardless of influence or counterinfluence at work, not all assimilations are acceptable as standard. The word *gas,* for example, is pronounced [gæs] and not [gæz] in American standard speech regardless of region; [opəm] or [opm] is not acceptable for *open.*

QUESTIONS AND EXERCISES

1. Define *assimilation.* What is the basis for assimilative change?

2. Give examples of assimilative pronunciations that are not considered standard in your community.

3. May the nasalization of the vowel or diphthong in words such as *on, aim, answer,* and *wrong* be accounted for on the basis of assimilation? Explain.

4. What is your pronunciation for the words *educate, don't you, won't you* and *culture?* Do they reveal assimilative influence?

5. Are there any conditions under which you are likely to avoid using assimilative pronunciations?

6. Are there any characteristic differences in vowel pronunciation and vowel production—e.g., degree of tension, place of articulation when you compare speakers from the "deep South," the Midwest, and the East for the following words: *Harvard, water, Texas, candy, marry?* Is the suggestion of nasality present for any of these regional speakers?

7. Listen to a television program that features an actor whose English has presumably been influenced by his native Spanish-speaking background. What pronunciation differences characterize this speech? Is this in keeping with your own experience with a person with a Spanish language background?

REFERENCES AND RECOMMENDED READINGS

Bronstein, A. J. *The Pronunciation of American English.* New York: Appleton-Century-Crofts, 1960.

Carrell, J., and W. R. Tiffany. *Phonetics.* New York: McGraw-Hill Book Company, 1968.

Chomsky, N., and M. Halle. *The Sound Pattern of English.* New York: Harper & Row, Publishers, Inc., 1968.

Falk, J. *Language and Linguistics.* Rochester: Xerox, 1973.

Greenberg, J. H., and J. J. Jenkins. "Studies in the Psychological Correlates of the Sound System of American English." *Word,* **20** (1964), 157–177.

Hanna, P. R., R. E. Hodges, J. S. Hanna, and E. H. Rudorf. *Phoneme-Grapheme Correspondence as Cues to Spelling Improvement.* Washington: U.S. Dept. of Health, Education, and Welfare, 1966.

Jakobson, R., G. M. Fant, and H. Halle. *Preliminaries to Speech Analysis.* Cambridge: M.I.T., 1965.

Miller, G. A., and P. E. Nicely. "An analysis of perceptual confusion among some English consonants." *Journal of The Acoustical Society of America,* **27** (1955), 338–352.

Thomas, C. K. *An Introduction to the Phonetics of American English* 1958. New York: The Ronald Press Company, 2nd ed., 1958.

Winitz, H. *Articulatory Acquisition and Behavior.* New York: Appleton-Century-Crofts, 1969.

Chapter 7

Improving Your Voice

In earlier chapters (Chapters 2 and 3) we learned how voice is produced and gave some consideration to the role of voice as a component of speech. We shall apply this information in the present chapter. In addition, we shall arrive at practical answers to three key questions relative to voice. These are:

1. What is an effective voice?
2. How can I exercise voluntary control to use voice effectively?
3. How can I improve my voice to make it a sensitive and effective instrument to reveal my thinking and feeling so that I can secure the responses I want my listeners to make to my speaking?

WHAT IS AN EFFECTIVE VOICE?

From the viewpoint of the speaker an effective voice is one that attracts no undesirable attention either because of the manner in which it is produced or because of the acoustic end product. An effective voice must necessarily be appropriate to the age, sex, and physical makeup of the speaker. An effective voice is a responsive instrument. It must be able to reflect the reactions the speaker makes to the person or persons in the communicative situation. It must also be capable of reflecting the selective speaker's responses to his own reactions. An effective voice, by virtue of being selectively responsive, is able to express the feelings and to communicate the meanings the speaker intends the listener to receive.

From the viewpoint of the listener an effective voice is one that can be heard without conscious effort or strain. It is a voice that is consonant with the speaker's content and that helps to make the content readily intelligible. The voice should be pleasant to hear, or at least have no unpleasant quality that produces a negative listener reaction. The feeling of pleasure, however, should not dominate the listener's reactions so that it distracts the listener, for more than a moment, from what the speaker is saying. Though a listener may appreciate that he is hearing a better than usual voice, the response should not be one that might appropriately be made to a singer's vocal production. In brief, the listener's "enjoyment" of a speaker's voice should be passive and unconscious. An effective voice should neither interfere with nor distract from the meanings a listener is supposed to receive from the speaker. On the positive side, an effective voice is one that enhances the listener's capacity for the reception and decoding of the speaker's messages.

Objective characteristics

The qualities of an effective voice discussed above are essentially subjective. Objectively we may consider several characteristics for effective voices:

1. ADEQUATE AND CONTROLLED LOUDNESS. An effective voice should be as loud as the speaking occasion demands. It should be heard with ease by all persons in the audience and yet not disturb any listener because of its loudness. The voice should be well controlled, changing in volume according to the significance of the content. Though the voice may become subdued when the content is not significant, it should never be so subdued as to be difficult to hear. If the speaker is engaged in conversation, there should be no need to ask him to repeat because of a failure to hear him. Neither should we wish to withdraw because our eardrums are assaulted with "boom that threatens burst."

2. VARIETY OF PITCH. Whether in conversation or in a public speaking situation, the speaker's voice should have variety of pitch. The pitch, of course, should vary with the intellectual and emotional significance of what is being said.

The extent of the pitch range should not be forced so that unpleasant, poorly sustained tones are produced. Whether the pitch is relatively high or low, the voice should have the support of an adequate supply of breath. The extent of the pitch range varies considerably from person to person. Most of us, however, can increase our range considerably with comparatively little effort. How to accomplish this will be considered later.

3. GOOD TONE QUALITY. An effective voice should be clear. Clarity is achieved when a voice has no fuzziness, harshness, breathiness, or rasp. The voice has good tone when it does not sound throaty, husky, raspy, or in any way forced. On the positive side, good tone quality is resonant, alive, and vibrant. It reflects and conveys the changes in mood and in feeling that accompany the nuances of thought the speaker wishes to convey to his listeners.

4. RATE AND TIMING. The well-controlled voice must reveal a sense of timing. If what is spoken is not timed to the speech content, the audience, and the situation, the significance of the content will be impaired.

It sometimes becomes necessary for a speaker to control his rate of utterance—the presentation of his thought products—in a way inconsistent with his personality. Some of us tend naturally to move, think, and in general to behave slowly. Others behave at a faster pace. Our external speech must, however, vary according to the needs of our listeners rather than the inclinations of our personalities. (Applications of this point are made in the discussions on reading and public speaking.)

5. RESPONSIVENESS. An effective voice not only should reflect the feelings and meanings the speaker wishes to communicate but also should reveal that the speaker is observing and responding to the reactions of his listener or listeners. If the speaker observes signs of boredom or of restlessness, it may be that his lack of vocal variety has induced such effects. Evidence of listener strain that suggests difficulty in hearing should be met with an increase in loudness, provided, of course, that the listener's hearing is not so poor as to impose abnormal demands on a speaker's vocal efforts.

Tonal variety—changes in loudness, pitch, rate, and quality that are consonant with and adjustable to the changes in a speaking situation—characterizes a responsive speaker. A flexible, adjustable voice should be able to reflect feelings of sympathy, deference, respect, and appreciation as well as the more negative feelings of irritation, annoyance, or rejection, if indeed these feelings are called for by the situation. We hope that no speaker makes a specialty of being proficient in expressing unpleasant reactions without developing at least equal aptitude for the more pleasant vocal responses.

IMPROVING YOUR VOICE

Hearing your voice and analyzing it

You are too close to your own voice to know how it really sounds to others. The surprised look of the person who hears his recorded voice played back for him, the look that says, "Is this really my voice?" attests to this unfamiliarity. It also provides mute evidence for the need most of us have to hear ourselves as others hear us so that we may learn how to improve our voices.

There are a variety of mechanical devices that can help us to listen to our voices and respond to what we hear much as other listeners do. Tape and cassette recording devices are now available in professional clinics, speech and hearing clinics, stores selling musical and speech recording equipment, and in many homes. We need to emphasize that both the recording instrument and the playback equipment must have appropriate range and high fidelity for the speaking voice. A good recording is essential. However, a good recording played back on a low fidelity instrument or one with high fidelity in ranges beyond the speaking voice will provide a poor vocal product. Cheap instruments or ones intended for music rather than speech are of little value to the student who is truly concerned with making an objective evaluation of his own voice.

Assuming the proper recording and playback instruments, adequate conditions for recording should be observed. These include a minimum of environmental noises and no interference through echo or reverbera- tion. The voice should be recorded in situations and conditions that simu- late or include (1) casual and serious conversation; (2) reading aloud of a newspaper column or editorial; (3) literary prose; and (4) public ad- dress. The speaker turned self-listener should then analyze his voice as a basis for asking himself a number of questions for making judgments. The questions should include:

1. Is my voice conveying the feelings and enhancing the meanings I intended to communicate?
2. Is my voice easy to listen to? Is it pleasant?
3. Is my voice adequately loud, controlled, varied and appropriate in its variety?
4. Is the pitch range appropriate and wide enough in range to avoid monotony?
5. Are the tones clear and well sustained?
6. Does the voice reflect the personality and image I have of myself? Am I pleased with this image?

The speaker with the courage to ask himself these questions, and to listen objectively for answers, should be motivated to work so that all the answers can ultimately be positive. The discussions that follow should help to bring about changes, when necessary, toward that end.

Voice and personality

The relationship between voice and personality is considered in detail in Chapter 10. We shall observe that our evaluation and judgments of personalities is considerably influenced by what the voices reveal to us. All too often we have only the voice of the speaker as the basis for our value judgments. For most of us the voices that come to us by way of the mass media influence our opinions as much or more as the visual images that go with them. Faces can be made up, harsh lines eradicated or added, and other cosmetic features modified so that they match the per- sonalities or at least our stereotypes of the personalities that are sup- posed to be portrayed. Politicians as well as actors who make acting their primary profession are aware of this. However, even the trained voice is controlled by the speaker and not an external on-the-spot and for-the- purpose manipulator.

Those of us who prefer radio to television respond to the speech of the performers to determine those who are preferable, acceptable, and not acceptable as personalities. We like some announcers, commentators, and newscasters. We are neutral in regard to others, and a few leave us feeling irritated. Whatever the reaction is, unless the diction is conspicu- ously faulty, our judgments and anticipatory attitudes are based largely on how the individual voice affects us.

The way a voice affects us is not a hit-or-miss affair. Recent research by Markel and his associates (1972)[1] indicates that "messages on the voice quality band of the speech channel are related to personality traits. . . ." Based on judgments by college students, Markel and his associates derived four voice quality profile groups. The vocal factors for judgment were quality, loudness, and tempo (rate of utterance). The profiles are summarized as follows:

Loud-Fast: Bright; self-sufficient, resourceful.

Loud-Slow: Bright; aggressive, competitive; confident, self-secure; radical; self-sufficient, resourceful.

Soft-Fast: Bright; enthusiastic, happy-go-lucky; adventuresome, thick-skinned; confident, self-secure; radical; phlegmatic, composed.

Soft-Slow: Bright; aggressive, competitive; enthusiastic, happy-go-lucky; adventurous, thick-skinned.

We might note that this study did not include negative voice qualities such as huskiness, excessive nasality, monotony, etc. The importance of the study is in its conclusion that we do make value judgments of personalities based on vocal attributes. We do have stereotypes of personalities associated with voices. Thus, even in the day of non-heroes and anti-heroes, when "good guys" and "bad guys" are no longer identified by the color and shape of their hats, we still make judgments based on voice alone. Mass media directors take advantage of this knowledge of our prejudices in casting or training their characters. Perhaps this is most conspicuously so in daytime "soap operas." Directors can count on our preestablished reactions, our stereotypes, in the selection or direction of actors relative to voice. So, who is to be liked or disliked, and who may need some time before we make our judgments, can all be predetermined. We can be expected to identify the outright bad character almost as soon as he has finished with his first sentence. The forthrightness of the hero or heroine, the suffering mate, the rare friend, and the blunt if not altogether honest anti-hero are all revealed to us through their voices.

We recognize, of course, that many times the stereotypes are wrong. Some very fine persons have very poor voices. And some very bad characters have excellent and deceptive voices. The fact remains, however, that our initial responses tend to be consistent with the stereotypes. If we, as speakers, have no opportunity to modify the initial responses of the listeners, then the stereotyped response, whatever it may be, will remain.

In responding to our own voices, we should determine whether we are

[1] Markel, N. N., Phillis, J. A., Vargas, R. and Howard, F. "Personality Traits Associated with Voice Types." *Journal of Psycholinguistic Research,* **1,** 3 (1972), 249–255.

revealing the personality we want revealed. Is there a suggestion of a whine when no whine is intended? Does the voice reveal aggression when aggression is not meant? Does the voice suggest irritability, indifference, annoyance, fatigue, boredom? Are the suggestions consistent with the actual situation? If they are not, their recognition may be enough for the speaker to eliminate them. If, however, they reveal traits of personality that are truly those of the speaker's, recognition alone will not be sufficient. An approach that emphasizes the need and wish to change is then in order.

It is important to appreciate that behavioral habits often outlive their initial purpose. So, particular manners of voice and diction may persist and tell of a personality and of attitudes that are no longer those that are in keeping with the person as he feels and wishes to be revealed to his listeners. The dynamics, adjustments, and maladjustments of yesteryear may still linger in current speech behavior. Voice as well as diction (articulation and pronunciation) are motor acts and thus tend to persist unless there is awareness and conscious, directed effort to change. Fortunately, in most instances such effort is rewarding and usually results in a modification of vocal and oral habits so that the modified personality may be reflected.

How to go about making modifications, if they are needed, are considered in the discussion that follows. However, there is no assumption that all changes for the better are invariably related to personality modifications. Our emphasis will be on techniques for effective voice production, without remedial implication.

LOUDNESS AND BREATH CONTROL

An effective voice, as we indicated earlier, must be adequately loud. That means that the volume of the voice must be under the voluntary control of the speaker so that, as the occasion demands, the voice may be appropriately soft as well as appropriately loud.

Control of loudness is established through control of breathing. Specifically it is a matter of learning how to release air so that the expiratory part of the breathing cycle is coordinated with the act of vocalization. That is, air is forced between the vocal folds that have approximated so that voice may be produced (see discussion related to Figure 2–2 and 2–3 in Chapter 2). Air intake (inspiration), except for persons having a pathology of the respiratory mechanism, is usually accomplished with ease. The establishment of exhalation that is gradual and subordinated to the needs of vocalization sometimes requires instruction.

Controlled breathing is best established through voluntary action of the muscles constituting the front and sides of the abdominal wall. (See Chapter 2 for a review of the breathing process.) We may become readily aware of abdominal breathing by observing a sleeping or thoroughly relaxed person. Observation will reveal that in inhalation the abdominal area moves forward; in exhalation the abdominal area recedes. In terms of muscular activity this means that the abdominal muscles relax in inhalation and contract in exhalation. When the contraction of the abdominal muscles is brought under voluntary control, we can, through an act of will and responsive abdominal muscles, determine how long and how much contraction is to take place. Breathing is then under control. (Such control, of course, is useful only for purposes of speech. For ordinary life purposes not related to speaking it would become a nuisance to have to think about breathing.)

To become aware of abdominal activity the following exercises are suggested:

1. Lie on a couch or bed. Place your hands gently on the abdominal area immediately below the ribs. Inhale as for normal breathing. Your hands should rise during inhalation and fall during exhalation. If this does not happen—if there is a tendency for the abdominal area to pull in and fall during inhalation—then the abdominal activity is incorrect and should be changed.

2. Repeat the first exercise from a sitting position and then from a standing position. Make certain that the abdominal wall expands—pushes out—on inhalation, and contracts—pulls in—on exhalation.

3. Inhale fully and then breathe out slowly, hands still on the abdominal muscles. Repeat by sustaining the sound *ah!* while exhaling. (Do not force the exhalation to a point of discomfort, but become aware of when the discomfort point is reached. This is important because it will help you to anticipate breath needs while talking.)

4. Inhale fully and then count out evenly and slowly without noticeable pause between numbers. Maintain even pitch and loudness. Stop before you feel any need to force your breath. Note the extent of the count. Did any breath escape during the brief pause? If so, repeat the exercise, and this time avoid wasting breath. At the rate of two digits per second, it should be possible for almost all adults to count at least to fifteen and for most adults to count to twenty on one sustained breath. Practice this exercise until at least a count of fifteen is achieved.

5. Repeat the exercise *whispering* while counting. What number did you reach? It should be lower than for vocalized counting because more air is expelled for whispered speech than for voiced speech. Practice this exercise until the initial count is extended by 20 per cent.

6. Repeat exercises 4 and 5, reciting the alphabet rather than counting. Make certain that no breath is wasted *between the enunciation* of the letters.

7. Breathe in fully and count out in groups of three, pausing the equivalent of a digit after each group. Do not exhale during pauses. If no breath is wasted, it should be possible to reach the same number as in straight counting. Repeat, pausing after each four numbers.

8. Follow the instructions for exercise 7, but substitute the recitation of the alphabet for counting.

9. Count in groups of three, but this time exert pressure on the abdominal muscles with the hands on each third number. The exertion of pressure should produce increased loudness. Extra breath is used, and the count should be less than in exercises 4 and 7.

10. Remove the hands from the abdomen and repeat exercises 4, 6, 7, and 8.

11. Repeat exercise 9, without the hands at the abdomen. Pull in the abdominal muscles directly to force out the additional air necessary for increasing the loudness on the third numbers.

12. Count out from one to ten, beginning with a voice barely audible (but *not* whispered) and ending in a voice just below a shout.

13. Reverse the sequence of exercise 12 from a very loud voice to one that is barely audible but not whispered.

14. Say each of the following sentences on a single breath:
  (a) Let us do what must be done.
  (b) Bob, try to act your age!
  (c) Together now, let's haul away.
  (d) All aboard! Everybody aboard!
  (e) No! You can't make me do it.
  (f) Even the longest road must have a turning.
  (g) Ben Franklin warned that a man's a fool who makes his doctor his heir.
  (h) The storm turned the stream into a torrential river.
  (i) Jones learned that he was considered a wise man by just becoming a respectful listener.

15. Imagine three situations in which you must give single loud, clear commands in the interest of safety. Announce these commands.

16. Try the following couplets on a single breath. Even if you pause at the end of the first line, avoid exhaling at the pause or inhaling for a second breath:

  (a) Of all the tyrannies on human kind
      The worst is that which persecutes the mind.
              —POPE, *The Hind and the Panther*

(b) Those who in quarrels interpose
Must often wipe a bloody nose.

—GAY, *The Mastiffs* (*Fables*)

(c) Though his behavior was various
It was always reliably nefarious.

—J.E., *The Variable Man*

Adequate loudness

The exercises suggested above are intended to assist in establishing voluntary control of the loudness of voice through breathing. Adequate loudness, however, should not be a matter of breath use alone. Proper resonance and ease of voice production should make it unnecessary, in conversation at least, for energetic breathing to be used. Energetic breath usage is a worthwhile achievement, but for most speech purposes it should not replace the less effortful reinforcement of tone through resonance. In fact, with public address systems so widely available, if skillfully employed, a speaker is rarely required to use anything but a conversational voice regardless of where he may be speaking.[2] The voice that rings the rafters need no longer be an objective for either private or public speakers. Reinforcement of tone through resonance will be discussed later in the chapter.

THE PRODUCTION OF CLEAR TONES

Voice or tone, we know, is a result of the activity of the vocal folds. Earlier we learned that the vocal folds are set into action to produce voice as a result of the integrated activity of muscles of the larynx. Voice is produced when the vocal folds are brought together to set up resistance to the column of air being forced up from the lungs. When the vocal folds are apart, so that the column of air is free to flow through them, quiet, unvocalized breathing takes place. For the present we shall be concerned with the vocalization of good tones, easily initiated.

A good tone is clear and free from the interference of tension or strain. It is produced with ease, sustained with ease, and appropriately reinforced. Tonal impurities result from tensions of the muscles of the neck and throat which interfere with the free action of the laryngeal muscles. This in turn prevents proper action of the vocal folds. Tonal impurities may also result from inappropriate resonance, for the most part related to the nasal cavities. The problem of nasality will be considered later. Our immediate concern will be with the initiation and maintenance of tone.

---

[2] Amplification material should be tested in advance and adjusted to the physical characteristics of the room. Such factors as position of microphone, distance of the speaker from the microphone, and voice intensity level need to be determined for the individual speaker, the mechanical equipment, and the properties of the room or auditorium.

Initiation of tone

To initiate a good tone the vocal mechanism must be ready for vocalization. This means that the vocal folds must be brought together a moment before the column of air is forced up to set them into action. The vocal folds must be tense enough to set up resistance to the flow of air, but not so tense that the resistance is too great to permit breath to blow them apart. The speaker can determine his own *readiness for vocalization* by trying the exercises that follow:

1. Contract the throat muscles as if you are about to swallow. Note the sensation of the contracted muscles. Open the mouth as if to produce the sound *ah*. Do the throat muscles still feel as they did in swallowing? If they do, they are too tense for the initiation of good tone. Note the sensation of contracted throat muscles so that you will know what to avoid.

2. Yawn *gently* with mouth half open. Then breathe in and out through the mouth. Note the feeling of air in the back of the throat. Contrast this sensation with that of swallowing. If the yawning is gentle the throat should be relaxed. This is the state of muscle tonus you wish to achieve while talking. If the throat still does not feel relaxed, then try the next two exercises.

3. Sit back in a chair and let your head drop to your chest. Permit your head to hang from the neck as a dead weight. Yawn gently and then take three or four breaths through the mouth. Note the sensation. Swallow and contrast the tonus of the throat muscles in swallowing with that of gentle yawning. Repeat the yawning and mouth breathing. Fix these sensations in your mind.

4. Stand erect, but not rigid. Repeat exercise 3 in the standing position.

5. In a standing position, with throat muscles relaxed, say the vowel /ɑ/. Then try /ɔ/, /æ/, /u/ and /i/. Go from one vowel to the other without pausing. Throat tension will necessarily increase for the vowels /u/ and /i/ if the proper vowel values are to be produced. Try, however, to avoid undue tension.

6. Open your mouth as if to yawn gently, but instead of yawning say *ha, how, ho, ha, haw, ho.* Then try the sentence *Who am I?* (The purpose of opening the mouth *as if to yawn* is to make certain that the vocal mechanism is ready for vocalization before an attempt is made to initiate the tone. In addition, the act of *almost yawning* requires a relaxed, open throat that is essential for a good tone.)

7. With a relaxed throat, count from one to ten, accentuating the activity of the lips and tongue. Become aware of oral activity in the *front of the mouth*. Now count from one to twenty. If there is any tendency

for the throat muscles to tighten, stop, recapture the "yawning sensation," and begin again.

8. Repeat exercise 7, reciting the letters of the alphabet rather than counting. Continue to accentuate lip-tongue activity. If such activity has not been habitual, it is likely that your lips will feel tired. This is an excellent indication that you are following directions. With practice, the feeling of lip fatigue will disappear.

9. Read the following selections aloud, maintaining a relaxed throat. Make certain that you are *ready for vocalization* before you begin to speak. If at any time your throat muscles begin to tighten, stop reading and go back to exercises 3, 4, 5, and 6.

(a) Martha and Maud walked about the garden.
(b) Lawrence enjoyed talking but avoided all argument.
(c) Audrey and Alfred won honors for their abstract drawings.
(d) Niagara Falls produces an endless flow of water for energy and power.
(e) An ohm is a unit of electrical resistance.
(f) Robert Louis Stevenson observed that to travel hopefully may be a better thing than to arrive.
(g) The novelist Conrad held that "Only in men's imagination does every truth find an effective and undeniable existence."
(h) Centuries ago Horace advised, "What cannot be removed, becomes lighter through patience."
(i) In his famous *Walden,* Thoreau observed, "It is true, I never assisted the sun materially in his rising; but doubt not, it was of the last importance only to be present at it."

Breathiness (the fuzzy voice)

There is an element of danger that a relaxed throat and easy initiation of tone may result in a breathy voice quality because of associated partial relaxation of the vocal folds. This will happen, of course, only if the vocal folds are not brought close enough together to prevent "leakage" of air when vocalization takes place.

To be able to overcome breathiness, it is first necessary to become aware of a breathy voice quality. Speech that is intentionally whispered employs breath that is not used for vocalization. Fricative and stop-plosive consonants, especially those that are voiceless, are breathy sounds. You can feel the breath by placing your hand in front of your mouth while saying sentences such as:

1. Sheila threw the pots and pans out of the house through the open window.
2. Harry, the hatless hero, caught cold while playing ball.
3. The foghorn sounded as the ship slipped down the bay.

4. Peter and Paul both liked pumpkin pie.
5. Sam was fond of ham and cheese sandwiches.

Voiced consonants and all vowels, unless intentionally whispered, should be produced without any of the breathy or aspirate quality that characterizes the fricative and voiceless stop-plosive consonants. The following sentences should be spoken so that a minimum of breath is felt if your hand is held before your mouth.

1. The runner ran a mile.
2. There are more widows than widowers in our nation.
3. As the day began, there was a roaring blizzard.
4. Our man will win the relay.

Breathiness may result from carrying over the aspirate quality of a fricative or plosive consonant to the vowel that follows. To prevent this kind of assimilative influence, care should be taken not to prolong the aspirate consonants, and to produce them only with as much aspiration as is needed to identify the sound. The sound /h/ is particularly wasteful of breath, especially if prolonged.

The following pairs of words should be spoken so that there is no more aspiration on the vowel or diphthong of the second than there is on the first. (There should be *no aspiration on the first.*)

eel	heel	eye	tie
ill	hill	ell	tell
am	ham	at	cat
ooze	whose	ear	fear
old	hold	are	far
ire	hire	out	pout
awl	haul	eat	sheet
awe	paw	air	chair

The following sentences should be spoken with emphasis on the vowels and care taken not to carry over the aspirate quality of the consonants to the vowels.

1. Come home, Henry. All shall be forgiven.
2. Hate can kill men—the haters as well as the hated.
3. A vagrant's life is not always happy.
4. A harried husband is likely to remember a happy bachelorhood.
5. The horn honked as the car turned around the corner.
6. He came to scoff and so he did though no others found cause for scoffing.

Reinforcement of tone: resonance

If we depended upon the energetic use of breath to produce audible voice, speech would be fatiguing. Fortunately, as has already been pointed out, except for public addresses before a large audience, energetic use of breath is only occasionally necessary. Vocal tones are reinforced by the resonating cavities that are part of the speech mechanism. The chief resonators are the cavities of the larynx, pharynx, mouth, and nose. If these cavities are not obstructed by organic growths such as enlarged tonsils or adenoids, or by muscular tensions created by the speaker, reinforcement of tone is easy to achieve.

There is little we can or need do about the *larynx as a resonator.* In the absence of any organic pathology the larynx will function automatically to reinforce the tones produced within it by the action of the vocal folds. Laryngitis will interfere with laryngeal resonance. A person suffering from laryngitis will do well not to talk. If the condition is persistent or recurrent, a visit to a physician is recommended.

The *pharynx* functions best as a resonator when it is relatively open and relaxed. When the walls of the pharynx become tense, the voice tends to lose mellowness, and becomes metallic. Higher-pitched sounds are reinforced at the expense of low-pitched sounds. The overall result is an unpleasant voice with poor carrying power. How to achieve a relaxed pharynx (throat) was discussed earlier (see pages 117–118) and might be reviewed at this point.

The mouth is the most modifiable of the resonators and is readily subject to voluntary control. The different vowels are produced as a result of changes in the size and shape of the oral cavity plus some modification in the tensions and shape of the upper part of the pharynx. Variations in the shape of the mouth are brought about by changes in the positions of the lower jaw, lips, tongue, and soft palate.

Oral resonance is generally improved if the speaker makes a conscious effort to emphasize lip and tongue activity. This is what is generally meant when singing teachers direct their students to "place the tone forward in the mouth." Though front-of-the-mouth activity should be emphasized, it should not be so exaggerated as to attract attention to itself rather than to the resultant speech content.

The nasal cavity refers, of course, to the area above the roof of the mouth, and not to the nostrils (nose). Appropriate nasal reinforcement will be discussed later.

The exercises that immediately follow are intended to help to create awareness of tongue and lip activity and oral reinforcement of voice.

Exercises to create awareness of oral resonance

1. Observe your mouth in a mirror as you produce these vowels in pairs:

/u/ and /ɪ/
/o/ and /e/
/ɔ/ and /ɛ/
/ɑ/ and /æ/

2. Produce all the front and back vowels in sequence, without stopping between vowels. Note the change in lip, tongue, and jaw position.

3. Say *tic, tac, toe, we will go* several times with awareness of oral activity.

4. Combine the sounds /t/, /p/, and /w/ with each of the front and back vowels.

5. Practice the following sentences and verses that emphasize front-of-the-mouth sounds. Make certain that the breath is controlled and the voice well sustained.

(a) Who is there? It is I.
(b) Bing, bang, beat the drum!
(c) Heigh, ho, away we go!
(d) The wind whistled through the trees.
(e) We wish you were well.

(f) A dwarf sees farther than the
giant when he has the giant's shoulder
to mount on.

—COLERIDGE, *The Friend*

(g) Carson in *The Sea Around Us* talks of the growth of huge submarine volcanoes that build up large lava cones on the floor of the ocean.

(h) Weep on! and, as thy sorrows flow,
I'll taste the luxury of woe.

—THOMAS MOORE, *Anacreontic*

Nasal resonance

Just how important the nasal cavities are for the reinforcement of sound still remains to be determined. That the nasal resonators are important cannot be denied. The sounds /m/, /n/, and /ŋ/, though articulated orally, are resonated in the nasal cavities and emitted through the nose. That is, the soft palate *is lowered* for the production of these sounds.[3] In connected speech, sounds in close proximity to nasals, like the vowels in *men* and *name,* are at least partly reinforced through nasal resonance. This type of assimilated nasality, if excessive, is considered undesirable in American-English speech. How to avoid excessive nasality will be considered later.

Appropriate nasal resonance lends considerable roundness and carry-

---

[3] Tongue activity is, of course, also involved in the production of nasal sounds. For /m/, the tongue has "relaxed" in the mouth. For the /n/, the tongue is raised and the tongue tip is in contact with the upper gum ridge. For the /ŋ/, the back of the tongue is raised and is in contact with the lowered soft palate.

ing power to the voice. We may become aware of nasal reinforcement through sustained humming. Make certain that the throat muscles and the tongue and the soft palate are relaxed, and the jaws almost but not quite together. Close the lips so that they barely touch. Initiate a humming sound on a sustained breath. Place the thumb and forefinger lightly on the sides of the nostrils. The hum should be both felt as well as heard.

The vibratory effect and fullness resulting from appropriate nasal reinforcement of tone can be appreciated by comparing a sentence such as *Many merry men may marry* with a sentence containing no nasal sounds such as *Do you wish six fish?*

To establish nasal reinforcement, the following exercises are suggested.

Exercises to establish nasal resonance

Begin each exercise with a relaxed throat, tongue, and soft palate. Sustain an even tone through controlled, gradual, abdominal contraction.

1. Hum gently on a sustained breath. Repeat three or four times.

2. Blend a hum with the vowel /ɑ/, making certain that the soft palate is raised for the vowel.

3. Produce the sound /n/ and blend with the vowels /ɑ/ and /ɔ/. Hold the /n/ at least twice as long as in normal conversational speech.

4. Repeat exercise 3, beginning with the /ŋ/. Try /ŋɑ/, /ŋɔ/, /ŋou/, /ŋu/.

5. Chant: Mabel and Mary want a man to marry,
They do not mind a Tom or a Harry,
They merely mind that he might tarry.

6. In the following sentences and verses emphasize the nasal consonants by doubling their normal length.
   (a) Noah was considered to be a moody man.
   (b) The moon is now well within man's universe of achievement.
   (c) An old Persian maxim advises that persons with long tongues may have shortened lives.
   (d) In his *Pudd'nhead Wilson's New Calendar* Mark Twain observed: "Man is the only animal that blushes. Or needs to."
   (e) In his essay *Of Vanity* Montaigne noted: "There is no man so good who, were he to submit all his thoughts and actions to the laws, would not deserve hanging ten times in his life."

   (f) When musing on companions gone,
We doubly feel ourselves alone.

   —SIR WALTER SCOTT, *Marmion*

(g) Sunset and evening star,
   And one clear call for me!
   And may I hear no moaning of the bar,
   When I put out to sea.
           —TENNYSON, *Crossing the Bar*

Deviations from normal nasal reinforcement

Insufficient nasal resonance, or *denasality,* may usually be attributed to obstructions to or within the nasal passages. Adenoidal tissue, if enlarged, will prevent sound from getting to the nasal cavities for reinforcement. Growths or restrictions within the nasal cavities prevent proper reinforcement or emission of nasal sounds. Extreme tension in the region of the nasopharynx may produce an effect comparable to an actual obstruction. The most frequent obstruction results from the common cold when nasal catarrh clogs the passages. Regardless of the cause, insufficient nasal reinforcement of tone results in a flat, lifeless voice. Unless there is severe organic pathology requiring medical attention, the exercises described above for the establishment of nasal resonance should help in overcoming denasality.

Excessive nasality is a defect opposite to that of denasality. It results usually from an overrelaxed soft palate that fails to rise when necessary in order to block off the stream of breath for nonnasal sounds. In some instances excessive and inappropriate nasality is associated with a general muscular sluggishness and an "I don't care" attitude on the part of the speaker. If attention is directed to speech activity, it will be found that the jaw, lips, and tongue as well as the soft palate are sluggish.

If the muscular sluggishness has a physical basis, medical attention is indicated. If the basis is in an attitude, speech exercises alone will not help greatly to overcome the nasality. If, however, excessive and inappropriate nasality has been learned unconsciously, and the will to change is present, the following exercises should be of help.

Exercises to overcome excessive nasality

1. *Raising the soft palate.* Stand before a mirror and yawn with a wide-open mouth. Note that the soft palate is raised while the yawn is maintained. Repeat and become aware of the feeling when the soft palate is elevated.

2. With mouth closed, try to elevate the soft palate. Then open the mouth to produce the vowel /ɑ/. Permit the soft palate to drop and intentionally produce a nasalized /ɑ/. Then raise the soft palate to produce a nonnasal /ɑ/. Capture the sensation of the elevated soft palate when the vowel sound is produced. Repeat for the vowels /ɔ/ and /ʊ/.

3. Close your nostrils by pinching them. Say /ɑ/. Repeat with open nostrils. There should be little or no difference in the sound either way. Repeat for all the back vowels.

4. Say /ŋ/ while observing and feeling the action of the soft palate. Then say /ɑ/. The soft palate should be lowered and relaxed for /ŋ/ and raised for /ɑ/. Alternate between the two sounds until there is immediate awareness of the difference in palatal position.

5. Place a cold hand mirror under your nostrils and produce a prolonged /ɑ/. If the soft palate is raised, there should be no clouding of the mirror. Practice until there is no clouding. Then repeat for all the back vowels.

6. Repeat exercise 5, for the front vowels. Avoiding clouding will be somewhat more difficult, but should soon be established. The vowels /ɛ/ and /æ/ may require special attention.

7. Pinch your nostrils closed and say each of the sentences that follow. If there is a feeling of stuffiness in the nose, or pressure in the ears, then the soft palate is not blocking off the passage of air to the nasal cavity. Make a conscious effort to raise the palate.

    (a) Here is where I wish to stay.
    (b) All aboard! The boat is about to leave.
    (c) The expected reply arrived too late.
    (d) The sky was red, the clouds ships of fire.

8. Say the following pairs of words with attention to the activity of the soft palate. The soft palate should be raised throughout the articulation of the second member of the pair.

moo	boo	nail	sail
me	be	no	go
my	die	me	tea

9. Practice the following words, making certain that the soft palate is elevated as soon as the nasal consonant is completed.

meek	moose
may	now
my	nerve
mat	nuts
neighbor	kneel
more	news

Associated nasality

The only sounds in American and English speech that require intentional nasalization are /m/, /n/, and /ŋ/. In connected speech, however, sounds in close proximity to the nasal consonants are almost always slightly nasalized. The nasalization is an assimilative effect resulting from the manner of articulation of /m/, /n/, and /ŋ/. Specifically, one of three things may happen: (1) The lowered soft palate may not be raised soon enough to prevent the following vowel from being somewhat nasalized. This would account for nasalization of the vowels, and occasionally consonants, in words such as *me, mail, not,* and *news.* (2) The soft palate may be lowered while the sound preceding the nasal is articulated, as in words such as *am, sing, and,* and *own.* (3) The soft palate may not be completely elevated because of the influence of preceding as well as following nasal consonants, as in *man, known, mountain,* and *mangle.*

There is little point in trying to avoid all traces of assimilative nasality. This feat could probably be achieved, but the required effort would be great, and the manner of articulation so self-conscious and precise as to be undesirable. It is important, however, that the amount of assimilative influence be kept to a minimum so that the articulation as a whole does not become characterized by nasality.

The exercises recommended earlier to gain control of the soft palate are directly applicable to overcoming excessive associated nasality. Emphasis on front-of-the-mouth activity for vowel production is also important. In addition, the following suggestions should be of help.

1. Where the nasal consonant precedes the vowel, lengthen the nasal consonant. This will afford the added moment of time needed to elevate the soft palate. The result should be a reduction of assimilated nasality on the sound that follows.

(a) Practice on the following sound combinations. At first exaggerate the duration of the nasal to a marked degree. Then reduce the degree of exaggeration, but maintain the nasal consonant for a time you consider about twice as long as normal.

/m/ : /ɑ/	/m/ : /ɛ/
/m/ : /ɔ/	/m/ : /æ/
/m/ : /u/	/m/ : /eɪ/
/m/ : /i/	/m/ : /aʊ/

(b) Repeat the foregoing exercise, prefixing the sound /n/ and then /ŋ/.

(c) Practice saying the following words, exaggerating the length of the nasal consonants.

may	more	not	never
mar	mood	gnaw	knee
mug	map	know	new

(d) Practice saying the following sentences, taking care to increase the length of the nasal consonants:

We may move in November.
Mary may marry Ned next May.
The mouse gnawed at the new twine.
Mabel mailed the note to her mother in Maine.

2. Where the nasal consonant follows the vowel, emphasize oral activity for the production of the vowel. This is especially important for front vowels and for the diphthong /aʊ/, which tend most often to be nasalized.

(a) Practice on the following sound combinations:

[æ m]	[æ n]	[æ ŋ]
[ɛ m]	[ɛ n]	[ɛ ŋ]
[eɪ m]	[eɪ n]	[eɪ ŋ]
[i m]	[i n]	
[aʊ m]	[aʊ n]	

(b) Practice careful enunciation of the following words:

amber	can't	angle
emerald	another	length
I'm	kind	single
ohm	own	sung

(c) Incorporate the words of the foregoing exercise into sentences such as the following:

Amy dislikes wearing emeralds.
The deer's antlers were two feet in length.
We sang a single song.
Amber is a kind of yellow-brown.

3. Where nasal consonants precede and follow the vowel, both lengthen the first nasal and emphasize oral activity for the vowel.

(a) Practice on words such as the following:

mean	moan	meandering
minnow	unknown	remembering
main	number	drowning
many	namely	cringing
meant	mingle	crowning
moon	banging	grinding
mine	numbing	frowning

(b) Practice careful enunciation of the following:

Men manifest their personalities by their conduct.
For months on end the snow showed no signs of melting.
The moon spread a silvery blanket over the meadow.

> Men sometimes sing mournful songs without living mournful lives.

(c) Practice items 5 and 6 of the previous "Exercises to Establish Nasal Resonance."

WIDENING THE PITCH RANGE

In the chapter on the components of speech (Chapter 3), we discussed the significance of pitch changes for communicating thoughts and feelings. The point was emphasized that thought pitch changes tend to follow emotional changes, pitch modifications in American speech are used to give intellectual significance to our words. It follows, therefore, that a voice that is narrow in pitch range tends to limit its user in communicating speech content. In addition, of course, the pitch-monotonous voice is not likely to attract attention or to maintain whatever initial attention the speaker may have.

Optimum pitch

In the absence of any pathology, there is a natural level at which the pitch of the voice can vary with greatest ease and effectiveness. Unfortunately there is considerable evidence to indicate that many persons use a habitual level that is not the natural best one for them. The result is that both pitch variety and voice quality suffer.

To determine the natural or optimum pitch level the following instructions should be followed:

1. Relax the throat muscles. Take a moderately deep breath and produce a well-controlled *ah* at whatever pitch level seems normal for you. Note the pitch of the sound.
2. Repeat, but this time produce a sound a step lower in pitch.
3. Continue, going down a step at a time, until you have produced the lowest-pitched tone you can. Do not strain for an abnormally low pitch.
4. Go back to the initial pitch. Now produce tones on an upward scale.

It should be possible for you to go up in pitch from the initial tone about twice the number of pitch levels you moved down. If this is the case, you are using your natural or optimum pitch level. (The optimum pitch level, for most persons, is *approximately one-third up from the lowest tone* the individual can comfortably produce.)

An alternate method of determining optimum pitch is to match tones with the notes of a piano. Produce tones down to as low a level as feels comfortable. Match each tone with a note on the piano. Then go up the scale as high as you can. Select a tone approximately a third of the way up from the bottom as the optimum pitch level for you.

Make a mental note of the optimum pitch level. Learn to recognize how it feels to produce this pitch and how it sounds. Most exercises to widen pitch range will be based on the *optimum or natural pitch level as the point of departure.*

If the pitch level at which you habitually initiate a tone and the determined optimum pitch level deviate significantly (by more than two tones), then work to bring the two levels closer together. There is no need for exact correspondence between habitual pitch level and optimum level. It has been found, however, that superior speakers tend to use their optimum pitch as their most habitual, or frequently used, pitch level. For this reason it is recommended for persons interested in voice improvement.

Habitual pitch

Although even a monotonous speaker does not have a voice limited to a single pitch, most of us tend to initiate and speak at a level and speak within a range that includes a recurrent or habitual pitch. If this pitch happens to be the optimum one, or no more than a level higher or lower than the optimum pitch, then the speaker has no need to be concerned about exercises for maintaining vocalization at or near the optimum pitch. If, however, the optimum and habitual pitch are more than two full steps apart as equated on a musical scale, then the exercises for optimum pitch are very strongly recommended.

Habitual pitch may be determined by a relaxed (but not overrelaxed) reading of a 50- to 75-word paragraph of material with relatively neutral content. Choose a simple passage, with words easy to pronounce and free of great challenge to the mind or to the feeling. Read the passage three or four times in a intentionally monotonous manner, but avoid dropping the voice to the extreme lower end of the pitch range. Instead, let the voice come and be sustained as it will, and note the level at which it is sustained. This is probably your habitual pitch. Record the reading, play it back, and compare it with a recorded reading of the same passage in which you emphasize vocalizing at optimum pitch. A passage such as the following may be of help.

> Considered as a chemical compound, water is an oxide of hydrogen and oxygen. Ordinary water is represented by the chemical formula H_2O. Seldom, however, is water so pure as to contain only hydrogen and oxygen. Though every schoolchild now knows that water is a compound, it was once regarded as a single chemical element. The English chemist Cavendish proved that water was not an element but a compound.

How wide should one's pitch range be? In general terms the answer is "As wide as necessary to give adequate expression to your thoughts and feelings." A practical and experimentally observed answer is that most good speakers employ a range of an octave or more. Poor speakers, more frequently than not, have a narrow pitch range. Most persons use a range narrower than they are capable of using, tending to concentrate on the lower parts of the pitch range.

Because the normal pitch range is about two-thirds up and one-third down from the optimum pitch, there is more room for variety if the upper pitch levels are developed. By no means, however, should low pitch levels be ignored. Nor should we strain for higher pitches that cannot be easily reached or supported.

Pitch change in singing vs. speaking

Before leaving our general discussion of pitch changes in speaking, a reminder is in order. Though singing is an excellent medium for establishing and extending pitch range, the method of employing pitch changes in singing is different from that of speaking. In the first place, as indicated in an earlier discussion, almost all pitch changes in singing are discrete. The singing voice moves in separate steps from note to note with each sound held longer than it is likely to be in speaking. Syllables within a sung word are spoken on distinctively different tonal levels. This is not usually the case in speaking. Most vocal changes in speaking are subtle. Except where a word is to be made conspicuous for the purpose of emphasis, a distinctive change in level is not likely to take place in conversational speech or in nonmelodramatic public speech. If we compare the pitch changes in the spoken and sung first line of the song *America,* the differences should become clear.

A second difference between pitch changes in speech and in singing should be noted. In singing, a pattern of pitch changes is established and then repeated with occasional modification. The repetition of pattern in singing constitutes melody. Such repetition is to be avoided in speaking where it constitutes monotony rather than melody. The pitch changes in speaking must be correlated with variations in thought and feeling. In English and American speech, subtleties of ideational content are conveyed through such changes. Patterned changes tend, therefore, to interfere with meaning and to impair effective communication.

Flexibility and responsiveness

It is axiomatic that a flexible, responsive voice requires voluntary control for production and an awareness of what is produced. The speakers must learn to appreciate his own vocal limitations and to evaluate what he hears in the voices of others. A widened pitch range can be achieved only after the speaker realizes fully the extent of his present habitual range. This requires sensitive and discriminating listening. Unless differences can be heard, practice and exercise cannot be put to fruitful use. Training in hearing differences is essential for any aspect of voice improvement, whether it is for breath control, tone initiation, or a widened pitch range.

Exercises for widening pitch range

1. Determine your natural or optimum pitch by one of the methods described above. Then say the sentence *I am John Jones,* initiating it on your optimum pitch level. Practice saying the same sentence, initiating the first word on succeeding lower levels until you reach the lowest comfortable pitch level. Begin again, going to the highest comfortable level.

2. Check your optimum pitch on a piano. Repeat exercise 1. Work for a range of at least one octave.

3. Begining at your optimum pitch level, count down a tone at a time, as low as you can with comfort. Begin again, this time counting up. Do you go about twice as high up as you can down? Work to accomplish this.

4. Repeat exercise 3, using the syllables [la], [na], [da], [mi], [meɪ], and [deɪ].

5. Review the discussion on kinds of pitch changes (pages 41–45). Then answer the following questions.

 (a) How many kinds of inflectional changes are there? How is each used in English-American speech?
 (b) What is a step? How does it differ from a slide?

6. Count from one to fifteen, using an upward inflection on the numbers five and ten, and a downward inflection on fifteen.

7. Recite the alphabet, using a falling inflection on each third letter.

8. Say the word *yes* to indicate (a) decision, (b) doubt, (c) irony or sarcasm.

9. Say the word *no* so that by means of pitch change you indicate the following:

 (a) Emphatic negation,
 (b) Uncertainty or doubt,
 (c) Interest,
 (d) Surprise,
 (e) Annoyance.

10. Repeat exercise 9, using the sound /m/.

11. Say the sentence *I will do it* so that the following meanings are suggested:

(a) Determination,
(b) Surprise,
(c) Pleasant agreement,
(d) Annoyance and doubt,
(e) Resignation.

12. Say the sentence *You're a fine fellow* in ways that will bring out the following meanings:

(a) Admiration for the person addressed.
(b) Encouragement,
(c) Dislike,
(d) Surprise at the discovery of the person's qualities.

13. Say *No* (a) so as to make it fill a short space of time, (b) double the initial utterance time, (c) triple the initial utterance time. What is the difference in feeling and meaning with the change in length of utterance?

14. Now say *No* (a) as if you are biting into the word, (b) you are enjoying the opportunity, (c) as if you are "stomping" on the word, (d) in a barely audible whisper, (e) to indicate that you are not at all certain that you really mean "No."

15. Repeat, having a friend listen, and find out whether you and your friend are in agreement by what you intended in your varied utterances of the single word *No*.

16. Pronounce the words, *Please, come here* so that they will constitute:

(a) A polite request,
(b) An entreaty,
(c) A polite command,
(d) An abrupt command.

17. Pronounce the sentence *I like him* to bring out the following meanings:

(a) A direct statement of fact,
(b) A contradiction of the literal meaning of the words,
(c) Irritation and surprise that anyone could conceivably accuse you of liking *the likes of him*,
(d) Indecision as to your feelings about *him*,
(e) Indication that your liking is for *him* and not for anyone else,
(f) An answer to the question "Who likes him?"
(g) An aggressive answer to the question "Who could possibly like someone like him?"

18. Read the following selections using pitch variations to emphasize changes in thought and in feeling.

(a) During its first twenty years my teaching followed a single pattern. Questions and discussion were encouraged and were fun, but lectures were the focus.

Today, lectures are on the defensive. Almost everything we would like students to know we can place in their hands via paperback. They can read faster than they can listen to us, and print is durable; they can go back if they miss something or forget.

All this is true, but the points don't add up to the conclusion that lectures are passé. One of my most memorable learning experiences was a course Thornton Wilder offered, once only, at the University of Chicago. The classroom was in fact an auditorium, and it was invariably packed. If there was a single question or comment from the floor I don't remember it, yet the exhilaration of those hours! I would leave the auditorium walking on air.

—HUSTON SMITH, *Two Kinds of Teaching*
The Key Reporter, *Phi Beta Kappan,* 38:4 (1973)

(b) There is nothing we receive with so much reluctance as advice. We look upon the man who gives it as offering an affront to our understanding, and treating us like children or idiots.

—ADDISON, *Spectator*

(c) There are two ways of being happy: we may either diminish our wants or augment our means. Either will do, the result is the same. And it is for each man to decide for himself, and do that which happens to be the easiest. . . .

—BENJAMIN FRANKLIN

19. Select a passage of 100 to 150 words from one of your favorite columnists or editorial writers in which the writer is angry about a situation or feels strongly about an issue. Read the passage aloud to communicate both the thoughts and the feelings of the writer.

20. Paraphrase the selection so that you are conveying the same ideas in words and constructions mostly of your own. Read your selection aloud to convey the underlying thoughts and feelings.

QUALITY

Most of our discussion of voice quality has been from the negative side. We have considered undesirable qualities such as breathiness and excessive nasality. There is a positive side to voice quality that is associated with the mood, feelings, and emotions of the speaker. Because voice quality is related to the nonintellectual aspects of behavior, it is not a subject that can be directly taught. The person who *feels what he says* need not be told what voice quality to use to reveal his feelings. The changes in muscle tone which naturally accompany changes in feeling will help to produce the appropriate voice quality. The overrestrained, inhibited person who tries to use an intellectual approach to quality will only succeed in conveying the idea that he does not really feel the way he would like the listener to think he feels. The responsive speaker who initiates tone properly and who uses an appropriate and flexible pitch range and rate of utterance need not concern himself about what voice quality to use. In the absence of any mental or physical disturbance, it is likely to come naturally and spontaneously.

Although we believe that quality of voice is generally a by-product of a state of being, there is always a possibility that in a given instance it may reflect a past rather than a present state. On occasion vocal habits may become reinforced and "fixed" and may suggest an attitude or a feeling no longer entertained by the speaker. The best way to make certain that this is not so, or to determine to modify the situation if it is so, is to have a recording made and to listen to the playback as objectively as if the voice were not your own. If the voice does not reflect the state you feel, or at least the feelings or attitude you intended to convey, compare your voice with that of another speaker who is successful in the expression of his states of affect, and try to do with your voice what you admire in the other speaker. Do not, however, violate your own personality by trying to speak like another speaker. Be yourself, but be certain that your voice reflects the self you wish to be, and at any given moment, the aspect or state of being of yourself you wish to reveal.

EXERCISES

Determine the underlying mood of each of the selections that follow, and then read them aloud to reveal the mood.

1. During the whole of a dull, dark, and resoundless day in the autumn of the year, when the clouds hung oppressively low in the heavens, I had been passing alone, on horseback, through a singularly dreary tract of country, and at length found myelf, as the shades of evening drew on, within view of the melancholy House of Usher. I know not how it was—but, with the first glimpse of the building, a sense of insufferable gloom pervaded my spirit.

—POE, *The Fall of the House of Usher*

2. A poor Relation—is the most irrelevant thing in nature,—a piece of impertinent correspondency,—an odious approximation,—a haunting conscience—a preposterous shadow, lengthening in the noontide of our

prosperity,—an unwelcome remembrance,—a perpetually recurring mortification,—a drain on your purse,—a more intolerable dun upon your pride,—a drawback upon success,—a rebuke to your rising,—a stain in your blood,—a blot in your 'scutcheon,—a rent in your garment,—a death's head at your banquet,—Agathocles' plot,—a Mordecai in your gate,—a Lazarus at your door,—a lion in your path,—a frog in your chamber,—a fly in your ointment,—a mote in your eye,—a triumph to your enemy, and apology to your friends,—the one thing not needful,— the hail in the harvest,—the ounce of sour in a pound of sweet.

> —CHARLES LAMB, *Poor Relations*

3. "And the earth was without form, and void; and darkness was upon the face of the deep."

> —GENESIS

4. ". . . For the sea lies all about us. The commerce of all lands must cross it. The very winds that move over the lands have been cradled on its broad expanse and seek ever to return to it. The continents themselves dissolve and pass to the sea, in grain after grain of eroded land. So the rains which rose from it return again in rivers. In its mysterious past it encompasses all the dim origins of life and receives in the end, . . . the dead husks of that same life. For all at last return to the sea—the ever-flowing stream—."

> —RACHEL L. CARSON—*The Sea Around Us*
> (New York: Oxford University Press, 1951, p. 216.)

5. Why do our joys depart
   For cares to seize the heart?
   I know not. Nature says,
   Obey: and man obeys.
   I see, and know not why,
   Thorns live and roses die.

> —LANDOR, *Why Do Our Joys Depart*

6. I strove with none, for none was worth my strife,
   Nature I loved, and next to Nature, Art;
   I warmed both hands before the fire of life,
   It sinks, and I am ready to depart.

> —LANDOR, *On His Seventy-fifth Birthday*

7. Jenny kissed me when we met,
   Jumping from the chair she sat in;
   Time, you thief, who loves to get
   Sweets into your list, put that in:

Say I'm weary, say I'm sad,
    Say that health and wealth have missed me,
Say I'm growing old, but add
    Jenny kissed me.
    —LEIGH HUNT, *Rondeau*

8. Sunset and evening star,
        And one clear call for me!
    And may there be no moaning of the bar,
        When I put out to sea,

    But such a tide as moving seems asleep,
        Too full for sound and foam,
    When that which drew from out the boundless deep
        Turns again home.

    Twilight and evening bell,
        And after that the dark!
    And may there be no sadness of farewell,
        When I embark;

    For though from out our bourne of Time and Place
        The flood may bear me far,
    I hope to see my Pilot face to face
        When I have crost the bar.
        —TENNYSON, *Crossing the Bar*

SUMMARY

In the absence of any organic pathology or abnormality of personality, it should be possible for each of us to develop an effective voice.

An effective voice is appropriate to the age, sex, and physical makeup of the individual. It reflects the person's inner responses and enhances the communication of thoughts and feelings.

Objective characteristics of an effective voice include (1) adequate and controlled loudness, (2) variety of pitch, (3) good tone quality, and (4) appropriate rate and timing.

Voice improvement begins with an awareness of the sound of one's own voice and an appreciation of its limitations. Voice and personality are closely related. If you recognize the reactions others have to your voice, you can estimate the personality picture your listeners have of you because of your voice.

Control of loudness is established through controlled abdominal breathing. Energetic breathing should not replace proper reinforcement of tone through resonance.

The production of clear, easily produced pleasant tones requires integrated activity of the muscles of the larynx and the pharynx. A tone free from tension and strain can be produced if the throat is relatively relaxed and the vocal folds *ready for vocalization* when voice is initiated.

Breathiness and excessive nasality are common defects of voice quality. Both can be avoided through the establishment of proper attitude and good muscle tone. *Appropriate nasal resonance* lends fullness and carrying power to the voice. A lack of nasal resonance is associated with obstruction to or within the nasal passages.

A flexible pitch range is best established on the *optimum or natural* pitch level of the voice. The optimum pitch is approximately one-third the distance above the lowest tone within the pitch range that can normally be produced. Superior speakers, as a group, use a pitch range of at least one octave.

Voice improvement can take place only with the active and intelligent cooperation of the person who feels the need for such improvement. The speaker must become aware of his limitations and learn what to do to overcome them. This is so whether the limitation is one of pitch, loudness, quality, or an underlying defect of personality that is manifest in a deficient voice.

Review selections for voice improvement

The selections that follow are intended for practice in all the aspects of voice improvement considered in this chapter.

1. *An Elegy on the Death of a Mad Dog*

Good people all of every sort,
   Give ear unto my song,
And if you find it wondrous short,
   It cannot hold you long.

In Islington there was a man,
   Of whom the world might say,
That still a godly race he ran,
   Whene'er he went to pray.

A kind and gentle heart he had,
   To comfort friends and foes;
The naked every day he clad,
   When he put on his clothes.

And in that town a dog was found,
   As many dogs there be,
Both mongrel, puppy, whelp, and hound.
   And curs of low degree.

This dog and man at first were friends;
   But when a pique began,
The dog, to gain some private ends,
   Went mad, and bit the man.

Around from all the neighbouring streets,
    The wondering neighbours ran,
And swore the dog had lost his wits,
    To bite so good a man.

The wound it seem'd both sore and sad
    To every Christian eye;
And while they swore the dog was mad,
    They swore the man would die.

But soon a wonder came to light,
    That showed the rogues they lied—
The man recovered of the bite,
    The dog it was that died.

        —OLIVER GOLDSMITH

2. *The Lady's Not For Yearning*

Please to listen, my fair lady,
    I've a lyric in my soul;
I've a loving, lilting lyric
    That I would give you, give you whole.

But the lady cannot listen,
    She has a heart, her own, in thrall,
She might hear yet not attend me
    Should I repeat, repeat it all.

        —J.E.

RECOMMENDED READINGS

ANDERSON, V. A. *Training the Speaking Voice,* 2nd ed. New York: Oxford University Press, 1966, chaps. 1–6.

BOONE, D. *The Voice and Voice Therapy.* Englewood Cliffs, N.J.: Prentice-Hall, Inc., 1971.

BRODNITZ, F. S. *Keep Your Voice Healthy.* New York: Harper & Row, Publishers, Inc., 1953.

BRONSTEIN, A. J., and B. F. JACOBY. *Your Speech and Voice.* New York: Random House, Inc., 1967, chaps. 1 and 2.

DENES, P. B., and E. H. PINSON. *The Speech Chain.* New York: Bell Telephone Laboratories, 1963, chaps. 1 and 4.

EISENSON, J. *Voice and Diction: A Program for Improvement.* New York: Macmillan Publishing Co., Inc., 1974, chap. 1.

FISHER, H. B. *Improving Voice and Articulation.* Boston: Houghton Mifflin Company, 1966.

HANLEY, T. D., and W. L. THURMAN. *Developing Vocal Skills*. New York: Holt, Rinehart and Winston, Inc., 1962.

HEINBERG, P. *Voice Training*. New York: The Ronald Press Company, 1966, chaps. 1 and 5.

MARKEL, N. N., J. A. PHILLIS, R. VARGAS, and F. HOWARD. "Personality Traits Associated with Voice Types," *Journal of Psycholinguistic Research*, 1, 3 (1972), 249–255.

OGILVIE, M., and N. S. REES. *Communication Skills: Voice and Pronunciation*. New York: McGraw-Hill Book Company, 1969, chaps. 1 and 2.

VAN RIPER, C., and J. V. IRWIN. *Voice and Articulation*. Englewood Cliffs, N.J.: Prentice-Hall, Inc., chap. 13.

Chapter 8

Improving Pronunciation & Articulation[1]

PURPOSE OF CHAPTER: EASE OF COMPREHENSION

The objective of the discussion and the related practice materials in this chapter is to provide a basis for the student to improve his articulation and pronunciation so that he can enhance his effectiveness as a communicator. As noted earlier, atypical speech—speech that deviates from an acknowledged standard for which the speaker is motivated—attracts attention to itself and away from the speaker's intended meaning and purpose. Speech production that falls within accepted and acceptable standards permits the listener to concentrate on the content of the utterance, rather than on the manner in which the content is expressed.

For varied and numerous reasons many adults who speak the English language do so in a way that seems to direct attention to the manner, rather than the content, of speaking. The listener may, after a short time, adjust himself to the differences in the speaker's manner and have little or no difficulty in following what is being said. Sometimes, however, the adjustment may be difficult. Occasionally the speaker may even be through with what he has to say before the listener has made the required adjustments. As a result, comprehension will at best be partial. At worst, there is impaired communication and limited comprehension.

CAUSES OF FAULTY DICTION

Foreign-language influence

The speaker for whom English is a second language and who produces English speech sounds in a manner closer to the sounds of his native tongue than to those of American speech is likely to have some difficulty in communicating his meanings. He may, of course, have something so decidedly worthwhile to say that the listener will make the necessary

---

[1] The term *diction* will be used as synonymous with pronunciation and articulation. In a broader sense the term *diction* is used to denote choice of words as well as the quality of speech sound production, pronunciation, intonation, and inflection. In the narrowest sense *diction* is limited to proficiency of speech sound production in contextual utterance.

effort to understand him. Even such a speaker may lose something of his effectiveness because of the special effort required for comprehension.

Many native-born speakers may have learned English from someone for whom it was a foreign language. For persons exposed to foreign-language influence, their spoken English may sound as if it were a second language learned as adults. Our adjustments in comprehending such speakers are occasionally as great as if they were actually foreign born.

This tends to be the situation when foreign-born persons migrate to the United States and settle in communities with relatives or friends within which cultural values may be maintained, and the native language used as the primary medium for communication. Often the children born to immigrant families hear and acquire their parents' language as their first language, and learn American English as a dialect influenced by the first language.

Mechanical faults

Sometimes the difficulty with the production of speech sounds is on a mechanical basis. There may have been some difficulty in childhood with one or more of the organs of articulation that made conventional sound production difficult. A substitute sound or an alternate manner of producing a particular sound may have been learned. A tongue-tie, for example, may have required that a *d* or a *t* be produced behind the lower teeth rather than behind the upper teeth; the *s* may have been learned as a laterally emitted sound because of malformations of dental structure. In any event, if the acoustic end result is significantly different from that heard when the articulators execute conventional movements for the production of American-English sounds, diction is to be considered faulty.

Imitation

Occasionally the reason for the faulty diction is purely imitative. As a child the speaker may have imitated an adult who, for one reason or another, spoke with faulty diction. Having no basis for exercising discriminative judgments, the child unwittingly may form the habit of faulty sound production. These habits, unless corrected, tend to persist into adult life.

Nonstandard and substandard speech

Another reason for faulty diction is the influence of nonstandard or of substandard speech in the environment of the speaker. As children, we have little choice in the matter of the speech we learn. We learn what we hear. If it is either substandard or nonstandard speech, that is what we hear and learn.

Whatever the reason for faulty pronunciation and articulation, the content of this chapter is intended to help the interested and motivated speaker overcome his speech faults or his differences. The sounds to be studied are those that have been found to cause most difficulty for native as well as foreign-born persons. Descriptions of the sounds, word lists, and other exercise materials will be provided.[2]

THE PHONETIC APPROACH TO ARTICULATION IMPROVEMENT

The most frequent place of articulation

If we examine Table 6–2, we may readily note that many of the sounds of American-English speech are produced at or near the upper gum ridge. At this point, by contact with the tongue tip the sounds /t/, /d/, /l/, and /n/ are produced. A fraction of an inch behind the gum ridge, articulatory contacts are made for the sounds /s/, /z/, /ʃ/, /ʒ/, /tʃ/, /dʒ/, and one of the allophones of /r/. It becomes important, therefore, to become acquainted with the apparently favored place of articulation for American-English speech.

For speakers who have been exposed to foreign-language influence, it may be of some help to know that most spoken languages seem to have favored places of articulation. In French, Spanish, and Italian many sounds are produced by contact between the tongue tip and the upper teeth.[3] In German, the point of contact is a bit lower. Because many of the sounds produced at these contact points correspond to the sounds of American-English speech, the tendency to carry over foreign-language articulatory habits becomes readily understandable. The need for a considerable amount of practice to overcome this carry-over should also be clear. A study of the diagram of the mouth should provide a visual aid for becoming acquainted with the alveolar (upper gum) ridge area (see Figure 8–1).

[2] We are aware that there are conflicting interests and influences—cultural, socio-economic, and political—relative to the acceptance of standards and that there are advocates for multiple standards for speech and for speakers. Such standards include variations in syntax, pronunciations, and word usage. We are not arguing for or against any one position. However, the materials that follow are based on the authors' personal beliefs that at least a knowledge and an ability to use a standard American English would certainly not be a negative factor in an individual's progress and effectiveness in a community of his choice. Certainly the investment of federal and local funds, and human effort, suggest that most of us are at least interested in achieving some well-recognized standard of proficiency before deciding to reject it for another standard. The ultimate choice is a personal one, based on highly and varied individual motives and dynamics. We think it is wise that when the individual choice is made, it be based on knowledge rather than indifference or a lack of information.

[3] Speakers of dialects of Spanish such as those spoken by Americans of Mexican parentage or by immigrants from Mexico and South America as well as those from Puerto Rico would be likely to show dental contact articulation as a carry-over influence. Similarly, Cajun (French) dialect influence may be expressed in dental articulation for sounds produced with gum-ridge contact by most American-English speakers.

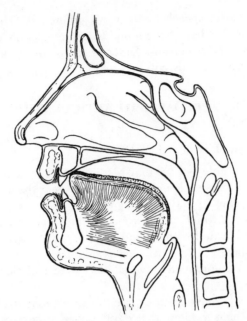

FIGURE 8–1. Diagram of the mouth showing contact point for /t/, /d/, and /l/. Essentially the same tongue tip and gum ridge contact is made for the /n/. The /n/, however, is produced with a relaxed and lowered soft palate.

INDIVIDUAL STUDY OF TROUBLESOME SOUNDS IN AMERICAN-ENGLISH SPEECH

/t/ as in *ten*

We shall begin our study with the consonant /t/. It has been our experience that if the contact point and manner of articulation for /t/ is mastered, it becomes an excellent point of reference for the articulation of other American-English speech sounds.

To produce the /t/ as in *ten* or as an isolated sound, the tongue is extended so that the tongue tip comes into contact with the upper gum ridge. The sides of the tongue near the tip are in contact with the upper gum. Farther back, the sides of the tongue are in contact with the upper molars. The tense, extended tongue is held in this position for a fraction of a second. Then, as suddenly and completely as possible, the tongue is retracted with a resultant slight "explosion" at the tongue tip. If the hand is held in front of the mouth, this "explosion" should be felt as a puff of breath.

The /t/ sound as just described occurs whenever the /t/ is in a stressed syllable and is immediately followed by a vowel as in *ten, ton, atone, attend,* and *intact.* /t/ as in *ten* may be described as a lingua-alveolar, voiceless, stop-plosive consonant.

In producing the /t/ sound as just described the following cautions should be observed:

1. Make certain that the tongue tip is in contact with the gum ridge and *not the upper teeth*. The contact, when broken, should be quick and complete.
2. Do not permit the tongue to slide so that contact is made between the front surface of the tongue and the gums. If this happens, the [ts] blend is likely to be produced.

Practice materials for /t/

/t/ in a stressed position followed by a vowel

Practice the following:

teach	tail	tact	toad
team	tell	tag	told
tick	ten	tog	tuft
till	tab	tube	tie
tin	tack	toe	tear
canteen	retain	intend	atomic
narcotic	attend	motel	retort
contain	contend	pretend	intone
detain	detect	baton	internal

1. Tina took her time telling us about her troubles.
2. Tiny Tim tiptoes through tulips.
3. Ted taught us to trap tigers.
4. The Catskills are replete with hotels and motels.
5. Teresa won a tea-tasting contest.

/t/ in an unstressed position as in *plenty, letter, rested*

The sound /t/ in an unstressed syllable followed by a vowel is produced in a less vigorous manner than when in a stressed syllable. The contact between tongue tip and gum ridge is not held as long as for a stressed /t/ and there is less breath puff following the breaking of the tongue contact. Care should be taken that the tongue contact is not so weakened that a variety of /d/ is produced or that the unstressed /t/ is entirely omitted.

The following words and sentences provide practice materials for the unstressed /t/:

ante	yeasty	hinted
quality	booty	lasted
beauty	zesty	inserted
scanty	justice	rusted
thirty	objected	wasted
vanity	dotted	coaster

1. Peanut butter sticks to the teeth.
2. Some people are sarcastic instead of witty.
3. This city is pretty after a rain.
4. A faulty radiator thermostat can be hurtful to an automobile's motor.
5. Literary critics are not often attracted to the beauties of reality.

Practice discriminating between the unstressed /t/ and /d/ in the following pairs of words and sentences:

latter	ladder
catty	caddy
fated	faded
grated	graded
hearten	harden
mentor	mender
knotted	nodded
otter	odder
writing	riding
wetted	wedded
butted	budded

1. The caddy enjoyed being catty.
2. The car's brakes grated on the poorly graded road.
3. Is the otter an odder animal than the beaver?
4. Tom's mentor taught him how to be an efficient mender.
5. Joe was heartened rather than hardened by the news.

Other varieties of /t/

According to context, the consonant /t/ varies somewhat as to manner of production and acoustic end result. Some of the more frequent variations will now be considered.

1. **/t/ followed by /θ/ or /ð/ as in *light things* and *at the*.** In combinations such as *at the, hit that,* and *light things,* it is permissible to produce the /t/ by contact between the tongue tip and upper teeth rather than at the alveolar ridge. The dentalized /t/ in these combinations is produced as a result of the assimilative influence of the next sound /ð/ or /θ/, which is articulated dentally.

For persons whose English speech is influenced by French, Spanish, Italian, or German, this variety of /t/ is likely to be the one habitually used. It is least likely to be defectively produced when foreign-born persons speak English.

2. **/t/ followed by /l/ or /n/ as in *little* and *button*.** When the /t/ sound is immediately followed by an /l/ or /n/ it is not necessary to remove the tongue tip from the gum ridge to complete the sound. Instead, the sides of the front part of the tongue break contact with the teeth to permit a *lateral* explosion. When /t/ is followed by /l/, as in *little, bottle, settle, cattle, fettle,* and *mortal,* the explosion is emitted orally.

In words in which the /t/ is followed by an /n/, as in *bitten, button, cotton,* and *mutton,* the tongue position is maintained in going from the /t/ to the /n/. In effect, a nasal explosion takes place. If the hand is placed in front of the nostrils, a nasally emitted puff of air may be felt.

There is a marked tendency to substitute a laryngeal click (glottal catch) for the /t/ when followed by /l/ or /n/. This substitution, in American speech, is generally considered substandard. The speaker may check on this tendency by placing his hand at the larynx while pronouncing the list of words and sentences that follow. If a "click" is felt, it is likely that a glottal catch is being submitted for the /t/. To avoid this tendency, special attention should be paid to the prescribed manner of articulation for /t/ in [tl] and [tn] contexts.

cattle	capstan
dottle	distant
gentle	flatten
mantel	kitten
mental	Latin
nettle	lenten
raffle	mitten
spittle	molten
subtle	mutton
whittle	batten

1. The blacksmith flattened the brittle metal.
2. The bottle and kettle on the mantel lost a battle to the little kitten.
3. Mutton and cattle fattened in the gentle mountain valleys.
4. Even a subtle engine rattle can frighten an automobile owner.
5. Stella was smitten with the poetry of her lover's letters.

3. **/t/ followed by /s/ as in posts.** In contexts in which /t/ is immediately followed by an /s/, the tip of the tongue is permitted to slide forward a bit in anticipation of the /s/. Care should be taken not to omit the /t/ sound entirely, especially in combinations where the /t/ is preceded as well as followed by an /s/. The fine articulatory movements required for the [sts] combination increase the tendency for the omission of the /t/.

Practice on the following contexts should help to focus attention on precise articulation required for [ts] and [sts]:

its	lots	insists
eats	facts	posts
meats	pots	rests
heats	flights	pests
feats	paints	ghosts
jets	jests	roasts

1. The ghosts of fallen men parade on military posts.
2. The last acts of plays should be best.
3. The hard facts of life frequently prevent the attainment of the heart's desire.
5. The two casts of actors made bets about the prospective costs of their films.

Additional practice material for /t/ in varied contextual positions

1. Practice so that a /t/ is produced in unstressed as well as in stressed positions:

tall	doted	nuts	exterior
tile	eaten	oats	yet
tool	fitter	pastel	zesty
tan	goatee	quite	pitted
tin	halter	rusts	tentative
ton	iota	statistics	potato
tune	jetty	trout	spatula
antler	kitten	until	sprinted
butler	latter	veteran	toasted
cantle	matter	witty	crusts

2. Practice the following sentences, paying special attention to the /t/ sounds:

(a) The pitter-patter of little cat's feet drove the terrier to its wits' end.
(b) The veteran captain looked at the rusted pits in his freighter's plates.
(c) If Cotter had invested better, he would not have been ten thousand dollars in debt.
(d) The butler brought in a platter of roasted mutton.
(e) The fateful bell tolled ten times.
(f) One of baseball's greatest hitters was the late Roberto Clemente of the Pittsburg Pirates.
(g) It's not too wise to take tips from race track touts.
(h) Mark Twain frequently recalled that the best time of his life was during his stint as a river boat pilot.
(i) We've been told too often that "politics is the art of the possible."
(j) It takes practice to use an electric typewriter, but mistakes come with little or no extra troubles on the typist's part.

3. The following selections might be practiced with emphasis on /t/ for sound production, with meaning a secondary factor:

(a) Oh, East is East and West is West, and
    never the twain shall meet,
Till Earth and Sky stand presently at
    God's great Judgment Seat.

> —RUDYARD KIPLING, *The Ballad of East and West*

(b) What country ever before existed a century and a half with-
    out a rebellion? . . . The tree of liberty must be refreshed
    from time to time with the blood of patriots and tyrants. It
    is its natural manure.

> —THOMAS JEFFERSON, *Letter to William Stevens
> Smith* (November 13, 1787)

(c) Work consists of whatever a body is *obliged* to do, and Play
    consists of whatever a body is not obliged to do.

> —MARK TWAIN, *The Adventures of Tom Sawyer,*
> Chapter 2

(d) Will Fortune never come with both hands full
    But write her fair words still in foulest letters?
    She either gives a stomach and no food;
    Such are the poor, in health; or else a feast
    And takes away the stomach.

> —WILLIAM SHAKESPEARE, *King Henry IV*, Part II

(e) I told my heart that all was bright,
    That time alone would set things right,
    I told my heart love had not died,
    My rude heart answered that I lied.

> —J.E.

/d/ as in *done*

The consonant /d/ as in *done* is articulated in essentially the same
manner as the /t/ in *ten*, except that /d/ is voiced. The /d/, like /t/,
is a variable consonant. The varieties of /d/ parallel those of /t/. Faults
in articulation also parallel those for /t/, the chief fault being the tendency toward dentalization. A second tendency to be avoided is the substitution of /t/ for /d/ in words in which the /d/ is final and voiced. This
fault may be especially noted in German-born persons or in the speech
of persons who had had German as an early influence. The reason for this
is that the final /d/ does not occur in German.

The following lists of words and sentences provide practice material
for the /d/ sound:

deal	kneading	dread
dig	seedling	fled
daily	midriff	held
dab	riddle	plaid
dog	caddy	bard
dues	waddle	cord
dome	model	hoard
dumb	poodle	node
deter	bundle	mild
dial	muddle	ground

Distinguish between initial /t/ and /d/:

team	deem	term	derm	doe	toe
tip	dip	tuck	duck	tog	dog
ten	den	too	due	town	down
tan	Dan	toe	doe	tile	dial

Distinguish between final /t/ and /d/:

/t/	/d/	/t/	/d/
seat	seed	mat	mad
kit	kid	knot	nod
lit	lid	cult	culled
ate	aid	girt	gird
prate	prayed	hurt	herd
felt	felled	bite	bide
vent	vend	write	ride
went	wend	tight	tied

Additional practice materials for /d/ and /t/

1. Trade unions sometimes make so-called "Bread and Butter" demands in contract talks.

2. Delia delighted in dressing up for dances.

3. Dunson wanted to drive his herd of cattle to Sedalia after fording the Red River.

4. To drain Holland, the Dutch built the most extensive dike system in the world.

5. Gideon started to fiddle in the middle of his duties.

6. Denton, a dentist, persisted at his drilling of the rootless tooth.

7. The poet Yeats rhetorically asked, "How can we tell the dancer from the dance?"

8. Hatreds and animosities engendered in youth are all too frequently husbanded and maintained into adulthood.

9. The midshipman shuddered with cold as eight bells tolled above the deck.

10. Alice went to a tea party with the White Rabbit and the Mad Hatter.

11. He that is not handsome at twenty, nor strong at thirty, nor rich at forty, nor wise at fifty, will never be handsome, strong, rich, or wise.

—GEORGE HERBERT, *Jacula Prudentum*

12. 'Tis beauty truly blent, whose red and white
Nature's own sweet and cunning hand laid on:
Lady, you are the cruell'st she alive,
If you will lead these graces to the grave
And leave the world no copy.

—WILLIAM SHAKESPEARE, *Twelfth Night*, Act I, scene 5

13. Henceforth I ask not good-fortune, I myself am good-fortune,
Henceforth I whimper no more, postpone no more, need nothing,
Done with indoor complaints, libraries, querulous criticisms,
Strong and content I travel the open road.

—WALT WHITMAN, *Song of the Open Road*, I

14. The blessed damozel leaned out
From the gold bar of Heaven:
Her eyes were deeper than the depth
Of waters stilled at even;
She had three lilies in her hand,
And the stars in her hair were seven.

—DANTE GABRIEL ROSSETTI, *The Blessed Damsel*, I

15. It was down in Old Joe's Barroom
On the corner by the square
The drinks were served as usual
And the usual crowd was there.

On my left stood big Joe McKennedy,
His eyes were bloodshot red.
He turned to the crowd around him,
These were the very words he said.

"I went down to the St. James Infirmary
"To see my baby there.
"She was stretched out on a long white table
"So pale, so cold, and so fair."

—*Saint James Infirmary Blues* (traditional)

/s/ as in *see*

The consonant /s/ is a high-pitched, voiceless, lingua-alveolar fricative that requires careful and precise articulatory action for its production. The adjustments involve the following:

1. The entire tongue is raised so that the sides of the tongue are pressed firmly against the inner surfaces of the upper molars.
2. The tongue must be slightly grooved along the midline. Air is forced down along this groove.
3. The tip of the tongue is placed about a quarter of an inch behind the upper teeth. The tongue tip is almost in position for a /t/. (Persons not able to attain this adjustment will probably find it easier to place the tongue tip against the lower gums.)
4. The teeth are brought in line, with a very narrow space between upper and lower teeth.
5. The breath is directed along the groove of the tongue toward the cutting edges of the lower teeth.
6. The velum is raised to prevent nasal emission of the sound.

The use of a mirror is recommended for the practice of the consonant /s/. The recommended articulatory position is represented in Figure 8–2.

In producing the /s/, special care should be exercised to avoid having the tip of the tongue touch either the upper teeth or the gum ridge. Neither should the tongue tip be permitted to slide down to protrude between the rows of teeth. The first articulatory error will result in the pro-

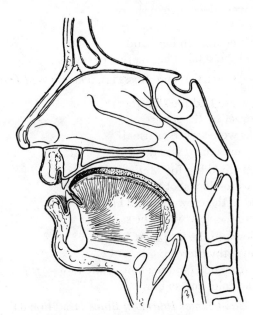

FIGURE 8–2. Representative tongue position for /s/ and /z/.

duction of a [ts] blend or a lateral sound resembling a voiceless /l/. The second articulatory error will result in an infantile, lingual, protrusion lisp resembling a /θ/.

Persons who habitually produce /t/ and /d/ sounds with dental rather than gum-ridge contacts are likely to lower the tongue tip for the production of /s/. The result, in most cases, is the production of a dull, low-pitched sound.

In some instances the articulatory adjustments just described do not help to produce the desired result—a high-pitched, sibilant sound. Occasionally the person, possibly because of an unusual mouth structure, must make individual adjustments to arrive at the same acoustic end result. With some articulatory adjustments, a low-pitched sound may be the best that the individual can hope to produce. Most persons, however, regardless of articulatory mechanism, can learn to produce an /s/ that acoustically resembles the high-pitched fricative described above.

Apart from the matter of articulation, the sound /s/ in American-English speech presents difficulty to the foreign born because of the many ways the sound is spelled. The most frequent representation is the alphabet letter *s*; other representations include *ss* as in *lass*, *sc* as in *scene*, *c* as in *pace*, and *x* as in *hoax*. The foreign-born speaker of English can be forgiven his failure to know when to produce the sound /s/ if we realize the many ways the letter s can be sounded. In addition to the /s/ we have /ʒ/ as in *treasure*, /ʃ/ as in *sure*, and /z/ as in *was*. To add to the foreign-born speaker's consternation we have the "silent" *s* as in *aisle* and *island*.

Practice materials for /s/

Because of the frequency of the /s/ in English speech, proper articulation for this sound is of special importance. Practice producing the sound as an isolated (single) phoneme, then incorporate the sound in nonsense syllables such as the following:

seep	sut
sig	saip
sape	sauk
ser	serl
saff	sile
sook	sone

Vowel sounds may be prefixed or added to these syllables to produce new combinations such as *aseep, seepa, awsut, sutee*.

If the /s/ cannot be "controlled" and mastered directly, it may help to begin with a /t/ produced with a lingua-alveolar contact and to work for the production of a [ts] blend. Words such as *eats, its, hates, hats, lets, pets, boots, punts, notes, pots, coats* are recommended for practice in establishing the [ts] blend.

Additional practice material

sage	asset	dose	ace
sap	blister	else	face
seem	costly	horse	brass
cellar	duster	ice	miss
slide	fasting	kiss	cuts
slit	gusto	less	sits
soap	hassle	mice	since
sob	acts	worse	sills
submarine	cluster	abbess	spaces
snub	mister	progress	spices

The combinations [sts] and [sks] are somewhat difficult because of the quick and precise tongue movements needed in their production. The following word lists and sentences provide practice material for these and other troublesome combinations:

boasts	mists	flasks
costs	nests	husks
firsts	rests	masks
hosts	basks	risks
jests	casks	tasks
lasts	disks	whisks

1. Steve slipped on the icy sidewalk.
2. Several sparrows made nests of the corn silk and rice husks they stole from the silo.
3. Asps are suspected of being sneaky snakes.
4. The mystic spread his fingers, relaxed his wrists, and foresaw six trysts.
5. Stephen insisted that he saw six ghosts stalking serenely across the sered grass to the desolate house.
6. Sally and Spike were set six tricks on their slam bid of seven spades.
7. Ross basted the roast breast of lamb with a spicy sauce.
8. Counterespionage can be seen as the science of turning a spy against himself.
9. Some scholars consider *War and Peace* to be Tolstoy's masterpiece; others consider *Resurrection* the Russian novelist's greatest work.
10. The center snapped the pigskin ball at the quarterback's signal.
11. The Snark missile soared skyward above the Pacific sunset west of Vandenberg Air Force Base.
12. The beast seemed at peace as he relaxed in a soundless sleep.

/z/ as in *zoo*

The sound /z/ is produced like the /s/ (see Figure 8–2), except that there is accompanying vocalization for /z/. The spellings for /z/ are many and varied. The more frequent orthographic representations include *z* as in *zoo*, *zz* as in *buzz*, and *s* as in *nose*.

Persons who have difficulty with the articulation of the /s/ are also likely to find the /z/ troublesome. The element of vocalization, however, may make the acoustic defects less apparent than in the case of the /s/.

Practice material for /z/

zero	easel	ease
zigzag	wizard	phase
zipper	lazy	boughs
zither	hazard	awes
zany	mused	cause
zap	buzzard	claws
zombie	closed	gauze
zouave	frozen	doze
zone	noses	hose
zircon	dozen	rose

Sentences:

1. The buzzard zigzagged lazily, perusing the boughs of the trees below.
2. Closing a zipper can sometimes be a hazardous business.
3. Hayes played zestful music on his zither.
4. The wizard wore a zircon above his grizzled eyebrows.
5. A morals clause in a contract is usually honored by nonobservance.
6. The sun rose to its zenith above the Tropic Zone.
7. Ezra's electric razor buzzed and left a smell of ozone along with most of his beard.
8. A fine spring zephyr eased the pains of the frozen winter season.
9. The frenzied musician paused to rub resin on his bow before his last musical stanza.
10. Zelda was puzzled as she sought to reason with her husband, who had bought an expensive bronze nozzle for their leaky garden hose.

There is a marked tendency among persons of Spanish and German background to substitute voiceless /s/ for /z/. This tendency, shared by many American speakers in the production of final /z/, breaks down the phonetic distinction between words such as *pays* and *pace, as* and *ass, prize,* and *price.* Practice on these pairs and the following exercises should help to maintain the phonetic differences between /z/ and/s/:

/z/	/s/	/z/	/s/	/z/	/s/
ayes	ice	graze	grace	prized	priced
braize	brace	his	hiss	quartz	quarts
close	close	loser	looser	rods	rots
doze	dose	razor	racer	spars	sparse
buzz	bus	seizing	ceasing	tens	tense
phase	face	news	noose	welds	welts

1. Cows graze with little grace.
2. The big Navy base fills two bays.
3. The insurgents' strategy was to seize new territories before ceasing hostilities.
4. Buzz takes the crosstown bus to his office.
5. The keys to the codes were sewn into the cryptographers' coats.
6. The price of rice has been on the rise.

Additional practice material for /s/ and /z/

1. There is no faith, and no stoicism, and no philosophy, that a mortal man can possibly invoke, which will stand the final test in a real impassioned onset of Life and Passion upon him. Faith and philosophy are air, but events are brass.

    —HERMAN MELVILLE, *Pierre*

2. As I would not be a slave, so I would not be a master. This expresses my idea of democracy. Whatever differs from this, to the extent of the difference, is no democracy.

    —ABRAHAM LINCOLN, *Letter*, 1858

3. The human heart has hidden treasures,
    In secret kept, the silence sealed;—
The thoughts, the hopes, the dreams, the pleasures,
Whose charms were broken if revealed.

    —CHARLOTTE BRONTË, "Evening Solace," I

/ʃ/ as in *she*

With the consonant /s/ as a basis for articulation, the /ʃ/ sound should be easy to master. Compared with /s/, the /ʃ/ is produced with the entire tongue drawn back slightly and broadened. (See Figure 8–3.) The stream of breath is forced over a broad surface rather than through a narrow groove as for the /s/. In addition, the /ʃ/ is usually produced with slight lip-rounding. Acoustically, /ʃ/ is a lower-pitched sound than /s/. Phonetically, /ʃ/ may be described as a *voiceless, blade-tongue, fricative sound.*

The sound /ʃ/ is represented by many spellings. The most common

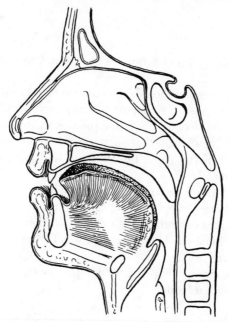

FIGURE 8–3. Tongue position for /ʃ/ and /ʒ/.

is the combination *sh* as in *she*. Other frequent combinations include *ti* as in *ration,* *si* as in *tension,* *ci* as in *delicious,* *ch* as in *machine,* and *s* as in *sugar.*

The similarities in orthographic representations for the /s/ and /ʃ/ as well as the similarity in manner of articulation may cause foreign-born speakers some confusion. Practice before a mirror provides a visual aid to distinguish between the /s/ and the /ʃ/. Try the following pairs:

shy	sigh	she	sea
shell	sell	ship	sip
shay	say	shine	sign

Practice material

shade	action	ash
sham	cushion	brush
sheep	blushing	dash
shed	gracious	flesh
shy	nutritious	gush
ship	ocean	hash
show	rendition	posh
shop	spacious	rash
shun	tension	quash
shut	wishing	wash

Sentences:

1. The wolf showed no passion for shams and shunned sheep's clothing.
2. Oceangoing vessels should have ship to shore radios.
3. Charlotte shopped for chartreuse window shades.
4. Elections are anxious times for politicians, even those with conscienceless "machines" that show devotion without emotion.
5. By the end of the game the shadows had pushed across the stadium's artificial turf.
6. The Ocean Shore restaurant serves delicious fish dishes.
7. Sheila's Alsatian shepherd dog dashed into the sagebrush.
8. The musicians rushed through their rendition of "Satisfaction."
9. When she blushed, Alicia Shinnert was the most gracious showgirl in Cheyenne.
10. The ship's captain finished washing, shaved, and carefully wiped his razor with a tissue.

/ʒ/ as in *pleasure*

The sound /ʒ/ is produced like /ʃ/ (see Figure 8–3) with accompanying vocalization. /ʒ/ usually occurs medially in English words. The sound may occasionally be heard at the end as in *rouge* and *mirage*. It does not occur initially in any English word. The most frequent spellings for /ʒ/ are *s* and *z*.

Practice material

azure	intrusion	treasure
casual	measure	vision
confusion	pleasure	garage
conclusion	seizure	mirage
decision	usual	prestige
division	usurious	rouge
explosion	derision	camouflage
fusion	incision	television

Sentences:

1. An azure sky is usually a pleasurable sight.
2. The seizure of the payroll was prevented by the intrusion of the police.
3. Rouge, properly applied, creates an illusion of good health.
4. The explosion was followed by confusion.
5. A mirage is a visual delusion.
6. Evasion and indecision seldom help in reaching conclusions.

7. The politician's tone was casual as he measured his debating opponent's indecision on the issues.
8. The right to defend against invasion of privacy and the need to resist illegal searches and seizure, despite government camouflage and confusion, is an obligation of a democratic society.

/tʃ/ as in *chest*

The sound /tʃ/ is a blend of /t/ followed immediately by /ʃ/. It presents no special difficulty to native American or English speakers. The sound may be troublesome, however, for speakers for whom English is not a first language and in whose native language the /tʃ/ does not occur. For example, /tʃ/ may be troublesome to native French speakers because it does not occur in the French language. For such persons the expected tendency is to substitute the sound /ʃ/ for the affricate /tʃ/. For speakers who show this tendency, the following exercises should be helpful in creating an awareness of the difference between /tʃ/ and /ʃ/:

/tʃ/	/ʃ/	/tʃ/	/ʃ/
cheap	sheep	chief	sheaf
cheat	sheet	batch	bash
cheese	she's	watch	wash
chaffed	shaft	crutch	crush
chock	shock	catch	cash
chuck	shuck	ditch	dish
chide	shied	match	mash

Sentences:

1. It's a good idea to remove your watch before you wash your hands.
2. Chuck shucked the corn.
3. Chester had the appetite of a ditchdigger and put two dishes of hash and eggs down the hatch.
4. In *The Gold Rush*, Charlie Chaplin is shown chewing a stew of old shoe.
5. Chambers caught the robber chief before he could reach his cache of stolen cash.
6. Hutchins put a chair against the door, closed the latch, and lashed it shut with a cheap chain.

/dʒ/ as in *judge*

/dʒ/ is the voiced counterpart of /tʃ/. This voiced affricate may occur initially, medially, or finally. In *judge* and *George* it occurs both initially and finally. In *agent* and *engine* the voiced consonant blend /dʒ/ occurs medially.

The most frequent spellings for /dʒ/ are *g*, *j*, and *dge*, as in *age, jump,* and *fudge.*

French, Spanish, and German speakers may have difficulty with /dʒ/ because the sound does not occur in their native languages. There is a marked tendency for German speakers to unvoice /dʒ/ so that it becomes /tʃ/. Many American speakers tend to unvoice /dʒ/ when it occurs finally. Distinguish between /dʒ/ and /tʃ/:

/dʒ/	/tʃ/
gin	chin
jar	char
jeer	cheer
jump	chump
jigger	chigger
jug	chug
bridges	britches
ridge	rich
badge	batch

Practice material

general	merge	adjust
generous	bridge	agent
gin	carriage	changed
jaw	edge	imagine
job	manage	granger
join	purge	soldier
Jud	urgent	stranger

The following materials should be practiced with a view to avoiding the unvoicing of the final /dʒ/.

1. The judge broke his pledge and denied Jud's appeal.
2. Robin Hood wanted to cross the bridge but Friar Tuck didn't budge.
3. Georgina's ring was lodged in the fudge.
4. Jane has great courage and energy.
5. "They're just over the ridge, Sarge," the granger yelled.
6. Strong language will often emerge as a response to trouble, real or imagined.
7. In the students' pursuit of what is alleged to be knowledge, strange courses are offered at some colleges.
8. The general had an urge to purge his gin-drinking soldiers.
9. Large corporations often manage to merge with other large corporations to emerge as larger ones.

10. By age two, a large majority of children can speak the language of their parents.

/l/ as in *lily*

The /l/ is a lingua-alveolar, voiced, lateral sound. It is produced with the tongue tip in contact with the upper gum ridge. The portion of the tongue just behind the tip (the blade) is lowered to permit the air to escape over the sides. The middle part of the tongue is raised and spread so that the sides are in contact with the side teeth.

The /l/ sound may occur initially, as in *law, let, lad;* medially, as in *alone, also, elbow;* and finally, as in *ball, well, mail.* The spellings are either the single *l* or the double *ll*.

In articulating the sound /l/ make certain that the tip, and not the blade of the tongue, is in contact with the gum ridge. Avoid contact with the teeth.

Practice material

lee	lack	loose	labial
lead	lab	lower	locale
leaf	lamb	lobe	lawful
lick	lax	lock	lentil
lid	lob	luggage	labile
lisp	log	lumber	listless
lay	lot	Lear	lonely
lace	luck	silly	landlord
late	law	pulley	Leslie
led	laud	wily	linoleum
letter	loop	colic	liberal

Sentences and selections:

1. Mabel was able to buy a beautiful gold-painted table.

2. Insects don't usually collect around yellow electric light bulbs.

3. Though lost, love's labors are not tax deductible.

4. The legal fees collected by some lawyers are unconscionable.

5. The arrival of a letter means a lot to a lonely person.

6. Light-Fingered Louie was reputed to be able to lift the halo from an angel.

7. The lexicon of the English language includes a plethora of words with the letter *l*.

8. It took the landlubber one gale to learn the value of "sealegs."

9. Philip Marlowe is the principal character in Raymond Chandler's novels that include *The Big Sleep; Farewell, My Lovely; The Lady in the Lake; The Little Sister;* and *The Long Goodbye.* All of these tales were made into films, but only one, *The Big Sleep,* can be called a classic movie. This film, starring Humphrey Bogart and Lauren Bacall, is frequently available to the sleepless as a late flick on television.

10. The historical Wild Bunch was led by Butch Cassidy and the Sundance Kid, whose actual names were George LeRoy Parker and Harry Longbaugh. From their hideout called the Hole in the Wall, they looted railroads until the Pinkerton Agency and federal marshals actively challenged this form of self-employment. When life in the States became intolerable, Parker and Longbaugh elected to live in Bolivia, where some historians claim that the outlaws were killed by a fusillade of bullets fired by soldiers of that Latin-American country.

11. Perhaps the most valuable result of all education is the ability to make yourself do the things you have to do, when it ought to be done, whether you like it or not; it is the first lesson that ought to be learned; and however early a man's training begins, it is probably the last lesson that he learns thoroughly.

—THOMAS HENRY HUXLEY, *Technical Education*

12. Our revels now are ended. These our actors,
As I foretold you, were all spirits, and
Are melted into air, into thin air;
And, like the baseless fabric of this vision,
The cloud-capp'd towers, the gorgeous palaces,
The solemn temples, the great globe itself,
Yea, all which it inherit, shall dissolve;
And, like this insubstantial pageant faded,
Leave not a rack behind. We are such stuff
As dreams are made on, and our little life
Is rounded with a sleep.

—WILLIAM SHAKESPEARE, *The Tempest,* Act IV, scene 1

13. I hope that calm counsel and constructive leadership will provide the steadying influence and the time necessary for the coming of new and more practical forms of representative government throughout the world wherein privilege will occupy a lesser place and welfare a greater.

—FRANKLIN DELANO ROOSEVELT, *Message to Congress*
(January 4, 1935)

14. Edmund Burke held that for evil to triumph it is only necessary that people who believe and hold themselves to be good do nothing.

/r/ as in *rose*

There is considerable variation, as has already been indicated (see page 94), in the production and pronunciation of the /r/ sound according to context. In this section the /r/ as in *rose, ready, around, derive* will be considered.

Two ways of producing the /r/ when the sound is immediately followed by a vowel in a stressed syllable will be described. The first method is to raise the tongue tip toward the roof of the mouth. The tongue tip may be brought close to the gum ridge, but actual contact with the gum ridge is avoided (see Figure 8–4). The tongue tip may also be flexed slightly toward the back of the mouth. Compare this position with those for the /t/ and /l/ sounds.

The second method of articulating an /r/ before a vowel in a stressed syllable approximates the production of a vowel sound. The tip of the tongue is lowered, and the central portion of the tongue is raised toward the roof of the mouth where the hard palate ends and the soft palate begins. This is illustrated in Figure 8–5.

For both methods of articulation the /r/ sound is produced with accompanying vocalization.

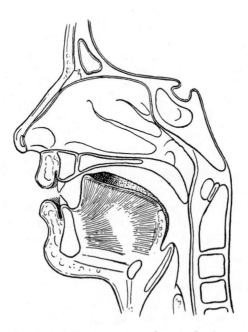

FIGURE 8–4. Tongue position for retroflex /r/.

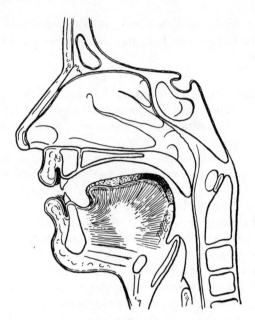

FIGURE 8–5. Tongue position for velar /r/.

Practice material

reed	represent	brigand
real	rap	career
rigged	rasp	drip
rim	rat	crater
rail	Roger	credit
rate	room	expressive
red	ruse	groin

Sentences:

1. The aviator's "Roger. Over and out," crackled through the radio of the ground control officer.
2. A short run of Red River forms the Texas-Arkansas border.
3. The war between Britain's Yorks and Lancasters was no bed of roses for the poor farmers who were taxed to support their ruling and quarreling lords.
4. Through the stories of Zane Grey many readers ride the western ranges in their armchairs.
5. Some persons who may not relate to Zane Grey prefer to travel to the dark corners of Europe with Eric Ambler.
6. Reaching for the right words is properly a writer's hardest work.
7. The brilliant actor and director Laurence Olivier is the first per-

former to have been awarded a lordship of Britain for his artistic contributions.

8. Some persons are content with moral victories; however, realists take pleasure in reminding them that races are won by those who cross the line first.

Words beginning with *p* and *b* (*proud, brown*) may be troublesome. Because of the lip activity involved, the /r/ may be produced with excessive lip movement. The result is an infantile sound resembling a /w/. Other difficult combinations are /gr/ and /kr/ as in *green* and *crumb*. The practice words that follow emphasize the more difficult combinations:

preach	breach	creed	grease
prig	brim	critter	grid
pretty	brittle	crepe	grail
primp	brain	crest	Greta
praise	braise	crag	grab
prate	breast	craw	groom
prawn	brad	cruise	group
prune	broil	crust	growl

/r/ as in *true, through, dry*

Another variety of /r/ approximates a fricative sound in manner of articulation. It is produced by placing the tip of the tongue close to, but not quite touching, the gum ridge. When air is forced over the tongue tip, a fricative /r/ sound is produced (see Figure 8–6). When this variety of /r/ occurs in the initial position, the sound is vocalized. When it occurs after a voiceless sound, as in *three* and *tree*, the /r/ may be completely or partly unvoiced. The sound is described as a *postdental fricative*. It is most likely to be heard after tongue-tip consonant sounds such as /t/, /d/, and /θ/.

trio	thread	dribble
trim	threshold	drift
trail	threat	dray
tram	thrash	drench
truth	throb	drag
troll	throttle	drum

1. Three-foot drifts built up at the tree line, and more snow threatened.
2. Price counted his sure tricks before trying to draw trumps.
3. Crandall, the ace pitcher, threw three straight strikes.
4. Drew nearly drowned in the rocky stream.
5. The legendary sheriff Pat Garrett was responsible for the deaths of

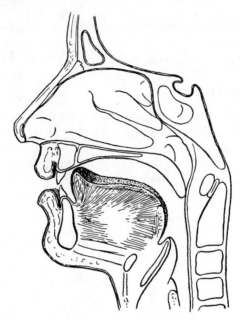

FIGURE 8–6. Tongue position for fricative /r/.

rustlers Charly Bowdre and Tom O'Follard as well as their better known crony, Billy the Kid.

6. His heart throbbing, Drummond dragged himself across the threshold.

Linking /r/ and intrusive /r/

Earlier we discussed the regional tendencies relative to the use of /r/ in words in which the letter *r* is final in the spelling (see pages 85–87). The /r/ in contexts such as *far away, for us, fear it* is usually heard as a *linking sound* between vowels. If we listen to the production of the linking /r/ we may note that it is produced with less vigor and is of shorter duration than the initial /r/ or the /r/ in a stressed position. Acoustically, the sound is much like the /r/ in unstressed syllables, as in the words *berry, merry, carry,* and *ferry.*

Practice the following phrases:

hear it	dare I	mere inch
bore in	dire act	wore out
for a time	bear under	dare us
fire away	dear aunt	four ounces

Occasionally an /r/ sound is intruded where the spelling of the word does not include the letter *r.* The /r/ may be intruded in combinations such as *law and order, idea of it, banana ice cream, vanilla* and *orange.*

The use of the intrusive *r* is generally considered substandard, and so this practice is not recommended.

By way of practice, the following sentences should be spoken slowly, and intrusive *r*'s avoided:

1. The idea of these exercises is to avoid an intrusive /r/.
2. Law and order should be maintained, but never used as a rallying cry for those who would subvert the law only to maintain order.
3. The sailor bought a banana in Manila.
4. Barbara asked for a vanilla ice cream cone.

/l/ and /r/ contrasts

For most native speakers of English the acoustic difference between /l/ and /r/ is clear and readily differentiated. However, for many non-native speakers of English, primarily those whose first languages have either an /l/ or an /r/, but not both phonemes, the distinctions are not readily apparent. Actually the articulatory positions for the /l/ as in *lip* and the /r/ as in *rip* are quite close.

Review the articulatory position for /l/ (see page 159) and the retroflex /r/ (Figure 8–4), then practice the following pairs of contrast words and the phrases that follow:

lead	reed	look	rook
lick	rick	law	raw
lid	rid	lump	rump
lace	race	lock	rock
lest	rest	low	raw
lack	rack	lie	rye

leaf on the reef   laid plans for the raid
lone roan   lie in the rye
wrap for a lap   right produces light

Additional practice material for /r/

1. Americans, who are accustomed to a degree of impartiality in the report of sports stories, are likely to be surprised at the fierce and outright partiality of Russian reporting. For example, sports writers for *Pravda,* or any other Russian newspaper for that matter, are likely to report a two-runner race between Ivan Russ and Joe American as follows: "Ivan Russ ran second; Joe American ran next to last."

2. Briefly stated, Parkinson's Law asserts that the more persons there are to do less work, the more time will be required for the work to be done. The "law" was formulated and promulgated by the British teacher and writer Professor C. Northcote Parkinson. The underlying principle

for the "law" was probably the result of a report of the British Royal Navy published after World War I. The report presented figures that revealed that after the demobilization of the World War I British Navy, the overall personnel was as large or larger than it had been at any prior time, including the period when the war with Germany was at its height.

3. Bryson was free with his promises. Usually Bryson's promises were no better than pie crust, made to be broken.

4. The nature of the relationship between professional literary critics and authors can be described as either necessarily symbiotic or purely parasitic. Here are two broadsides from partisan authors, spanning a century. First, an excerpt from Ralph Waldo Emerson's *Spiritual Laws:*

> There is no luck in literary reputation. They who make up the final verdict upon every book are not the partial and noisy readers of the hour when it appears; but a court as of angels, a public not to be bribed, not to be entreated, and not to be overawed, decides upon every man's title to fame.

In his book *Green Hills of Africa,* Ernest Hemingway, one of the truly great American writers of recent times, categorized critics as the "lice who live off the body of literature."

To make a critical judgment on the rhetorical armory of the two, Emerson fired at his literary targets as if with a scattergun loaded with birdshot, whereas Hemingway seemed to prefer a single round from a rifle.

/θ/ as in *thin*

/θ/ is a voiceless fricative sound. It is produced by placing the tip of the tongue either against the back of the upper front teeth or against the cutting edge of the upper teeth[4] (see Figure 8–7). Air is forced through the place of contact to produce the characteristic fricative quality.

/θ/ is represented by the letters *th* in the spelling of a word. The sound may occur initially as in *thin* and *through;* medially as in *athlete* and *mathematics;* or finally as in *bath* and *mirth.*

Some Americans who have been exposed to substandard speech influences tend to substitute a /t/ for the /θ/, especially in initial positions. Foreign-born persons who do not have the /θ/ sound in their first language tend to substitute an approximate sound for it. South German and Swiss speakers, for example, are inclined to substitute a dental /s/ for the initial /θ/. North German speakers are more likely to substitute a dental /t/.

---

[4] Some persons produce /θ/ by placing the tongue tip between the upper and lower front teeth.

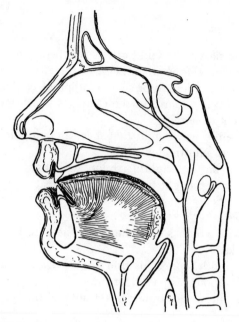

FIGURE 8–7. Representative tongue position for /θ/ (the postdental /θ/) and /ð/.

Practice material

theme	beneath	deathless
thank	both	anything
thick	cloth	author
thin	death	bathtub
third	earth	strengthen
thought	fourth	everything
thaw	length	ruthless
theory	moth	orthodox
threat	myth	atheist
thyroid	uncouth	enthusiasm
therapy	zenith	slothful

Distinguish between /θ/ and /t/:

/θ/	/t/	/θ/	/t/
thank	tank	bath	bat
thinker	tinker	math	mat
myth	mitt	both	boat
eighth	ate	booth	boot
death	debt	oath	oat

Sentences:

1. Smith enthusiastically held forth on his theory that blood is thicker than water but thinner than beer.
2. Martha bought a length of thick mothproof cloth.
3. A third or even a fourth of something is worth more than a hundred percent of nothing.
4. Burt unhappily was taught that it is safer to hold to an orthodox myth than an unorthodox truth.
5. Ted North, batting eighth, tripled with two out, but the ninth batter was not thought to be a hitting threat.
6. Death and taxes are as ruthlessly inevitable as thinning hair to some males.
7. Few of us give thanks for some of the theories that come out of the "think tanks."
8. Sedgwick-Smith tapped his thin fingers against his pith helmet as he thought about his past tiger hunts.
9. Thaddeus threw his traffic ticket into a thicket of thistles and thorns.
10. The theme of the honest farmer who becomes a thief after suffering an injustice runs through the cultures of many nations.

/ð/ as in *that*

/ð/ is the voiced cognate of /θ/. It is represented by the letter *th* and may occur initially, medially, or finally in the pronunciation of a word.

There is no certain way of knowing whether a particular word should be pronounced with /θ/ or /ð/. There is a tendency, in initial positions at least, for words that are meaningfully significant and stressed in a sentence—nouns, verbs, and adjectives—to be pronounced with the voiceless /θ/. Pronouns, articles, and conjunctions—words that are likely to be weak in a sentence—are more likely to be pronounced with the voiced /ð/. The words *thumb, think, throw, thick, them, the, than* exemplify these tendencies. Words ending in silent *e* preceded by a *th*, as in *bathe* and *soothe,* are usually pronounced with a /ð/.

Foreign-born persons who are inclined to substitute a /t/ for a /θ/ are likely to substitute a /d/ for /ð/. This kind of substitution may also be heard in substandard and nonstandard American speech, and is heard in Black English.

Practice material

them	bathe	although
that	breathe	another
there	clothe	brother
these	with	either
those	blithe	father

though	loathe	northern
they'll	scythe	smother
they've	teethe	logarithm

Distinguish between /ð/ and /d/:

they	day	then	den	lather	ladder
thine	dine	there	dare	loathe	load
though	dough	thy	dye	tithe	tide
those	doze	lithe	lied	father	fodder
breather	breeder	they'll	dale	than	Dan

Sentences:

1. They passed through the town the other day.
2. Things aren't what they used to be in the good old days, but then again, they never really were.
3. Old Howard shouted "There's gold in them there Sierra Madres," and dared Curtin and Dobbs to find the gold with him.
4. Matthew loathed carrying loads of cement up the ladder.
5. The brothers sped hither and thither in a general dither.

Additional practice material for /ð/ and /d/

1. The man who goes alone can start today; but he who travels with another must wait till that other is ready.

> —HENRY DAVID THOREAU, *Walden*

2.   . . . I would give
    All that I am to be as thou now art!
    But I am chained to Time, and cannot thence depart.

> —PERCY BYSSHE SHELLEY, *Adonais*, XXVI

3. I have done one braver thing
       Than all the Worthies did;
    And yet a braver thence doth spring,
       Which is, to keep that hid.

> —JOHN DONNE, *The Undertaking*

4. They breathe truth that breathe their words in pain.

> —WILLIAM SHAKESPEARE, *King Richard II*, Act II, scene 1

/ŋ/ as in *ring*

/ŋ/ is a velar nasal sound. It is produced by having the raised back of the tongue in contact with a lowered soft palate while the vocal folds are in vibration. (See Figures 8–8 and 8–9.) /ŋ/ is a continuant sound that is emitted through the nose.

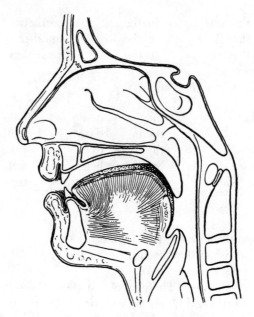

FIGURE 8–8. Tongue position for /ŋ/.

Except for possible confusion between the /n/ and the /ŋ/, there is seldom any difficulty in the actual articulation of the velar nasal consonant. There is some tendency, however, to add either a /g/ or a /k/[5] following the /ŋ/ so that all words containing /ŋ/ are pronounced with either /ŋg/ or /ŋk/. For the most part this tendency may be traced to the influence of a foreign dialect. A second influence may be attributed to the speaker's inability to remember just how the particular word should be pronounced. A third influence is a direct result of the manner of articulating the /ŋ/. If the soft palate is raised before the tongue contact is broken, a /k/ or /g/ sound is produced. To avoid adding a /k/ or/g/ when only the velar nasal consonant is desired, the speaker must watch his articulatory timing. Specifically he must make certain that the back of his tongue is moved away from his soft palate before the soft palate is raised to block off the nasal passage.

Practice with phrases such as the following should be of help in establishing timing and control of the velar nasal consonant: *long ago, going away, Long Island, coming and going, running on, bringing it up, ring a bell, spring is here, King of England, swing along.*

The /ŋ/ is represented by the letter *n* or the letters *ng*. It usually occurs in words in which the letter *n* is followed either by a *k* or a *g* in the same syllable, as in *sink, tinkle, sing,* and *single.* /ŋ/ is generally not heard in standard speech in combinations where the *n* and the *g* that

[5] German speakers, however, tend to omit the /g/ and /k/ and use only the /ŋ/.

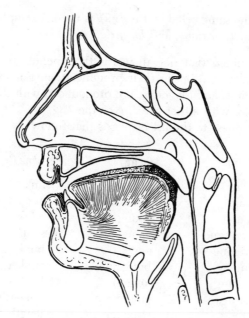

FIGURE 8–9. Tongue position for /k/ and /g/.

follows are in different syllables, as in *ingrate* and *congratulate*.

To know how to produce an /ŋ/ is not enough. We must also know whether the velar nasal is to be followed by a velar plosive /k/ or /g/, or by some other sound. There is, of course, only one certain way to learn the pronunciation of a word with velar nasal consonants. The certain way is to learn each word individually, using an unabridged, up-to-date dictionary as a guide. A second approach is to learn the so-called "rules" for the use of the velar consonants in English speech. These follow:

1. When the word ends with the letters *ng* or *ngue*, the pronunciation calls for the /ŋ/. Examples include *thing, rang, tongue*, and *harangue*.

2. Usually, when a suffix is added to a root word that is pronounced with the /ŋ/, the pronunciation calls for the /ŋ/. Examples include *things, rings, singer, longing*, and *ringing*.

    The exceptions to this general tendency include the comparative and superlative of the adjectives *long, young*, and *strong*, e.g., *longer, longest; younger, youngest; stronger, strongest*. These have the /ŋ/ followed by /g/.

3. Where the letters *ng* are medial in a root word, as in *finger, tingle, hunger, tangle, extinguish*, and *single*, standard pronunciation calls for the use of /ŋg/. An exception is the pronunciation of *gingham* as [gɪŋəm].

4. In combinations in which the letter *n* is immediately followed by *k*,

c, or *x* in the same syllable, the /ŋk/ is used. Examples include *ink*, *yank, distinct, anxious,* and *larynx.*

It should be noted that not all words that include the letters *ng* in their spelling call for a /ŋ/ in their pronunciation. For example, words such as *range, singe,* and *longevity,* are pronounced with the combination /ndʒ/ rather than with either the /ŋ/ or the /ŋg/.

Apply these "rules" to the list of words that follow:

/ŋ/	/ŋg/	/ŋk/
wing	tingle	link
rang	spangle	anchor
young	younger	wink
meringue	elongate	sank
evening	anger	bunk
ringing	bungalow	trinket
longing	longest	lynx
springs	jangle	strength[6]
strong	stronger	length[6]
banging	Congo	tanker
bung	bungle	bunk
tang	tangle	tank

Additional practice material for /ŋ/ in various contexts

The following sentences and selections are intended for general practice and review:

1. The banging grew stronger, then the doors swung open.
2. The Wrangler of the Blue Wing Spread walked in, spurs jangling, anger on his elongated face.
3. Evening was long gone, but the young cowhands in the Long Branch were far from their bunkhouses.
4. "I'm a-calling you out, Younger," Wrangler Jennings said, his voice low, lying like a cold spring fog against the plankings of the floor.
5. Younger took the longest drink of his life before gambling what might be his last card.
6. He clinked two gold eagles from his winnings, then the whole Long Branch saw his left hand slipping under the table.
7. Younger winked at the Barman, who was reaching for his table-leg, preparing to swing it in self-defense.
8. Raising his glass in his right hand, Younger said challengingly,

---

[6] The words *strength* and *length* are acceptably pronounced as either [strɛŋkθ] or [strɛŋθ] and [lɛŋkθ] or [lɛŋθ].

"Jennings, this paint-thinning elixir is the strongest thing about. So, if you'll be joining me, show it by reaching for a glass and bringing it here."

9. Jennings sunk deep into some fast thinking. He hankered after the boring of card-sharping Younger, but by his anxious figuring the gambler had some angles that yet needed turning.

10. "Would rankle to be drinking the same poison you're taking," Jennings said.

11. Both were anchored to their spots, freezing and quieting the Long Branch, a silence soon breaking with the cocking of two .44s.

12. We're apologizing and paying our respects to the writings of Zane Grey and Earnest Haycox, and we're taking the opportunity of allowing how this sagebrush saga may be continuing in the next edition of *Basic Speech*.

—Contributed by Arthur M. Eisenson

Selections:

1. Sherrington, the eminent English neurologist, described an awakened brain as "an enchanted loom where millions of flashing shuttles weave a dissolving pattern, always a meaningful pattern though never an abiding one."

2. The humming bird
   Taking to wing
   Hovering over a new grown
       thing,
   The humming bird
   Quivering,
   Pulsating,
   Fixing time,
   Encompassing motion,
   Quick sipping a potion
   From its nectared thing
   Brings wordless word
   of spring.

       —J.E.

3. A man—I let the truth out—
   Who's had almost every tooth out,
   Cannot sing as once he sung,
   When he was young as you are young,
   When he was young and lutes were strung,
   And love-lamps in the casement hung.

       —William M. Thackeray, *Mrs. Katherine's Lantern*

/w/, /hw/, and /h/

/w/ and /hw/ words such as *what, when, where, whim, whip, whirl, whisk, white, whole, whoop,* and *why* may be pronounced with either /w/ or /hw/. Individual pronunciation will usually be determined by what was current in the dialect area in which the speaker was brought up. However, not all words that are spelled with *wh* are pronounced with either of the bilabial glide sounds. *Who, whom, whose* and compounds of these words (*whosoever, whomsoever*), and *whole* and its compounds are pronounced with an initial /h/. Thus *whole* and *hole* are homonyms, but *while* and *wile* may or may not be homonyms, depending on the individual's pronunciation of *while*. Similarly *what* and *watt*, *where* and *wear*, and *whale* and *wail* may be considered optional homonyms.

Determine the pronunciation of the following in your home community, and compare the practice with that of a friend or fellow student reared in a different area of the country.

walk	wheel	whip	whoosh
wale	when	whir	whopped
whom	where	whisk	whomp
wharf	whet	whisper	whoopee
what	which	white	whorl
wheat	whiffle	whole	why

Do you make a distinction in the pronunciation of the following pairs?

whale	wail	whey	way
what	watt	whir	were
when	wen	which	witch
where	wear	while	wile

Practice the following to make the indicated distinctions, reading across the columns.

/h/	/w/ *or* /hw/	*initial vowel*
hale	whale	ail
hitch	which	itch
hair	where	air
her	whir	err
hay	whey	"A"
high	why	I
hack	whack	ack
hen	when	en

Emphasize distinctions for /h/, /w/ or /wh/ and the words with initial vowels in the following sentences:

1. While Wendy practiced her wiles, Will was walking on air.
2. After hitching the horse to the wagon, Walter felt itchy all over.
3. Walker had to remind Watts that to err is human, and not a cause for wailing.
4. With a sad air Wilbert asked, "Where is my hair of yesteryear?"

/h/ as in *hen, hit, hot, hungry,* and *hut*

The sound /h/ is a voiceless fricative that results from the emission of air between the vocal folds. The degree of fricativeness depends on the immediately following sound, so that there is more evidence of fricative quality in *he* and *him* than in contexts with more "open" vowels such as in *how* or *hot*. British Cockney dialect speakers tend to drop the /h/ in the key words above. Some American speakers fail to make a distinction between *hit* and *it, hill* and *ill, hail* and *ail*. Such failure may be considered substandard.

In words such as *huge, humanity, humility,* and *humor* some speakers "blend" an initial /h/ with an immediately following palatal glide /j/ to produce, in effect, a distinctive partially voiced palatal fricative sound. This may be represented by the symbols /hj/ or /ʃ/.

Practice materials

Make a clear distinction for the initial sounds in the following pairs:

habit	abbot	ham	am	heave	eve
hack	ack	heat	eat	heart	art
hand	and	hall	all	harm	arm
haft	aft	home	ohm	haul	all
Hague	ague	head	Ed	heel	eel
hair	air	hate	ate	hear	ear

Maintain clear distinctions in the key words in the following sentences:

1. The abbot wore his priestly habit throughout the whole, hot and humid day.
2. Helen added to her austere air by the way she combed her hair.
3. Because of the heat, Henry could hardly eat.
4. Hal hauled all of the furniture into the hall.
5. Hubert boasted that while he had a good right arm, no harm would come to either Helen or Ellen.

What is your pronunciation for the following words: *human, humid, humility, huge, Hewlett, Houston?* Check your pronunciation with a friend brought up in a different geographic region.

THE VOWELS OF AMERICAN-ENGLISH SPEECH CONSIDERED INDIVIDUALLY

/i/ as in *free*

A glance at the vowel diagram (Figure 6–6 and Figure 6–9) will reveal to us that /i/ is a high front vowel. It is produced with a considerable degree of tension of the lips. The blade of the tongue is raised high so that it is almost in contact with the anterior part of the hard palate. The lip position approximates a tight-lipped grin.

The sound /i/ has many orthographic representations. The most frequent spellings include *e, ea, ee, ei, is* and *ie*. These are indicated in the following transcriptions:

be	[bi]
tease	[tiz]
see	[si]
receipt	[rɪsit]
machine	[məʃin]
yield	[jild]

Practice material for /i/

each	alleviate	agree	key
eager	conceivable	appeal	quay
ease	displeasing	believe	Erie
east	illegal	Dixie	eerie
eel	intriguing	discreet	frieze
eerie	machinery	esteem	freeze
ether	precedence	esprit	heal
even	subpoena	police	heel
green	unceasing	receive	lea
meager	unseasonable	species	lie

1. Pass the green peas, please.
2. Did Adam or Eve rule in the Garden of Eden?
3. The wild geese beat their wings against a bleak sky.
4. An effective team possesses *esprit de corps.*
5. A queen bee has other bees eager to follow.
6. Even an eel may be intriguing.
7. He was served a subpoena when he indiscreetly refused to answer the policeman's appeal.
8. Beans are likely to be eaten at evening meals.

9. Socrates said he was not an Athenian or a Greek, but a citizen of the world.
10. Beasley was displeased with Zina's teasing.

/ɪ/ as in *hit*

One of the differences in manner of production between /i/ as in *free* and /ɪ/ as in *hit* is in the degree of articulatory tension for the two vowels. The sound /ɪ/ is produced with a relatively lax tongue. In addition, as may be observed from Figure 6–6, the tongue position is slightly lower for /ɪ/ than for /i/. The lip position for /ɪ/ is approximately a relaxed smile contrasted with the tight-lipped grin for /i/.

The most frequent spelling for /ɪ/ is the letter *i*, as in *bit, sit, lit, inn.* Less frequent spellings include *u, ui,* and *e* as in *business, build,* and *English.*

Some speakers use the vowel /ɪ/ for the final *y* in words such as *pretty, very,* and *city.* For most speakers, however, final *y* is likely to be pronounced with a vowel closer to that of *free* rather than the vowel /ɪ/ of *hit.* The reader might determine for himself which vowel he approximates for words ending in the letter *y.* The following list of words should be of some help.

key	catty	kit
sea	city	sit
pea	petty	pit
lea	leggy	lit
knee	knotty	knit

Do you know any speakers who fail to make a clear distinction between the vowels /i/ and /ɪ/? What language or dialect influence may account for this? Distinguish between /i/ and /ɪ/ in the following word pairs:

beat	bit	leak	lick
deem	dim	meat	mit
eat	it	neat	knit
feet	fit	peek	pick
heat	hit	sheep	ship

In the following sentences the first underlined word has the vowel /i/ and the second /ɪ/. Keep the distinction clear:

1. Our team counted on Tim.
2. Joe's feet were not fit for the race.
3. The heat hit us suddenly.

4. The sheep arrived by ship.
5. "I won't eat it," insisted Ned.

Additional practice material for /ɪ/

ill	business	addict
imply	differ	admit
Indian	fill	agile
infer	hymn	begin
indicate	pick	cryptic
ink	quilt	eclipse
inn	sieve	instill
it	trip	mystic
ingot	women	respite
Italy	wishes	until

inch by inch	little intake
kindred spirit	bitter pill
spin inside	dig in
silver tip	six slips

1. We stopped at an inn during our trip to Italy.

2. It was done as quickly as a flick of the eyelid.

3. The Indian mystic made his few cryptic remarks as if he were intoning a hymn.

4. Intelligent action is adaptive and well directed.

5. Truth is not infrequently sacrificed for the sake of wit.

6. Pitt paid his bills with his winnings.

7. Bill Wilson, for fifty years a bachelor, had a ditty he repeated to himself six times whenever he felt in imminent danger of changing his singular state. Bill's ditty was:
   Needles and pins, needles and pins.
   If I marry Jill my trouble begins.

8. That he is mad, 'tis true: 'tis true
      'tis pity;
   And pity 'tis 'tis true.

   —SHAKESPEARE, *Hamlet*, Act II, scene 2

9. Pascal insisted that to ridicule philosophy is still to philosophize.

10. Swift did not consider after dinner a good time for thinking. In his *Journal to Stella*, Swift held that immediately after dinner we are more inclined to drinking than to thinking.

/e/ as in *state*

The vowel /e/ is infrequently used as a pure vowel. More often the sound becomes a diphthong and might be more precisely represented as /eɪ/ in words such as *way, say,* and *blame.* /e/ as a pure vowel is produced with somewhat less articulatory tension than /i/ but more than for the vowel /ɪ/. As indicated on the vowel diagram (Figure 6–9) and in Figure 6–6, it is front and midhigh. When used, /e/ is likely to appear either in an unstressed syllable as in *chaotic* or in a syllable in which the sound is immediately followed by a voiceless, stop-plosive consonant /p/, /t/, /k/ as in *cape, plate,* and *cake.*

The difference between /e/ and /eɪ/ is not phonemic. That is, there are no words in our language that would be distinguished in meaning from one another on the basis of the use of the pure vowel /e/ or the diphthong variant /eɪ/. The same word may have /e/ in one context and become /eɪ/ in another.

In the sentence "She wore the cape all day," it is likely that the word *cape* would be pronounced [kep] and *day* as [deɪ]. In another context such as "She wore a long cape" the word *cape* might very well be pronounced with the diphthong /eɪ/ rather than the vowel /e/.

The words that follow include examples of the most frequent orthographic representations for /e/ or /eɪ/. The letter *a* is probably the most frequent spelling; *ay, ai, ea, ey,* and *ei* are also represented as in *date, rate, sale, make, stain, paint, ray, steak, vein, they.*

Practice material for /e/ or /eɪ/

ace	caged	acquaint
age	fading	byplay
ague	failure	delay
ail	feinted	dismay
aim	hasten	enrage
angel	haven	entree
bail	lazy	gainsay
bait	reigning	persuade
dame	strafed	portray
deign	zany	repay

1. Angel food cake, well made, is good date bait.

2. The caged animal was enraged by the zany tactics of the keeper.

3. The portrait was of a quaint dame who reigned in ancient days.

4. It is hard to gainsay an aged male.

5. Maine is a New England state.

6. The weary lover could not say whether his lady was pale or his love had become stale.

7. Clayton Cain was fond of saying:

"They who get themselves in jail
May not taste of cakes and ale."

8. There is something in a face,
An air, and a peculiar grace,
Which boldest painters cannot trace.

—SOMERVILLE, *The Lucky Hit*

9. The wasting moth ne'er spoil'd my best array;
The cause was this, I wore it every day.

—ALEXANDER POPE, *Paraphrases from Chaucer*

/ɛ/ as in *met*

The vowel /ɛ/ differs from /e/ in that it is produced with less articulatory tension and with a slightly lowered front tongue position. (See Figures 6–6 and 6–9.)

/ɛ/ is usually represented by the letter *e* in word spelling. Less frequent spellings are *a* as in *any*, *ay* as in *says*, *ai* as in *said*, and *ea* as in *head*.

Additional specimen words that contain the vowel /ɛ/, when spoken according to acceptable standards, include *beg*, *best*, *bend*, *elk*, *enter*, *elm*, *said*, and *breast*.

A nondistinctive variant of the vowel /ɛ/ is heard in words such as *their*, *fare*, *bare*, and *dare*. These words are also pronounced with the diphthong /ɛə/ and the omission of the final /r/ by many New York City, Southern, and eastern New England speakers. In General American speech the words are more likely to be pronounced with the vowel /ɛ/ followed by /r/ or by the vowel blend /ɛɚ/.

Practice material for /ɛ/

ebb	beckon	attest
echo	check	behead
edge	deaf	detest
egg	feather	fret
elder	gesture	inept
elevate	guess	instead
elfin	meant	intend
ends	pleasant	invest
energy	ready	regret
enter	settle	request

1. Many men are not meant for marriage.

2. Ted and Ed elected to settle their bets on Wednesday.

3. The men of finance were ready to settle their debts.

4. The deaf men gestured to beckon their friends.

5. Pent-up energy can be spent for pleasant ends.

6. Not many men admit that they aspire to be among the ten best-dressed.

7. An investment is characterized by careful investigation and the expectation of a small but steady increase in capital; speculation is characterized by more guessing, greater hopes, and frequent regrets.

8. . . . The bell invites me.
   Hear it not, Duncan: for it is a knell
   That summons thee to heaven or to hell.
      —SHAKESPEARE, *Macbeth*, Act II, scene 1

9. Life that dares send
   A challenge to his end,
   And when it comes, say,
      Welcome, friend!
      —CRASHAW, *Wishes to His Supposed Mistress*

10. The rest to some faint meaning make pretence,
    But Shadwell never deviates into sense.
      —JOHN DRYDEN, *Mac Flecknoe*

Make a clear distinction between the vowel /ɪ/ and /ɛ/. The word pairs and sentences that follow should help to bring out the differences between these two front vowels.

bid	bed	mill	mell
hid	head	nil	knell
id	Ed	pil	pell
kin	ken	sit	set
lid	led	rid	red

1. Ben kept his wood in a bin.
2. Fred was kin to Ken.
3. When a hen sets she sits.
4. Bess hid under a hat with a broad felt brim.

/æ/ as in *hat*

/æ/ is a low front vowel. It is heard rather regularly throughout the United States in the standard pronunciations of the words *rat, mash, rack, angle,* and *gather.*

In some parts of the United States there is a tendency for speakers to substitute the vowel blend /ɛə/ for the sound /æ/. In the General American speech area many speakers use a vowel that belongs to the phoneme /ɛ/ rather than /æ/ in words such as *marry, Harry,* and *parry* in which the vowel is followed by the sound /r/.

The vowel /æ/ is usually produced with a lax tongue, though a tense variety of /æ/ is produced by some speakers. A tendency that should be avoided is the production of the vowel /æ/ with excessive tension and accompanying nasality. See Figure 6–6 for tongue position.

The reader may use the following word list and sentences to determine his own practice for words that have the vowel /æ/ in acceptable pronunciation.

Practice material for /æ/

cat	shall	carry	parrot	drank
band	fact	marriage	sand	family
back	fad	carriage	land	fancy
crack	bags	wrapped	grand	handy

sad sack	atomic blast
rag bag	mad dash
pact for action	random facts
dank camp	Yankee band
packed bags	dandy candy

1. The groom lifted his bride out of the carriage and carried her into the house.
2. The angry members of the family banded together to prevent the marriage.
3. Random thoughts may include both facts and fancy.
4. Parrots can repeat, but cannot establish, facts.
5. Harris planned to make concessions, but he began with several demands.
6. Barrett did not understand Calvin's complaint about being asked to carry coals to Newcastle.
7. Provided a man is not mad, he can be cured of every folly but vanity.

   —JEAN JACQUES ROUSSEAU, *Émile*

8. Pam was fond of ham sandwiches and tacky candy.

/a/ as in *ask*

As a pure vowel, /a/ is rarely used by most Americans. It is more often used as part of the diphthong /aɪ/[7] as in *I, my,* and *ice.*

/a/ in both sound and manner of articulation is a "compromise" somewhere between /æ/ as in *gather* and /ɑ/ in *calm.* Some speakers, principally from the eastern New England area, use the vowel /a/ in the words *path, bath, ask, park,* and *laugh.* Other speakers may use either /æ/ or /ɑ/ for these words. Which do you use? Consistency is recommended but by no means prescribed. See Figure 6–6 for tongue position.

Review material

Front Vowels

1. It is when we try to grapple with another man's intimate need that we perceive how incomprehensible, wavering, and misty are the beings that share with us the sight and the warmth of the sun.

    —Joseph Conrad, *Lord Jim*

2. "Yes", I answered you last night;
    "No", this morning, sir, I say:
 Colors seen by candle light
    Will not look the same by day.

    —Elizabeth Barrett Browning, *The Lady's "Yes"*

3. In skating over thin ice our safety is on speed.

    —Ralph Waldo Emerson, *Prudence*

4. Battles, in these ages, are transacted by mechanism; with the slightest possible development of human individuality or spontaneity, men now even die, and kill one another, in an artificial manner.

    —Thomas Carlyle, *The French Revolution*

5. No sadder proof can be given by a man of his own littleness than disbelief in great men.

    —Thomas Carlyle, *Sartor Resartus*

6. The very hair on my head
 Stands-up for dread.

    —Sophocles, *Oedipus Colonus*

7. Experience is the name everyone gives to his mistakes.

    —Oscar Wilde, *Lady Windermere's Fan*

---

[7] See page 195 for a discussion of the diphthong /aɪ/.

8. I can resist everything except temptation.

  —OSCAR WILDE, *Lady Windermere's Fan*

/ɑ/ as in *calm*

/ɑ/ is produced with the tongue in about as low a position as it is likely to get without using direct external pressure. Such pressure is applied when a physician uses a tongue depressor and asks the patient to say "ah." The patient is asked to say "ah" because in the production of the sound he relaxes and flattens his tongue and so permits the doctor to see the back of his throat. /ɑ/ is a low, back, lax vowel. The mouth is "open wide" and the lips are unrounded. See Figure 6–8 for tongue position.

The vowel /ɑ/ is most frequently represented in spelling by the letter *a* or *o*. Other individual spellings include *e* (*sergeant*) and *ea* (*heart* and *hearth*). In words such as *ah, alms, barn, farm, psalm,* and *balm* the sound /ɑ/ is consistently heard throughout the United States.

In the words *not, hot, cog, fog,* and *grog* the vowel is represented by the letter *o*. These words, however, are also frequently pronounced with the vowel /ɒ/ and occasionally with /ɔ/.

The vowel /ɑ/ is also heard occasionally in the words *office, coffee, long,* and *song*. The vowels /ɔ/ and /ɒ/ are, however, more frequently used in these words.

Practice material for /ɑ/

ah	Antarctic	afar
alms	archives	alarm
artist	armory	bazaar
barber	balmy	becalm
cargo	bombardment	disarm
dart	departed	discharge
farthing	dishearten	disembark
father	guardian	shah
hearth	pardon	spa
harbor	remarkable	unharmed
qualm	swamped	unscarred
sergeant	unqualified	vanguard

ardent farmer	large barn
calm harbor	army sergeant
honest art	harsh marshal
far star	doll cart
artful father	charming palms

1. Fathers are not all guardian angels.
2. Calm waters are well charted.

3. The harbor was bombarded but no person was harmed.
4. The alarm was heard from afar.
5. What was the cargo on Noah's ark?
6. A coat of varnish may prevent tarnish.
7. The Bard of Avon wrote many sonnets.
8. Tom, who was a hod carrier, also shod horses when he had the time.
9. All Hollywood stars do not enjoy their parts.
10. Charles thought that Marcus was balmy for sending cargo to the arctic.

/ɒ/ as in *clog*

In manner of articulation and in acoustic impression, /ɒ/ is somewhere between /ɔ/ as in *fall* and /ɑ/ as in *calm*. The vowel /ɒ/ is produced with the tongue in a low and relatively lax position. The lips usually are slightly rounded. See Figure 6–8 for tongue position.

No list can be given or words for which the vowel /ɒ/ is consistently used throughout the United States or even in any major speech region. The sound is more likely to be heard in eastern New England than elsewhere, but its use is by no means confined to this area.

The vowel /ɒ/, as we noted, may be heard in words such as *not, hot, cog, fog*, and *grog*. The use of the vowel /ɑ/, however, is more frequent in these words.

The vowel /ɒ/ may also be heard in words in which the spelling includes the letter *o* followed by a voiceless fricative or a nasal consonant. Such words include *off, lost, cost, loft, long*, and *song*. The vowels /ɔ/ and /ɑ/ may also be heard for these words.

Other words in which the vowel /ɒ/ may be heard, but probably less frequently than either /ɔ/ or /ɑ/, include *horrid, foreign, orange, porridge*, and *florid*. It may be noted that in each of these words the letter *o* is followed by a single or double letter *r*.

/ɔ/ as in *call*

/ɔ/ is a mid-, low, back vowel produced with slight tongue and lip tension and lip-rounding. The most frequent spellings for /ɔ/ include *a* as in *call, aw* as in *awful, au* as in *taught* or *taut, ou* as in *sought*, and the single letter *o* as in *horse*. See Figure 6–8 for tongue position.

In many words, including some of those just presented, the vowels /ɒ/ or /ɑ/ may be heard instead of /ɔ/.

The interested reader may test his own practice in regard to the use of /ɔ/, /ɒ/, or /ɑ/ by pronouncing the following lists of words and sentences. The first column is a list of words that are most likely to have the vowel /ɔ/ consistently used. The words of the other columns may also be pronounced with the vowels /ɒ/ or /ɑ/.

Practice material for /ɔ/ and /ɒ/

hawk	doll	collar
call	song	foreign
bought	long	borrow
calked	wrong	horrible
ought	soft	sorrow
taught	coffin	torrid
wall	cost	forest
August	lost	orange
auto	off	porridge
maul	mock	dollar

1. Calmly the frog sat on a log at the edge of the water.
2. He lay on a cot in the jungle to escape the torrid heat.
3. For long he had considered it wrong to be confined to his office.
4. He became taut as he came close to the object he sought.
5. Laura was taught that to borrow even a dollar was to invite sorrow.
6. In *The Course of Empire* De Voto warned that the dawn of knowledge is usually the false dawn.

7. Men must be taught as if you taught them not.
   —POPE, *Essay on Criticism*

8. The horn, the horn, the lusty horn
   Is not a thing to laugh to scorn.
   —SHAKESPEARE, *As You Like It*, Act IV, scene 2

/u/ as in *ooze*

/u/ is characterized by a greater amount of lip-rounding than any of the other vowels in American speech. The back of the tongue is arched, tense, and high. See Figure 6–8 for tongue position.

The most frequent spelling for /u/ is *oo* as in *school, too, fool,* and *ooze;* other spellings include the single letter *o* as in *do* and *to; u* as in *dupe;* and *ou* as in *coup* and *soup.*

If prolonged, /u/ may change to the diphthongal variant /ʊu/. This modification of /u/ is similar to the changes of the vowels /i/, /e/, and /o/ to the nondistinctive diphthongal variants /ɪi/, /eɪ/, and /oʊ/.

Practice material for /u/

boon	blooming	accrue
coop	druid	ado
doom	lampoon	afternoon
food	prudent	brew

group	ruler	buffoon
move	spoofing	grew
rude	toothsome	recluse
rumor	troopers	shrew
swoon	truant	threw
troupe	truthful	zoo

1. It takes more than two afternoons to tame a shrew.
2. Fools as well as flowers bloom in the afternoon.
3. The rumor grew as the time flew.
4. A truant from thought needs a rude awakening.
5. Truth makes no demand that the truthful be ruthless.
6. They who carve on tombstones are uncouth if they insist on telling the truth.
7. Hubert was one of the few students who utilized the information he accrued in school.

/ʊ/ as in *pull*

/ʊ/ is a high, back, lip-rounded vowel. The tongue is relaxed and in a slightly lower position than for the vowel /u/. Though the vowel /u/ may occur either initially, medially, or finally, /ʊ/ occurs only medially. The spellings include *u* as in *pull, full,* and *bull; oo* as in *book, took, wood,* and *look.* Other spellings include *ou* as in *could* and *should* and *o* as in *wolf.*

In many words of native English origin, especially those spelled with *oo,* practice varies in the use of /u/ or /ʊ/. The reader may test his own inclination by pronouncing the words *root, roof, broom, hoof,* and *soot* and attending to whether the tongue feels tense or relaxed when the vowel is articulated. If it is tense and the lips are very rounded, the sound /u/ is probably being produced. If the tongue feels relaxed and the lips are less rounded, the vowel sound is probably /ʊ/. See Figure 6–8 to compare the positions of the tongue for the two vowels.

The distinction between /u/ and /ʊ/ may be brought out by comparing the pronunciations of the following pairs of words:

pool	pull
shoe	shook
boo	book
fool	full
too	took
croon	crook

The vowel /ʊ/ is also heard in the unstressed syllables of the words *casual* and *gradual* and for *to* when it is followed by a word beginning with a vowel or diphthong as in *to England* and *to Iowa.*

Practice material for /ʊ/

bush	bullet	forsook
could	bosom	Lynbrook
foot	butcher	mistook
good	cooking	neighborhood
put	crooked	overlook
shook	pudding	partook
stood	pulley	pulpit
took	should	retook
wolf	wooden	sugar
would	woolen	understood

1. The cook made the pudding in such haste that she forgot to add sugar.
2. The crooks used a wooden pulley to lift their loot.
3. It was understood that the debate was to allow for refutation.
4. A spook needs no rubber heels to be unheard on foot.
5. Goods once woolen are now made of materials once wooden.
6. After a hail of bullets, the soldiers retook the fort in Old Brooklyn.
7. Brooks, a bookish man, was fond of cookies.

/o/ as in *boat*

/o/ is a tense vowel made with the raised portion of the tongue in a mid-back position and the lips rounded. /o/ is infrequently used as a pure vowel. It is most likely to be used as a pure vowel in words in which a stop-plosive sound follows the vowel as in *goat, oat, oak,* and *open.* In words where the sound is final, /o/ is likely to be lengthened and blended with /ʊ/ to become /oʊ/ as in *go, sew, toe, bone, owe, soul,* and *home.* (See page 198 for further discussion of /oʊ/.) In general, a lengthened /o/ is likely to become the diphthong /oʊ/. See Figure 6–8 for the tongue position for /o/.

The most frequent spelling for /o/, as may be noted in the key words, are *o, oe,* and *ou.*

Practice material for /o/ or /oʊ/

oaf	boulder	below
ocean	coma	bestow
ode	comely	crow
oh	folder	dough
ohm	frozen	explode
only	growing	flow
own	loaded	foe

boast	moaning	hollow
beau	poser	sorrow
bones	precocious	tomorrow
nose	slowly	untold
roam	soldier	woe

1. Joe Stoke holds that though sticks and stones may break your bones, names can also harm you.
2. The grouse were hunted with loaded guns.
3. Tomorrow is time enough for sorrow.
4. The beau grew bolder as his love grew older.
5. The boasting gave way to moaning as the foe approached.

Review material

Back vowels

1. To sorrow,
    I bade good-morrow,
And thought to leave her far away behind;
    But cheerly, cheerly,
    She loves me dearly;
She is so constant to me, and so kind.

    —John Keats, *Endymion*

2. Last night we saw the stars arise,
    But clouds soon dimmed the ether blue:
And when we saw each other's eyes
    Tears dimmed them too!

    —George Darby, *Last Night*

3.   My only books
        Were women's looks,
And folly's all they've taught me.

    —Thomas Moore, *The Time I've Lost in Wooing*

4. Time stoops to no man's lure;
    And love, grown faint and fretful,
    With lips but half regretful
    Sighs, and with eyes forgetful
Weeps that no loves endure.

    —Algernon Charles Swinburne, *The Garden of Proserpine*

5. Those who in quarrels interpose
    Must often wipe a bloody nose.

    —John Gay, *The Mastiffs* (*Fables*)

/3/ or /3˞/ as in *curl*

/3/ and /3˞/ are mid-central vowels. In their production the middle of the tongue is arched toward the roof of the mouth (see Figures 6–9 and 6–7). The two vowels are essentially the same in their manner of production and acoustic end result. The sound /3/ acoustically suggests the sound /r/. The vowel /3˞/ contains more than a mere suggestion of the /r/ sound. It is, in effect, a vowel /3/ blended with the sound /r/. See Figure 6–7 for tongue position.

Whether the speaker uses /3/ or /3˞/ usually depends upon his practice relative to the pronunciation of words spelled with a medial *r*. Those speakers who are inclined to pronounce the sound /r/ whenever the letter *r* appears in the spelling are likely to use the vowel /3˞/ or the combination /3r/. Those speakers who are likely to pronounce /r/ only when the spelling includes the letter *r* immediately followed by a vowel are also likely to use the vowel /3/.[8] In eastern New England and in Southern speech, /3/ is usually heard in words such as *curl, hurl, word, fir, girl, burn, whirl, earn,* and *kernel*. In General American speech, the same words are likely to be pronounced with the vowel /3˞/.

The spelling of words in which /3/ or /3˞/ is used usually includes the letters *ur, or, ir,* or *ear*. An interesting exception is the word *colonel*.

Some speakers substitute the sound blend /3ɪ/ for the vowel /3/. The acceptance of this substitution depends upon the practices of the speech area in which the speaker lives. Persons who wish to avoid the substitution of /3ɪ/ for /3/ might practice the regular inclusion of the /r/ sound following the vowel to produce either a distinct /3r/ combination or the sound /3˞/.

Differences in speaker usage may be determined by an analysis of the pronunciation of the following words:

cur	cursive
heard	hurting
burr	burden
mirth	murmur
occur	occurring
demur	demurring

Practice material for /3/ or /3˞/

certain	ascertain	avert	inter
curl	bestirred	demur	refer
earn	concerning	deter	aver
err	determine	observe	stir
first	discursive	occur	purr

[8] See page 86 for a discussion of practice in the use of /r/.

guerdon	disturbing	preserve	swerve
hurt	excursion	rehearse	stern
mirth	impersonal	reverse	surf
sermon	indeterminate	taciturn	spur
terse	uncertain	unfurl	third

1. Gertrude considered Thurston to be a person of sterling worth.

2. Merton determined to be stern as he worked.

3. A good merchant is seldom taciturn.

4. A pretty curl may make up for a lack of learning.

5. The pilot of the excursion boat averted an accident.

6. A stirring sermon may produce a rebirth of religious fervor.

7. To earn her keep, the farm girl churned the butter.

8. Burton told a story of a girl named Myrtle and her friend Earl. Myrtle complained that even in summer Earl was stern and cool and lacking in affection. When asked about her plans, Myrtle replied, "I'm not certain, but I think that when spring returns I'll just have to change my Earl."

9. Cursed be the verse, how
          well so e'er it flow,
      That tends to make one worthy
          man my foe.

> —ALEXANDER POPE, *Epistle to Dr. Arbuthnot*

10. There once was a girl named Myrtle
    Whose mind was exceedingly fertile
    She trained her purple pet turtle
    A three-foot fence to hurtle
          Poor Myrtle
          Poor turtle
    Had Myrtle trained her turtle to skirtle
    It would have been better than a one-time hurtle.

> —J.E.

/ʌ/ as in *cup*

/ʌ/ is a midvowel produced with a relatively relaxed tongue arched toward the middle or back of the palate. (See Figure 6–7.) It is heard only in stressed syllables either at the beginning or middle of words. The most frequent spellings are *u* as in *up*, *cup*, *but*, and *hum* and *o* as in *come, some,* and *comfort.* Less frequent spellings are *ou* as in *touch* and *double* and *oo* as in *blood.*

There is a tendency for some speakers, possibly as a result of influences emanating from the southern part of England, to substitute a vowel close to /ɑ/ in words usually pronounced with /ʌ/. This tendency appears to be especially strong for words spelled with the letter *o*. The reader may check his own practice by comparing his pronunciations of the following pairs of words:

donkey	dunk
come	cut
done	dub
some	summary
comfort	cunning

Practice material for /ʌ/

blood	lunge	assumption
blunder	mumble	asunder
brother	mutton	begun
bud	once	benumb
club	rubber	construct
does	sprung	discussing
double	tongue	percussion
gun	trouble	rebuff
honey	umpire	undone
love	unctuous	unsung

1. Get up, Duncan, the night is done, and greet the new day's sun.
2. Hud grumbled and mumbled throughout the supper meal.
3. In some schools it was once a custom to identify the poor student by a dunce cap.
4. Sometimes the bee keeps on making honey because he is in a rut.
5. Numbskulls as well as witches can create double trouble by their mumbo jumbo.
6. The fight for freedom, once begun, is a fight that is never done.
7. The rough, bumpy sea gave the landlubber much trouble.

8. Not a face below the sun
   But is precious—unto one.
   —Sir Edwin Arnold, *Facies Non Omnibus Una*

/ə/ as in *about* (first vowel) and *sofa* (second vowel)

/ə/ is a midvowel, produced with a relaxed tongue in a position slightly lower than for /ɜ/. (See Figure 6–7.) Except as part of a diphthong, the sound /ə/ is used only in unstressed syllables as in the first syllable of the words *attend, about, alone,* and the second syllable of *sofa, soda, taken, bacon,* and *fracas.*

The vowel /ə/, though limited in use to unstressed syllables, is nevertheless probably the one most frequently used in American-English speech. Two related features of American-English speech explain the high frequency of usage for the vowel /ə/. One is that most words of two or more syllables have at least one unstressed syllable. The second is that "function" words—prepositions, conjunctions, etc., regardless of number of syllables—are usually spoken as if all syllables were unstressed.

We may *be*gin to *be*come *a*ware *of* how of*ten* /ə/ may oc*cur* if we read *the* pres*ent* sen*tence* *a*loud. Each of the italicized syllables may appropriately be pronounced with the vowel /ə/.

Further practice may be had by saying the following sentences aloud as if they were parts of conversations. The spellings of the words should not be permitted to exert undue influence on the pronunciations.

1. The woman was about to leave the room.
2. The paper was full of frightful items of news.
3. The older brother attended to the needs of the younger one.
4. We who are about to die, salute you.
5. It rained and rained from morning to night.
6. Around and about went Ursula looking for Ella.
7. Eva enjoyed okra in her luncheon salad.
8. Edna and Stella planted azaleas and petunias in their garden.

/ɚ/ as in build*er*, hard*er* (General American)

/ɚ/, like /ə/, is used only in unstressed syllables. It is used in place of /ə/ by those speakers who habitually pronounce medial or final *r*'s whenever the letter occurs in the word spelling.

The vowel /ɚ/, like /ə/, is a mid-central vowel produced with a relatively lax tongue. Unlike /ə/, however, /ɚ/ is characterized by an /r/ coloring. This characteristic is produced either by raising the tip of the tongue from behind the lower gum ridge or by arching the middle part of the tongue a bit higher than for the /ə/ sound. See Figure 6–7 for tongue position.

The reader may check his own tendencies relative to the vowels /ə/ and /ɚ/ by analyzing his pronunciations of the italicized syllables in the words tak*er*, farth*er*, wond*er*, and bitt*er*.

The difference between /ɝ/ and /ɚ/ may be brought out by attending to the vowels in the stressed and unstressed syllables in the words *murmur, murder, further* and *burner.*

Review material for central vowels

1. Werther had a love for Charlotte
   Such as words could never utter;

Would you know how first he met her?
  She was cutting bread and butter.

· · ·

Charlotte, having seen his body
  Borne before her on a shutter,
Like a well conducted person,
  Went on cutting bread and butter

— WILLIAM M. THACKERAY, *Sorrows of Werther*

2. George M. Cohan uttered a terse complaint that we are "hurried and worried until we're buried, and there's no curtain call."

3. Hunter was perturbed about sleeping in an upper berth. He worried that if he turned or stirred an accident might occur.

4. Tom Tucker and his brother Merle sang at supper.

Questions and exercises on the study of vowels

1. How do vowels differ in articulation from consonants?

2. What consonants closely resemble vowels in their manner of production?

3. Why may it be said that the consonant sounds /m/ and /n/ may well be considered nasal vowels?

4. In what way do the sounds /w/ and /j/ resemble vowels? How about /r/ and /l/?

5. Transcribe phonetically your pronunciation of the following words: *fee, bean, people, been, pill, state, plate, hat, mat, ask, path, too, school, blood, hook, roof, broom, boat, stall, ball, hog, log, father, balm, curl, surly, above, rudder.*

6. Do any of your pronunciations vary from those of other speakers in your own social and educational class? Indicate the differences through the use of phonetic transcriptions or, if a recorder is available, by recording and playing back your version of how you and other speakers brought up in different regions vary in pronunciation.

7. Transcribe the italicized words of the following sentences as you would pronounce them in ordinary conversational speech.
  (a) *The* race is *to the* quick and that's *the way* to place *your* bets.
  (b) Three *and* four are the same *as* five *and* two.
  (c) Is this book *for* me or is it *yours?*
  (d) *The* hour has come, *let's* eat.

8. Transcribe each of the following according to your habitual pronunciation: *asunder, burn, curtain, furnace, further, pearl, plunder, stern, turn, under, upper, yearn.*

DIPHTHONGS

Dipththongs are vocalic glides that are uttered in a single breath impulse. In a strict sense, the word *diphthong*, which literally means *two sounds*, should not be used for what is actually a *continuous gliding vowel* sound. The conventional phonetic symbolization suggests that a diphthong contains two sounds. A better interpretation of the symbols would be that the first element of the diphthong represents the approximate intial sound, and the second element represents the approximate final sound of the glide. For example, the diphthong /ɔɪ/ is initiated with the vowel /ɔ/. The organs of articulation are then continuously modified to produce a continuous change of sound until the diphthong is concluded with what approxiates the vowel /ɪ/.

The diphthongs /aɪ/. /ɔɪ/, and /aʊ/ are phonemic. Each represents a distinctive sound unit. Each serves as a basis for enabling us to distinguish beween spoken words in the same ways as do vowel and consonant phonemes. Not all diphthongs, however, are phonemic. For example, though we may recognize an acoustic difference in pronunciation when *gate* is pronounced [get] or [geɪt], we would recognize the intended word with either pronunciation. Similarly, we know what day of the week is signified whether we hear *Tuesday* pronounced as [tjuzdɪ], [tɪuzdɪ], or [tuzdɪ]. The nonphonemic diphthongs include /eɪ/, /oʊ/, /ɪu/, and /ju/.

There is another group of sounds that might also be studied among the nonphonemic diphthongs. These sound combinations occur in the speech of persons who omit the medial and final /r/ in their pronunciations. This group of vowels includes /ɪə/, /ʊə/, /ɔə/, /oə/, and /ɛə/ in words such as *hear, dear; poor, sure; floor, door; horse, wore;* and *dare, fair.* These will be discussed later.

/aɪ/ as in *ice*

The diphthong /aɪ/ is most frequently represented orthographically by the alphabetic letters *i* at the beginning and middle of words and *y* as the final letter of words. Many persons use the vowel /ɑ/ for the first sound of the diphthong to produce the blend /ɑɪ/. This pronunciation is frequent enough among cultured speakers to be accepted as standard.

The words *ice, ire,* and *aisle* contain the diphthong /aɪ/ in the initial sound.

In the words *mine, timely,* miner the diphthong appears medially. In *sky, by, tie, wry* the diphthong /aɪ/ is used as the final sound.

Practice material for /aɪ/ or /ɑɪ/

aisle	aspiring	aside
buy	beguiling	butterfly
diagram	declining	behind
drive	designing	byline
height	devise	despite
island	inviting	hindsight
mine	reminder	lifelike
side	requited	overripe
riot	unlikely	skyline
time	unsightly	twilight

1. Dinah made a beguiling bride as she walked down the aisle.
2. The wise use others' hindsight for their own foresight.
3. The high spires appeared to be aglow in the twilight.
4. Ina aspired to an iron-clad knight.
6. Simon noted that time and tide are not on the side of those who are righteous but idle.
7. Mike aspired to make his foresight as wise as his hindsight.

/aʊ/ or /ɑʊ/ as in *now*

The now famous line "How now brown cow?" contains, in each of its words, the diphthong /aʊ/ or /aʊ/. In this sentence, it may be noted, the diphthong is consistently represented by the letters *ow*. Another frequent spelling is *ou* as in *mouth, out, flout, bound,* and *sound.*

There is a rather strong tendency to use the vowel blend, /æʊ/ rather than /aʊ/ or /aʊ/, in some parts of the Eastern speech areas (New York and the Middle Atlantic States) and in parts of the South. The use of /æʊ/ is usually considered substandard in the North, but is generally acceptable (is less likely to attract unfavorable attention) in the South. Occasionally the triple vowel combination /æaʊ/ or /æaʊ/ is heard for the standard /aʊ/ or /aʊ/.

The combination /aʊ/ rather than /aʊ/ is frequently used throughout many parts of the United States. It has the prestige of usage by persons of education and culture.

Practice material for /aʊ/ or /aʊ/

count	about	allow
doubt	announce	bow
gown	astound	brow
mouth	dismount	cow
out	impound	how

owl	profound	now
proud	rebound	plough
shout	resound	sow
south	unfounded	thou
town	ungrounded	vow

1. The threat of showers shrouded the day in gloom.
2. The horseman failed to dismount but fell to the ground.
3. However unfounded, the rumor spread throughout the town.
4. Even as thou, a cow or a sow may look profound.
5. Take counsel with yourself before deciding to mouth your thoughts aloud.
6. The scoundrel's last wish was that he might see his proud wife wearing a shroud.
7. The stout plowman preferred mounds of flowers to crowds of people.

/ɔɪ/ as in *soil*

The diphthong /ɔɪ/ is appropriately used in words such as *oil, toil,* and *toy.* The most frequent spelling equivalents in English are the letters *oi* at the beginning and middle of words and *oy* at the end of the words.

The vowel blend /ɜɪ/ is occasionally heard substituted for /ɔɪ/ by some New York City speakers. This substitution is considered substandard. In the speech of some Southerners the phonemic difference between /ɔɪ/ and /ɔ/ breaks down, the speakers using a lengthened vowel /ɔː/ for the more generally acceptable diphthong /ɔɪ/.

The following word list and sentences are intended to provide practice material for words in which the use of the diphthong /ɔɪ/ is recommended as standard. Avoid the use of either /ɜɪ/ or of /oɪ/. The latter is a substitution occasionally heard in parts of the Middle Atlantic States.

Practice material for /ɔɪ/

oil	join	employ
toil	point	enjoy
soil	poison	annoy
voice	rejoice	recoil
choice	oyster	deploy
boy	coin	adroit
coy	cloy	convoy
soy	spoil	avoid

1. Memories of things once enjoyed still leave us with an aching void.
2. A slippery oyster can be enjoyed only by the well poised.
3. The oil that burns may be an ointment for the burned.
4. The cackling chicken is no longer noisy when it becomes a broiler.

5. The royal family exploited the citizens to provide themselves with the coin of the realm.
6. The spoils of battle are seldom worth the toil of battling.
7. A voice too coy may be a voice to cloy.
8. Boyd enjoyed the play at the Savoy.
9. Soybeans and poi may be employed in royal dishes.
10. The noisy boys annoyed McCoy.

/eɪ/ as in *bay*

The diphthong /eɪ/ is pronounced as the first letter of the alphabet. It may be used instead of the vowel /e/ in such words as *nail, aim, lace, fame, pray, way,* and *bewail*. It may also be heard in such words as *date, berate,* and *ache* and in the second syllable of *today*. The use of the diphthong /eɪ/ rather than the vowel /e/ depends on speech context. The difference in pronunciation between /ə/ or /eɪ/ will not result in differences in meaning for any English word. (See page 179 for practice material.)

/oʊ/ as in *toe*

The diphthong /oʊ/ is pronounced as the alphabetic letter *o*. This diphthong, or the vowel /o/, is used in such words as *only, owner, ocean, pillow, open,* and *coal*. Whether the speaker uses the vowel /o/ or the diphthong /oʊ/ is almost entirely an automatic matter determined by the speech context. In this respect it is parallel to the use of /e/ or /eɪ/, discussed earlier. (See page 188 for practice material.)

/ɛə/ as in *their*

The diphthong /ɛə/ is used instead of the more frequently heard combination /ɛr/ by persons who omit the medial and final /r/ sound in their pronunciations. It is likely to be heard in such words as *air, fair, there,* and *scare*.

Some speakers tend to substitute the diphthong /ɛə/ for the vowel /æ/ or /a/ in such words as *last, fast, class, path* and *bath*. This substitution is generally considered substandard.

Practice material for /ɛə/ or /ɛr/

air	mare	despair
bear	their	forbear
care	wear	impair
dare	affair	prepare
fair	beware	tableware
hair	compare	welfare
lair	declare	repair

1. The unwary bear was trapped in his own lair.

2. Most men forbear to express their feelings about how women care for their hair.
3. The heirloom, a fine set of silver tableware, has a rare design.
4. A bachelor, unable to bear children, may still write about their welfare.
5. The heiress seemed beautiful beyond compare.
6. Our share of night to bear,
   Our share of morning.

> —EMILY DICKINSON, *First Series, Life*

7. Dairlington was ever beware of Fairlington because, despite his name, his behavior was nefarious.

/ɔə/ and /oə/

The diphthongs /ɔə/ and /oə/ are likely to be used by persons who are inclined to omit /r/ from their pronunciations, except when the letter *r* is immediately followed by a vowel. These are the same speakers who use /ɛə/ rather than /ɛr/ for words such as *there* and *welfare*.

Speakers who regularly include /r/ sounds whenever they occur in the spelling of words are likely to use /ɔr/ or /or/ in the same contexts. Practice in regard to /oə/ and /ɔr/ or /oə/ and /or/ varies, though not with complete consistency, along the following lines.

The pronunciation of words such as *accord, horse, lord,* and *north* follow fairly uniform usage throughout the United States: /ɔə/ for the "r-dropping" speakers and /ɔr/ for the others.

There is greater variability between /ɔ/ and /o/ in the pronunciations of the words *board, mourning, course,* and *more.* Most Americans are likely to pronounce the words with either an /o/ or and /or/. "Native" residents of New York City are likely to use the vowel /ɔ/ for all of these words, thus making no distinctions between *horse* and *hoarse* or *for* and *four.* Except in the New York City area, most Americans are likely to use /ɔ/ for *horse* and *for,* and /o/ for *hoarse* and *four.*

The reader may check his own practice by comparing his pronunciations for the following pairs of words:

> *border* and *boarder*
> *horse* and *hoarse*
> *morning* and *mourning*
> *war* and *wore*

The following words are usually pronounced with either /ɔr/ or /oə/, depending on regional tendency relative to the final /r/

cord	import	perform
course	lord	short

/ɪə/ as in *dear*

This diphthong, as noted earlier, is used by persons who omit medial and final /r/ sounds from their pronunciations of words such as *dear, fear, near, arrear, beard,* and *cheerful.* In the General American speech area, all of these words are properly and more frequently pronounced with the combination /ɪr/ rather than the diphthong /ɪə/.

/ʊə/ as in *poor*

The vowel blend /ʊə/ is likely to be used in words such as *poor, cure, sure,* and *tour* by those speakers who tend to omit the /r/ except in words in which the r is followed by a vowel. Speakers who regularly pronounce the /r/ sound whenever the letter r appears in the spelling of a word are likely to use the combination /ʊr/ rather than the diphthong /ʊə/.

/ju/ as in *use*

In our study of the consonants, the sound /j/ was described as a *glide.* It should be apparent that one could easily justify listing /j/ as a vowel rather than as a consonant. In keeping with this point of view, the sound blend /ju/ may justifiably be considered a diphthong. It is pronounced as the letter *u* of the alphabet. See Figure 8–10 for initial tongue position for /j/.

The combination /ju/ is heard in the words *few, feud, cube, pewter,*

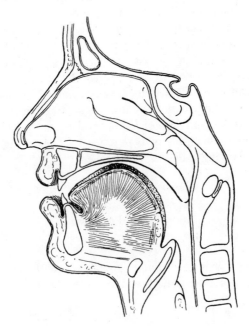

FIGURE 8–10. Tongue position for /j/.

music, use, eulogy, and *union.* It may also be heard in *Tuesday* and *new.* Many cultured speakers, however, pronounce *Tuesday* as [tuzdɪ] and *new* as [nu].

The diphthong /ɪu/ is used by many speakers instead of /ju/ in words such as *beauty, cube, muse, fuse,* and *views.* The difference between /ɪu/ and /ju/ is not phonemic. It is likely that most speakers use both of these diphthongs without being aware of the difference between them.

In initial positions, as in the words *use, eulogy, unique,* and *union,* /ju/ is regularly used.

Questions and exercises on the study of diphthongs

1. Define a diphthong.

2. Distinguish between phonemic and nonphonemic diphthongs.

3. Transcribe phonetically your pronunciation of the following words: *fear, dear, pail, maze, mate, wait, pear, rarely, like, high, flow, Joe, stone, bone, rope, elope, billow, escrow, boor, gourd, Moor, soil, join, boy, Roy, more, wharves, floor, down, gown, stout, doubt, endure, skewer, fewer, news, music.*

4. Indicate phonetically any frequently heard variations in the pronunciation of these words.

5. For any of the words above, are the variations you hear consistent for speakers according to the geographic area from which they came?

6. Are any of the variations related to social or economic factors? Specify which.

RECOMMENDED READINGS

The list that follows includes texts that contain discussions and practice materials that should be of help to the student who wishes to pursue further the *phonetic* approach to the improvement of diction.

ANDERSON, V. A. *Training the Speaking Voice,* 2nd ed. New York: Oxford University Press, 1961.

BRIGANCE, W. N., and F. A. HENDERSON. *Drill Manual for Improving Speech,* rev. ed. Philadelphia: J. B. Lippincott Co., 1955.

BRONSTEIN, A. J. *The Pronunciation of American English.* New York: Appleton-Century-Crofts, 1960.

CARRELL, J., and W. R. TIFFANY. *Phonetics.* New York: McGraw-Hill Book Company, 1960.

EISENSON, J. *Voice and Diction: A Program for Improvement.* New York: Macmillan Publishing Co., Inc., 1974.

FAIRBANKS, G. *Voice and Articulation Drillbook,* rev. ed. New York: Harper & Row, Publishers, Inc., 1960.

OGILVIE, M., and N. S. REES. *Communication Skills: Voice and Pronunciation.* New York: McGraw-Hill Book Company, 1969.

THOMAS, C. K. *Handbook of Speech Improvement.* New York: The Ronald Press Company, 1956.

THOMAS, C. K. *An Introduction to the Phonetics of American English,* rev. ed. New York: The Ronald Press Company, 1958.

VAN RIPER, C., and J. V. IRWIN. *Voice and Articulation.* Englewood Cliffs, N.J.: Prentice-Hall, Inc., 1958.

WINITZ, H. *Articulatory Acquisition and Behavior.* New York: Appleton-Century-Crofts, 1969.

Chapter 9

Speech, Language, & Meaning

How to Mean What You Mean When You Have Something to Say

> The situations which prompt people to utter speech include every object and happening in their universe. In order to give a scientifically accurate definition of meaning for every form of language, we should have to have a scientifically accurate knowledge of everything in the speakers' world.
>
> LEONARD BLOOMFIELD[1]

Speech, viewed as a form of human species-specific behavior, is a communicative system in which the meanings we wish to convey go through the following transformations: (1) A message is generated in the brain (mind) of the speaker. (2) The message is encoded into the form of language common to the speaker and the listener. (3) The message is converted into neural signals that are sent to the muscles of the speech mechanism where they are transformed into articulatory patterns (acoustic signals). (4) The acoustic signals are then decoded by the listener. Thus, as the linguist Fromkin[2] points out, "the input signal that presumably starts as a string of individual discrete sounds organized into phrases and words ends up as a semicontinuous signal that the receiver must change back into the original string of discrete units."

Essentially two kinds of decoding take place: a decoding of sounds, and a decoding of the meaning of the sounds. It is possible for one to

[1] Leonard Bloomfield, *Language* (New York: Holt, Rinehart and Winston, 1933), p. 139.
[2] V. A. Fromkin, "Slips of the Tongue," *Scientific American*, **229**:6 (December 1973), 110–117.

occur without the other, as the conversation between Alice and Humpty Dumpty suggests.

WHICH IS TO BE MASTER?

"When I use a word," Humpty Dumpty said in a rather scornful tone, "it means just what I choose it to mean—nothing more or less."

"The question is," said Alice, "whether you *can* make words mean so many different things."

"The question is," said Humpty Dumpty, "which is to be master— that's all."

The conversation between Humpty Dumpty and Alice raised questions that have still not been answered. Can words be made to mean anything we want them to mean? Which is to be master—the speaker or the words? And how does the listener know which meaning of the words or of a context of words is intended by the speaker?

We will be able to arrive at answers when we decide two fundamental questions: (1) What do we mean my meaning? (2) How do words get their meanings?

MEANING

In a broad sense, meaning is the differential way we respond to situations (things, persons, places) or ideas. Our responses vary from time to time. Strictly speaking, we never respond the same way twice to any situation. So, also, no situation is ever precisely the same at any two moments. It follows, therefore, that every situation has more than one potential meaning and that each response is an expression of a meaning.

The house we live in undergoes constant change. The wood ages. New and differently colored paints are applied. The roof is patched or a new roof put on top of the old leaky one. Flowers are grown and wither and die. Time and the seasons bring changes. If we are aware of our responses to the physical features of our house, we begin to appreciate that they are subject to constant change. Notwithstanding all of these changes, however, there is a core of consistency in our responses. Our particular house is not likely to change its location to any significant degree. It is located on a given street or a road in a particular village, town, or city. We have no difficulty in recognizing it as our house despite the modifications.

When we talk about meaning, we usually have in mind the relatively constant significance that things, persons, places, or ideas have for us. The *boss*, whoever else he may be, is someone for whom we work. Our *house* is the place in which we live. The sun is a source of light and energy regardless of whether it is visible or when it rises or sets.

There is another way of considering meaning which allows for constant semantic change. We might say that meaning is the way we respond, at the moment of responding, to any situation when all its aspects are considered. The *boss* then becomes not just someone we work for, but the sum total of our responses at a given moment because of the way he behaved when we arrived ten minutes late. Our *house* may be one thing when we think of its cost and the size of the mortgage, and something else again when we think of who is living in it. Its meaning includes shoveling snow during the winter, mowing the lawn during the summer, and raking leaves in the fall. The specific meanings of our *house* are as varied and as many as the number of times we respond to it. Its conceptual meaning is the residual of all our responses and the potential for the residual for determining future responses.

FACTORS THAT DETERMINE MEANING

Most words considered alone have so many possible meanings that it becomes necessary to consider what factors determine a particular meaning. "A word is not a crystal, transparent and unchanged; it is the skin of a living thought and may vary greatly in color and content according to the circumstances and the time in which it is used.[3]

The *circumstances* and the *time* cover considerable territory. They include the external conditions at the time a word is used, the relationship of the given word to a context of words, the attitude of the speaker toward the person to whom he is speaking and/or to what he is saying. These, and at least two other factors we shall consider, determine the meaning of a particular word.

External conditions

Is a *fireman* a person who puts out fires or keeps them going? On a steamship or train or a diesel locomotive a fireman keeps a fire going. In a home community a fireman is one whose job it is to help put out fires *in places where they are not wanted.* No sane fireman either starts fires everywhere or puts them out anywhere he may be. The special circumstances or external conditions help to determine the meaning of the word.

Circumstances include our expectations based on direct or vicarious experiences with an object, a situation, or a relationship. How *fast* is *fast?* If a trip between two points is usually made in an automobile in 30 minutes, and varying traffic conditions on occasion make it possible to cover the distances in 25 minutes, and on other occasions in 35, then is 25 fast and 40 minutes slow? A conventional automobile travels fast when it is going over 60 miles an hour, a propeller-driven airplane travels fast at 200 miles per hour, and a jet-powered plane is not traveling fast unless

[3] Justice Oliver Wendell Holmes—quoted in *Yankee From Olympus* by Catherine Drinker Bowen (Boston: Little, Brown, 1944), p. 396.

its comparative ground speed is at least 600 miles per hour. This speed, however, would be slow for a supersonic plane.

Verbal context: The sentence as the unit of meaning

By this is meant the relationship of a given word to other words with which it is used in context.

> "Are you sure you're going to marry the best man?" a
> radio comedian asked a bride-to-be on a quiz program.
> "Yes," the bride-to-be assured him.
> "That's funny," the comedian quipped. "I thought you're
> going to marry the groom."

Of the many possible meanings a word may have, the particular meaning usually becomes evident when the word is used in context. When context alone is not enough, the special conditions under which a word is used help to limit word meaning. There is little danger that the bride will be confused between *her* best man and *a* best man.

Some words sound alike but do not even have a common core of meaning. In context these words—*homonyms*—seldom if ever cause confusion to the literate. The number *eight* is not apt to be confused with the verb *ate*. The sentence *Two drinks may be too many drinks* contains a pair of homonyms. Verbal context helps to make their meanings clear as well as to give meaning to the sentence as a whole.

The amount of verbal context necessary to limit or clarify a meaning is highly variable. As we indicated, it is sometimes necessary to "spell out" the special conditions of a verbal formulation to bring out one meaning where several meanings are possible. For example, there are several possible meanings for the statement *John Jones watered his stock*. Some of these are brought out only if we know something about John Jones as a person. What is his vocation, avocation, and reputation for honesty? For example, if John Jones is known to be a farmer, the words *watered* and *stock* and the statement as a whole have different meanings than if John Jones is the head of a business corporation that has just issued stock for sale to the public. Still a different meaning would develop if we knew that John Jones happened to be a horticulturist who was fond of a particular *flower called stock*. If John Jones turned out to be a gentleman farmer as well as the head of a corporation, we would need to know *when* the watering took place, and to inquire about the nature of the *stock* for the statement *John Jones watered his stock* to have any particular meaning. In brief, verbal context is helpful only when it is sufficient to take care of special circumstances for limiting and defining the meanings of individual words as well as multiple word formulations. If we had a paragraph rather than a single sentence about Mr. Jones, we could keep our thoughts about him in order. For example, it should help to be informed:

John Jones, the head of the National Skyhook Corporation, was convicted of falsifying his company's assets and watering his stock. Jones was sentenced to three years on a state prison farm. Among his specific tasks was to water the stock daily and to keep the barn clean.

Attitude of the speaker

When we knew how a speaker feels about what he is saying, when we are aware of his personal attitude, we are in a better position to understand the meaning of his words. The speaker's attitude may be a momentary one or may be moderately habitual. The speaker may be irritated or annoyed at the moment he is speaking. What the speaker means by his words, at such moments, is likely to be colored by his immediate personal attitude. The "No" of an angry individual may in effect mean, "Don't ask me now."

When we know the habital attitude, or position of a speaker on a subject or issue, we increase the likelihood that we will understand the meanings of his utterances. The words *coexistence with the Communist world* have different meanings for the members of the Communist party in general than they do for members of either the Republican or Democratic parties in the United States. In the early 1960s *coexistence* seemed to express a different attitude for members of the Communist party in good standing within the Soviet Union than they did for Communist party members in China. *Coexistence* and *détente* assumed still different meanings in the 1970s.

We need not confine our examples of meanings as related to attitudes to citizens of nations with divergent political and social philosophies. Many American husbands insist that they have learned to compromise issues with their wives by accepting their wives' interpretation of *compromise*. And some American wives insist that they have learned to *compromise* by *conceding*. Is the *flexible* person one who can appreciate another's point of view or is he one who lacks the courage of his convictions and bends or yields to the assertions of another who speaks with conviction, or as if he had conviction? The more we know about the speaker, his personality and his attitude, the better we are able to understand the meanings of the words he uses.

Manner of speaking

The way in which an individual speaks his words—his manner of utterance—is intimately associated with his immediate personal attitude. Feelings are readily reflected in voice (see pages 39–40). Voice tones may belie intended meanings and reveal the speaker despite himself.

Frequently the speaker uses a vocal tone, or an inflection, or a slow rate to give special significance to a word or words. *Yes* spoken with an upward pitch glide may be a more effective way of saying "No" than the word *no* spoken with a downward pitch glide. If the sentence *Yes, I'll do it* is spoken slowly, with a slight upward pitch glide on *yes*, the speaker is probably revealing unwillingness but resignation for a task. The same words, spoken rapidly and with a downward pitch glide on *yes* and *do*, reveal willingness and determination for the task.

Manner of utterance includes more than vocal pattern. The facial expression, the gestures, the total bodily action at the time of speaking are elements that give meaning to words. These elements have been discussed in some detail in earlier chapters (see "The Components of Speech" and "Nonverbal Communication").

The referent

Few if any words have inherent meanings. Words acquire meaning through a process of association. Through association most words come to "stand for" characteristics of the objects or actions or experiences. Still other words "stand for" relationships between actions and objects or experiences. To know the meaning of a word we must be able to determine, at any given time, what the word stands for. We must, in brief, know which association out of many possible associations the word calls forth in our minds. When we are able to do that, we have defined the *referent* of the word and so have placed appropriate limitations on the meaning of the word.

Common reference

Words would have little value in communication if they had meaning only for the speaker. Words are the coin of communication because they have some common meanings for many members of a group. The shared meanings are a result of common experiences which persons of a given group must necessarily have. However individual our reactions may be in regard to the weather, or our jobs, or our homes, if we live in a particular community many aspects of our reactions are approximately alike. These approximations or similarities of experience and response are the basis for the common references to words. The meaning of words listed in a dictionary represent the highest common factors of the various meanings of the words based on common experience. These may be referred to as *denotative meanings*.

APPROXIMATION OF UNDERSTANDING

We manage to get along in our social and business world through the use of words that we understand only approximately. Identity of meaning and of understanding is probably never achieved. For the ordinary purposes of living, approximations are usually adequate. Whether we would get along better with one another if a more complete understanding were possible is debatable. It may even be that we actually would love our neighbor less rather than more if we understood fully what he meant by the words he spoke.

In any event, the degree to which we understand one another's meanings is determined in part by the similarity of past experiences between the speaker and the listener. The greater the number of common experiences, the greater will be the likelihood that the speaker will respond essentially the same way to the spoken words. In brief, common meanings depend on common responses to words and to related experiences or objects.

The blind men in the fable derived different meanings from their contacts with the elephant because at a crucial moment the blind men shared no common experiences. From the point of view of seeing persons, all the blind thought the others were wrong because no two of them were responding to the same part of the elephant, and none of them was responding to the elephant as a whole. For words to have even approximately the same meanings for two or more individuals, those individuals must be able to respond to the same situation, considered not in part but as a whole.

HOW WORDS ACQUIRE MEANINGS

Although, as we indicated earlier, the sentence is the unit of meaning, we do not learn the meanings of sentences by direct and recurrent exposure to the same verbal formulations. The number of possible sentences we are capable of understanding is theoretically infinite, even though the most learned person has a finite number of words in his vocabulary. We may and do, however, learn what individual words may mean and what they are likely to mean when in sentence context. For the present we shall consider a few factors that determine how words acquire meanings.

Association

Words acquire meanings through a process of association. As a result of experiences, an event, an object, or a relationship becomes associated with a word. If the experience is vivid, or highly significant, or occurs frequently, a connection is made between the event, or object, or relationship and the associated word. In time the word comes to *stand for* or symbolize the associated experience.

The child learns the word *doll* after the toy object and the word are presented together often enough for the association to be formed. When the child responds to the word *doll* in much the same fashion as she (or he) responded to the object doll, the word *doll* means the object doll. So, also, the child learns other words.

As the child matures and has experiences, he continues to make associations and learn new words. Sometimes he has several different experiences associated with the same word. The child may learn that water is associated with drinking and swimming and cooking and washing. Thus he learns that a word may have more than one meaning. In time the child, as he grows up, may come to the conclusion that a word may have as many different meanings as he has ways of responding to it. He may eventually conclude that a word may have one core meaning and various shades of meaning. To the small child *mother* may mean the person who is the comforter and the feeder and the linen-changer and the lullaby singer-at-night. *Father* may mean the person who comes home in time for supper and who walks the floor with him at night and who talks roughly but usually does what mother tells him.

KINDS OF MEANING

Personal vs. objective meanings

If we study our responses to situations or to words, we can appreciate that some of them are highly personal and individual. We are not surprised to find that other persons do not respond as we do to the same situation. A particular tune is not just a Burt Bachrach or Bob Dylan melody; it is *our song* because we heard it when we began to think as *we*. But the tune, because it has a certain time and rhythm, is also a specific kind of melody. The same situation may have a *personal* or *subjective* meaning and an *impersonal* or *objective* or *informative* meaning. Words, which stand for situations, similarly may have personal meanings and objective meanings. The word *mother* has innumerable personal meanings, many of which are highly sentimental. The objective meaning of *mother* is almost rudely abrupt. *A mother is a female parent.*

Another way of arriving at the difference between a personal and objective meaning is to compare the implications of two statements that include the term *mother*. Suppose James Wilson says to his friend Tom Smith, "I think that Bob's wife is a fine mother." Such a statement might be considered a value judgment. It is an expression of what Wilson considers to be qualities, not in any way indicated, of what constitutes *motherhood,* as well as *fine motherhood.* All we know, if we know anything at all about Wilson's statement, is that he seems to approve of Bob's wife as a mother. At a later time, Wilson may be walking down a street with his friend and meet and greet a child and a woman. As Wilson and his friend Tom Smith continue on their way, Wilson may then say, "Oh, by the way, that was young Bob Jones and his mother." In this statement mother has objective and denotative meaning. The word *mother* in this instance referred specifically to the familial relationship between two persons, without regard to any value judgments or personal assessments about the relationship.

Meanings may be personal without being sentimental. Following are some examples of personal (value judgment) statements and observations:

- I studied for my exams; Joe crammed for his.
- I take my time about coming to a decision; Tom can't make up his mind.
- I have a sense of humor; Bob is silly.
- Mary has an open mind; Sue is just plain putty.
- I have backbone; you are rigid.
- My observation was witty; yours was sarcastic.
- Steve is fearless; Ned is irresponsible.
- My grandson is going through his "acting out" stage; my neighbor's kid is emotionally disturbed.

We may note that despite their subjectivity the statements are so worded that an objective core of meaning of the key words can be recognized. Unless there is an objective core—a common ground of understanding—shared meaning is not possible.

Affective connotation

Some words more than others are associated with experiences of feeling. The feelings may be pleasant or unpleasant, mild or strong. Though these words have meanings listed in the dictionary, more frequently than not the dictionary does not list among their objective meanings the responses the words arouse in us. When we refer to people as "dogs," "kooks," "old bats," or "squares" we express our feelings rather than our thoughts about them. Feelings of a different sort are usually expressed when we use terms such as "chicks," "sweetie," "toots," or "monkey face." In the middle 1970s "She's outrageous" was about as good as "She's far out." Somehow, at least in our youth culture, such terms and observations had acquired positive and complimentary values.

Many terms, such as those included above, are especially useful when we need to express affect in our language. The choice of words that a man may use to indicate his feelings as well as his thoughts about a woman goes beyond ordinary definition or designation. It makes an affective difference whether a female person is referred to as a "woman," "young woman," "lady," "gentlewoman," "wife," "wench," "mistress," or "Ms." It also makes a difference if she is referred to merely as "that female."

Terms of respect, including *Sir, Your Honor, Your Excellency, Your Worship*, are significant for their affective implications.

Affective language makes it possible for us, in writing as well as in speaking, to reveal how we feel about what we think. The thought in the following paired sentences remains essentially the same. Our feelings about the thoughts are different:

The issue was so grave that the president was unwilling to be hurried into a decision without first weighing all the facts.

The president didn't know enough to make up his mind.

We had roast capon for dinner.
We had cooked, desexed chicken for supper.

Her intellectual curiosity and deep sympathy naturally directed her to choose psychiatric social work as a career.

She has always been a busybody, prying into other people's affairs. No wonder she chose to become a psychiatric social worker!

However, there is more than an affective difference between "Her face could stop a clock" and "Her face could make time stand still."

Almost any word may have affective value according to its manner of use. The sentences above illustrate the significance of word context to modify an essential idea with feeling tone. A more usual way of adding feeling to thought is through voice change. This method is considered at some length in the discussion on the components of speech (Chapter 3).

SYMBOLS, WORDS, AND LANGUAGE

Symbols

The sounds that make up our words mean nothing unless two or more human beings agree on a meaning. The agreement is usually tacit. As children we learned combinations of sounds and their associated meanings. The process is called *learning to speak*. If we wish, however, we can more actively agree that certain things will stand for other things. Two persons may formulate a code for private communications. The persons may agree between themselves that their *code symbols* will stand for whatever they choose. They may choose visible symbols such as puffs of smoke, or red lights, or white lines. They may decide that a red light means *stop* or that a double line on a highway means *do not cross*. They might just as readily have decided that a red light means *go*, and a double white line means *crossing is permitted*.

Persons may agree on using symbols that require direct contact for communication. A handshake or a pat on the back, as is the case in some secret societies, may be given a specific meaning. Symbols may be of as many kinds or combinations of kinds as there are senses. Symbols may be based on smells or sights or sounds or physical feelings. Whatever the basis of the symbol system, there is seldom if ever a necessary or inherent connection between the symbol and that for which the symbol stands.

The possible exceptions are the sound symbols (words), such as *buzz,* *hiss,* and *switch, smash, crunch,* which, when spoken, may suggest the thing or act for which they stand.

A *symbol* is a convenient artifice which, by tacit acceptance or active agreement, comes to stand for something. The something for which a symbol stands or which it symbolizes may be an object, a relationship, an experience, a feeling, an attitude, or a concept.

Speech symbols

Speech symbols are audible and/or visible. They are commonly called words and gestures. *Audible symbols* are conventionalized (agreed upon) sounds produced by actions of the lips, tongue, teeth, palate, vocal muscles, and lungs. *Gestures* are conventionalized actions produced by the hands, arms and shoulders, facial muscles, and occasionally other parts of the body.[4] Whether audible or visible, we normally produce speech symbols without the need to restort to instruments or devices outside the human body. Instruments and devices, however, may be employed to transmit symbols (the telephone or radio) or to make them more easily discernible (the loud speaker system).

A *spoken language,* as we usually think of it, consists of a system of audible symbols. Tonal patterns, manner of articulation, and customs of sentence structure and word relationships (syntax) are involved in our concept of a spoken language. The patterns and customs differ according to the language spoken. These differences give us English and French and Chinese and all other spoken languages. A *written language* is a system of visible symbols that usually stand for spoken symbols. In Chinese and some other Asiatic languages, the written and spoken systems are separate.

Symbol reaction

The ability to deal with symbols is a distinctive human achievement. Symbol behavior characterizes man alone. Animals as high in the scale as the chimpanzee occasionally approximate man's achievement, but the approximation is rarely close enough for the brightest chimpanzee to be able to compete successfully with a human being even of subnormal intelligence.

The distinctive difference between us and the animal in respect to symbol behavior is that we are able to reserve judgment and action. The animal is not. We are able to learn that something *may stand for* something else. We do not ordinarily confuse *stands for* with *is.* We are able to evaluate the situation which amounts to our saying to ourselves, "The symbol stands for something *only if conditions are the expected ones,*

---

[4] The term *pantomime* is usually used for total body actions.

only if there is nothing unusual in the present situation to call for a different reaction."

The workingman on a construction job may expect a whistle to blow at lunchtime and at quitting time. He may, however, stop even if the whistle fails to blow. On the other hand, he may continue for a brief time *after* the blowing of the whistle if present conditions call for such behavior. The riveter with a hot rivet in his hand is not likely to drop his material merely because the whistle has blown. He is more likely either to continue putting the rivet in the metal or to place the rivet where it will be out of harm's way.

For most of us a green light stands for "go." We do not, however, insist that a green light be present in order to make us go. Some road crossings have no lights. We "go" or "stop" according to the total situation. Occasionally, if there is urgent reason for speed, we may "go" on a red or yellow light. What we do is to evaluate the situation that involves the symbol and the usual reaction to it. If the conditions warrant it, if there is nothing unusual in the total situation, we react in the conventional or customary way. If unusual conditions prevail: if, for example, a child is crossing against a red light, or an automobile is stalled in our path, or another car is "going through" a red light, we do not feel compelled to "go" merely because we are faced with a green light.

If we were to respond to a symbol in a consistent and invariable way regardless of the set of conditions, we would then be reduced to an animal level of behavior. The symbol would then have become completely identified with the thing with which it is associated. The dog who was trained (conditioned) to respond to expect food at the ringing of a bell continued for a long time to salivate and show other responses to food whenever he heard the particular bell ring, even though food was no longer presented to him. Another dog, having learned to recognize the sound of an opening door, would run to the door every time he was able to hear it being opened, even though he did not wish to leave the house. Such behavior reveals an inability to evaluate, to reserve judgment while conditions are being surveyed and assessed. This may be designated as *signal responses.*

When we respond to symbols without reservation and in an invariable manner, we are behaving below our highest level of capability. Such behavior may take place when we are tired, or emotionally disturbed, or intellectually distracted. As an occasional incident of a total pattern, nonevaluative behavior has significance according to the occasion. If, however, nonevaluative reaction characterizes the general behavior of a person, he has given up the most important feature of human behavior. He is no longer exercising the distinctively human capability to withhold or delay a response until it has been determined that conditions are appropriate for the expected response to be made. He is behaving in a low-level, *unconditional manner.*

Specific (differential) responses

There is another important way in which our ability to deal with symbols differs from that of animals. We are able to use symbols to convey highly specific ideas and to get highly specific responses. We are able to use symbols to present shades of differences in ideas, and to respond to symbols that stand for concepts or objects nearly alike but different in some important respect. We can think and talk about water, hot water, cold water, lukewarm water, distilled water, and other kinds of water. The animal is able to make his wish for quenching his thirst known by going to his customary place for getting water and hoping that someone will observe him going there. If he is not observed, he may bark to attract attention and then repeat his action. If the dog is given water he has the choice of drinking it or rejecting it. He is not able to specify what it is about the water that dissatisfies him: nor is he able to indicate what kind of water would be more to his liking. Most human beings who have learned to speak can be more specific in revealing their likes or dislikes. We are able to ask for a drink as specialized as "a coffee soda with vanilla ice cream, whipped cream, and chocolate sprinkles."

Through our ability to deal with symbols specifically, we are able to present specific situations through words, and to get specific responses. Through specific symbol use accompanied by vocal coloring and gesture, we are able to convey innuendoes and implications in our thinking. We are able to be either blunt or subtle, cruel or gentle, kind or unkind, according to our thoughts and feelings.

NONSYMBOLIC LANGUAGE

As human beings we are ordinarily capable of dealing with symbols in specific ways. As indicated in an earlier discussion, it is, however, not always necessary or appropriate that we do so. Sometimes, and for some of us rather frequently, the situation in which the symbol is used requires that a general rather specific response be made. When acquaintances on meeting greet each other with "How are you?" a report of health status is seldom expected. The "Fine, thank you" response, even though it may be literally untrue, is nevertheless appropriate for the speech situation. This kind of word usage is not specifically symbolic. Its symbolic value is general and pertains to the situation as a whole rather than to the individual words or even to the statement per se.

Language is also used without regard to the specific symbol value of words when we speak to express our feelings rather than our thoughts. The language of love and of hate, of tender feelings and of violent emotions, is nonspecific and nonsymbolic. If it were otherwise, persons in love would accuse one another of talking nonsense in the early stages of their romance. If words were always specifically symbolic, we would not, when angry, call one another names that are impossible of literal application.

Words, then, may be symbolic and highly specific. When there is such need, those of us who are normal are ordinarily capable of using symbols on this high intellectual level. We do not, however, always need to use words on this high intellectual level. It is frequently appropriate to use words nonspecifically and nonsymbolically. This point is considered at some length in the discussion on the functions and levels of speech (see pages 2–7).

WHICH IS TO BE MASTER?

This is an appropriate time to return to the question at the opening of the chapter: *Which is to be master*—the words or the speaker of the words? The words spoken or the person responding to the words?

Taboos

Whenever we respond to words as if they had powers and potentials other than those we give them, we are permitting the words to be our masters. To some degree almost all speakers permit themselves to be victimized by words. There are some words we do not speak in polite society; there are other words we do not speak with propriety in mixed company, even though the words may be known, understood, and used by all members of the company regardless of sex. In brief, even in our highly civilized society some words are considered *taboo*. The largest number of taboo words are those referring to biological functions, sex, illness, and death.

Attributed power

Words also become our masters when we respond to them as if they had the characteristics or powers of the things for which they stand. We react as word victims when we avoid using words for fear that their use might somehow cause undesirable events to happen. Many small children have been hushed, scolded, or slapped for innocently asking about a sick person, "Will he die?" Some elderly persons will not use and do not like to hear of anything that is *terminal*.

Overgeneralization

In still another way we reveal that we are sometimes the victims rather than the masters of our words. In some parts of the United States a person is viewed with negative reservation merely because he is a Yankee. In many parts, and in many countries, an alien—any alien—is held suspect. In other parts, or among certain groups, to call a person a Republican or a Democrat is to indicate his undesirability as a member of society. Among some groups of Republicans or Democrats, a person who is a liberal is, without reservation, considered undesirable. For some industrialists, a labor leader cannot possibly be considered an acceptable member of society. And many labor leaders return the compliment, or lack of compliment, to industrialists.

Southerners and Northerners; Republicans, Democrats, and Socialists; industrialists and union leaders share the fault of *overgeneralization*. When the Northerner reacts to all Southerners as he has learned, correctly or incorrectly, to react to one or more Southerners, he is overgeneralizing. When a labor leader assumes that every industrialist by virtue of his being an industrialist is necessarily opposed to the workingman, the labor leader is overgeneralizing. He is responding to the word as he did to a particular person with whom the word is associated. Unfortunately he is also responding to the person as he responded to the word. And in each response of the "Oh, he's a ——" type, there is considerable margin for error.

MAKING MEANINGS CLEAR

Narrowing the approximations

The point has been emphasized that we communicate only approximate meanings. Exact communication of thought is not possible except under circumstances difficult to conceive. These circumstances would require that the speaker and listener have identical experiences in regard to the language symbols used, and identical reactions to the experiences. It is obvious that if we were reluctant to communicate except where listener and speaker showed identical experiences, there would be little or no communication. Speaking would be a lost art.

Though precise communication of meaning is not possible, moderately accurate communication is within the limits of our capabilities. The basic task is one of *narrowing* the extent *of the* approximation so that there is a reasonable chance that speaker and listener are responding to essentially the same symbol situation. This may be accomplished through at least two approaches.

Increasing respect for listener

The first approach calls for increasing the respect we have for our listener. If we are speakers genuinely interested in communicating ideas, we must be willing to talk in language understandable to our listeners. We must be willing to take pains to select not only words but sentence constructions for their meanings. Our words should be so presented that our meanings become apparent. That implies that when a speaker uses language he should have reason to believe that (1) the words are within the known vocabulary inventory of the listener; (2) the particular meaning of the possible meanings of the word is likely to be recognized by the listener; (3) the language context, sentence structure, and speaking situation make it likely that the particular meaning is brought out. It makes a difference whether a statement such as "I need gas" is spoken at an automobile service station, at a dentist's office, or over the telephone to a clerk of a utility company.

All of this is another way of saying that words are symbols, and *stand for* things. If we really wish to be understood we must make our symbols stand *as near as they can* for the same things in our listeners' minds as they do in our minds *at the moment of speaking*. The meanings of the word symbols we use are not inherent in the words. They are in our minds. We must not assume that the same meaning—the same response to the symbol—will occur in the listener merely because it is present in us.

Are we sure of what we mean?

Unless we can, without doubt or indecision, answer "yes" to this question, we have no right to expect our listener to figure out what we mean. If we are hazy in our thinking, our approximations will be wide of the mark. If our feelings are so strong that our listeners respond to the affective tones (the manner) rather than to the words (the matter) of our speech, we will not be making our meanings clear. Our feelings will have intruded themselves in the way of our meanings.

Determining the intention of the speaker

Essentially, when a listener tries to determine what a speaker intends by the words he uses, he is indicating his respect for the speaker. Because words in and out of verbal context are capable of many meanings, the matter of *intention* is often crucial. Dialogues such as the following between husband and wife may suggest what may develop if either fails to recognize the intention of the other.

> "Darling, mother wrote that she is coming for a visit next week. Do you mind?"
> "No, not at all, why should I mind?"
> "Well, if you cared for me, even if you didn't for mother, you would mind in a nice way. You might even be glad that mother is coming so I wouldn't need to worry about her."
> "Oh, I didn't know you worried about your mother. Is anything wrong?"
> "See, you don't even care enough for me to know when I'm worrying, about mother, or anything. No wonder you don't mind. You don't mind about mother, or what I wear, or how I feel, all you do care about is——."

Listener attitude

Because words may have many meanings, understanding is what emerges out of a relationship between a speaker and a listener. If it is our purpose to understand what a speaker is trying to communicate by the words he uses, we must not only hear his words, but become sensitive to the intentions of the speaker. To understand a speaker we must learn to listen to what he intends his words to mean. If our own intentions prevail, if we assume that verbal utterances necessarily mean what we would mean if the utterances were ours, understanding will suffer. If it is our sincere wish to understand the persons with whom we must talk and interact, then we, as listeners, must behave as generously as if we were about to be speakers. We shall have more to say on this point in our discussion of speech and personality (Chapter 10).

The general semantic approach[5]

The general semantic approach emphasizes the use of aids and devices for narrowing the approximations to make meanings clear. The most widely used of the semantic devices is the *subscript*. The subscript is an index used to indicate that among a number or series of similar words or terms, the particular word or term is *different* in some important way or ways from the others. For example, $horse_1$ is *not* $horse_2$, is *not* $horse_3$. . . . $Industrialist_1$, is *not* $industrialist_2$, is not $industrialist_3$. . . . Union $leader_1$ is *not* union $leader_2$, is *not* union $leader_3$. . . .

A second frequently used semantic device is the *dating of terms*. In effect, dates are a special kind of index. They are used to emphasize that *meanings change with time*. We can readily understand that John $Jones^{1950}$ is *not* John $Jones^{1960}$, is *not* John $Jones^{1970}$. . . . A span of thirty years would be expected to make a difference in John Jones' appearance, physical endurance, and thinking. We should also be able to understand that United States foreign $policy^{1960}$ was *not* United States foreign $policy^{1970}$, and may *not be* United States foreign $policy^{1980}$. . . .

A third device is the use of *modifying terms* to limit the extent of a generalized statement. Such terms include *seems to me, I believe, I think, from my point of view, etc.* We can evaluate the effect of modifying or conditional terms by comparing the following paired statements:

John Smith is reactionary in his political thinking.
As I see it, John Smith is reactionary in his political thinking.

Living in the suburbs is dull.
I find that living in the suburbs is dull.

Moving pictures are a waste of time.
For me, moving pictures are a waste of time.

---

[5] Semantics is a subdivision of linguistics dealing with word meanings. The *general semanticist* employs the study of symbols and meanings in an effort to improve human adjustment.

This kind of modifying terms reveals the speaker's awareness that his judgments are subjective. In effect, the speaker is saying that he has come to a personal conclusion based on his own observation and that he is speaking only for himself. Other modifying terms limit the condition or conditions according to which a statement may be valid. *Conditional terms* include *at the present time, in our country, in our culture, under existing conditions,* etc. Comparing the following will point up the differences:

> The struggle for power between labor and capital is inevitable.
> *Under existing conditions,* the struggle for power between labor and industry is inevitable.

> Women are dependent persons.
> *In our culture,* women frequently become dependent persons.

The use of semantic devices has serious shortcomings as well as virtues. To use them often in spoken language would result in a somewhat cumbersome phraseology. Too many modifying terms give the listener an impression that the speaker is either overcautious or insecure. It is difficult for a speaker to sound convincing if his statements are characterized by many *if*'s, *and*'s, and *it seems to me*'s. The outstanding value of the semantic devices is to create a feeling and a point of view as to the need for accuracy in language usage. This point of view is expressed by Wendell Johnson:

> A considerable amount of practice in using the devices is essential—if one is to develop the "feel" for their semantic significance. Once this "feel" is acquired to a reasonably high degree, one need not use the devices outwardly or actually, except now and then when they are especially to be stressed. Otherwise, their use is a matter of mutual understanding between speaker and listener . . . , an agreement or bargain.[6]

Another general semantic device is the use of quotes around specific words. When a particular written word is modified by quotes, we indicate that we are using the word in a special way and an individual way, that we are aware, and are cueing our reader, of this unusual use. Unfortunately it is difficult to hear "quotes" when one is a listener. Some speakers help the listener to overcome this difficulty by gesturing "quotes"

[6] Wendell Johnson, *People in Quandaries* (New York: Harper & Row, 1946), p. 224.

with the index and middle fingers of the hands as a particular word is uttered. When a speaker with a general semantic orientation uses "quotes," he is trying to indicate to his listener that he is aware of his subjectivity or of the individual extended meaning he is giving to a word, and he hopes that the listener will take this into consideration as he evaluates what he hears.

PRACTICAL APPLICATIONS

At this point the reader may be posing a pertinent question. He may be asking himself and the author: "Now that I know more about the meaning of meaning, what am I supposed to do about it?" Some answers to the anticipated question were implied in the present chapter. An effort was made to establish a point of view or attitude toward speech and language which would be helpful in our thinking and in our speaking. In later chapters we will make more specific applications of our study of meaning. We will learn how to apply our information as conversationalists, public speakers, or public readers. We will see how an understanding of meaning can be of help in the preparation and delivery of spoken material. We will also see how the point of view of *proper evaluation* of language and speech situations may help us to reduce the terrifying influence of the bogey called Stage Fright.

SUMMARY

Meaning is the way we respond to situations. The meaning of a word is the way or ways we are able to respond to the word.

Words have relatively constant or core meanings and less constant subjective meanings. The meaning of a given word is determined by several factors which include:

1. The circumstances and the time the word is used.
2. The verbal context and construction.
3. The attitude of the speaker.
4. The manner in which the word is spoken.

Listening and speaking are decoding-encoding processes.

Words have little value in communication unless speaker and listener share a common reaction to them.

Identity of meaning is not possible. At best we are able to understand only approximately what we hear.

Few if any words have inherent meanings. Words acquire meanings through a process of association.

Words may be said to have personal, subjective meanings and objective meanings. Objective meanings are found in the dictionary. Personal meanings vary with the individual.

Some words are frequently associated with feelings rather than thinking. Such words may be said to have *affective connotations.*

A *symbol* is something that *stands for* something else. Human beings are intellectually superior to animals because they are usually able not to confuse *stands for* with *is.* Human beings are able to make evaluative judgments about symbol situations. Animals are not able to evaluate or reserve either judgment or action to symbol situations. In addition, human beings are able to use symbols to convey highly specific ideas and to get highly specific responses. Animals do not possess this ability. Human beings, however, do not always react or need to react to symbols on their highest level of capability.

Meanings can be made clear by narrowing the area of approximation. This aim may be accomplished by having the speaker place himself more completely at the disposal of the listener. The speaker must take the trouble to use words in such a way that (1) the words are likely to be within the vocabulary inventory of the listeners; (2) the particular meaning of the word is likely to be recognized by the listener; (3) the language context clarifies word meaning; and (4) speaker and listener respect one another's intentions.

We are not likely to make our meanings clear unless (1) we have a strong wish to do so, and (2) we are certain of what we mean when we speak.

Another way of clarifying meaning is through the approach of the general semanticist. This approach emphasizes technical devices such as *subscripts, dates, modifying terms,* and *conditional terms* and a general understanding that the speaker is saying what he has to say with "semantic modifiers" implied even when they are not specifically stated.

QUESTIONS AND EXERCISES

1. (a) What is the meaning of *meaning?* (b) What factors determine the meanings of a word? (c) Over which of the factors does a speaker have control? (d) Why is identity of meaning seldom possible?

2. (a) What is a symbol? (b) What is a symbol reaction? (c) When is language used in a nonsymbolic way?

3. Why is the sentence rather than the word the unit of meaning?

4. How many meanings do you have for the words *case, charge, front, matter, pot, gun, run, shop, water?* Check your list of meanings against those given in an unabridged dictionary. Bring out the various meanings of one of these words by using it in several different sentences.

5. Bring out as many meanings as you can for the word *yes* through changes in the manner of utterance. Through gesture or pantomime.

6. What is the first reaction (meaning) you have to the words *liberal, conservative?* Check your reaction with those of five friends or acquaintances. Were the reactions consistent with their known attitudes?

7. Differentiate between the objective meaning and your personal meaning for the following words: *Chinaman, father, college, fascist, snake, lizard, statesman, winter, childhood, politician, bachelor, international banker, chauvinist, liberated.*

8. Indicate the relationship between language and symbols. What kind of symbols do we use in spoken language?

9. Differentiate between an evaluative reaction and a signal reaction. List five words to which you are especially inclined to give signal reactions. Can you explain why?

10. Are there any words considered *taboo* in your social group? Can you account for the basis of the *taboo?*

11. What is the linguistic fault of *overgeneralization?* List five examples in which editorial writers or newspaper columnists reveal this fault.

12. Are there any taboo words today that were not present before the civil rights movement?

13. What has been the effect of "women's lib" on the use of language in public places and in mixed company?

RECOMMENDED READINGS

EISENSON, J., J. J. AUER, and J. V. IRWIN. *Psychology of Communication.* New York: Appleton-Century-Crofts, 1963, chap. 7.

FROMKIN, V. A. "Slips of the Tongue." *Scientific American,* **229**:6 (December 1973), 110–117.

HAYAKAWA, S. I. *Language in Thought and Action.* New York: Harcourt Brace Jovanovich, Inc., 1964.

HEBB, D. O., W. E. LAMBERT, and G. R. TUCKER. "A DMZ in the Language War." *Psychology Today,* April 1973, pp. 55–62.

JOHNSON, W. *Your Most Enchanted Listener.* New York: Harper & Row, Publishers, Inc., 1956.

"Communication," *Scientific American,* **227** (Sept. 1972). This entire issue is devoted to communication, animal and human.

Chapter 10

Speech & Personality

WHAT IS PERSONALITY?

In our discussion of meanings we presented an underlying notion that meanings are the many ways persons respond to events, including verbal events. The term or verbal event *personality* is an excellent example of one with a multitude of meanings. The inquisitive student with time to investigate the meanings, the implications, of the multifaceted term personality might, time permitting, discover more than fifty definitions in the psychological literature. Investigations in the popular writings among the "How to Improve Your Personality" type of books and articles might increase the "definitions" with each writing. We shall, therefore, not undertake a survey of the literature, but instead move to our concept of *personality*.

As we shall use the term *personality*, we shall emphasize two related aspects: (1) A personality is as the person behaves. (2) A personality is for the most part what the individual thinks of himself.

The behaving individual, if he is at all sensitive to his behavior, has some awareness of the effect he has on others. In some instances he may exaggerate this effect and in others underestimate it. In any event, the "feedback" influence of the individual's own behavior is an influence that determines future behavior. Personality, therefore, is a product of interacting influences, the resultant of "forces" of the individual acting upon other persons in the environment and the return influences of the environment on himself. Because the resultant is an estimate or judgment of one person, the forming and ever-modifying personality becomes and is continually becoming what the individual thinks of himself. Diagrammatically, the interacting forces may be represented as shown in Figure 10–1.

We make varying impressions and leave more or less lasting impressions upon others according to the immediate and residual effects of our behavior. Such impressions are an important product of the personalities of *the others*. An individual may be considered either aggressive or charming or inconsiderate or thoughtful by virtue of the "same" overt act. Thus, a man in a crowded bus who gets in the way of another male passenger to make it possible for a woman passenger to occupy a newly vacated seat may create several different impressions. The woman in the situation may consider the intruding man to be a gentleman because he did not take the seat for himself. The obstructed male, especially if he is

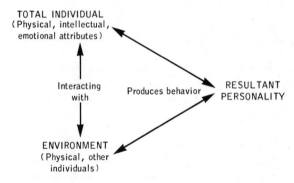

FIGURE 10–1

not as tall or husky as our first man, may consider our "gentleman" to be an aggressive bully. Still another observer may consider him foolish for not following the—or his—principle of every man for himself. Each, according to his own light, and his own inclinations, is exercising a judgment and making his own interpretation of the observed behavior of someone else.

An individual may seem to have more than one personality according to relatively established and yet different patterns of his behavior in "typical" situations. An employee may behave as a docile Mr. Milquetoast on his job and yet be an autocratic and short-tempered Mr. Bangs in his home. An employer, by contrast, may be as harsh and indifferent as his labor-management contractual obligations permit him to be, and yet be a sensitive, considerate husband and father. These seemingly inconsistent and contrasting patterns of behavior may stem from underlying common dynamics. Some individuals must express their aggression and their hostilities somehow and somewhere. They may choose to express such feelings and attitudes according to their own judgments of how their overall needs are best served. So, a cold and indifferent boss may find it the better part of wisdom to be a considerate husband and father in contrast to a timid employee who finds it necessary to "rule his roost."

Personality, it appears, is easier to describe than to define. It is the sum total of our reactions and interactions. It is each of us somehow identified as an *I*, acting as a resultant of an organized complexity of forces making adjustments to a continuously changing environment. Personality is neither constant nor wholly consistent, nor should constancy and consistency be the individual goal. Except for those who may confuse immobility with stability, unvarying and completely predictable behavior has little virtue. The normal adult abandons the behavior of his childhood, however successful such behavior may have been in satisfying his early and immediate needs. This includes the kind of talking—the speech behavior —that may be acceptable in a child but would characterize the adult as being childish and immature.

THE MAKING OF A PERSONALITY

While many factors and forces combine with temporary and maintaining influences to produce *a personality* (note the *a* to emphasize unity), there are six aspects of the question of personality we believe should be emphasized.

1. Personality is the expression of many physical, environmental, and psychological forces and influences; some are inherited and others are acquired. For example, how one is likely to look is a physical factor. How we estimate and respond to our "looks" and what appearance we present in terms of our "looks" are products of environmental and psychological factors.
2. Personality is the expression of the individual's judgments and values and the attitudes that are initially shaped and continually modified by interaction with a culture at large and a subculture, or subcultures, in particular. We are citizens of a country (culture at large) and live in a community, are members of a family, attend given schools, work at special jobs (subcultures in particular), etc., etc.
3. Personality, with its many possible meanings, nevertheless implies that there are two prevalent kinds of reactions: (a) those that determine what, at a given time and in a given situation, an individual is likely to do; and (b) those that influence the reactions or effects on others of the behaving person—the personality-in-action—with whom we happen to be concerned.
4. The developing personality anticipates certain reactions from members of his environment and modifies whatever behavior he might otherwise express in the light of these anticipations.
5. The individual's *self-concept,* the image the individual has of his own personality, is determined by his anticipation and the realization or outcome of these anticipations as he responds to the reaction he has evoked.
6. A personality is the expression of the "essence" of the individual's relatively enduring traits organized in a relatively consistent manner so that it becomes possible to expect a line or mode of behavior from the personality in action. A *trait* may be any particular or distinguishable enduring way in which one individual differs from another.

PERSONALITY AND SPEECH: RELATED DEVELOPMENT

Personality is expressed in each act of our behavior. Beginning with the moment of birth and the accompanying cry, virtually all of our behavior is accompanied by some act of inner or overt speech. At birth, crying is purely reflexive. It is a product of physiological activity involving the muscles of the body as a whole, including those of phonation (vocalization). Cries of healthy, newborn babies sound pretty much alike. So, for a brief time at least, are their personalities, which may be characterized as indefinite or nebulous. As infants become conscious of being alive, as they become aware of physical changes and of their responses to them, as they begin to have needs, there is more vocalization. The vocalization is expressive, and the expressions of personality make their appearance. The happy baby reveals his happiness by "contented sounds." The unhappy baby keeps himself and others busy by crying; we label him a "colicky baby." If he does a fair amount of cooing but does not overlook the usefulness of vigorous crying, we may think of him as a "determined baby."

As small children learn to use words, physical activities are usually accompanied by speech; the small child behaves and talks about his behavior. He plays and talks aloud—to himself and to others. He begins to entertain ideas and to work out problems. He expresses not only his wishes and his feelings but his thinking as well. The small child reveals in his speech that he is conscious of what is going on about him. He tells us of his strivings and of his adjustments; his speech indicates that intellectually, physically, and emotionally he is functioning as an integrated entity. We become aware of the child as a unique human being and as a personality.

The child growing up reveals his development and growth through speech. Speech development reflects intellectual, physical, and emotional "growing up"—or failure to grow up. Almost all conscious behavior is accompanied by some form of speech. Consequently, speech—words and the way they are used—begins to stand for the adult. If, through speech, a man tells us that he has not given up speaking and thinking as a child, we think of him as infantile. If a man's concepts are narrow and his abstractions inappropriate, we think of him as dull. Through the words and voice we hear, we form impressions of people we may never see. The personality pictures we have of radio performers are based entirely on their speech. If we are able to observe a man's actions, we have a more complete basis for forming a judgment of his personality. Right or wrong, we assume that the person is as he speaks.

Through speech we exercise control over our environment. The infant accomplishes control through crying. The infant has relatively few needs, so that crying is generally adequate as a method of control. Many of the infant's needs are anticipated for him, so frequently even crying is not necessary. The child has more needs than the infant, and less is done for him in anticipation of his wishes and wants. The child, therefore, must use language for a satisfying existence. The child who fails to develop adequate language must either reduce his wants or be frustrated. We know that children whose vocabularies are inadequate for their environment tend to be frustrated. They reveal frustration through crying, temper tantrums, and other nonverbal means of expression.

The maturing individual, with his complexity of wants and wishes, has an increased need to use language in order to control his environment. Through speech he satisfies some of his wants and wishes, and agrees to delay in the satisfaction of others. Through speech the maturing individual adjusts to his environment and assists the environment in adjusting to him. Maturity implies ability to make necessary adjustments. It implies knowing when to yield, when to compromise, and when to be insistent on having one's way. It implies knowing how to establish a balance between an individual's demands and the demands of his environment. The mature, well-adjusting personality does not make excessive demands on his environment. Neither does he permit the environment to make excessive demands on him.

The personality we reveal through speech is the result of a continuous process of growing. Though growth is a continuous process, it is not always a smooth and even process. Speech develops and parallels intellectual, physical, and emotional growth. When the three aspects of growth are well integrated, speech and personality are well integrated. Disturbances in growth, temporary or permanent, are reflected in the individual's speech. From time to time, minor disturbances are to be expected. They are part of the "normal personality." Perfection in speaking at all times and under all circumstances rarely, if ever, occurs. The "normal personality" does not strive to achieve perfection in speaking at all times and for all occasions. Some margin for error must be allowed for speech behavior as well as for behavior in general.

THE NORMAL WELL-ADJUSTING PERSONALITY AND SPEECH BEHAVIOR

Vocabulary

In our discussion on conversation in the next chapter we emphasize the need for the speaker to respect his listener if he—the speaker—is speaking to somebody with an expectation of being understood. So, a normal speaker makes an initial selection of words—says what he has to say in words the listener should be able to understand. In any speaking situation, in conversation or in public speaking, the normal speaker observes his listener for reactions, for "feedback" so that he may learn from the observed reactions whether he has been understood. If the reactions suggest a lack of understanding or of the speaker's intention, the normal speaker adjusts his words or his manner of speaking and tries again. In short, the normal speaker realizes that unless he is speaking only for or to himself, he must make verbal adjustments to his listeners. Such adjusting does not imply speaking down or using a vocabulary limited to the first thousand or two thousand words most frequently used in our language. Adjusting does imply taking the trouble, when necessary, to define unusual words or words used for a special meaning. Further, it implies the use of examples and the expansion of explanations or the rephrasing of a statement so that the speaker's message, or the point of the story, may be understood.

Voice

The voice of the speaker, the variation in its attributes—loudness, quality, pitch range, and the rate of utterance—should reveal the thinking and feeling of the speaker and be appropriate to the speaking situation. The listener should not need to ponder what the speaker's vocal changes mean because the vocal changes should be consonant with the speaker's meanings. The voice should sound emphatic when the speaker wishes to be emphatic, without suggesting aggression or hostility. The speaker's voice should be able to invite attention to an idea or a shade of meaning or a state of feeling, and yet not be obvious or infantile. The speaker's voice should be easy to listen to and readily heard and yet not be overloud. Control of the attributes of voice requires inner control and a constant response to the listener's reactions. Ordinarily, the speaker's wish to accomplish these objectives is sufficient to ensure the accomplishment.

Gestures

The speaker who is well adjusted has probably incorporated gestures as part of his expressive verbal behavior. Gestures are used to reinforce his meanings and to communicate his feelings. In any speaking situation the well-adjusting speaker uses gestures as he does his words, with an attitude of respect for his listeners. If the gestures get in the way of his ideas, if the response to them is negative or inappropriate, the use of gestures must be modified. Occasionally speakers reveal anxiety or discomfort through the repeated use of a movement or an action that is tic-like and distracting. If this is the case, the gesture should be controlled. For the most part, however, gestures tend to be produced "naturally" and accompany the speaker's verbal behavior without need for conscious concern.

NORMAL SPEAKER-LISTENER RELATIONSHIPS

A normal relationship between speaker and listener necessarily implies a wish for mutual understanding. Underlying this wish, or attitude, as we have emphasized elsewhere, is an obligation to appreciate the intention of what is said. This means that the speaker must have insight into his own intentions. He must know not only what he is saying, what he wishes his listeners to understand, but also what he really intends by his utterances. The listener, for his part, must not ignore intention if, for some reason, the utterance—the words used—seems not to be consonant with the intentions. Words, as we know, have many meanings, and words in sentences may have special meanings. The well-adjusting speaker should be able to project himself into the role of the listener and to be objective about whether what he is saying and the manner of his speaking are likely to communicate his thoughts, his feelings, and his intentions. The listener, in turn, should be fair minded. Such state of mind becomes possible if the listener does a bit of projecting on his own and assumes that what he may have to say when he becomes a speaker may also be understood or misunderstood, according to the listener-to-be's ability to appreciate intention as well as literal meanings.

A well-adjusting person is aware that some words and some ways of saying some words are likely to produce negative emotional reactions. The well-adjusting speaker avoids loaded terms, or at least the "loaded" way of using some words unless, for some special reason, this is his conscious intention.

We shall try to highlight some of the difficulties we have with our verbal behavior in the discussion of personality maladjustments and speech. We hope that from this approach the reader will gain insights into what might be avoided if he wishes to be considered a well-adjusting person.

PERSONALITY MALADJUSTMENT AND SPEECH

Speech of the moderately maladjusted

How, through speech, do we recognize the not-so-well-adjusted individual? We learn much from the voice we hear. There is the voice that whines when there is no occasion for whining. There is the voice that apologizes for being heard when the speaker has a right to be heard. There is the voice that "shouts down" even in the face of no opposition. There is the voice of the irritable and the voice of the plaintive. There is the voice of the person who for too long has enjoyed ill health and only regretfully admits being well. All these, and others, are the voices of not-so-well-adjusted personalities.

The not-so-well-adjusted tell us much about themselves in the words they speak and in their responses to the words they hear. Language content may be narrow and limited. The not-so-well-adjusted individual may specialize in a single subject that is laboriously presented in pseudoconversation without regard to time, place, or number of previous repetitions. Listeners may have to hear, for the nth time, about the oh-so-big-fish that got away, or about numerous allergies, or about a precocious grandchild, nephew, or niece. What the speaker has to say may be interesting or even fascinating—but only the first or second time at an appropriate place.

The one-topic specialist frequently makes a poor listener. He speaks his piece but reveals no willingness to listen. Over the telephone he has his say and then, perhaps even rudely, cuts the conversation short. The listener is left with a mouthful of unspoken words and an elevated blood pressure. If we interpret the behavior of the one-topic specialist as mere rudeness, we may be wrong. Probably a more nearly correct interpretation is that this kind of speaker feels that he cannot make adequate responses on another person's level of thinking. Narrowness of language content is probably a reflection of a speaker's limited ability in a world of words other than his own.

Not all the not-so-well-adjusted are one-topic specialists. Some avoid words on any topic. Their part of a conversation consists of a begrudgingly emitted "uh-uh," or an occasional "umm." Still others are experts on almost any topic. You start it and they take it over. They listen just long enough to take off with a "now, let me tell you about my experience." From that time on, the conversation becomes a monologue. Some of it may be entertaining or even funny, but essentially it is a pseudoconversation with a giving or at least a production of words, but without a willingness to be receptive, to listen to the words of another.

These speakers reveal considerable difficulty in getting along in a world of words, at least when the words are not, for the most part, their own. The nonverbal grunter is probably insecure about what his verbal responses should be. He avoids saying the wrong thing by saying next to nothing. He reveals, however, that he is aware of social proprieties by punctuating what he hears with his occasional grunts. The expert-on-any-topic speaker does not take a chance on misunderstanding what someone else may have to say to him. By taking over, he makes his further understanding of speech unnecessary. What he fails to understand is the give-and-take nature of conversation; what he succeeds in making his listeners understand is that, as a speech personality, he is inadequate.

Somewhat related to the nonverbal grunter is the speaker whose conversational responses consist of a few set but not always pat phrases. Instead of an "uh-uh" we might get a "how nice," or "lovely," or "you don't say" to what we do say. A response from a limited inventory of responses is made to a speech situation without regard to the nature or intent of the situation. Occasionally the set phrase may have a grandiose ring and include a "Why, that's just devastating," or "Isn't it simply divine!" Profanity and slang are other resources of the speakers of set phrases. This kind of limited language usage, if it is characteristic of the speech responses of an individual, may indicate rigidity of personality. It may also indicate the individual's inability or unwillingness to attend to speech closely enough to make appropriate, rather than set or stereotyped, responses.

The literal speaker

Of another kind is the speaker who insists that the words you speak and he presumably is trying to understand must mean what he means when he uses the words. He will take a word out of context and argue with you about its meaning. Frequently he forgets that the context includes the manner of speaking, the nature of the speech situation, and the sequence of events that led up to the use of the word. For this occasionally verbose but almost always rigid personality, words may mean only what he or the dictionary permits them to mean. This speaker may know many words, but he does not know the ways of words. He may even pursue the study of words as some persons pursue the accumulation of money. A large vocabulary, a memory for literal definitions of words, an exactness and precision of speech, round out the picture. Unfortunately formalized rigidity of thinking and of language usage are the products of the study. Conversations with such a person are not easy. One must be on guard not to use a word in any but the conventionally accepted sense. A conversation becomes a verbal inspection. Each meaning must be in its expected place, or else. . . .

The noncommunicative speaker

For those of us who are at least moderately well adjusted, or adjusting, and who use speech for social contact and communion, it may come as a surprise that some less well-adjusted persons speak only to communicate. Because of this limitation these persons seem noncommunicative. In effect, they are, because speaking for them is generally a one-way affair. A message is spoken, information is verbalized, or a directive given. Unfornately, because there is no personal contact, the speaker does not find out whether he has been understood. Often the "message" is presented without adequate preparation or opportunity for the listener to become ready for what he is to receive. There are no social amenities. There is no verbal equivalent of the Navy's "Now hear this, now hear this." The noncommunicative speaker goes directly to his task; he speaks his piece and assumes that he is through. If the listener indicates that he has not understood this speaker, perhaps only because the listener was not quite ready for the message, the speaker may repeat verbatim what he said the first time. The utterances are likely to be logical, precisely articulated, with each word usually meaning what the dictionary denotes it to mean. Because some listeners may be somewhat less logical and more adjustable, they may not be able to appreciate the appropriateness of this speaker's remarks. All too often the remarks of those who speak presumably only to communicate fail to show an awareness of the situation—the time, the place, and the background and interests of the listener or listeners.

It is quite likely that the noncommunicative speaker is not aware of his own intentions in speaking. He speaks to empty his mind, to get rid of thoughts and words, rather than to share them with others. Perhaps he may feel that his job, if not his duty, is done. He seems to speak to say what he must, rather than to establish contact and so become more truly involved in a communicative situation.

Misevaluations

The not-so-well-adjusted individual is what he is in part because of the way he evaluates what he hears. His evaluations are self-centered. Too often this person fails to determine the intentions of the speaker to whom he is presumably listening because his own intentions get in the way. In contrast, the well-adjusted personality evaluates what he hears in terms of the particular speaker and the background and occasion of the speech. He does not confuse words with the host of meanings that words may have. The well-adjusted personality recognizes that few if any words have inherent meanings, that his use of a word may differ in significance from another person's use of the "same" word. The well-adjusted personality would not feel slighted or insulted because a neighbor's child called him a "silly-willy." First, he would consider that a child is using the phrase. Then he might conjecture that, for this particular child involved, "silly-willy" may be a term of endearment. Finally, he might ask himself what "silly-willy" meant to him. If after pondering the question, he could come to no conclusion, he would decide that this question was one not really worthy of an answer, and so why bother about it after all!

The special aptitude most of us have for misevaluating the words of others is dramatically presented by Dorothy Parker in her story "*Here We Are.*" The scene is a compartment on a train. The characters are two newlyweds. One of the predicaments they talked themselves into follows:

"I guess I will take this darned old hat off," she said.

"It kind of presses. Just put it up on the rack, will you, dear? Do you like it, sweetheart?"

"Looks good on you," he said.

"No, but I mean," she said, "do you really like it?"

"Well, I'll tell you," he said. "I know this is the new style and everything like that, and it's probably great. I don't know anything about things like that. Only I like the kind of a hat like that blue hat you had. Gee, I liked that hat."

"Oh, really?" she said. "Well, that's nice. That's lovely. The first thing you say to me, as soon as you get me off on a train away from my family and everything, is that you don't like my hat. The first thing you say to your wife is you think she has terrible taste in hats. That's nice, isn't it?"

"Now, honey," he said, "I never said anything like that. I only said——"

"What you don't seem to realize," she said, "is this hat cost twenty-two dollars. Twenty-two dollars. And that old horrible blue thing you think you're so crazy about, that cost three ninety-five."

"I don't give a darn what they cost," he said. "I only said—I said I liked that blue hat. I don't know anything about hats. I'll be crazy about this one as soon as I get used to it. Only it's kind of not like your other hats. I don't know about the new styles. What do I know about women's hats?"

"It's too bad," she said, "you didn't marry somebody that would get the kind of hats you'd like. Hats that cost three ninety-five. Why didn't you marry Louise? You always think she looks so beautiful. You'd love her taste in hats. Why didn't you marry her?"

"Ah, now, honey," he said. "For heaven's sakes!"

"Why didn't you marry her?" she said. "All you've done, ever since we got on this train, is talk about her. Here I've sat and sat, and just listened to you saying how wonderful Louise is. I suppose that's nice, getting me all off here along with you, and then raving about Louise right in front of my face. Why didn't you ask her to marry you? I'm sure she would have jumped at the chance. There aren't so many people asking her to marry them. It's too bad you didn't marry her. I'm sure you'd have been much happier."[1]

Levels of significance

The newlyweds in Dorothy Parker's story involved themselves in difficulty because of the failure to appreciate that speech has varying levels of significance. Their states of mind and feeling brought about a verbal entrapment from which neither could escape without the help of the other. Their special situation could and should excuse their dilemma, their temporary, we hope, inability to distinguish between speech as an emotional expression and speech to convey and interchange thought. Faced with the overwhelming situation of the first hours of their marriage, they forgot the importance of the trivial. But many not so newlywed husbands and wives continue to make comparable errors and verbal misevaluations. For some, there is no such occasion as a casual conversation. "How are you?" spoken as a social gesture evokes a detailed account of their medical ailments, past and present. A parting, "So long, hope to see you soon" is likely to result in an actual visit the next day. Feelings may be hurt if the unwitting extender of the invitation did not seem to expect or be prepared for the visitor. All too often, words spoken in jest

[1] From "Here We Are" in *The Portable Dorothy Parker*. Copyright 1943 by Dorothy Parker. Used by permission of The Viking Press, Inc., New York.

are remembered and taken literally and seriously. Weeks after a conversation, the not-so-well-adjusted individual recalls the precise words he has heard and confronts and confounds others with them.

PERSONALITY ADJUSTMENT THROUGH SPEECH

A well-adjusted personality responds to language as part of a total situation in which the language is used. The not-so-well-adjusted individual, and especially the neurotic personality, overlooks one or more significant parts of the situation, and responds inappropriately. Faced with a problem, the neurotic does not have a thorough enough talk with himself. Evidence of research workers reveals that neurotics actually resist a complete verbalization of their problems. The neurotic fails to recall important elements in the situation that created the problem. This memory failure limits the amount of information he must have to arrive at a proper solution. It reduces the likelihood of arriving at a normal, discriminative response.

Insight and speech

Both well-adjusted and poorly adjusted persons talk to themselves. The important difference is that the well-adjusted persons know when and how to do the talking. It is only through talking things over with oneself that insight is attained. Insight is nothing more than a verbalization of a person's problems so that he appreciates how he should relate to them. If the not-so-well-adjusted personality seeks better adjustment, he must learn how to talk to himself. Well-adjusted persons control their behavior through the use of language. Some of the language is subvocal and some is gesture. Adequate adjustment can take place when the individual learns how to speak to himself and for himself in ways appropriate to the situation. Fortunately man can do more with language than talk himself into quandaries and dilemmas. Through speech he can solve his problems and make adjustments to the world in which he lives. In essense, therapy for self-adjustment is a learning process. The learning is achieved when the person knows how and when to speak to himself in appropriate ways to control his own conduct.

Objective listening to one's self

It is important for us not only to be well adjusted, but also to sound and act the part. Though we do not have the gift "to see ourselves as others see us," we can hear ourselves as others hear us. A variety of recording and playback devices make hearing ourselves possible. The most desirable setup for hearing ourselves as others hear us is to be recorded "candidly." But even an intended recording may have great therapeutic values. One adolescent boy with a "cracked, falsetto, alto voice" cringed when he heard his voice played back for him. He pleaded for the help he resisted before he had the opportunity to hear himself. By hearing ourselves we may be able to learn why our listeners do not interpret us as we would like. We may begin to appreciate why the thin voice with the oversupply of rising inflections is not a persuasive voice; or why our listeners took in deadly earnest something we intended in fun. In short, if we are not satisfied with the personality picture others seem to have of us, hearing ourselves as others hear us may provide a basis for making changes.

Reflected behavior

In one sense, we are able to see ourselves as others see us. We tend unconsciously to imitate the physical behavior of those we observe. Looking at a tense individual makes us feel tense and may make us feel uncomfortable. If we regularly become uncomfortable in the presence of another person, we may avoid the person who is the cause of the discomfort. Further, we may conclude that the individual who is the cause has an unpleasant personality. We may come to the same conclusion in regard to persons who are overrelaxed and "sag." Such persons make us feel tired. It is well to remember that we do unto others as they do unto us. If others fidget in our presence, it may be because we make them fidget. If they become tense, it may very well be that they have "caught" the tensions from us. If our listeners slump when we talk to them, they may merely be reflecting our own appearance.

Our gestures as well as our voice and words reveal our personalities. Gestures, as part of the total act of speech, influence communication and help to determine the response we get in speaking. Our actions may contradict our words. A facial grimace or a smile may reveal our attitude more truly than the words we use. The relaxed appearance, the tense look, the tired or bored look, all reveal attitudes that are parts of personality. Through our actions, whether or not accompanied by words, others make assumptions about us and adapt to us. Unfortunately we cannot study our own actions as well as we can our voices and our words. We can, however, study our responses to the actions of others, and then apply some of the conclusions to ourselves.

SUMMARY

Personality is the impressions we make on others and ourselves as a result of our behavior. Personality is most readily expressed in our speech. Through speech we not only express our personalities, but also make adjustments and modifications of behavior which reflect growth and change. Our use of language, voice, and gesture reveals our abilities to get along in our environment. Through speech we can talk ourselves into maladjustment. Fortunately speech is also the means of modification for correcting maladjustment. A proper evaluation of speech, from the point of view of the speaker as well as the listener, will prevent maladjustment.

Sensitivity to the effects of our speech behavior on others should help us to modify undesirable personality aspects.

QUESTIONS AND EXERCISES

1. What is your concept of personality? Explain how it is possible for one individual to have more than one personality. How do you form your judgments of the personalities of persons you meet for the first time?

2. Tune in to a television "soap opera." As soon as you hear each performer speak, form an immediate estimate of his personality. Is your estimate that which the script writer would want you to have?

3. Explain how disturbances of speech and personality are related.

4. Read one or more speeches or essays of three of the following: (a) Harry S. Truman, (b) Franklin D. Roosevelt, (c) Richard Nixon, (d) Robert Kennedy, (e) Martin Luther King, Jr., (f) Buckminster Fuller, (g) Sam Erwin, (h) Lyndon B. Johnson, (i) Abba Eban.
Indicate how each reveals his personality through his words and turn of phrase. For those you have seen on television, in film, or in person, describe characteristic gestures and how they are manifestations of the personality.

5. Are there any radio or television performers who irritate you? Why?

6. Are there any newspaper columnists to whom you object, not because of what they have to say, but because of the way they say it? Indicate, by specific quotation, what you find objectionable. Correct the quotation (edit it) so that it becomes more acceptable to you.

7. Describe briefly some personality characteristics of persons you know who fall into one of the following categories:
   (a) The infantile individual.
   (b) The person with a minute speaking vocabulary.
   (c) The expert-on-any-topic speaker.
   (d) The aggressive asserter.
   (e) The "Well, if that's how you feel about it" type.
   (f) The person who regularly overlooks or misunderstands the intention of the speaker.

8. What speech activities would you recommend for each of the above as aids in the modification of personality?

RECOMMENDED READINGS

EISENSON, J., J. V. IRWIN, and J. J. AUER. *The Psychology of Communication.* New York: Appleton-Century-Crofts, 1963, chap. 19.

FERGUSON, L. R. *Personality Development*. Belmont, Calif.: Wadsworth Publishing Co., Inc., 1970, chaps. 3–5.

HAYAKAWA, S. E. *The Fully Adjusted Personality*, in S. I. Hayakawa (ed.), *Our Language and Our World*. New York: Harper & Row, Publishers, Inc., 1959.

JOHNSON, W. *Your Most Enchanted Listener*. New York: Harper & Row, Publishers, Inc., 1956.

MERLOO, J. A. M. *Conversation and Communication*. New York: International Universities Press, 1952.

STAGNER, R. *Psychology of Personality*. New York: McGraw-Hill Book Company, 1965, chaps. 7–12.

Chapter 11

A Speaker & a Listener

The Basic Ingredients of Conversation

> Most of the successful people I've known are
> ones who do more listening than talking. If
> you choose your company carefully, it's worth
> listening to what they have to say. You don't
> have to blow out the other fellow's light to let
> your own shine.
>
> BERNARD BARUCH

At the peak of protest over the war in Vietnam, the draft, and ROTC, while angry students were occupying faculty offices, classrooms, and even presidential suites, an advertising agency, Campbell-Mithun, Inc., purchased a full-spread advertisement in *Time* magazine. Featured was the huge, contorted face of a man—eyes sharp and narrow, mouth agape, teeth bared, with lips spread, obviously spewing forth vehement, passionate speech. Immediately beneath his lips were three words: talk, talk, talk. Curiously the picture exposed only a part of one ear, emphasizing, perhaps symbolically, the advertiser's message: "What this country needs is a good 5-minute listener," also a quaint twist to Thomas R. Marshall's celebrated aphorism.[1] Offering free buttons inscribed "I'm a listener," the advertiser also demonstrated an awareness of the fundamental elements vital to all successful communication, namely the inseparable links that must join the sender of the message with the receiver, thereby transforming a meaningless monologue into a shared dialogue. "Talk can arouse, but of itself it cannot heal," the writer warned, but "To listen— *truly* listen—is to begin the healing process a wounded nation needs."[2]

---

[1] Marshall, two-term Vice President with Woodrow Wilson, often brought wit and humor to his routine task as the Speaker of the Senate. During a tiresome debate, as one senator droned on about the "needs" of the nation, Marshall turned to John Crockett, the chief clerk of the Senate, and made his famous remark, "What this country needs is a good five-cent cigar."

[2] *Time*, October 5, 1970, pp. 60–61.

In this chapter we shall continue our examination of basic speech concepts as revealed in social conversation (speaking and listening), recognizing that the ingredients of successful interpersonal communication apply to all other forms, including discussion, debate, public speaking, and reading aloud. Not everyone is going to participate in group discussion or debate, and there are some who would avoid the public platform, but there is no place to hide from the daily conversations we inevitably encounter in our homes, dormitories, and classrooms, in our social and business contacts on the local, national, and even international levels. Some occupations depend largely on skillful interviewing techniques, and few if any of us secure a job without a face-to-face encounter with a prospective employer. This everyday, ongoing exchange in sheer volume alone completely dwarfs our uses of other communication forms, including the mass media.

Yet until recently we have given scant attention to discovering what happens during conversation, assuming that normally intelligent persons with adequate skills in reading, writing, and speaking would *ipso facto* become adequately skilled conversationalists. It simply has not happened. As the cynical André Gide observed, "Everything has been said already, but as no one listens, we must always begin again." The outcry of students during the late sixties and early seventies bemoaned the failure of the Establishment—parents, teachers, and employers who didn't, couldn't, or wouldn't "listen." It soon became painfully apparent that highly intelligent persons of all ages, possessing rich, cultural backgrounds and a wide assortment of communication skills, were often notoriously inept in their use of this aspect of interpersonal communication.

Brickman in his popular newspaper cartoon, "The Small Society," vividly portrays a communication breakdown on the family level. Mensch, the father, with fists clenched and one arm raised defiantly, shouts at his bearded, barefoot, bead-bedecked, hippy son, Ethnic, "Why must we always have meaningful dialogue? Why can't we just talk like everybody else?" Mother, vainly wringing her hands, stands helplessly in the generation gap between the irate father and cynical son as Ethnic, eyes closed and arms folded, demonstrates through his nonverbal gestures that he is probably no closer to a "meaningful dialogue" than is his father.

Happily a growing body of knowledge about conversation and listening is available to assist us in understanding and developing our skills in interpersonal communication—skills that can be learned, perhaps even taught. And one of the principal purposes for studying basic speech is to help us develop our skills as conversationalists, perhaps thus enabling us also to discover the secrets of meaningful dialogue.

The listener about to be a speaker as well as the speaker who must be prepared to be a listener must both bear in mind that conversation, in common with all communicative efforts, requires at least two persons engaged in interacting roles. Whether the conversation has as its purpose the clarification of an issue to arrive at "the truth of the moment" or the enjoyment of an anecdote, at least two active persons are needed. At any given time only one can be a speaker and the other must be a listener.

THE ORIGIN AND PURPOSE OF CONVERSATION

When our civilization was young and still without books, conversation provided the primary means of learning and transmitting the cultural patterns and traditions to each new generation. Even with the appearance of written communication, the necessity for oral discussion remained as the best and most frequently used means of understanding and bringing out the meanings in the written word. Educators and students generally agree that learning is promoted in the classroom permeated with planned, purposive conversation known as classroom recitations or discussions. Reading alone is often inadequate without the testing and reinforcement of concepts through speaking and listening. Indeed, in our increasing reliance on the mass media and the spoken word, we are rapidly returning, as Marshall McLuhan reminds us, to the primitive state where oral-aural communication formerly predominated. The home, once a sheltered haven with its library and study as the principal sources of information, has increasingly become a "communication center" loaded with telephones, tape recorders, and television sets fed by satellites and laser light beams, but all dependent on the spoken word and the listening ear.

Conversation, like other forms of communication, begins and sustains itself as intrapersonal communication, so-called "inner speech." Without silent speech—those conversations we hold with ourselves, even while we talk with others—no communication is possible. We are all afflicted to some degree with the Walter Mitty syndrome, generating through inner speech our ideas, hopes, and dreams. We may smile at the old-timer who when asked why he talked to himself so much offered two reasons: first, he liked to talk to a good man and, second, he liked to hear a good man talk. He was simply more audible in his intrapersonal communication than some of his detractors and was trying out his ideas on himself before offering them to others. The lady who asked "How can I know what I think until I've heard what I say?" expressed, perhaps unknowingly, a fundamental element in communication theory as well as the integral relationship between speech and thought. Our ability to hear ourselves before we speak aloud, to listen to ourselves while we speak, and to restate the thoughts we receive from others when they speak to us determines in large measure how close we come to achieving meaningful dialogue.

The purposes and topics for conversations—some planned, others accidental, and many by chance—are as varied as the motivations that bring people together. Through conversation we find friends, meet strangers, exchange ideas, get and give information, console and scold, share our victories and defeats, and sometimes even annoy ourselves and others.

Except as limited by good taste there are no limits to the subject matter of social conversation. It nearly always begins with a "Hi, how goes it? what da yuh know?" But if the casual chatter ever gets beyond the "How are you" stage, for which we rarely want an answer, the topic will likely continue to focus on the "personal" concerns of each participant. This, in an important sense, is as it should be if a knowledge of the subject is a prime criterion for its selection. Indeed, the speaker with knowledge as well as insight into himself has a fascinating topic for conversation, provided that he is not fascinated too long at a time and is capable of appreciating that other speakers may entertain a comparable fascination. Next to themselves, most persons are likely to be interested in talking about their friends. In a sense, this topic is a projection of the primary interest—still themselves.

Some of our supremely satisfying moments come through conversation that opens in the realm of trivia and may even conclude on a note of trivia, or, if the participants are fortunate, on a note of levity. The immediate purpose of most social conversations is the shared pleasure of talking—and of listening. On some occasions it may even reach the ultimate in intellectual stimulation. Dr. A. Whitney Griswold, in his Convocation at Brown University's 191st academic year, caught the essence of conversation at its best when he described it as "an exchange of thought that leaves all parties to it a grain wiser"—and occasionally we may indeed experience one of those rare moments when we may manage to touch or be touched by wisdom.

THE INTERVIEW

The chances of increasing our wisdom are often greater in the interview, a highly formal type of conversation. It is marked by prior planning and more structured procedures. A useful means of securing information, and often a necessary requisite for securing employment, the successful interview requires careful preparation by both parties. Still, many of the same conditions prevail in both interviewing and social conversation, enabling the preceptive participant to learn much about dyadic (person to person) communication from both types of experience.

Primary responsibility for preparation, planning, organization, and timing rests with the interviewer—of course, with the cooperation and consent of the interviewee. If, for example, you are preparing a speech on academic freedom, you may want to secure interviews with prominent faculty members, the president of the local chapter of the AAUP (American Association of University Professors), the dean of faculties, and perhaps even the university president. You will probably also want to seek opinions from members of the business community outside the Groves of

Academe. The problems of establishing mutually satisfactory times and places are yours. When you seek the appointments, you will also want to be as specific as possible about the topics for discussion, e.g., tenure, right of dissent, loyalty oaths, etc. The success of your interview will depend on your advanced planning—your selections of questions as well as their phrasing and sequence.

In the actual interview, after you have established some degree of rapport you should restate the *purpose* of your interview and explain your *intended use* of the information and opinion you receive. A tape recording may prove helpful if your respondent is willing, but he or she may also speak less freely, and you will need to avoid the temptation of allowing the recorder to do your listening for you.

To help minimize losses of information and to avoid mistakes, you should restate succinctly the major items of information and opinion either during the interview or at the close. Anyone interviewed by a reporter for the town or college newspaper is often shocked and dismayed to see quotation marks around certain inflammatory statements attributed to him that he is sure were pure figments of the reporter's imagination. Someone in that dyadic interchange not only failed to use feedback appropriately or ethically but may also have deliberately distorted the message. Euphemistically we may refer to this as "creative interviewing."

A student anxious to improve his or her skills in speech communication will take advantage of every opportunity to participate in interviews, even seeking out situations perceived as potentially uncomfortable, but which may in reality provide stimulating intellectual experiences. The information thus gleaned will often add credibility and support for subsequent speeches and will also give you needed practice for facing a prospective employer when you fill the role of interviewee.

CHARACTERISTICS OF A GOOD CONVERSATIONALIST

Conversation, whether casual or structured, can be no better than its participants. It may, however, be much worse. Usually it reflects the personality traits and attitudes of the participants, intermixed with the speaking and listening skills they bring together during the course of the conversation. Clearly a person successful in one situation might prove inadequate in another setting, and a conversational trait acceptable to one group might prove anathematic to another. Thus, in attempting to isolate conversational standards and norms we always risk the danger of oversimplification and stereotyping. Further, the rapid shifting in speaker-listener roles that normally occurs during social conversation or in the one-to-one interview renders many concepts equally applicable to both parties. Nevertheless, we may still seek with profit the answers to the question: What general characteristics as senders should we cultivate to improve our conversational behavior? Later in the chapter we will offer suggestions to the listener, many of them equally relevant for the speaker.

1. A GENUINE INTEREST IN OTHERS. As we have already noted, the subject of greatest interest to people is "people." And the people most conversationalists are interested in talking about are themselves. One reason we may forget the name of a newly introduced person is our over-riding concern with ourselves and the impression we are making on our new acquaintance. In most of our informal social conversations the topics are highly personal ones about our families, homes, and our states of health, followed perhaps by politics and matters of national and interna-tional interest. The skillful conversationalist, however, is able to move out of the egocentric sphere toward a sensitive concern for the interests and needs of others. Though we may never lose our egocentricity, we may happily discover that great personal satisfaction can be derived from giving pleasure to others. A good conversationalist is one who realizes that normal human beings want to enjoy living, and he must be willing to do his part to make living enjoyable. Egocentric and egotistic self-absorbed persons may perhaps succeed as public speakers, but they are not likely to become good conversationalists.

2. A SKILLFUL APPRAISAL OF THE OCCASION. The behavior of speakers, their choice of topics, their manner of speaking, the words used, and even the clothes worn are determined in some measure by the conversational situation. The rebellion of the late 1960s and early 1970s against the con-ventions and norms of the so-called Establishment radically changed, for better or for worse, some of our notions about appropriate conversational conventions. The move was toward greater informality in dress for all occasions and less concern for adapting language patterns to radically different settings. The blue jeans were considered by some to be as ap-propriate for a visit to the president's office as to the lounge of the dormitory. And language patterns once reserved for members of the same sex were employed freely, even in conversation with conservative mem-bers of the Establishment.

In all probability succeeding generations will develop their own dis-tinctive characteristics, and perhaps be equally shocking to the present student population. A person on the radical fringe, if he is determined to remain inflexible in his conversational approach, should not be surprised if his behavior alienates even some of those who share many of his beliefs. As we have already noted, the interview—a highly specialized form of conversation, and one more directly controllable by one or both partici-pants—calls for language and behavior patterns appropriate to the occa-sion; so it is surprising that students seeking employment in a conserva-tive office are often bewildered when they fail to impress a "square" employer with their "far out" appearance and speech patterns.

3. WARY AND PRUDENT ENGAGEMENT IN CONFRONTATION. Many conver-sations raise differences of opinion, and one of the highly refreshing ex-

periences of college living includes the lively give-and-take, the clash of ideas that enliven the classroom, the dorm, the snack bar, and the college green. The excellent conversationalist, however, avoids turning every occasion into a forensic bout. The individual whose opening response to nearly every remark is, "Well, now, on the other hand . . ." will probably end up convincing no one. Differences of opinion should be aired and persuasion practiced, but no participant should be made to feel ignorant or that his opinion is unworthy of a decent hearing. Persuasion, when it takes place in conversation, should be practiced as a gentle art. When it ceases to be gentle, it is probably out of place. One of the highly satisfying aspects of conversation is that it offers a laboratory in which we can test our ideas and receive direct feedback before offering them to larger groups. But as Francis Bacon cautions, "Discretion of speech is more than eloquence."

4. TOLERANCE. If the conversationalist is to avoid the pitfalls of hasty confrontation, he must generate the wholesome qualities of tolerance, recognizing that we all have weaknesses and shortcomings. He must not assume that a person who disagrees with him is necessarily wrong. Neither will he feel compelled to "show up" another person, even if he knows that the other speaker is mistaken. High on the list of insufferable individuals and inadequate personalities is the one who is always right, who makes undeniable assertions, nonnegotiable demands, and who, moreover, has the facts to prove it. The good conversationalist knows that there may be a wrong time for being right, and does not confuse being right with being righteous. As a general rule he extends himself as far as possible to make the other fellow "look good."

5. A BALANCED SENSE OF HUMOR. Most of the foregoing qualifications will be seasoned by a good conversationalist with a healthy sense of humor. As we shall point out later, humor if skillfully used can serve the public speaker's needs in many ways, but as a double-edged sword it can also destroy. In conversation, wit and apt rejoinder have their places only if they are as enjoyable to the listeners as to the speaker. Oscar Wilde and James Whistler may have been brilliant speakers, but they were poor conversationalists. Their remarks, scintillating but caustic, were more pleasurable to overhear than to hear. Their "retorts perfect" were stoppers to conversation. Some participants on the late TV talk shows are probably better entertainers than models for good conversation. And as Will Rogers once observed, "Everything is funny as long as it is happening to somebody else." Still, the ability to tell an amusing story and to listen to one without interruption even when you've heard it before are necessary skills for the conversationalist. Dr. Martin Grotjahn, Clinical Professor of Psychiatry, in his exhaustive study of humor concludes that "One's sense of humor develops in gradual stages during a lifetime. Every step is connected with the mastery of a new anxiety, and

each conflict mastered at the different developmental stages is marked by a growth of the sense of humor."[3] While we often laugh to keep from crying, our ability to laugh at ourselves helps us develop a sense of proportion about life and people, an invaluable asset for the social conversationalist.

6. GIVE SERIOUS ATTENTION TO THE LANGUAGE STYLE OF CONVERSATION. We pay a high compliment to a public speaker when we describe his delivery and style as conversational. Indeed, the platform lecturer usually succeeds only as he approximates the articulate conversationalist. One of the shortcomings of the students of the late 1960s and early 1970s, despite their lip service to the values of effective communication, was their seeming contempt for a vivid communication style, their use of jargon, at times colorful, but which more often described nothing and degenerated into what one newspaper writer described as "non-verbal ineloquence." Another editor blamed the violence and obscene rhetoric that plagued our campuses and streets in part on the inability of youth to express themselves adequately with language.[4] Bernard Rosenberg in his *Dictionary for the Disenchanted,* published in 1972, defined the overused word "Like" as "an all-purpose expletive. Along with 'you know,' 'hopefully,' 'dig,' and 'man,' it has so enriched American English that we can henceforth do without most of the remaining 600,000 words that still clutter out-of-date dictionaries."[5]

The student of conversation and public speaking would do well to ponder the words of George Orwell in his classic essay, *Politics and the English Language,* revived again by a *Time* correspondent during the 1973–1974 Watergate hearings. "If thought corrupts language, language can also corrupt thought," wrote Orwell in the 1940s, but his words are particularly applicable to our own troubled times. "One ought to recognize," he said, "that the present political chaos is connected with the decay of language and that one can probably bring about some improvement by starting at the verbal end."[6]

7. CULTIVATE EXPERIENCE AND KNOWLEDGE. As a requisite for good conversation, we must not overlook the advantage of having something to say that is worth saying. It is obvious that the broader our experiences, the greater our background for conversation. The more one knows about the workaday world, about life and people, the better acquainted he is with literature, art, music, history, and all that makes up human knowl-

---

[3] Martin Grotjahn, *Beyond Laughter* (New York: McGraw-Hill Book Company, 1957), p. 73. By permission of the author.

[4] "Violent Protest: A Debased Language," *Time,* May 18, 1970, p. 15.

[5] Cited by Melvin Maddocks in *The Christian Science Monitor,* January 11, 1973, p. 7. Also see Norman Cousins, "The Stammering Society," *Saturday Review World,* March 23, 1974, p. 4.

[6] Stefan Kanfer, "Words from Watergate," *Time,* August 13, 1973, p. 20.

edge, the better prepared he is for conversation. The substance of conversation is human experience, direct and vicarious. The ability to verbalize our experiences and the desire to share our ideas with others go a long way toward the making of a conversationalist.

THE NATURE OF LISTENING AND LISTENERS

But good conversation demands good listening. Just like love and marriage, "You can't have one without the other," or so Bing Crosby and other crooners assured your parents in the fifties and sixties. Unhappily we have only recently discovered and studied intensively the role of the receiver of the message. Thanks to the pioneering work of Ralph C. Nichols and others and the recent scientific research by Carl H. Weaver, we now enjoy a clearer understanding of listening theory and more reliable guidelines for the improvement of listening skills. Some of the subsequent ideas that appear in this chapter are in Dr. Weaver's perceptive volume *Human Listening: Process and Behavior,* which not only analyzes past research findings but offers practical suggestions and exercises to upgrade listening behavior.[7] Techniques for improving our listening include learning as much as possible about the process, and examining introspectively our own listening behavior.

Many commonly held misconceptions about listening clutter our attempts to improve the practice. Some persons consider the capacity for listening to be an aspect and correlate of intelligence and so view it essentially an intellectual function. Another school of thought considers reading and listening skills alike, since in both situations a receiver is attempting to sort out, remember, and assimilate input data. Weaver's analysis of research suggests "that listening capacity is a unitary process of handling data," not necessarily synonymous with intelligence and quite distinct from reading. While intelligence certainly influences our capacity for both reading and listening, the two processes are different, each demanding its own special skills. When we listen and remember, we hear different items of information than when we glean the same material from the printed page. One readily apparent difference rests with the opportunity a reader enjoys of rereading a particularly foggy line without personal embarrassment. As listeners, we may feel reluctant to ask our respondent to repeat an idea lest we be considered stupid.

Much of our listening effectiveness depends on our ability to focus attention on the mass of competing stimuli and to select those elements relevant to the task at hand. In Chapters 15 (pages 323–328) and 18 (pages 390–393) we will consider in more detail the perverse nature of

[7] Carl H. Weaver, *Human Listening: Process and Behavior* (Indianapolis: Bobbs-Merrill, 1972). Also see Ralph G. Nichols, "Factors in Listening Comprehension," *Speech Monographs* 15 (1948), 154–163.

attention, which is partly controlled by the determination of the listener to pay attention, and which is partly beyond our control. At a cocktail party when you are in the middle of your most exciting story and notice the eyes of your conversational companion shift and stare across your shoulder, you can be sure that he or she is still "paying attention," but not to you. The story wasn't as lively as you thought; it may have offended; some words may have held no meaning for your companion; or a figure more attractive than your ideas caught his or her eye. A friend who wears a hearing aid confessed that he often turns it off when the conversation becomes dull, boring, or incomprehensible, turning instead to the more exicting realm of intrapersonal communication. All listeners have their own built-in hearings aids which they can switch off and which in spite of their best efforts accepts input in spurts rather than continuously.

A few years ago we thought that men were better listeners than women, but supporters of Women's Liberation would not be surprised to hear that scientific studies have yet to produce any conclusive evidence of a sex difference. The studies do, however, bear out the long-revered French axiom about the fundamental distinguishing features of sex: *Vive la différence*. Women still tend to talk about different matters and are more inclined to listen to different stimuli and at different levels than men. Perhaps the Women's Liberation Front will ultimately eliminate "girl talk," eradicating even our speaking and listening differences, but for the moment, at least, this distinction persists. Further, we need to recognize that each individual, irrespective of sex, listens differently because of the particular physical and mental set, the cultural background, and biases—the total frame of reference in which the message is received.[8]

Many of the following suggestions for the improvement of listening skills apply to public speaking as well as to one-to-one and small-group listening. In subsequent chapters we will include material designed for the speaker and the listener in an audience setting. At this point we are primarily concerned with the receiver of the messages.

CHARACTERISTICS OF A GOOD LISTENER

Listening seems so natural a part of our behavior that we tend to assume that the extent of our ability to listen is fixed and cannot be altered. Like any other habit or behavioral change, the conditioning process is laborious, and the progress, at best, usually slow. We can, however, through conscious effort and special training techniques increase our efficiency as listeners. In the conversational one-to-one setting,

[8] See Cheris Kramer, "Women's Speech: Separate but Unequal?" *Quarterly Journal of Speech* 60 (February 1974), 14–24.

whether in the school, the home, or the business concern, we can distinguish the characteristics of the poor listener. Fortunately many of the personal qualities necessary for building the skills or subskills of listening are within your control and subject to your command. Some of them include:

1. A DETERMINATION TO LISTEN WITH MAXIMUM EFFICIENCY. This suggestion may sound as pious as our parent's admonitions to "Be Good!" or "Pay attention!" But the truth of the matter is that most of us shirk at the tasks of listening. Good listening requires effort. As readers, we can poke along with a word at a time or force ourselves into using our eyes more effectively. The same holds true for listening where sheer determination to change our basic habits is a necessary first step. Moreover, it is not easy for most of us to curb our tongues and concentrate instead on our ears, but such self-discipline offers rich rewards in improved human relations and actual learning.

2. CONSCIOUS CONTROL OF EMOTIONS AND BIASES. We listen with our prejudices, emotions, biases, and our loves and hatreds. If a speaker violates one of our cultural attitudes, our listening ears may snap shut almost before the speaker has opened his mouth. If we can control our emotional responses to the loaded words and nonverbal cues the speaker sends in our direction, we can at least hear him out and thereby grasp the essentials of the message. The maturity to control our emotional evaluations of the speaker's verbal and nonverbal messages and instead concentrate on his ideas will raise our listening efficiency.

The rise of blood pressure in the listener and the subsequent listening loss often stem from the inaccurate or false inferences we draw from the symbols, verbal and nonverbal, that come from the speaker. If as a listener you can block that urge to explode and can instead question and probe, you may happily discover that no real cause for disagreement exists. At the very worst you will at least receive a more accurate conception of your respondent's ideas, unpleasant or irrational though they may be. Perfect understanding, even if possible, will not ensure perfect agreement. In fact, it may promote the exact opposite. A progressive young minister blamed his dismissal on the clear communication of his liberal message to his conservative congregation. "That's why they fired me," he said. Still, many of our heated disputes during conversation rise out of our failures to listen. The breakdown and misinterpretation of the message were triggered in the listener by emotional biases that were quite unrelated to the speaker's message.

3. FULL UTILIZATION OF FEEDBACK. One of the advantages of casual conversation is the opportunity it affords the listener to respond directly to the message, thereby helping the receiver to sort out incorrect inferences. Indeed, effective listening requires us to let the speaker know that we are responding to the message. Our posture, our facial expressions,

our nods of assent or approval, even our frowns and scowls are indications of good listening. But we need to go beyond the "uh-huh" stage to what Dr. Weaver calls "reflecting the message of the talker." Your conscious effort to restate the speaker's idea, coupled with questions that draw out the speaker, will reveal your genuine interest in what is being said, and will also help fix the ideas in your mind or correct any initial misconceptions. You will not, for example, attempt to refute a premise until you can restate, to the satisfaction of your respondent, the position he or she holds.

4. A SENSITIVITY TO REFERENTIAL DIFFERENCES. A frequent cause of misunderstanding occurs because the speaker and the listener do not share the same referents for the words used to express ideas, concepts, or values. The background language experiences of each may be quite different. Such variations are readily apparent in cross-cultural and intercultural communication even when two people share the same mother tongue. An American girl, for example, if told she was homely would react negatively, whereas an English girl would take no offense because the word in England connotes no hint of ugliness, but instead a wholesome simplicity that would make her quite attractive to the opposite sex. Observers have often noted that a major communication barrier between the two principal English-speaking nations is language.

Nuances in speech, as in dress and in manners in general, vary as cultures vary. American "nuances," the words spoken and the way they are spoken, differ as they also do among other English-speaking peoples. They differ individually according to the personalities of the individual speaker and the sensitivities of the speaker in the conversational situation. There is no lack of nuances in the conversations of people who speak English in the many different ways English is spoken.

5. CONSTRUCTIVE USE OF SPARE LISTENING TIME. Through the use of compressed speech we know that individuals are capable of listening to some information faster than the normal speaker can deliver the words. Of course, the speed of delivery and of the subsequent comprehension depends on the complexity of the material. Some abstract, esoteric concepts may indeed need to be repeated. In many cases, however, we enjoy some extra listening time that we can use profitably to review and rethink the speaker's message. Above all, we need to avoid the strong temptation to "wool-gather."

6. A KEEN INTEREST IN THE SUBJECT. Avoid prejudging a subject: it may turn out to be as interesting as the one you want to introduce when your turn arrives. Further, the "truth" may often appear in seeming trivia, in light treatment of a subject, in the choice of an anecdote. Assume that virtually nothing is really said by chance, and more may presently become significant. Don't, however, assume the attitude of a psychoanalyst who becomes constantly concerned with "What did he really mean by that remark?" The patient listener may soon find out.

CHARACTERISTICS OF A GOOD CONVERSATION

Given two or more well-adjusted persons who are willing to share the pleasure of talking, *and of listening,* good conversation will likely occur. The chances for successful dialogue are enhanced if the participants are willing, as the occasion may demand, to assume the responsibility for guiding the talk and for helping all to share in the exchange. As one wishing to promote excellent conversation, you will want to observe some of the following guidelines:

1. Choose an initial subject that is inoffensive but interesting to any normal participant. Even highly controversial topics may legitimately enter the discussion, perhaps challenging your ingenuity, self-restraint, and listening skills.
2. Encourage participation from all who are present by drawing out the shy and thereby possibly discouraging the overenthusiastic talker.
3. Avoid prolonged periods of silence, but do not become anxious because of moments of quiet. Knowing how to ask a question and knowing when and how to change from one subject to another are skills vital to the good conversationalist.
4. Do not drag out a topic so that discourse becomes either boring or strained.
5. Make an effort—better, make it a point—to relate and address yourself to all members of the conversational group. Avoid the occasional temptation—by words, tone, or gesture—to speak to selected members as if they were special initiates of a subgroup. At all times the prevailing attitude and spirit must be one of talking with, and not of talking at, others.

In summary, good conversationalists are adequate human beings with the commensurate skills of a speaker and a listener. Sensitive to the feelings of others, they have genuine interests outside themselves and appreciate that people may disagree without being disagreeable and recognize that all "truth" rarely resides in one person. Good conversationalists recognize that human behavior is characterized by strivings that include the wish for pleasurable living. They do whatever they can to make living pleasurable. In brief, a good conversationalist is a good human being who knows how to talk, when not to talk, and how to listen so that the pleasure of talking may be shared and further conversation may be created.

Some of the characteristics of good conversation frequently appear in radio and television talk shows as well as in classical and current literature. Harry Reasoner, in his commentaries for American Information Radio, often reports his real or imagery conversations over a glass of his special lemonade with his conservative neighbor, Gus. In the following conversation with a friend who is a judge, the two discuss the highly controversial topics of pornography and movie censorship. Despite the seemingly inconsequential nature of much that is said, some shrewd insights emerge during the exchange.

Nudism in the courts[9]

A friend of mine is a judge and I ran into him the other day in our favorite restaurant. "How's the judging business?" I asked him. "Well," he said, "up until the last few months it's been pretty much the same old thing. What with all the plea-bargaining going on, the calendar being so clogged and all—it hasn't been a joy, I can tell you. But lately we've been getting into this pornography thing," the judge said.

"You mean . . . ?" I guess I said.

"That's right," said the judge. "Some other judges and I have been looking at some of the movies they've been showing around town—both in the theatres and in those little peep show places. I've never seen one of those so-called sex shows," the judge said. "It's the kind of thing you don't find judges going to much on their own." I said I could understand that. "Oh, I remember a couple of grainy old black and white stag films years ago at the Harvard smokers," the judge said, "but never anything like this." The judge sighed and said, "We must have looked at at least 20 movies." Well, twenty movies is a lot of movies . . . more than most people see in a year. I asked my friend the judge why he and his associates had to look at so many of them.

"Well, you see," the judge said, "there's a lot involved here. You've got what is called the right-privilege decision factor—oh, let me tell you . . . there's a lot to it. For instance," the judge said, "they just handed down a ruling in California that you can't have bottomless dancing in the same place where liquor is sold."

I told the judge that maybe there was some sense to that . . . but if the bottomless *dancers* weren't worried about dancing bottomless while guys stand around pouring down the liquor, why should the court be so concerned.

"That's just it," the judge said. "Another complexity."

"You see," the judge said, "according to the California

[9] "The Reasoner Report," December 14, 1972. Printed by permission of Harry Reasoner.

thing, topless is O.K. but bottomless is out unless liquor is not served. So right there is a morality issue with more than one side."

"But back to the movies," I said. "How bad are these movies you're looking at?" "Well," the judge said, "I saw one the other afternoon called—XXXXXXXXXXXX—well, call it anything you want to—and this was a bad movie. The girl couldn't act her way out of a paper bag, the guy had a serious case of acne, and the sound was terrible. Both of them were out of synch. The color values were very spotty, too—and in one case the color correction wiped out all the greens. Terrible," the judge said. "I certainly wouldn't spend five dollars to go to see it on 42nd Street."

I explained that wasn't really what I was asking when I asked how bad the picture was . . . that I was thinking more along the lines of morality. "Well, there again it's hard to say. When I saw my first one," the judge said, "I was dumbfounded. My first thought was, I wonder how they got these singularly unattractive people to undress and allow themselves to be photographed even if they didn't do anything—which they did. By the sixth or seventh picture, the whole thing was a crashing bore."

"But," sighed the judge, "we'll have to do some deciding on this thing, and I'll probably have to sit through a lot more of these terrible things."

My friend the judge said that he's had an idea in the back of his mind for sometime now regarding legislation against obscenity. "If we could make it illegal to bore people to death, we might be able to crack this thing," he said. Maybe he's got a point there.

QUESTIONS AND EXERCISES

1. Prepare a five-minute speech in which you contrast the qualities of a person with whom you like to converse with some one you prefer to avoid. In the speech you may wish to describe recent conversations you found enjoyable or trying.

2. If you have access to a small tape recorder, carry it with you for a day and record (with permission) some of the conversations you have with your friends. Analyze the selection of topics and variety or lack of variety in language used in the exchanges.

3. List five topics of conversation that would be suitable for mixed groups of educated men and women, five that would be more suitable

for men than for women, and five that would be especially suitable for women. Justify your selections.

4. Divide the class into groups of 4 to 6 persons, delegating one to serve as host for the conversational setting. Pick a subject such as (a) Rock Music, (b) Cleaning up the Environment, (c) Men as Cooks, (d) Women in Politics, (e) What Is the Purpose of a College Education? (f) The Season's Most Popular Play.

5. Write three questions that a host might be prepared to ask on each of the topics suggested in exercise 4 in order to keep the conversation going.

6. Select a day and keep a log of all your conversations. At the end of the day analyze the nature of the subjects covered by topic and general purpose.

7. Recall a conversation—in which you were involved or that you overheard—in which something did go wrong. Why? How could the confusion or misunderstanding have been avoided?

8. Samuel Johnson, the English literary figure, was recognized as a great conversationalist. He has been described as a person "of large heart and frame, proud and humble, tender and just, hungry for all that is human, radiating wisdom which was fresh from life." Search your memory for the best conversationalist you have known. Describe one of your conversations with this person.

9. Write out one or more interesting items of information in preparation for a class discussion on the following topics:

    (a) The Pollution Problem
    (b) The Energy Crisis
    (c) Objectivity in TV News
    (d) Ethics in Government
    (e) Intercollegiate Athletics

10. Analyze the conversations or interviews on television to determine how the moderator helps the participants to observe the practices or rules that govern conversation-discussion. Prepare a short speech explaining the techniques.

11. In an informal classroom discussion, analyze the best means for managing a long-winded talker in a campus rap session.

12. Francis Bacon in his essay *Of Discourse* wrote: "And generally, men ought to know the difference between saltiness and bitterness. Certainly, he that hath a satirical vein, as he maketh others afraid of his wit, so he had need be afraid of others' memory."

    (a) What did Bacon mean?
    (b) What is the proper place of wit in conversation?

13. Prepare a short speech in which you affirm, deny, or qualify the statement that "knowledge is the death of talk."

14. Pick out a total stranger on campus and attempt to draw him or her into conversation. Compare your experience with the conversations you hold regularly with your friends.

15. What are the chief differences and objectives between relatively unstructured "open-end" conversation programs on radio or television and those that use conversation as a format but are structured or controlled?

RECOMMENDED READINGS

BIANCOLLI, L. (ed.). *The Book of Great Conversations.* New York: Simon & Schuster, Inc., 1948.

BROWN, CHARLES T., and PAUL W. KELLER. *Monologue to Dialogue: An Exploration of International Communication.* Englewood Cliffs, N.J.: Prentice-Hall, Inc., 1973.

EISENSON, J., J. V. IRWIN, and J. J. AUER. *The Psychology of Communication.* New York: Appleton-Century-Crofts, 1963, chaps. 15, 19, 20.

JOHNSON, W. *Your Most Enchanted Listener.* New York: Harper & Row, Publishers, Inc., 1956.

LEE, IRVING J. *How to Talk with People.* New York: Harper & Row, Publishers, Inc., 1952.

MORTENSEN, C. DAVID. *Communication: The Study of Human Interaction.* New York: McGraw-Hill Book Company, 1972, chap, 7.

NICHOLS, RALPH G., and L. A. STEVENS. *Are You Listening?* New York: McGraw-Hill Book Company, 1957.

OLIVER, ROBERT T. *Conversation: The Development and Expression of Personality.* Springfield, Ill.: Charles C Thomas, 1961.

PEAR, T. H. *The Psychology of Conversation.* London: Nelson, 1939.

PRIESTLEY, J. B. *Talking.* New York: Harper & Row, Publishers, Inc., 1937.

WEAVER, CARL H. *Human Listening: Processes and Behavior.* Indianapolis: The Bobbs-Merrill Co., Inc., 1972.

Chapter 12

Group Discussion

> So far as minds are concerned, the art of
> democracy is the art of thinking independently
> together.
>
> ALEXANDER MEIKELJOHN

As we chat together during a social gathering, enjoying a casual conversation, someone is apt to raise an issue that touches a responsive cord in the group. He or she may have sensed a campus or community problem such as a suspected increase in friction between students and police, traffic snarls on main street, a recent drug bust, or the impact of the energy crisis on the environment. As individuals we may want more information, and as our awareness of the problem increases, we feel a strong desire for appropriate answers and perhaps even a justification for some concerted, cooperative action.

In the course of social conversation, topics usually shift too rapidly to permit a full exchange of information and more than a cursory examination of possible solutions. More often the members of a social group possess neither sufficient knowledge of the subject nor a recognized leader capable or willing to coordinate the discussion. Often the mood and the time or the place are not right for investigating the topic in depth. But when several participants feel the need to pursue an issue, to search out the facts, to explore possible courses of action, the conversation becomes directly and specifically purposeful. We then have left social conversation and are ready to engage in some form of structured group discussion.

NATURE AND PHILOSOPHY OF DISCUSSION

Discussion that emerges from social conversation is unanticipated and unplanned. The dangers of a superficial analysis based on inadequate information, thus leading to false solutions, is an ever-present hazard. In the social setting we are frequently reluctant to raise emotionally loaded issues or turn a friendly gathering into a potentially explosive confrontation. Even so, despite the impromptu character of social conversation, several features of formalized, planned discussion are likely to appear. For one thing, the participants feel the need for answers and solutions unlikely to emerge from social conversation. Second, they want to share information, seek additional evidence, and exchange opinions, thereby discovering new methods and programs for resolving their common prob-

256

lems. Third, one of the participants in the original conversation group often assumes temporary leadership, guiding the more formal behavior of the conversationalists-turned-discussants.

Most formalized discussions—and those we shall consider in this chapter—are planned and anticipated. The participants understand the purpose of the meeting and are willing to direct their thinking and speaking toward the discovery and dissemination of knowledge. From these shared communication experiences there may happily emerge the solution to a common problem or at least a deeper understanding of the issues yet unresolved.

This is not to say that the discussion method will magically convert or cure those who may purposefully use the techniques to confuse and to block group action. Nor will it always save any of us from falling heir to emotional hang-ups and the ever-present danger of indulging in specious reasoning and illogical behavior. Our hope, however, is that as individuals learn to use the discussion method, reasoned decisions—often based on consensus—will emerge more frequently. Persons intent on inquiry have points of view of their own, but should try to maintain the attitude of an earnest seeker intent on giving fair attention to every idea presented. Open-minded without being empty-headed, discussants may hold strong contentions and opinions but intently avoid a contentious or opinionated attitude. They cheerfully agree to disagree without becoming disagreeable.

Formal discussion and debate appear at all levels of government, education, and business. Indeed, freedom of speech and the awesome responsibilities such freedom places on individuals in our society determine in no small degree the success of democratic institutions. As Lord Macaulay reminds us: "Men are never so likely to settle a question rightly as when they discuss it freely." Admittedly, the process is imperfect, due in large part to the inadequacies of the participants. Suppression of democratic discussion not only violates First Amendment guarantees but may often give a distasteful, pernicious doctrine more publicity than open discussion would have afforded. And if it is truly obnoxious or malicious, discussion provides an excellent means of unmasking the sophistry.

In this chapter you will find many of the principles, techniques, and forms of discussion applicable to classroom practice or to use by the general public. But before examining the means for improving the process, we need to clarify some basic premises fundamental to a philosophy of discussion and debate in a free society.

We believe that:

1. Discussion and debate furnishes the best method of objective inquiry into questions of policy or value.
2. Citizens reach the most satisfactory solutions to problems when issues are resolved through unlimited discussion and debate.

3. In times of crisis and emergency, discussion may prove impractical; nevertheless, when solutions are achieved democratically, they are inherently superior to authoritarian and autocratic decisions.
4. Discussion and debate functions most satisfactorily when employed by mature, educated, responsible participants who have thoroughly researched the topic.
5. The techniques of discussion and debate must be learned and developed through training and practice.
6. No one type of discussion or debate is inherently superior to any other. The determining factors are the problem, the audience situation (if any), the knowledge of the participants, the time limits, and the degree of necessity for an immediate decision.

PURPOSE OF DISCUSSION

In general and specific purpose, discussion groups and sessions vary widely to include problem-solving, teaching, indoctrination, negotiation, encounter groups, collective bargaining, and group therapy, to name a few. Some discussions are designed for an audience; others are limited to small groups in which all members participate. We will not cover the area of group therapy but will confine our focus toward "problem-solving" discussion in which objective inquiry is an essential feature.

Objective inquiry

Discussion at its best represents a project in group thinking. If it is to be of value to the participants or to a possible audience whose members may also become active ingredients, the discussion process must be motivated by an orderly, systematic, objective approach. Fundamental then to our whole study of discussion is an understanding of John Dewey's classic description of *How We Think* and of the processes we follow in seeking a solution for a problem. Dewey's familiar five steps in reflective thinking correspond closely to the scientific method used in experimental research and represent a systematic rather than a random method of searching for truth.

The five logical steps in Dewey's plan are

1. Locating and defining the problem—sensing a felt difficulty.
2. Exploring the problem—defining, delimiting, analyzing the difficulty.
3. Examining suggested solutions—exploring each suggested solution.
4. Choosing the best solution—through evidence and reasoning.
5. Securing acceptance of the best solution—testing its efficacy.

Ewbank and Auer, two pioneers in the field of speech communication, used Dewey's five steps to show the close relationship between debate and discussion. They considered them to be *one process* "along a continuum of inquiry and judgment."[1] Both discussion and debate use essentially the same methods of inquiry and, as we shall see in this chapter and in the next, the similarities outweigh the differences. They move, often hand in hand, toward the same goal—democratic decision-making. One reason for treating discussion first is that it should always precede formal debate (if such is necessary) in working along the continuum toward the best solution.

Decision-making

Clearly, few discussions accomplish all five steps at a single session. Some may conceivably begin with step 3. Few discussions plod slavishly through all five steps. Informal debate may occur at almost any stage of the process, but usually assumes a more formal character at about step 4 or 5. On a particular problem, it may take months or years to achieve the acceptance of a workable solution. This is often hard for youth to accept and difficult for adults to understand. Yet it occasionally becomes necessary for discussants to realize that some problems have no apparent solutions. To insist on finding a solution to every problem may result only in finding a poor one. The best solution is sometimes no solution.

The decision to reach no decision is more likely to result from informal discussion arising out of social conversation than it is from planned discussion. When people get together for the purpose of finding a remedy for a problem, one or more of the participants is likely to have a workable solution in mind. But even in planned discussion, all proposed plans are often weak in one or more important respects. One community found its present water works defective and inadequate. After a long series of discussions and investigations, at least four methods were offered as solutions to the problem:

1. Patch up and expand the present plant.
2. Purchase water from an adjoining community.
3. Run pipe to a nearby Great Lake.
4. Build a completely new reservoir, using an adjacent river as the water source.

No one scheme satisfied all the citizens or the town council who finally selected plan 4 as less than perfect but probably the best possible solution.

Some limitations

Discussion is often slow and time consuming. It does not always enable people to arrive at decisions or to formulate a course of action. It gives persons with limited knowledge a chance to talk. (Fortunately it

[1] H. L. Ewbank and J. J. Auer, *Discussion and Debate* (New York: Appleton-Century-Crofts, 1951), p. 33.

also gives them a chance to learn.) Discussions and the behavior of people taking part in them are unpredictable and sometimes unpleasant. What happens cannot always be anticipated. Most of these criticisms are probably valid. But they are criticisms of the characteristics inherent in a democratic society.

Even the most enthusiastic advocate of discussion would hesitate to recommend the full discussion process, from investigation to consensus, as the best method for emergency action. Times of crisis may demand quick action under the direction of a person recognized as superior in a given situation. But even during the Cuban crisis in the fall of 1962, President Kennedy and his advisors engaged in lengthy discussion before making the decision to set up the blockade. We can conclude that some emergency situations cannot wait for complete or even partial consensus. Often the leader must take action (or no action) opposing at times the best judgment of some members.

Discussion, because of its relative informality, often makes sustained and logical presentation of argument difficult. Listeners wishing to hear a concise and orderly presentation of argument either in favor of or in opposition to a proposition are not likely to get it in discussion. Neither are they likely to be presented with clear-cut alternatives to a recommended course of action. When action is necessary and the group has failed during the discussion to reach a general agreement and they wish to hear or engage in argument pro and con on a specific possible course, the time for preliminary discussion has ended and we are ready for debate.

WHAT SHALL WE DISCUSS?

Local, national, and world events, personal, religious, and educational problems furnish the issues from which exciting discussion sessions develop. Any question that interests and perplexes people is a likely topic, but if the discussion is to be held before an audience, the precise selection ought to be geared to their needs and interests. A lively topic for the PTA might be less than scintillating for the Lion's Club. The questions themselves are usually classified as *fact, value,* or *policy*. Each type or a combination of the three is suitable for private or public discussion and lends itself to your classroom sessions.

1. QUESTIONS OF FACT. Since in many cases we can consult the *World Almanac* or a good encyclopedia for the exact answer, questions of *fact* need to be carefully selected for discussions. But facts are not always that easy to discover. Recall the endless discussion of the so-called facts surrounding the energy crisis that hit the world in the fall of 1973 when the Mideast war broke out. It seemed that no one, least of all the common citizen, knew whether the shortage of oil was real or a contrived ploy of the oil companies to increase their profits. Other questions of fact sur-

rounding the energy crisis, demanding investigation and discussion, included such topics as "Will year-round daylight saving time actually save energy?" "Is it possible for the United States to achieve self-sufficiency by 1980?" "Will nuclear energy provide a safe source?" These and other topics call for a wide assortment of data and expert opinion, coupled with a careful analysis and interpretation of all the available "facts."

2. QUESTIONS OF VALUE. When we discuss questions such as "Do present grading practices improve the quality of education?" or "Is violence ever a justifiable method of dissent?" or "Should political campaigns be completely financed by the government?" we are dealing with questions of value. The answers we seek touch on educational philosophy, standards of personal conduct, moral issues, and the rightness or wrongness of certain practices.

3. QUESTION OF POLICY. The best avenues for discussion usually appear in questions that attempt to determine future action or policy. After our disengagement from Vietnam in 1973, many people were concerned about future military commitments and considered such questions as "What policy on bilateral military agreements would best serve the United States?" and "How should the United States administer aid to sovereign nations?" Clearly any discussion of these complex topics will also require that the discussants ferret out all the *facts* and consider carefully the *value* implications of any proposed *policy*.

Question form

You have already noted that all the above subjects were cast as questions rather than as declarative sentences or mere topics. While a profitable discussion might ensue from such topics as "Military Assistance," "Foreign Economic Policy," or "*Détentes* with Russia," the question form helps delineate, prescribes the limits, and points toward a specific area of investigation. A declarative sentence or proposition such as "United States foreign military assistance should be discontinued" implies debate or advocacy rather than inquiry. A discussion of the above questions related to our military posture throughout the world might ultimately lead to a debate, but in the early stages of discussion, open-ended questions promote a healthier climate for the investigation of available facts, alternative proposals, and possible solutions.[2]

Timely or timeless questions

Even though we have accomplished the objective of placing a man on the moon, questions concerning "outer space" and our continuing commitment to further experiments and possible cooperation with the

[2] Some of the afore-listed questions were suggested by the NUEA Committee on Discussion and Debate for 1974–75.

Russians will render astronautical questions timely for many years. Discussion of "lift-offs," however, assumes immediate timeliness when the Congress considers massive financial cuts in the space program. Some questions, usually considered *timeless,* have been around for a long time and show no signs of leaving. "How can we avoid an economic recession?" and "What kind of educational program best promotes good citizenship?" will be discussed as long as we experience dips and rises in the economy and consider schools a training ground for public service. The group still faces the task of making the timeless questions as relevant to their audience as it may be to the discussants. The study group, for example, may thrill to new revelations about the philosophy of Spinoza, but the topic would offer special problems in timeliness for public discussion. Questions that focus on immediate, pressing problems will usually promote a lively, stimulating session.

Provocative questions with widespread popular appeal

Questions for discussion should be controversial, thought-provoking, and of genuine interest to the audience as well as to the speakers. Sometimes questions are of concern to selected audiences with specialized interests. "What kind of college calendar will best promote quality education?" is probably of greater concern to the students, teachers, and administrators of that institution than to the general public. The skill and insight of the program planners into the concerns and needs of the group will determine the success or failure of the discussion.

Clear, precise, fair phraseology

Lengthy, double-barrelled, involved questions lead to confusion rather than to understanding and thought. "Will gas rationing and the relaxation of environmental controls solve the energy problem?" is a two-pronged question and is better stated as two separate questions for purposes of discussion. "Should we adopt a radical program of socialized medicine?" not only begs the question with two loaded adjectives, "radical" and "socialized," but also implies a yes or no response, usually leading to debate rather than to inquiry. If stated, "How can we best meet the health needs of our citizens?" the door opens to a fair discussion of voluntary and compulsory health insurance and their various modifications.

POSSIBLE QUESTIONS FOR DISCUSSION

As you and your colleagues search for suitable questions for discussion, some of the following topics may give you a start. You will, of course, want to phrase the topics in *questions form,* making sure they meet the tests of *clarity, unity, relevance, timeliness,* and *fairness.* Keep your questions "single" and "open-ended."

1. Inflation
2. University Governance

3. Financial Support for Higher Education
4. Campaign Financing
5. National Defense
6. World Government
7. Mass Transportation
8. Nuclear Energy

SMALL-GROUP DISCUSSION FORMS

If we consider all possible modifications of the discussion format, a nearly unlimited variety exists, and as participants you will want to try as many different types and combinations as possible. They range all the way from the informality of the dialogue and guided conversation to the formality of the symposium and formal debate. The audience in some instances consists merely of the discussants, while in other forms the spectators may witness and then ultimately join in the discussion.

Those usually carried on without a witnessing audience include the *dialogue, guided conversation, the study group, classroom discussion, colloquium,* and the *conference.* The *dialogue,* which is best illustrated by the interview, is treated in Chapter 11, pages 242–243.

The guided conversation

Often referred to as *informal discussion,* the guided conversation sometimes emerges from a social situation. During a social gathering a group discovers a problem of mutual concern and resolves to investigate, study, and discuss it together under the direction of a leader. Occasionally they invite experts or resources persons with special information on the topic to join the group. This does not absolve group members from study and preparation. Moreover, inviting experts may actually turn the meeting into a lecture forum, thus radically changing the discussion method.

Groups intent on guided conversation may also find it helpful to meet for an organizational session, elect a leader, and subdivide the topic. All members should read and study the subject broadly, but each also should assume individual responsibility for seeking factual information and opinion in special areas. The so-called *study group* and *classroom discussion* often follow the format of the guided conversation. When special experts are added, the discussion is usually referred to as a *colloquium.* Further suggestions for organizing and participating in the *informal discussion* are:

1. A small group numbering twenty or less.
2. An informal atmosphere, marked by good fellowship and punctuated with good humor.
3. Short, spontaneous remarks, preferably a minute or less.
4. A leader who keeps the discussion moving by stimulating the shy and reticent while patiently and tactfully discouraging the overtalkative.

5. Frequent summaries and assessments by the leader or other members to help ensure a unified, coordinated discussion.
6. Avoidance of the temptation to tarry over interesting nonessentials to the exclusion of prosaic essentials.

The conference

The term *conference* is used in various ways, often synonymously with *group discussion*. It also describes the meetings of educational, business, professional, and religious organizations. The Methodist Church, for example, holds its Annual and General Conferences, and the Speech Communication Association sponsors a yearly conference and frequent special conferences. These larger conferences are usually subdivided into a wide assortment of panels, symposiums, lecture forums, plenary sessions, and executive committee meetings. For our purposes, we are limiting the term *conference* to *small, private discussion groups* intent on finding a solution to a common problem.

The conferees in the small group may seek answers to personal problems (group therapy, sensitivity training) or they may attempt to find solutions to problems affecting widely divergent groups. During labor-management disputes the conferees often represent the union, the industry, the government, and the public. Occasionally conferees with no personal interest in a controversy are selected to ensure objectivity. Such is the case when an impartial board of arbiters seeks to settle disputes or make adjustments affecting the welfare of others. Often a major obstacle is the selection of persons satisfactory to all parties in the controversy.

Determinants of a successful conference

The successful conference operates in the best tradition of the *round-table discussion*. All members are relatively equal, ensuring a balanced group in terms of the potential importance of each participant. If any member sits at the table merely for the sake of form and his point of view is dismissed by common, tacit agreement of opposing members, the conference is unbalanced. A few years ago a common undergraduate complaint was that the students sitting on college committees with faculty members enjoyed few of the rights normally accorded to a committee member. More recently an increasing number of colleges and universities have granted voting privileges to the student representatives on various committees, establishing a more balanced structure. In any conference where the participants are rigidly committed to a position and unwilling to hear differing points of view, only the superficial appearance of a conference exists. A conference is successful only when all members listen with flexible as well as polite minds. This same "balance of power" must prevail in larger conferences where all legitimate, though divergent, points of view require fair representation.

A successful conference tolerates no inactive members. Each conferee is selected with the expectation that he will contribute substantially to the solution of the problem. Thus, whenever possible the number of participants is kept as small as is consistent with a fair representation of factions and opinions. A group larger than fifteen may lose the air of informality necessary for the easy give-and-take of opinion.

The leader of the conference must be a respected person, capable of dealing impartially and tactfully with persons holding divergent views. Of great strategic importance is the leader's timing ability. He or she must know how to avoid wasting time, and yet not appear to hurry any of the participants into reaching decisions they may not be ready, either intellectually or emotionally, to make or to accept.

For the bright and intelligent members of the group the frustration of waiting on slower members to grasp ideas is admittedly great. Occasionally, however, the plodders save the quick from serious errors. Shakespeare, perhaps, offers us some comfort for the built-in delays inherent in small-group decision-making. "Wisely and slow; they stumble that run fast."

BUILDING AN EFFECTIVE DISCUSSION

Preparation and participation

In discussion, where from three to twenty persons share the responsibility for talking, the temptation is strong to be incompletely prepared, comfortable in the thought that "George" will carry on somehow. Few other attitudes are so well designed to sabotage a discussion session. While not necessarily preparing in the same way, the discussant must equal the public speaker in thoroughness of preparation. No discussion will ever achieve merit until each participant prepares fully for the task.

Communication skills

To promote a relaxed atmosphere conducive to effective communication, the leader and the participants should give careful attention to the physical environment. For guided conversation, the seats should be arranged for easy exchange; for the panel or symposium, the tables, chairs, and speaker's stand must occupy positions conducive to optimum viewing and subsequent audience participation.

During the discussion the participants should strive to employ all the techniques of effective communication. They share equally the responsibility of transmitting ideas clearly and vigorously to members of their group and to any audience that may be present. When the situation permits, the speaking manner should resemble excellent social conversation. If possible the discussants for a public program should meet in advance and use every opportunity to converse about the problem under consideration. Even where the discussion opens with formal speeches, the leader or moderator should introduce the program in a manner designed to promote informality and to encourage audience participation. The speeches themselves, in the best tradition of public address, should follow the conversational mode of delivery.

Many of the personality conflicts during discussion sessions stem from our failures to communicate or to employ the language of conciliation. "Every thinking person knows that . . ." we say as we brand by implication as stupid or unthinking all who disagree with us. Or we ask, "Do you have any other suggestions to offer?" implying by our inflectional patterns and facial expression that we hope not, if they are as absurd as the previous ones. Popular TV cross-examination type shows like "Meet the Press," "Face the Nation," and William F. Buckley's "Firing Line" usually feature controversial figures and probe sensitive, emotional problems. The best interrogators and respondents are those in command of the facts, their emotions, and their phrasing.

Satisfactory interpersonal relationships

The emotional and personal relationships that inevitably accompany any kind of group interchange will play a vital role in facilitating or inhibiting analysis, thinking, and action. Group discussion usually brings to the table or platform a wide assortment of personalities, different age groups, and persons with various social, racial, and religious backgrounds. Objective inquiry and the search for truth are intermixed with status seeking, ego fulfillment, concealed loyalties, hidden agendas, and conflicting interests.

As we glance around the table, we are apt to see the expert in one-up-man-ship across from the timid soul, the supreme optimist next to the prophet of gloom, the axe-grinder alongside the conciliator, and the reflective thinker near the conclusion-jumper. While it is comforting to think of ourselves as one of the few "normal" persons at the table, we may also recognize most of these character types present in ourselves. The effective discussant makes every effort to keep the discussion idea-centered, to suppress the tendency to consider criticism of the ideas as personal attacks, and to avoid attacking individuals whose ideas are distasteful.

Most of us do not accept criticism of our ideas easily, considering it a personal affront. It is particularly agonizing when "one of our own" or a close friend questions one of our "best" ideas. Even when your nearest friend begs for a "frank, honest" judgment from you, he may in actual fact be seeking your approval and reinforcement for his latest "brainchild." This does not mean that you must always "hold your tongue," but it calls for tactful, careful wording, the use of questions rather than assertions, and a generous portion of praise intermixed with criticism. Even more important, we need to guard against our own defensive tendencies to consider criticism an affront to us personally.

Two additional suggestions for minimizing interpersonal conflicts include the development of group-centered rather than individual-centered attitudes, and careful attention to the physical arrangements for the meeting. For example, try to separate hostile members, but avoid seating them directly across the table from each other. As a participant you will want to give your enthusiastic support to group goals, try to establish friendly relationships with other members, concentrate on listening as well as speaking, and attempt to retain your good sense of humor. When you serve as discussion leader, whether appointed or selected by the group, you will bear special responsibilities for organizing and conducting the discussion. For additional information on the psychology of group behavior see Chapter 18, pages 397–399.

Effective leadership

The divergent personality types—the bright and the dull, the thick-skinned and the sensitive—present in any small group provide a stimulating challenge in understanding human behavior. Successful discussion does not necessarily require a sterile atmosphere free from the germs of dissension, where only sweetness and light prevail, but it does thrive best in an environment of mutual respect.

If the small group is to accomplish its purposes, careful planning, study, and participation in cooperation with a skilled leader is vital. As a potential leader you will want to familiarize yourself with the various forms of discussion, master the special techniques of each, and develop an understanding and appreciation of the philosophy of discussion. While it is not necessary for the leader to be an expert on the subject under consideration, it is important to find a liberally educated person, skilled in communication and possessing a sympathetic understanding of human relationships. Sometimes an expert on the topic makes a poor discussion leader because of his or her impatience with less well-informed participants, and possibly a resulting desire to dominate the discussion.

Obviously the leader needs to possess as many of the so-called desirable personality traits as possible. Tact, poise, confidence, a sense of humor, and the ability to make quick decisions are among the important characteristics. The leader must possess the talent for guiding the discussion courteously and fairly, drawing facts and inferences from the group, thus ensuring a final product that reflects group thinking at its best. In one study,[3] Wischmeier found that discussions under the guidance of a group-centered leader produced a greater degree of cooperation and more substantive contributions than those employing a leader-centered moderator. Some contrasting characteristics of each type of leadership are noted in the parallel columns:

[3] Richard R. Wischmeier, "Group-Centered and Leader-Centered Leadership: An Experimental Study," *Speech Monographs,* **22** (March 1955), 43–48.

Group-centered	*Leader-centered*
1. Leader clarifies and reflects member ideas without attempting to influence.	1. Leader interprets, rephrases, and modifies a member's contributions to conform with what he considers most important.
2. Leader makes few evaluative statements.	2. Leader freely evaluates the statements of the members and expresses approval or disapproval.
3. Leader is concerned with utilizing all of the human resources of the group and thus encourages all members to participate.	3. Leader makes little apparent effort to bring all members into the discussion so long as he feels that the group is progressing satisfactorily.

Paradoxically a majority of the discussants in Wischmeier's study felt that the more autocratic leader did the better job, perhaps suggesting that a leader must risk his or her own reputation as a so-called "dynamic" personality in the interests of group accomplishments. Inevitably some situations arise which seem to demand leadership bordering on the autocratic, but we can be sure when this happens that democratic decision-making has suffered some degree of setback. In general, the more nearly free and democratic the process becomes, the more successfully the discussion progresses. Moreover, discussion on this level requires greater self-discipline, clearer thinking, and more individual effort than is required under more autocratic control.

PUBLIC DISCUSSION

The discussions we have considered so far may be thought of as *private,* since the participants themselves comprise the audience. Another form, with roots deep in American culture, is the public discussion held and conducted by one group of participants for the benefit of another group. The listeners may be actually present and constitute an audience before whom the speakers carry on their discussion, or they may be at home listening and watching while the discussants appear before a microphone or a television camera. In either case we have *public* rather than *private* discussion.

In most public discussions the participants wish to stir up questions and comments from the audience. Every communicative situation demands a two-way exchange, but in public discussion, the dialogue is usually more audibly vocal than in public speaking. Indeed, the number and the quality of the questions and comments from the audience may well serve as indicators of the success or failure of the discussion. Even in radio and television programs, conducted without a studio audience, the listeners or viewers are often encouraged to phone in their questions. And all of us have caught ourselves during a radio or television program inserting our own comments or continuing the discussion in the family circle.

The *procedures* and the precise *form* of public discussion are determined by the purpose of the meeting and the size and nature of the audience. The following techniques, as a means of stimulating, coordinating, and promoting group action, often prove helpful.

PHYSICAL ARRANGEMENTS. Beyond hiring the hall and publicizing the meeting, someone must take the responsibility for arranging the tables and chairs to provide maximum audience viewing and participation. The "theatrical" elements in public discussion make it imperative that the planners and participants recognize and utilize the dramatic possibilities in each type of discussion.

WARM-UP SESSIONS AND ADVANCED PLANNING. Although participants in public discussion are selected because of their special knowledge in a particular field, prior planning is necessary to coordinate and ensure a meaningful and organized presentation. In the panel discussion and symposium, participants should meet in advance to set up an outline and clarify the divisions of the question.

BALANCED PARTICIPATION. Lodges, church groups, industrial organizations, and various closed groups sometimes employ discussion to indoctrinate the membership. We would warn that discussion under any circumstances may prove a poor propaganda tool, since heretical doctrines may inevitably intrude. We consider indoctrination as the basic purpose of public discussion to be an inappropriate if not unethical practice. Those in charge of a discussion have an obligation to make certain that all points of view are fairly represented.

PROMOTIONAL DEVICES. An imaginative planning board or leader can devise various means to promote a lively discussion and stimulate audience interest and participation. Film strips, movies, case studies, role-playing, or recordings coordinated skillfully with the leader's opening remarks often help to dramatize the problem and stimulate the discussion.

FORMS OF PUBLIC DISCUSSION

Although the varieties of form in public discussion are unlimited, most follow one of four basic patterns that we shall consider. These are the *panel,* the *symposium,* the *lecture forum,* and the *buzz session.* In a public-speaking exercise, you may already have participated in a lecture forum if a question period followed one of your speeches.

The panel

The panel is a guided conversation held in the presence of an audience. The speakers, usually two to six in number, are highly interested persons possessing special information on some phase of the problem. Seated on a platform in full and easy view of the audience, the panelists, under the direction of the leader, engage in conversation among themselves, but expressly for the benefit of the audience. Indeed, during most panel discussions the audience is ultimately invited to ask questions or to make comments. In a brief introductory talk the leader outlines the procedures and introduces the topic and panelists to the audience. Since each panel member usually develops a special aspect or point of view relative to the topic, he may outline this theme in a short opening statement. The dangers of this procedure sometimes offset the advantages by turning the panel into a symposium and thereby destroying the spontaneity and conversational informality of the discussion.

The *objectives of the panel* are to give the audience a better understanding of the problem under discussion and in some cases to encourage them to consider possible courses of action relative to the problem. The panelists may feel the need to fight their way through to some definite conclusions. More often, however, they are content with the creation of audience concern and the clarification of preliminary infor-

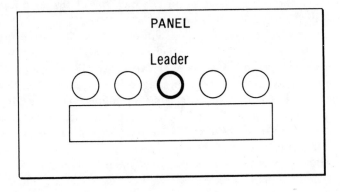

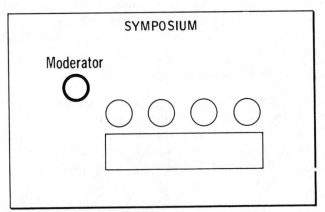

Figure 12–1. Possible seating arrangements for public discussions employing the panel or the symposium. A lectern is often preferable to the table in the symposium.

mation about the problem. An incidental but still exceedingly important contribution of a panel is to help persons realize that well-informed speakers may entertain different points of view and maintain respect for one another despite their differences.

When you serve as the moderator or leader, you bear a major responsibility for the success of the panel. Your duties include:

1. Creating a friendly, informal atmosphere conducive to a lively, good-natured discussion.
2. Clarifying procedures for the panelists and the audience.
3. Guiding tactfully the discussion toward previously established goals.
4. Phrasing questions designed to probe and draw out discussion on unexamined areas.
5. Keeping panelists aware of the audience.
6. Sensing the opportune time to open the discussion to the audience. (Spaced suggestions, implying later audience participation often help. "In a few moments a member of our audience may want to comment or question us about the statistics we've just presented." No sharp break in the discussion need occur at the point of audience participation.)
7. Recognizing yourself as the prober, organizer, mediator—not as the chief contributor, authority, or source of all wisdom. (The discussion should move easily and freely among panelists with no necessity for formal recognition of each speaker. If the leader enters the conversation after each contribution, the discussion session may be considered a failure.)
8. Alleviating hostilities if they arise through tact and possibly through self-directed humor.
9. Sustaining a clear, purposeful discussion by encouraging speakers to summarize the outstanding points as they develop. (As leader, you may summarize or encourage other panel members to assume some of this responsibility. You should not, however, call on any member to summarize without a forewarning.)

The *panelists* share the major responsibility for the substance of the discussion. The moderator's burden is considerably lightened if the speakers assist in carrying out their roles.

Your duties as a panel member include:

1. Preparation and research no less thorough than is required of the public speaker. (In some respects, as a panelist, if you perform well, you face a more demanding task than the public speaker; for you are required to shift, adapt, and integrate your ideas with those of four or five other persons.)
2. An understanding of the dramatic elements in the panel discussion. (Too many panels become oppressively dull because members seem unaware of the audience and of the necessity to "appear" interested,

alive, and alert. The danger of underplaying is far greater than any tendency to "ham it up.")

3. Suppression of the desire to give a "speech" or present your "facts" simply because you have them.
4. Recognition of the need for vocal projection and more precise diction.
5. Skill in speaking fluently and translating technical concepts into readily understandable words.
6. Tact, a sense of humor, and a willingness to engage in a controversial discussion without losing your good nature.

AUDIENCE PARTICIPATION: THE FORUM. Ultimately during the panel discussion the audience is invited to participate. They may direct questions to the speakers or submit their comments. No formal break need occur between the so-called panelists' portion of the program and the wider discussion including the audience. Indeed, the moment for audience participation will be determined by the interest of the audience and the awareness of the moderator to audience desires and a sense of timing. The moderator continues to direct and coordinate the discussion and recognizes the speakers from the audience. He may have to rule tactfully on the relevance of questions, reword if necessary, and sometimes direct them to specific panel members. At the conclusion of the forum the moderator should make a final statement, informally and briefly summarizing the areas covered.

The symposium

The major distinguishing feature of the symposium is its reliance on set speeches, carefully prepared in advance. Usually, three or four experts prepare five-to-ten-minute speeches on a specific phase of a general topic. Following the presentation of the prepared speeches, the speakers may enter into informal discussion, questioning and cross-questioning each other. Eventually, the audience is invited to participate in a forum, in which questions are directed to individual speakers.

The questions asked by audience members usually fall into one of three categories:

1. Those calling for more detailed explanation or further information from a speaker.
2. Those intended to give a speaker who is in essential agreement with the questioner an opportunity to expand or support an argument already stated.
3. Those intended to reveal weaknesses in the arguments of a speaker with whom the questioner is in disagreement.

The *objectives* of the symposium are similar to those of the panel. In general, the purpose is either to provide the audience with information or to give the listeners an opportunity to consider and compare the merits of two or more solutions to a problem. The symposium is better adapted to larger audiences and is conducive to a more orderly, formal presentation than is the panel.

The *success* of the symposium, like that of the panel, is determined largely by what has taken place during the preparatory stages. Usually a number of interested persons engage in the preliminary planning. Items they should consider include:

1. The choice and wording of a topic most likely to arouse audience interest. Questions often need to receive headline treatment. Instead of the prosaic "How can we best meet the medical needs of all our citizens?" a more lively and provocative title might read "Is your health the nation's business?"
2. Deciding on the basis of audience knowledge whether the objective should be to provide information or to consider the relative merits of solutions to a controversial issue.
3. The selection of speakers who can best contribute to the achievement of the objectives of the symposium. Care should be exercised to ensure adequate, fair, and balanced representation to all points of view.
4. The selection of a moderator acceptable to all factions and completely familiar with the discussion method and the precise techniques of the symposium.
5. Giving the moderator and the speakers an opportunity to become acquainted with one another as well as with the nature, objectives, and plan of the meeting.

The *duties of the moderator of a symposium* resemble in some respects those of the panel leader. They include:

1. Presiding at the meeting. [This responsibility involves (a) a short, provocative introduction of the general topic; (b) an explanation of the ground rules, governing time limits, and audience participation; (c) introducing each speaker; (d) making certain the rules and time limits are observed; and (e) recognizing members of the audience.]
2. Unifying the discussion by pointing up relationships between the speeches.
3. Eliciting questions and statements during the forum which will direct attention to different aspects of the problem.
4. Restating inaudible audience questions and rewording them when the meaning is obscure.
5. Concluding the meeting according to the prearranged schedule with a summary that ties together the main ideas in the discussion.

The lecture forum

The lecture forum is perhaps the most widely used type of public discussion, probably because it requires less preplanning by fewer individuals than any other type. It is also the least likely to generate a profitable discussion. It consists of a prepared lecture by a specialist, followed by audience questions. A moderator usually presides over the meeting, introducing the speaker and conducting the forum period.

If it were possible for people with formed opinions to be completely objective, the lecture forum might be an excellent way of presenting points of view as well as information on a controversial problem. Because objectivity is difficult, if not virtually impossible to achieve, once a speaker has formed an opinion, the listeners will likely hear a talk weighted or slanted toward the speaker's private opinion. Some discussion clubs remedy this problem by securing a series of speakers for successive meetings, each representing a different point of view on the same subject.

Some of the following suggestions will help to stimulate a profitable discussion during the forum period.

1. The sponsoring organization should select a moderator who is alert to the dangers and possibilities inherent in the lecture forum.
2. In his introduction of the speaker, the moderator should create an atmosphere conducive to discussion by alerting the audience to the forum period and inviting them to formulate their questions during the lecture period. Cards distributed in advance to the listener-participants may help them remember to write out their questions.
3. The moderator should design his own questions to point up areas of controversy.
4. In advance of the meeting the moderator might encourage various members to come prepared to ask questions. Once the ice is broken, audience questions usually flow freely.
5. The moderator should formulate a plan for the forum period designed to promote discussion of the significant points and prevent aimless wandering.

The advantage of the lecture forum is the ease of arrangement. The disadvantages are its lack of objectivity and the dangers inherent in loose structuring. These include the possibilities of no questions, poor questions, and "sounding off" speeches rather than questions. The result may be a dull, random discussion period involving no real group thinking. A good speaker may occasionally "save the day" by saying, "If I were a member of the audience, I would ask this question. . . ." A good moderator will plan questions just in case.

The buzz sessions

Often called "Phillips 66 buzz session" and named for its originator J. D. Phillips, this specialized technique is often employed with large groups as a method of stimulating the widest possible participation.[4]

[4] See J. D. Phillips, "Report on Discussion 66," *Adult Educational Journal,* 7 (October 1948), 181–182.

Although numerous variations in method are possible, buzz sessions usually follow this pattern.

1. During the introduction the leader of the buzz session explains the discussion procedure and outlines the problem. The leader's remarks may be followed with a panel, a symposium, or one or two experts who supply background information. From this discussion a single, specifically stated question such as "What is the most important contribution of X organization to our community?" is placed before the whole assembly.

2. The audience is divided into clusters of six persons who merely shift their chairs closer together and then take six minutes to find as many answers as possible. Speed is of utmost importance, so groups quickly select their leader and secretary and proceed immediately to formulate their answers.

3. After six minutes of the leader of the buzz session calls for order and asks each group leader (secretary) to submit a one-minute report of its answers. These are usually synthesized and recorded on a blackboard. Discussion then may continue, involving a selected panel or the whole audience. The leader continues to direct and integrate the discussion.

Obviously the buzz session demands a discussion leader who has planned the whole program with meticulous care—a person with contagious enthusiasm and one possessing a thorough familiarity with the entire discussion process. It likewise demands a high degree of homogeneity in the participating group. A primary virtue of the buzz session is the stimulus it offers toward 100 per cent participation in a large group. Further, the atmosphere of informality tends to carry over to the larger group, thus setting the stage for a lively discussion. Its drawbacks include the time-consuming process of explaining and setting up the mechanics of the program and the dangers of superficial answers based on less than adequate information.

Discussion agenda—outline plan

The following agenda illustrates how the students in one group organized their preliminary planning sessions, devised their methods of research, and finally outlined their presentation for the class.[5] They found a topic that concerned them personally and one that they and their audience considered to be within their sphere of influence and subject to their persuasive actions. Arranging a series of meetings, the group investigated and discussed as many as 27 problem areas before finally delimiting and phrasing the chosen topic in question form.

[5] Prepared by Mrs. Jean Metz, Director of Forensics at Sinclair Community College, Dayton, Ohio from a project by Cindy Doner, Brad Bixler, Dale Brandly, Mike Paluch, and Dennis Patterson for a class discussion on March 11, 1974.

After several preliminary meetings, they finally selected the question: "What can be done about the poor parking facilities at Sinclair?"[6] During these planning sessions, each member of the group accepted the responsibility for investigating the complete subject of parking at universities and colleges located in metropolitan areas. Later, particular individuals were assigned or volunteered to research specific aspects of the parking problem, interviewed key community and college figures, and devised questionnaires that were administered to various student groups.[7] Their instructor required them to keep their own personal log or journal of each group meeting, including their estimate of the following factors:

1. The contributions of each member.
2. The organization of each session.
3. The emergence of a leader, if no one was so designated earlier.
4. The specific achievements of the group during each meeting.

In preparation for the actual classroom presentation, the group was advised to spend at least one preliminary session in planning, outlining, and practicing for their appearance before the audience. They recognized that other members of the class, though painfully familiar with the frustrations of campus parking, had not attended the earlier group meetings and, therefore, needed to hear the topic discussed factually, logically, and in keeping with the essential features of the reflective thinking process we discussed earlier in the chapter (see pages 258–259). This agenda, of course, represents only one of several legitimate approaches and as you probe a particular problem, you will need to adapt your analysis to the specific issues and to the group considering the topic. The basic structure of reflective thinking, however, will permeate the total process from planning to presentation.

DISCUSSION OUTLINE

QUESTION: What can be done about the poor parking facilities at Sinclair?

Preliminary Group Activity:
1. Brainstorming session—27 possible topics listed.
2. Limiting possible topics—each student selected one and did initial research survey to determine:
    a. Is it really a problem?
    b. Are adequate resources available for research?
    c. Can it be covered well in the time available?
3. Topic area decided upon for discussion: Parking Problem at Sinclair Community College.

[6] By omitting the loaded term "poor" and substituting "to improve" for "about," they might have had a better statement of the question.

[7] See Chapter 11, pages 242–243 for information on interviewing and Chapter 13, pages 295–297 for help in gathering and recording evidence.

I. RECOGNITION OF THE PROBLEM
   A. Formulation of the Problem as a Question:
      1. What is the extent of the parking problem at Sinclair? (Question of Fact)
      2. Does Sinclair Community College owe its students adequate parking facilities? (Question of Value)
      3. What can be done about the poor parking facilities at Sinclair? (Question of Policy)
   B. Group choice: #3—Question of Policy.

II. DESCRIPTION OF THE PROBLEM
   A. History (obtained through interviewing Mr. Thomas Davis, City Planning Board Director of Transportation and Mr. Robert Barr, Director of Public Information at Sinclair.)
      1. Sinclair is part of the redevelopment plan for downtown Dayton.
      2. Land designated under the beautification project cannot be used for parking facilities.
      3. The Regional Transit Authority operates bus lines and is against increasing parking areas.
      4. In March, 1972, the college contracted Wilbur, Smith and Associates to study the present and future parking needs of Sinclair and make recommendations based on their findings.
         a. Results of study:
            (1) Present student transportation use:
               (a) 75% of students drive
               (b) 11% are passengers
               (c) 8% use buses
               (d) 5% walk
            (2) Sinclair has a low car occupancy rate (1.13 persons per car) because of irregular class schedules.
            (3) Patterns of use:
               (a) Peak time is 10:00 A.M.
               (b) Peak day is Monday
            (4) Space availability versus need:
               (a) Need—1,400 spaces
               (b) Available—790 spaces
            (5) Projections of need:
               (a) 1974—2,945
               (b) 1976—4,207
               (c) 1978—4,716
               (d) 1980—4,760
         b. Recommendations of study:
            (1) Purchase private land and construct multi-story parking facility adjacent to campus.
            (2) Re-structure present student parking area into additional multi-story facility.
            (3) Adopt student fees comparable to those of other schools with similar problems—University of Akron, Wayne State University, University of Cincinnati.
   B. Present effects of the problem (obtained through questionnaires formulated by the group and distributed to students).
      1. Present lot is too crowded.
      2. Student price is too high (65¢ per day).
      3. Walking distance to campus is too far.
      4. No security person on duty in the lot to ensure safety of car or students.

   C. Importance of the problem (obtained through combination of above interviews and questionnaires).

      1. Vast majority of students drive to campus.

      2. Mass transit facilities are not available to many areas of the city or suburbs.

      3. Student enrollment is expected to increase.

III. SUGGESTIONS OF POSSIBLE SOLUTIONS

   A. Short-range solutions:

      1. Cut down number of cars by encouraging use of buses.

      2. Promote use of car pools.

      3. Keep students informed about the problem to avoid misunderstandings.

      4. Stagger class schedule times.

   B. Long-range solutions:

      1. As soon as budget allows, construct proposed multi-story garage adjacent to campus.

      2. After completion of above, construct multi-story unit on present student lot.

      3. Utilize parking facilities at nearby Convention Center and run shuttle service to campus.

      4. Construct light rail transit system from suburbs.

IV. EVALUATION OF POSSIBLE SOLUTIONS

   A. Short-range solutions:

      1. More bus use:

         a. *Dayton Daily News* article:

           (1) Present service inadequate.

           (2) RTA negotiating with suburbs on contract service.

           (3) New buses could be obtained in one to three years.

           (4) County authorities are considering opinion sampling on suburban bus ridership.

         b. Federal decisions:

           (1) New Unified Transportation Assistance Program.

           (2) Money to states and cities on basis of population.

         c. *Business Week* study:

           (1) Stresses extensive bus system.

           (2) Suggests use of incentive approach (Denver system seems applicable to Dayton).

         d. Implementation of the above would involve too many interest groups to achieve any results in the near future.

      2. Use of car pools:

         a. Interview with Mr. Robert Statum, promoter of car pools at Sinclair showed minimum use at present.

         b. Group questionnaire showed 75% of students would join car pool if convenient; 85% would join in event of gas rationing or gas price of $1.00 gallon.

         c. *U.S. News and World Report* study:

           (1) People need incentives to join car pool.

           (2) Phoenix Mutual Life Insurance Co. offers $1.00 day.

           (3) Illinois Gov. Daniel Walker considering requiring state employees to join car pools.

           (4) Many companies offering reserved spaces to car pools.

           (5) San Francisco offers express lanes and reduced tolls.

           (6) Federal Highway Administration offers audio tape recordings to inform commuters how to form car pools.

         d. Sinclair could initiate reserved areas, publicize car pools by relating

them to energy crises, saving money, and could help in linking up interested students and geographic areas.
    3. Inform student body:
        a. Student Handbook listing activities could also discuss problem.
        b. Include information in yearly catalogue.
        c. Give periodic information in the student activity newsletter.
        d. This seems the best short-term solution.
    4. Stagger class schedules:
        a. Would involve extensive computer work.
        b. Student work schedules would probably not match classes which would result in an even bigger problem.
        c. Implementation only as a "last resort" measure.
    B. Long-range solutions:
    All possible solutions would have to be carried out, and would necessarily follow budgetary considerations.

V. DEVELOPMENT OF THE PLAN OF ACTION
    A. Group can aid in improving number of car pools through talking with fellow students.
    B. Group met with Mr. Norm Grant, Student Activity Director, and persuaded him to include parking information in the Student Activity Newsletter.
        1. The subsequent articles will contain information on incentives to join car pools.
        2. General information about the extent and reasons for current parking problems will be published periodically on the Sinclair campus.

SOURCES

BARR, ROBERT. Director of Public Information at Sinclair Community College, Interview.

"Bus Urge Grows," *Dayton Daily News*, February 27, 1974.

"Car Pools Gaining Coast to Coast," *U.S. News and World Report.* January 28, 1974, p. 66.

DAVIS, THOMAS. City Planning Board, Interview.

GRANT, NORM. Student Activity Director, Interview.

"Making Mass Transit Work," *Business Week*. February 16, 1974, pp. 74–80.

STATUM, ROBERT. Promoter of Car Pool Plans, Interview.

WILBUR, SMITH & ASSOCIATES, *Parking Study*. March 1972. Completed at the request of Sinclair Community College.

SUMMARY

Discussion is a mode of speaking—and thinking and living—possible only in a democracy. Its characteristics, basic philosophy, and limitations are also those of a democracy.

As contrasted with social conversation, discussion demands careful planning, skilled leadership, and intensive preparation by the participants. The purpose of discussion may be to impart information to an audience or to seek solutions to problems in any area vital to the participants and to any observers present.

Ideally, the process of decision-making through discussion closely approximates the scientific method, including *location, definition,* and *exploration* of the problem, coupled with the *examination* and *selection* of the best solution.

Discussion may occur on a private level in *dialogue, guided conversation, study groups, classroom* discussion, and the *conference.* Many forms and variations appear in public discussion, the most common being the *panel, symposium, lecture forum,* and *buzz session.* The nature of the proposition under consideration and the size and circumstances of the meetings will help determine the most appropriate type of discussion form.

QUESTIONS AND EXERCISES

1. Divide the class into several groups of four or more persons and select a problem for discussion. Each group should work out a complete agenda, following carefully the five steps in Dewey's process of reflective thinking. Record your discussion and write a critique evaluating the success of the group in following the agenda. Could any steps have been omitted? Would the discussion have been improved by omitting any steps? Tell why.

2. If you were going to set up a discussion program for an audience of 700 persons, which type of format (i.e., panel, symposium, lecture forum, buzz session) would you employ? Be prepared to defend your choice. What special circumstances would influence your selection?

3. Divide the class into groups of four to six and let each group pick a topic suitable for a panel discussion. The instructor or the group may wish to designate one person in each group to serve as the leader. If possible, record the panel discussion and then ask each participant to criticize the discussion according to the following factors:

   (a) Was the leader successful in keeping the discussion organized?
   (b) Which member or members of the group offered the best contributions?
   (c) If you were to use this same topic again for a panel discussion, what changes would you make in your preparation and participation?

4. After your experience in the panel discussion, what qualities do you consider most necessary for the leader?

5. Listen to a radio or television discussion program. Can you classify it according to any of the types mentioned in this chapter? Would another format have accomplished the purpose more satisfactorily? Were the major points of view adequately represented?

6. Select the campus issue you consider most timely and most desperately in need of a satisfactory solution. If you were to organize a public discussion on this question, what kind of discussion form would you employ? Who would you select as the leader? Participants? Be prepared to defend your selections.

7. Take the five steps in the process of reflective thinking and break each one into three subheadings. For example, under the second step, "Exploring the problem," you might include (a) the causes of the problem, (b) the economic factors, and (c) the political nature of the situation.

8. Select a general topic for discussion. Phrase the topic into a discussion question for a symposium. In a one-minute speech explain and defend your phraseology.

9. Attend a lecture forum and then write a short paper in which you discuss and evaluate the following:

    (a) The moderator's introduction of the topic and the speaker.
    (b) The question and answer period. Did the moderator use any devices to encourage questions? Was the speaker clear in formulating his answers? To what extent, if any, did the moderator participate?
    (c) Summaries. Did the speaker or moderator summarize at any point? Was the summary helpful?

10. Select a topic of current public interest or campus concern and assume that you will serve as the leader of a panel preparing to discuss this question. In outline form set up the specific subtopics and the order you would attempt to follow during the discussion. In a short speech be prepared to defend your selection of the subtopics and the order.

RECOMMENDED READINGS

BORMANN, ERNEST G. *Discussion and Group Methods: Theory and Practice.* New York: Harper & Row, Publishers, Inc., 1969.

CARTWRIGHT, DORWIN, and ALVIN ZANDER (eds.). *Group Dynamics: Research and Theory.* New York: Harper & Row, Publishers, Inc., 1960.

CORTRIGHT, RUPERT, and GEORGE L. HINDS. *Creative Discussion.* New York: Macmillan Publishing Co., Inc., 1959.

HARMS, L. S. *Human Communication: The New Fundamentals.* New York: Harper & Row, Publishers, Inc., 1974. Part Two.

HOWELL, WILLIAM S., and DONALD K. SMITH. *Discussion.* New York: Macmillan Publishers Co., Inc., 1956.

JACOBSON, WALLY D. *Power and Interpersonal Relations.* Belmont, Calif: Wadsworth Publishing Co., Inc., 1972.

KELTNER, JOHN W. *Group Discussion Processes.* New York: Longmans, Green & Company, Inc., 1957.

PHILLIPS, GERALD M. *Communication and the Small Group.* Indianapolis: The Bobbs-Merrill Co., Inc., 1973.

PHILLIPS, GERALD M., and EUGENE C. ERICKSON. *Interpersonal Dynamics in the Small Group.* New York: Random House, Inc., 1970.

SATTLER, W. M., and N. EDD MILLER. *Discussion and Conference,* 2nd ed. Englewood Cliffs, N.J.: Prentice-Hall, Inc., 1968.

UTTERBACK, WILLIAM E. *Group Thinking and Conference Leadership.* New York: Holt, Rinehart and Winston, Inc., 1950.

Chapter 13

Debate

> It's better to debate a question without settling
> it than to settle a question without debating it.
>
> JOSEPH JOUBERT

When Senator George McGovern set forth to win the Democratic presidential nomination in 1972, he issued a call to all potential nominees to join in debates across the country. His plea inspired a sardonic quip from one news commentator: "That's probably too good an idea for the gang to join in." The cynical journalist was right. Unfortunately no nominees for the highest office in the land have met in face-to-face debate since the exciting campaign of 1960 when an audience estimated as high as 85 million watched and listened as John F. Kennedy and Richard M. Nixon outlined the issues, submitted to cross-examination, and engaged in refutation and rebuttal.[1]

At that time Senator Kennedy and Vice-President Nixon had moved beyond the preliminary stages of discussion, namely the identification of the problems and an investigation of all possible solutions. Each man behaved and spoke as if he thought that his party had discovered the right answers, and each was feverishly attempting to persuade the American voters to accept his party's choice as the commander-in-chief for the next four years.

When the electorate, which now includes most college students, face a moment of decision, either on a national (with international implications) or on a local level (a water supply problem or school levy), the voters may engage in a long series of discussions, public and private, organized and disorganized. They may even call in experts to define and help to identify the problems, thereby investigating a wide variety of solutions. But eventually the citizens, directly or through their representatives, must make a choice and reach a definite decision, temporary or permanent.

In one community a discussion of the city's financial plight reached the referendum stage, and the voters finally decided the fate of the debate proposition: "*Resolved,* That a 1 per cent gross income tax be

---

[1] See *The Great Debates,* Sidney Kraus, ed., (Bloomington: Indiana University Press, 1962), for a thorough analysis. The Gallup Poll estimated 85 million heard at least one of the debates (*idem,* p. 148).

levied on all residents." Citizens' committees for and against soon sprang up, and the articulate debated the question informally at home, at places of business, at service clubs, and on the local television stations. A few days before the election two representatives for each side clashed in public debate, attempting to persuade the people to cast their ballots for or against the new tax.

During any small-group discussion a considerable amount of talk may approach actual debate. As discussants seek to define the problem, identify the issues, and probe for possible solutions, they may engage in informal debate as they use John Dewey's steps in reflective thinking. (See Chapter 12, pages 258–259 for Dewey's concept.) No sharp dividing line separates discussion from debate. They are not two distinctively and diametrically opposed concepts, but essentially an intermixture of two complementary elements of one process—democratic decision-making. Rational decisions are possible only if we are willing to explore, examine, test, and submit our ideas to the vigorous attacks of the opposition. No idea, however rash, foolish, or seemingly dangerous, is unspeakable. Forced into the public forum it may be unmasked as false. Suppressed, it festers, threatening all free inquiry. When we exclude discussion and debate, we turn inevitably to unthinking acquiescence, or to mindless violence, thereby perverting democratic processes.

DEBATE AND DISCUSSION COMPARED

When a group of discussants seek a solution to a problem and have reached a point where they are prepared to hear arguments *for* and *against* a specific proposal, they are ready for debate. We may define formal debate then as a clean-cut, pro-and-con argument between two persons or sides who are advocating a specific proposal for the solution of a problem. One side—the affirmative—supports or argues for (affirms) the proposition. The other side—the negative—argues against (denies) the proposition.

If we analyze the thinking process taking place *before* a group is ready to commit itself to a course of action, five fundamental characteristics of discussion and debate become apparent:

1. In discussion we usually begin with a problem and, through group thinking, strive toward a solution. When the group fails to reach a general agreement or a consensus during their discussion and the membership is clearly divided in its acceptance of a solution, the moment for debate has arrived.
2. Formal debate may then be the final step in the process of reflective thinking.
3. Debate begins with a proposed solution; a discussion member turns

debater after he has selected a solution and is prepared to support it with evidence and argument.

4. We usually phrase the solution as a resolution, a proposition, or a motion. In formal debate a proposition is always explicitly stated.

5. The debate format is usually structured formally to ensure fair and equal representation to both sides.

THE PROPOSITION

In discussion we are usually concerned with a general question, for example, "What kind of sewage disposal system is best for our town?" The topic implies general dissatisfaction with present arrangements. After a thorough investigation, including, perhaps, expert analysis, several solutions may claim our attention. Additional discussion may produce a specific point of view, stated in declarative form and constituting the proposition: "*Resolved*, That a chemical disposal plant be constructed for the purpose of sewage disposal." At this point speakers line up their evidence and arguments for and against a definitely stated point of view. Like discussion questions, debate propositions may concern *fact, value,* or *policy.* "Joe Smith murdered his wife" (fact). "Free enterprise is preferable to socialism" (value). "*Resolved*, That the Federal Government should control the utilization of energy in the United States" (policy).

Effective debating requires a good proposition, carefully phrased and marked by the following qualities:

1. *Debatable.* A proposition is debatable when it has two clear-cut sides. Unless sufficient evidence and argument permit individuals of intelligence and integrity to take opposing sides, the proposition is undebatable.

2. *Complete assertion.* A good proposition demands a complete assertion. A phrase or term such as "Compulsory Health Insurance" is incomplete and not debatable. The statement "*Resolved*, That the United States should adopt a program of compulsory health insurance for all citizens" is complete and debatable.

3. *Brevity.* A good proposition is stated in as brief a form as possible without sacrificing clarity. The following is an overworded proposition: "*Resolved*, That the United States Congress should work out a plan more like the British form of government." The same proposition is more briefly and effectively worded: "*Resolved*, That the United States should adopt a parliamentary system of national government."

4. *Single.* Avoid multipropositional statements. A good proposition necessarily centers about a single problem. We should not, for example, attempt to include a nuclear test ban, peaceful uses of atomic

energy, and general disarmament in one question. Although these problems are closely related, only one should appear in the phrasing of a proposition.

5. *Affirmative.* A good proposition is stated *declaratively* and asserts the position of the affirmative. The affirmative argues for a change in the existing state of affairs. It recommends the establishment or the abolition of a situation depending upon existing conditions. For example, students at a college with intercollegiate football might debate the question "*Resolved,* That intercollegiate football be dropped at X College." At another school without intercollegiate football, the proposition would be stated: "*Resolved,* That intercollegiate football be established at Y College."

6. *Impartial.* Keep the proposition free from emotional, question-begging terms that give special advantage to either side. We should avoid, for example, a wordy one such as "*Resolved,* That the United States should stop poisoning the atmosphere and condemning unborn generations to untold misery by unilaterally stopping all further testing of nuclear weapons." So stated, the proposition argues the case for the affirmative. A fairer statement might be "*Resolved,* That the United States should unilaterally stop all further testing of nuclear weapons."

ARGUING THE PROPOSITION

Before you meet in platform debate, you will face the intensive demands of analyzing the proposition and finding the evidence with which to build the strongest possible case. The initial preparation requires both sides to perform the following tasks:

1. *Defining all terms.* Even if the proposition is clearly stated and free from technical jargon, we can save needless talk in discussion and debate by defining our terms. Unless all words and phrases appearing in the debate are clear and mutually acceptable to both sides, it is impossible to grapple with the major issues themselves.

2. *Determining the specific issues.* Issues are like swinging doors, opening the way to both the affirmative and negative cases. Correctly phrased they pose questions to which the affirmative always answers yes and the negative usually answers no. The issues will be stated somewhat differently, depending on the kind of proposition under consideration. For propositions of *fact* and *value,* the questions probe for the truth or validity of the affirmative assertion. The prosecuting attorney (affirmative) in the Joe Smith murder case will ask and answer yes: "Did Joe have a motive?" "Did he have access to the weapon?" "Was he in, around, or near the scene of the crime?" In essence, the questions (issues) are designed to discover

the facts surrounding the case. For a question of *value,* the stock issues will focus on the moral, spiritual, aesthetic, or materialistic benefits that may or may not accrue from the proposition.

In the proposition of *policy,* the stock issues include questions that include fact and value, but are primarily concerned with the consequence of a new course of action. Anytime we face the problem of making a decision, we ask ourselves consciously or subconsciously certain ordinary, common, or stock questions. "Do I need to make this change?" "Will the change solve my problem?" "Is the change practical and desirable?" In debate we refer to these inevitable questions as the *stock issues:*

(a) Is there a need to change our present policy? Is the body politic sick?

(b) Will the change recommended by the affirmative remedy the condition? Will this remedy effect a cure?

(c) Is the proposed change practicable and workable? Is this "wonder drug" free from harmful side effects?

(d) Is the proposed change the best available solution? Is this cure better than any other possible remedy?

(e) Will additional benefits result from the adoption of the affirmative proposal? Will this remedy also serve as a tonic?

The stock issues are valuable to both the affirmative and negative mainly in the early stages of analysis. During the debate itself, the skillful debater avoids talking about the "need" and "our plan," phrasing each issue according to the specific proposition he is debating. On the question "*Resolved,* That Congress should be given the power to reverse decisions of the Supreme Court," the first stock issue (NEED) might include: "Has a small group of nonelected men usurped legislative functions, thereby thwarting the will of the people?" Since the proposition in this instance does not spell out the means of congressional reversal, the affirmative must also present a specific plan. They might advocate the overriding of Court decisions by a two-thirds vote of the Congress. If the question were on the abolition of capital punishment, the affirmative plan is included in the statement itself. The affirmative must establish (prove) the validity of all the issues. The negative may deny (rebut) all the issues or it may admit some and refute others.

Burden of proof

The *burden of proof* rests with the side that wants to change the present system. In legalistic language, *status quo* (the present system) is *presumed* to be innocent until the affirmative assumes its burden of proof and demonstrates the guilty condition of that system and shows why the affirmative plan would be better. The affirmative must not only show that the evils that exist in the present system are inherent in that system, but must also explain how their propositional plan will cure the evils.

The negative, on the other hand, must then assume the *burden of rebuttal* because if no protesting voice is raised to the affirmative proposal, the listener is obliged to accept it. In meeting its responsibilities, the negative enjoys a wider range of choices than the affirmative. If we think of the affirmative team as soldiers holding a fortress consisting of the stock issues (Need, Plan, Benefits), it is obvious that they must protect all the ramparts of the fort. The negative, on the other hand, may concentrate its fire on the weakest bulwark (issue) and by destroying it can invade the fort and put the affirmative to flight. If there is no need for a change, for example, it makes no difference how wonderful the plan may be. Put in everyday terms, the so-called "bargain" dress or car or golf clubs are no bargain at all unless we actually "need" them.

Comparative advantages case

In most debates on policy questions both sides will compare the advantages and disadvantages of life under the new affirmative system with continued existence under the old system or the status quo. This technique becomes the primary affirmative strategy in the so-called *comparative advantages case*. The affirmative accepts the basic goals of the present system, but will insist that these objectives will be achieved more satisfactorily under the affirmative plan. On the proposition: "*Resolved,* That a Federal World Government should replace the United Nations," the affirmative would probably agree on the goals and objectives of the United Nations, but maintain the "comparative advantage" of World Government over the UN as a peace-keeping agency.

Possible negative stands

The negative may reject the entire affirmative case, denying the existence of a problem and perhaps even maintaining that were one to exist, the affirmative program still would not work. Or the negative may recognize some weaknesses in the present structure, but insist that a few minor changes will remedy the problem. Using a different tack, the negative may admit the evils in the present system, but insist that the affirmative measure will not correct the ills. Further, the negative may brand the affirmative cure as worse than the illness. While the negative speakers are under no obligation to present a remedy, even when they share the affirmative's distaste for the present system, they may find it advantageous to offer a *counterproposal*. The negative then assumes the burden of proof and must demonstrate that the counterplan not only is superior to the affirmative remedy but also cannot under the statement of the proposition be adopted by the affirmative. On the Supreme Court question, for example, a negative proposal to permit three-fourths instead of two-thirds of the Congress to override the Court is not a counterplan. The affirmative would simply agree with the negative and win the debate under the statement of the proposition. On the other hand, President Franklin D. Roosevelt's proposal to increase the membership of the Supreme Court as a way of insuring his legislative program would constitute a counterplan, albeit, as Roosevelt discovered, not a popular one.

TYPES OF DEBATE

Formal debate

In traditional, formal debate an equal number of speakers, usually two, support each side. The speaking order usually follows this pattern, but the time limits may be changed as long as both sides receive equal time.

Constructive speeches

First affirmative	10 minutes
First negative	10 minutes
Second affirmative	10 minutes
Second negative	10 minutes

Rebuttal speeches

First negative	5 minutes
First affirmative	5 minutes
Second negative	5 minutes
Second affirmative	5 minutes

To meet various audience situations, it is possible to employ a multitude of forms, including problem-solving debate, heckling debate, debate forums, two-man debate, documentary debate, and courtroom debate.[2] The most commonly used variations are the following:

Cross-examination debate

Sometimes called the Oregon Plan because of its development at the University of Oregon,[3] this type of debate gives each speaker an opportunity to cross-examine the opposition and in turn to submit to cross-examination. Except for the first affirmative, the speakers step from cross-examination to the speaker's stand for their constructive speeches. A typical debate appears as follows:

[2] Most standard texts in argumentation and debate include complete explanations of each type. See H. L. Ewbank and J. J. Auer, *Discussion and Debate* (New York: Appleton-Century-Crofts, 1951), pp. 394–404; and Austin J. Freeley, *Argumentation and Debate*, 3rd ed. (San Francisco: Wadsworth, 1971), pp. 352–372.

[3] J. S. Gray, "The Oregon Plan of Debating," *Quarterly Journal of Speech Education*, 12 (April 1926), 175–180.

Speeches	Minutes
1. First affirmative speech	8
2. First negative cross-examines first affirmative	4
3. First negative speech	8
4. Second affirmative cross-examines first negative	4
5. Second affirmative speech	8
6. Second negative cross-examines second affirmative	4
7. Second negative speech	8
8. First affirmative cross-examines second negative	4
9. Negative summary (either speaker)	4
10. Affirmative summary (etiher speaker)	4
Total time	56

Aptly designed for audience situations, the cross-examination debate ensures close attention through the rapid give-and-take and the opportunity for direct clashes of the participants. Indeed, the debaters need to recognize and may exploit all the legitimate dramatic elements inherent in this type of speaking. But a word of caution is in order too! They must guard against the emotionally histrionic exhibition that plumbs the depths of *argumentum ad hominem* and descends to mere bickering and brow-beating. Below are some suggestions for the cross-examination debater:

1. Intensive preparation and practice to ensure clear, relevant, well-phrased questions.
2. Questions concentrated on one issue rather than scattered over the whole case.
3. Questions phrased to elicit short responses, preferably yes or no.
4. Questions designed to expose feeble evidence or specious reasoning.
5. A realization that the cross-examiners must know the answers to all the questions. They are not seeking information, but attempting to establish or weaken a contention.
6. Little or no editorial comment from the cross-examiner.
7. A close integration of the answers revealed during cross-examination with the development of the constructive speeches. (Too often the cross-examination and the constructive argument bear little relationship to each other.)

Direct clash debate

This modification encourages a careful analysis of the specific issues and promotes a direct pro-and-con consideration of one issue at a time. Using a traditional debate question and two to five persons on a side, the procedure is as follows:

1. *The analysis period.* With the affirmative opening the debate, each side takes six minutes to clarify its stand on *definitions, major issues, plans,* and *counterplans.* The purpose of the initial speeches is to

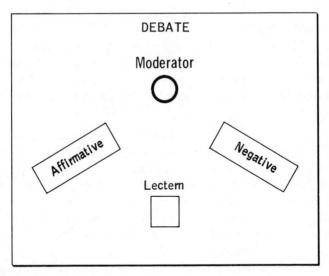

FIGURE 13–1. A typical platform arrangement for the cross-examination or the formal debate.

clarify the issues and determine those on which both teams agree to clash. If necessary each side may have an additional three-minute speech to support its analysis. Neither team needs to use all of its time, and the only evidence introduced is to establish the validity of definitions or the importance of the issues. It helps at this stage to place all the issues on the blackboard.

2. *The judge's evaluation.* The judge then comments on the issues, definitions, and plan, suggesting any necessary clarifications. He may select the issues for the clashes or permit teams to choose their own from the accepted list.

3. *The clashes.* The affirmative initiates the first clash with a four-minute speech designed to establish an issue. A negative speaker follows with a two-minute answer. Alternating two-minute clashes continue until each side has spoken an agreed number of times or until the judge declares one side the victor. In the second clash the negative initiates the issue with a four-minute speech and concludes the clash with the final two-minute speech. The affirmative opens and closes the last clash and the team winning two out of three wins the debate.

Clearly this style of debate places a premium on issue analysis, direct adaptation, incisive, extempore speaking, and immediate refutation. Indeed, when a team fails to answer directly or adequately the judge is asked to stop a clash and award the decision to the other side.[4]

[4] J. Garber Drushal, "Direct Clash Debate as a Teaching Procedure," *The Gavel*, 41 (November 1958), 5–6, 14, 16.

Parliamentary debate

This modification of traditional British debating provides a stimulating exercise for classes or forensic clubs. It gives all members maximum opportunity to speak briefly to the proposition for debate. Presumably, all participants have studied the question in advance. The procedure is as follows:

1. As members enter the room, those favoring the motion sit to the moderator's right and those opposing to the left. The moderator calls for order, announces the motion, e.g., "This House Would Rather Be Red Than Dead," and introduces the first speaker who has seven minutes in which to support the motion.
2. The moderator presents a speaker for the opposition who likewise has seven minutes. He or she is followed by pro-and-con seconding speeches of three minutes each.
3. The moderator then recognizes speakers from the floor, alternately for and against the motion, who may speak for not more than three minutes.
4. Any speaker except the first may be interrupted "on a point of information." The speaker may refuse to answer or even give a member the chance to ask his questions.
5. Only the following points of order are permitted: objections to irrelevant remarks; objections to unsuitable language; objections to behavior of a member.
6. At the end of a specified time, eighty or ninety minutes, the moderator recognizes speakers for the final summaries, first against and then for the motion. Each side has two minutes.
7. The moderator calls for a division of the house (vote), announces the winner and adjourns the meeting.

Obviously this style of debating requires a moderator with a heavy gavel and a complete knowledge of parliamentary procedure. It helps speakers develop a facile, extemporaneous style. There is a danger, however, that it may also encourage the speakers to count on and to develop verbal facility rather than to concentrate on the essentials of research and an analysis of the issues. Glibness at the expense of substance may well result.

PREPARATION FOR DEBATE

Everything we have said up to this point should help you prepare for a specific debate. Presumably, before taking sides, you engage in serious inquiry, examining the problem area and the various solutions. After the selection and wording of a proposition, you then face the task of developing a unified case and a speech that is coordinated with the constructive argument of your partner. These additional suggestions should prove helpful.

Investigate both sides

No debaters are completely prepared to defend their own positions until they thoroughly understand the arguments of the opposition; they must, therefore, find all the evidence (facts, opinion, motivations) supporting every possible contention on both sides of the question. Finally, they must concentrate on discovering all the available proof for their own contentions. Unhappily too many debaters place their faith in unsupported assertion, developing arguments and drawing conclusions based on inadequate or faulty evidence. While the affirmative must prove its indictment of the status quo, *every debater, affirmative and negative, must assume the burden of proof for all of his assertions.* To assert with vigor or vehemence is not enough.

Test the evidence

Proof in debate should depend primarily on confirming evidence. The assertions, premises, or contentions that tend to support or prove the affirmative or negative cases are true only if they can be established through evidence of fact and by authoritative or expert opinion. Fact, of course, is almost always preferable to opinion, which is used when facts are unavailable or seemingly contradictory. As you research your topic, you will look for all the available facts (examples, statistics, instances, analogies) and expert testimony that will strengthen your contentions. In debate, you are always dealing with *probable* truth rather than *absolute* truth; otherwise, there is no reason for debate. Further, two equally credible, authorative witnesses may observe the same facts but draw radically different inferences and conclusions.

In 1973 the nations of the world faced an acute energy crisis, one that the "experts" predicted would plague us, perhaps to the end of the twentieth century or beyond. Authorities in many fields from different parts of the globe searched for the "true" facts, undoubtedly found some, but reached widely different conclusions about the causes, the probable effects, and the best courses of action to pursue. Some called the "crisis" a contrived one and refused to accept the notion that an actual shortage of gas and petroleum existed. Most blamed the 1973 war in the Middle East and the Arab oil embargo as the proximate cause. Others faulted the Nixon Administration for not recognizing the early signs and acting sooner to avoid the approaching crisis. Even the environmentalists received their share of the blame for insisting on emission controls for our cars and industrial plants and laws regulating strip mining. The puzzling problems facing the debater include the evaluation of the facts and opinions. Some of the questions you will want to apply to your evidence and that of your opponent include:

1. Are the sources of evidence *primary* (firsthand, original)? Secondary sources (hearsay, quoted material) are always less reliable. A so-called "fact" in print is not necessarily a fact. It may be an outright lie, a deliberate distortion, or an inadvertent misquote.
2. Is the evidence verifiable? The written primary source is superior to the spoken word, unless you can produce a verified video tape recording.
3. Can you find a wide variety of recent facts and opinions that support your contentions?
4. Have you tested your statistical evidence for reliability and validity of sampling, source, and statistical significance? An ancient aphorism warns that "Figures don't lie, but liars figure."
5. Will the audience accept your authorities and are the facts and opinions consistent with their experiences? Until the judges accept, proof is incomplete.

Test the proof (reasoning)

Logical proof of your case will include a careful combination of *evidence* and *reasoning,* clearly and persuasively adapted to your judges. We reason by presenting evidence that points toward the truth or falsity of the proposition. Our line of reasoning usually develops from *causal relationships* or from argument by *example, comparison* (analogy) or from *sign.* To watch a line of argument develop (and to see how open it is to fallacious reasoning), let's examine the case of falling college enrollments to see how we might establish the truth or the falsity of the issue: "Are enrollments at our college going to decline next year due to low academic standards?"

Both the affirmative and the negative may have noted certain *signs* that seem to point to lower enrollments and perhaps to a decline in academic standards. Freshman applications are down, the administration is planning to close a dormitory, and there is talk of eliminating some programs. This *argument from sign* establishes no actual causal relationship with either facet of the issue. It is similar to the flag flying at half-mast or the cat scratching itself: the flag's position did not cause the death, nor the cat's scratching, the fleas. However, the affirmative may have discovered that neighboring Westovershew College has suffered falling enrollments over the past two years and that its academic standards were also low. They are attempting to establish through analogy the *effect* (falling enrollment) to a probable *cause* (low standards). They might also attempt to complete the causal relationship by asserting that unless our school raises standards (cause), we too will face declining enrollments (effect). If the negative, on the other hand, have uncovered a number of institutions with standards similar to Westovershew who have actually experienced rising enrollments, they cast serious doubt on the validity of the affirmative's causal argument. The decision will probably go to the team that has used inductive and deductive reasoning most expertly. They will have found the most reliable data and authoritative opinion and woven these factual threads into a persuasive fabric.

Stephen Toulmin, an English logician, offers a model for analyzing the often complicated arguments that twist their way toward proof of a contention. For Toulmin three essential elements, *Data, Warrant,* and *Claim,* provide the heart of his approach to an argument.

In inductive proof we move from the *specific* to a *general* conclusion. We move in the opposite direction in deduction, going from the general statement to the specific application. When we talk about evidence and data, we are referring to those inductive elements that enable us to draw a conclusion. "Everybody's doing it!" is our deduction drawn from an assumed perfect induction—a rare occurrence. See Chapter 16, pages 348–350, and Chapter 17, pages 376–378, for additional materials on inductive and deductive reasoning as well as causal reasoning.

The data or evidence leads us to a (claim) or conclusion by way of a (warrant) which contributes the reason or connecting causal link between the data and the claim. The *warrant* is frequently implicit in an argument and must be "broken out" or made explicit in order to test the causal link and ascertain what *backing* is necessary to establish the validity of the warrant. Failure to *support* the warrant adequately may destroy the *claim*. Moreover, the conclusion, itself, may also be hedged in with a *qualifier* and a *rebuttal*. Many variations and nearly unlimited expansions of the model are possible in the development of a complicated argument. The energy crisis can provide the setting to watch the model in operation.[5] In the winter of 1974 the U.S. Director of Energy tried to explain the fuel crisis to the Congress and to the public, many of whom shivered in cold homes, waited in line for gas, or saw their jobs vanish. One of the arguments on the Toulmin model would look something like the one shown in Figure 13–2.

Record the evidence

The old-fashioned picture of debate teams lugging huge stacks of books to the tables prior to the debate, though quaintly romantic, probably served no useful purpose. A better method is to devise a uniform system of note-taking, following a prearranged format satisfactory to both debaters. Then as the debate progresses, each can exchange readily understandable items of evidence. Each debater should develop a consistent system of note-taking, perhaps like those shown in Figure 13–3, which can also serve as a useful research tool for any type of public speaking.

[5] See Stephen E. Toulmin, *The Uses of Argument* (Cambridge, Eng.: Cambridge University Press, 1958).

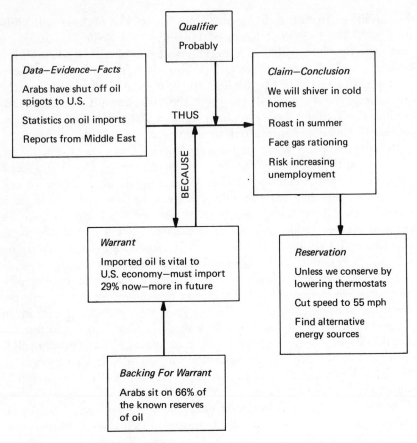

FIGURE 13–2. Toulmin Model.

The first item is an example of *evidence of fact* and the second, *evidence of opinion*.

During your research keep the following rules in mind:

1. Figure 13–3 represents only one of many ways to record evidence of fact and opinion. It is important, however, for teams to select a precise form and adhere strictly to it. *Be consistent in your note-taking.*
2. Select a uniform sized card (4 × 6 or 6 × 8). A 3 × 5 card is usually too small.
3. Place *one item* only on each card.
4. Use your own words whenever possible. Save direct quotation for authorities whose opinions carry real weight and whose words and phrases are in themselves impellingly persuasive.
5. Be sure to set off direct quotations with the appropriate marks. For your own words within a quotation, use brackets.
6. Identify the author and source. For many audiences one name and

Subject: Energy Supply & Demand	Author: John G. Winger et al., Energy Economics Division, Chase Manhattan Bank	Title: Outlook for Energy in the United States to 1985	Source: Chase Manhattan Bank, N.Y., June 1972, p. 8

Verbatim quotation from a study by the Energy Economics Division

All the various uses for energy are far too numerous to discuss individually. But they all fall within one or the other of five major market categories. They are listed below according to their current size:

Energy Market	% of Total
Industrial	32
Electric utilities	25
Transportation	24
Residential	14
Commercial	5
Total	100

Subject: Energy Conservation Insulation	Author: Joel Darmstadter & Milton Searl	Title: Growth in U.S.A. Energy Import De- pendence: Prospect and Options	Source: Hearings: U.S. Senate Foreign Relations Comm. May 30, 1973, p. 25

Researches from Resources for the Future, Inc. testified that "even if all new residential buildings in the United States were insulated in the most ideal way, this would cover only around 2% per year of the Nation's housing and thus would, for some years into the future, contribute only sparingly to reduced energy use in space heating."

FIGURE 13–3. A typical system of note-taking.

source is just like another. Simply because a writer made a statement and had it published does not give it the weight of actual authority. Establish the basis for the authoritativeness of your source.

Formulate a complete brief

The name *brief* seems to be a contradiction in terms, since it is far from short or lacking in length. It is the debater's complete logical outline of all the contentions on one side of the question. It likewise includes all the evidence of fact and opinion, placed in proper logical relationship to each premise or contention. It is not intended as the speaker's outline for the debate speech. If the speakers followed the complete brief for their presentations, their speeches would be stiff and colorless. We shall cover the "debate speech" in the following section of this chapter. Additional helps on outlining the actual speech are in Chapter 17, "Synthesis and Organization" (see pages 379–385).

When President Nixon delivered his State of the Union message on January 30, 1974, he urged the Congress to enact his comprehensive health insurance plan. Prior to his speech, Senator Edward M. Kennedy and Representative Martha Griffiths had submitted a different kind of plan to meet the same problem. The nation's lawmakers will probably debate this question, a favorite of college debaters for almost half a century. And regardless of the measure that the Congress passes, the topic in various forms will remain timely. During 1972–1973 the intercollegiate debaters across the country argued this proposition; one of the briefs that came out of that season is included here. You may wish to compare this plan with the Nixon or Kennedy proposals.

SAMPLE BRIEF

Prepared by Steve Thompson and Jim Wallace, members of the Ohio University debate team for the intercollegiate season, 1972–73.

PROPOSITION: *Resolved,* That the Federal Government should provide a program of comprehensive medical care for all United States Citizens.

Affirmative

INTRODUCTION

I. Immediate Cause for Discussion:
   A. Millions of poor people in the U.S. do not receive adequate medical care.
   B. Persons who cannot get adequate medical care have poorer health.
   C. The steadily rising costs of medical care make it increasingly difficult for all citizens to pay for medical services.
II. Origin and History of the Question:
   A. During the past century most of the nations of the Western World have adopted some form of comprehensive medical care for all of its citizens.
   B. The U.S. Government, state and local governments have provided increasing but inadequate support for general health programs.
   C. Medicaid represents an attempt by the government to assist poor patients.
III. Definition of terms:
   A. "Federal Government" refers to the central government as distinct from the governments in the several states.
   B. "Should" means ought to, and not necessarily will.
   C. "Comprehensive medical care" means the establishment of all-inclusive national health insurance for all persons in the U.S. including the following features:
      1. A federal licensing program for interns which mandates that upon completion of internship, they are required to serve for 24 months in an area with low physician/population ratio characteristics.

2. Administration of the program by the Department of Health, Education, and Welfare.
3. Financing of the program by a new progressive personal and corporate income tax.

IV. Admitted matter:
   A. The affirmative concedes that some people are financially capable of providing their own medical services.
   B. Some people are adequately covered through voluntary health insurance.
   C. The affirmative admits that the U.S. has one of the highest average standards of medical care in the world.

V. The issues are as follows:
   A. Do millions of poor receive inadequate medical care?
   B. Do citizens who cannot secure adequate medical care suffer with poor health?
   C. Are present programs such as Medicaid inadequate to meet the medical needs of a significant portion of the nation's citizenry?
   D. Will the affirmative program of comprehensive medical care provide adequate medical care for all citizens?

DISCUSSION

I. Millions of poor citizens in the U.S. do not have access to adequate care, for
   A. About 35 million Americans cannot pay for their medical care. National Urban Coalition, *Counterbudget*, 1971, p. 69. Robert S. Benson and Harold Wolman, ed. (New York: Praeger). Herbert Morais, *The History of the Negro in Medicine* (New York: Publishers Company, Inc., 1969), p. 207.
   B. Physician and hospital maldistribution prevent 40 million Americans from getting care. *Time*, "Health Care: Supply, Demand, and Politics," June 7, 1971, p. 86.

II. Citizens who do not get adequate medical care have poorer health, William C. Richardson, "Poverty, Illness and Use of Health Services in the United States," *Hospitals*, July 1, 1969, p. 40. Richard Kunnes, *Your Money or Your Life* (New York: Dodd, Mead 1971), pp. 98–99

III. Partial coverage programs under the present system such as Medicaid will always fail to cover the needs of the poor, for
   A. Partial programs are limited in coverage, for
      1. Those eligible for Medicaid included only one-third of those who are actually needy. U.S. Department of HEW, *Catastrophic Illnesses and Costs* (Washington: U.S. Government Printing Office), May 1971, p. 46.
      2. Even for those covered, Medicaid and Medicare leave substantial financial burdens. Eveline Burns, "The Nation's Health Insurance and Health Services Policies," *The American Behavioral Scientist*, June 1972, p. 717.
   B. Present-day partial programs are uncoordinated, for
      1. They are administered by many varied agencies of the government which are incapable of providing medical services to the poor. *New York Times*, March 17, 1970, p. 1.
      2. Lack of coordination keeps many away from medical care. Eveline Burns *et al.*, *Social Economics for the 1970's*, p. 108.
   C. The present system cannot provide adequate medical services in depressed areas, for
      1. Giving the poor medical purchasing power, as Medicaid attempts to do, has not guaranteed available medical services in deprived areas. Jeffrey Weiss, *et al.*, "An Essay on the National Financing of Health Care," *Journal of Human Resources*, Spring 1972, p. 142.
      2. Financial inducements cannot alleviate this problem. R. Finch, *et al.*, "The role of Prepaid Group Practice in Relieving the Medical Care Crisis," *Harvard Law Review*, February 1971, p. 896.

D. Any partial program of medical care for the poor will only promote inflation, thus denying even those who are marginally poor from getting care, for
1. A program designed for one segment of society will drive up the price of medical service. *Monthly Labor Review*, June 1972, p. 51.
2. Rising prices cause many persons to be priced out of care. Charles L. Schultze, *et al.*, *Setting National Priorities: The 1973 Budget* (Washington: The Brookings Institute, 1972), p. 223.

CONCLUSION

Therefore since:
I. Millions of poor citizens in the U.S. do not have access to adequate medical care, and
II. Those who do not get adequate medical care have poorer health, and
III. Partial coverage programs under the present system fail to cover the needs of the poor.
It is to be concluded that the Federal Government should provide a program of comprehensive medical care for all United States Citizens.

Negative

[This brief is designed to meet the specific arguments and plan proposed in the affirmative brief. A full brief would contain arguments and evidence to meet any possible case the affirmative might propose under the statement of the proposition.]

INTRODUCTION

[The negative brief contains essentially the same kind of material in the introduction that appears in the affirmative brief. Both teams, of course, must come to an agreement of the definition of terms or make definition one of the issues for debate. A good debate, however, will not focus on the definitions but rather on the central proposition under discussion.]

DISCUSSION

I. There is no need for the adoption of a program of comprehensive medical care for all U.S. citizens, for
A. Virtually all citizens in the U.S. have sufficient access to medical care today, for
1. Medical indigency does not exist, for
a. Statistical analysis reveals that poor persons make slightly more physician visits than do middle and upper income classes. Charles L. Schultze, *et al.*, *Setting National Priorities: The 1973 Budget* (Washington: The Brookings Institute, 1972), p. 224.
b. Actual field studies have demonstrated that financial barriers do not cause a significant amount of delay in seeking medical attention. Edward Suchman, "Stages of Illness and Medical Care," *Journal of Health and Human Behavior*, Fall 1965, p. 120. Roger Battistella, "Factors Associated With Delay in the Initiation of Physician's Care Among Late Adulthood Persons," *American Journal of Public Health*, July 1971, p. 1353.
B. Present medical programs have not led to categorization of the poor, for
1. In the most comprehensive Medicaid plans, all of the poor are covered, for,
a. New York Medicaid covers all persons with an income of up to $5000 per year. *New York Times*, December 18, 1972, p. 45.
b. If all state plans were as comprehensive as New York Medicaid, the

entire poverty population of the U.S. could be covered. Robert J. Myers, *Medicare*, 1970, p. 226. (Bryn Mawr, Pennsylvania, published for Mc-Cahan Foundation 1970).

C. An alleged lack of coordination of Federal Programs is not an inherent evil in the present system, for
    1. Under Title 19 of Medicaid, all states must coordinate all of their health and hospital programs. *Medicaid: State Programs after Two Years* (New York: The Tax Foundation, 1968), p. 56.
    2. A lack of coordination merely calls for an information dissemination campaign telling the poor how to obtain medical services.

D. Lack of medical services in depressed areas does not obviate the expansion of existing federal programs, for
    1. Several studies have shown that distance to medical care is not related to the rates of utilization. T. W. Bice, R. L. Eichhorn, P. D. Fox, "Socioeconomic Status and Use of Physician Services: A Reconsideration," *Medical Care*, May–June 1972, p. 269.
    2. The Emergency Health Personnel Act of 1972 will distribute 600 medical personnel to areas of low physician-population ratio. "Country Doctor, '72," *Newsweek*, May 8, 1972, p. 64.

E. Inflation will not prohibit expansion of existing Federal medical programs, for
    1. An increase in the supply of doctors has moderated inflation. Harry Schwartz, *New York Times*, November 29, 1971, p. 39.
    2. Wage and price controls have been successful in stopping inflation in the areas of health care. Harry Schwartz, *The Case for American Medicine*, 1972, p. 104 (New York: D. McKay Co., 1972).

II. The affirmative proposal is not practical, for
  A. Doctors would quit rather than work under National Health Insurance, for
    1. Doctors may find National Health Insurance so unacceptable that they would be unwilling to continue working. Robert Patricelli, "National Health Insurance Proposals: Leverage for Change?" *Bulletin of the New York Academy of Medicine*, January 1972, p. 125.
    2. Doctors have taken such action in the past, most notably in Quebec. "Crisis in Canada over a New Medicine Plan," *U.S. News and World Report*, November 23, 1970, p. 80.

  B. The lack of a fee barrier would overload the medical system, for
    1. The fee for service system restrains people from malingering, thereby overusing the system. Harry Schwartz, "Health Care in America: A Heretical Diagnosis," *Saturday Review*, August 14, 1971, p. 55.
    2. When the fee has been removed unnecessary operations have increased as they did after World War II under the United Mine Workers System of Health Insurance. Raul Tunley, *The American Health Scandal* (New York: Harper and Row, 1966), pp. 46–47.

III. The affirmative plan is undesirable, for
  A. It does not represent the best use of scarce resources, for
    1. No evidence shows that medical care really improves the overall health of the nation. Merwyn R. Greenlick, "The Impact of Prepaid Group Practice on American Medical Care: A Critical Evaluation," *Annals of the American Academy*, January 1972, p. 104.
    2. There is not enough money available to fulfill every human need. Robert M. Grosse, "Cost-Benefit Analysis of Health Service," *Annals of the American Academy*, January 1972, p. 97.
    3. The money used to finance the affirmative plan would save more lives if used in other areas, for
    a. Reducing the air pollution by 50% would increase life expectancy in the

United States by one year. Lester Lave and Eugene Seskin, "Air Pollution, Climate, and Home Heating: Their effects on U.S. Mortality Rates," *American Journal of Public Health,* July 1972, p. 915.
  b. Better housing in ghettos and depressed areas would substantially improve the health of the nation. Albert Schaffer *et al., Understanding Social Problems* (Columbus, Ohio: Charles E. Merrill Publishing Company, 1970), pp. 241–242.

CONCLUSION

Therefore since:
  I. There is no need for a comprehensive medical care program, and
 II. The affirmative plan is impractical, and
III. The affirmative plan is undesirable.
The negative urges the rejection of the proposition.

THE DEBATE SPEECH

In traditional debate with two-man teams, each speaker shares the responsibility of developing a part of the complete case. Combined with his colleague's speech, it constitutes the constructive argument on one side of the question. The general approach for typical debate speeches will appear somewhat as follows:

First affirmative constructive speech

  I. Introduction
   A. Focus attention on the topic, demonstrating its timeliness and importance; if possible select evidence or develop an illustration designed to encourage a sympathetic audience response to the affirmative position.
   B. State the proposition for debate.
   C. Define only the ambiguous terms or those that may lead to misunderstanding or controversy.
   D. Outline the entire affirmative case, indicating the major contentions each affirmative speaker will establish.
   E. Restate your major contentions.
 II. Body
   A. State the first contention (a part of the need issue).
     1. Establish through reasoned argument based on examples, analogy, statistics, and authority.

To develop the complete need issue, the first speaker may offer two or three but never more than five contentions. After establishing these contentions (need issue) the first speaker should probably outline the specific nature of the plan, if such is necessary. It is unfair to the negative and to the audience to withhold the affirmative plan until the second affirmative speech. Furthermore, the second affirmative needs more time to demonstrate how the plan will remedy the inadequacies in the present system.

III. Summary

    Every speaker in the debate should save sufficient time to restate succinctly the team case and his own contentions. It is likewise helpful to insert summaries, during the body of the speech, briefly restating each contention following the proof. Skillfully executed, the internal summary also helps to build the transition to the next contention. For example, "Thus, we can see that many states lack adequate resources to support public education. This brings us to our second contention that the lack of funds produces substandard schools."

First negative speech

1. Introduction
   A. Adaptation to the case of the affirmative. Acceptance, rejection, or reinterpretation of the affirmative definitions. If the negative challenges the definitions, the speaker must prove that the negative's interpretation is valid.
   B. Presentation of the entire negative case. This will depend on the negative approach (see the section "Possible Negative Stands," pages 288–289). The remainder of the introduction, body, and conclusion will follow the same general plan as the first affirmative's speech.

Second affirmative speech

The second affirmative speech depends largely on the negative stand. Still the speaker must complete the affirmative case by proving that the affirmative plan is the best possible remedy for the weaknesses of the existing structure. If the negative admits the need issue and presents a counterplan, the major focus of the second affirmative will consist of an attack on the negative plan, coupled with a defense of the affirmative proposal.

Second negative speech

This speaker completes the negative contentions through direct adaptation to the affirmative case. With absolute fairness and accuracy, the second negative indicates which of its arguments the affirmative has failed to recognize or answer adequately. At this point in the debate, the issues should be sharply drawn and the area of conflict narrowed.

Rebuttal speeches

With the exception of the first affirmative, all speakers should use a part of their constructive time for direct refutation of the opposition's contentions and arguments. A team that reserves all of its refutation for the rebuttal period will find itself hopelessly behind. During the rebuttal neither team may add major contentions to its case. For example, the affirmative cannot present its plan at this point, nor can the negative raise a new objection to the affirmative case. But new evidence, continuing adaptation, and fresh reasoning are necessary for an effective rebuttal. A major breakdown occurs when teams exhaust their ammunition during the constructive argument and are reduced to parroting "what my colleague just said." They need an abundance of "stopper" evidence.

A common error in rebuttal is a speaker's futile attempt to answer every piece of evidence and every shred of argument thrown against his case. At best the speaker presents a shotgun—scattered defense or an attack that scarcely damages the opposition. The skillful debater sifts the mountains of evidence to discover the major objections or issues, rarely more than two or three, and meets these squarely with the strongest possible evidence and reasoning. The following outline will prove helpful, if the debater realizes that adaptation to the particular circumstances of each debate is always necessary.

I. Introduction
   A. Refute one of the issues covered by the previous speaker.
   B. Indicate which issues still remain in contention.
II. Body
   A. Take each issue singly and state clearly.
   B. Indicate how the opposition attempted to establish it.
   C. Present your counterevidence and indicate the flaws in your opponent's reasoning.
   D. Summarize and show how this issue now affects both cases.
   E. Treat the remaining issues similarly or indicate that your colleague will deal with them.
III. Conclusion
   A. Summarize the entire debate.
   B. Contrast the advantages of your position with that of your opposition, appealing at the same time for the adoption or rejection of the proposition.

COMMON ERRORS IN DEBATE

ATTEMPTING TO CONVINCE THE OPPOSITION. This is a waste of time and yet debaters frequently deliver most of their speeches to the other team. An occasional remark directed to the opposition for its dramatic effect may be in order, but the primary target for your persuasion is the audience. Each team needs to show what acceptance or rejection of this proposition will mean to each member of the audience.

USE OF TECHNICAL DEBATE JARGON. Debate is essentially persuasive speaking designed to win the approval of the average person. It is not an esoteric exercise for the select few. As a debater you should understand what is meant by *burden of proof, status quo,* and *post hoc ergo propter hoc,* but you will be wise to avoid using any of these terms in the actual debate.[6] The same applies to the technical terms of a particular question. If you have to employ any of these terms, you must make sure that your audience understands the meaning. We often forget how long we studied to acquire an understanding of a technical term and erroneously expect our audience to grasp the concept immediately.

USE OF MEMORIZED SPEECHES. The so-called "canned" speech rarely succeeds in debate. After the first affirmative speech, all others must constantly shift and adapt their remarks to preceding speakers. All debate speeches are most effectively delivered extemporaneously, that is, thoroughly prepared, outlined, and rehearsed in advance, but neither memorized nor read from manuscript. In addition to the difficulties of adaptation, a memorized speech usually lacks the directness and spontaneity necessary for effective delivery. To anticipate arguments and devise rebuttal cards in advance are wise measures as long as the debater recognizes the necessity of adapting every argument to the precise case of the opposition.

A SARCASTIC, CONTENTIOUS ATTITUDE. Sarcasm in any speech is a highly explosive element, prone to injure both the giver and the receiver. A debater can be vigorous and enthusiastic without exhibiting bad manners. Moreover, a team that can maintain its poise, emotional equilibrium, and kindly sense of humor during the heat of argument adds immeasurably to its own persuasive appeal. An overemotional, sarcastic attack often incites audience sympathy for the victim and contempt for the promoter.

FABRICATION OF EVIDENCE. Debaters are sometimes accused of employing dishonest methods in their unholy desire to win an immediate verdict. A few may have succumbed to such temptation. To their dismay the audience or their opponents usually discover the deceit. Debate and discussion, as we have indicated earlier, are not the favored tools of the demagogue. He and the charlatan flourish best in an atmosphere where they are free from exposure.

UNWILLINGNESS TO CONCEDE AN ISSUE OR ARGUMENT. "He or she must be a great debater," runs the familiar axiom, "because they contradict everyone on everything." Nothing could be further from the truth. Skillful

---

[6] See p. 287 for the definition of burden of proof. *Status quo* means literally "the state existing." It is thus ridiculous for debaters to say as they often do "The *Status quo* can remedy the existing condition." *Post hoc ergo propter hoc* means "after this therefore because of this." The rooster who thought his crowing caused the sun to rise committed this fallacy. Vice-President Ford used this fallacy to inject humor into one of his speeches. The price of Fords, he remarked, went up by $150 after he was sworn in as Vice-President.

debaters know how much of the opponent's argument to accept without losing the debate. They are then in a stronger position to push their attack or strengthen the defense at strategic points.

RELIANCE ON LIMITED TYPES OF EVIDENCE. A common error is to place too much reliance on one type of evidence. Debate speeches sometimes appear as a mere recital of opinion. The wise debater looks for as wide a variety of evidence as possible, employing facts, witnesses, instances, statistics from which to draw inferences.

FAILURE TO IDENTIFY AUTHORITY. When available, fact is always superior to expert opinion. But on questions of probability we are sometimes forced to rely on opinion. Simply to attach a name to an opinion, however, lends no special significance to the opinion. The audience needs to know *who* the authority is and *why* his opinion makes a difference.

FAILURE TO EVALUATE AND VERIFY THE EVIDENCE. In our cliché-ridden world we often speak of the "simple fact of the matter." We would caution any speaker that even a so-called "well-known fact" may finally prove to be pure fiction. Often a declarative statement that sounds like a fact is instead merely an inference. *Fact:* We observe a man stagger. *Inferences:* That man is drunk? Crippled? Sick? None of these inferences may constitute a fact. He may, in fact, be "putting on an act." Thus, debaters need to generate a deep-seated suspicion of all sources and witnesses, rigorously testing them to determine their accuracy and reliability. Finally, we can safely draw one conclusion—facts are rarely "simple" and almost never "well known."

SUMMARY

Although debate often begins where discussion ends, it is frequently difficult, if not impossible, to draw a sharp dividing line. These two democratic techniques constitute cooperative, continuous forces in decision-making. But when we reach that stage of deliberation that requires action or no action and the participants need to hear clean-cut, pro-and-con arguments, they are probably ready for debate.

Like discussion, debate demands a fairly stated proposition of *fact, value,* or *policy.* Most often, debate concerns policy decisions and requires a formal question that is (1) debatable, (2) complete, (3) brief, (4) single, (5) affirmative, and (6) impartial.

Debaters on both sides of the question share the responsibility of *defining the terms, determining the issues,* and *assuming the burden of proof* or *rebuttal.*

Many different forms of debate are possible, the most commonly used being *formal debate, cross-examination, direct clash,* and *parliamentary.*

Preparation for debate involves the construction of a *case,* thoroughly supported with evidence of fact and opinion. The *brief* helps the debaters draw logical inferences and serves as a reservoir of evidence for each contention. The debate speeches usually include the *constructive argument* and the *rebuttal*. Although speeches are carefully prepared and rehearsed, they are always distinguished by careful adaptation to the arguments of the opposition and directed to the interests and concerns of the judges (audience).

QUESTIONS AND EXERCISES

1. Explain what is meant by the statement "Debate begins when discussion ends." Can you find exceptions to this general principle?

2. Distinguish between propositions of *fact, value,* and *policy.* Write an example of each.

3. Formulate debate propositions of policy on the following problems:
   - (a) Euthanasia.
   - (b) Federal financing of elections.
   - (c) Handgun legislation.
   - (d) United Nations police force.
   - (e) Control of nuclear weapons.
   - (f) Capital punishment.
   - (g) Disarmament.
   - (h) School bussing for integration.

4. Find a newspaper editorial with which you disagree. Develop a four-minute rebuttal speech. You will find it helpful to review the material on pages 303–304 dealing with rebuttal.

5. The modifications of traditional debate procedure covered in the preceding chapter are only a few of many in existence. Work out a "new" plan of debate and be prepared to defend your "modification" in a short speech to the class.

6. Select a proposition suitable for debate and indicate specifically (avoid stock issue phraseology) the issues. Take one issue and develop an affirmative or negative brief of that issue.

7. Using the same proposition define the terms. Do you believe that the affirmative and negative might disagree on the definitions of any terms?

8. Bring to class three examples of *evidence of fact; evidence of opinion.* In a three-minute speech indicate how you verified the facts and how expert or authoritative you consider the items of opinion.

9. Set up a series of classroom debates on vital topics of public or campus concern. The teams may consist of one or two persons and the time allotments for individual speeches may vary, but each side should receive equal time.

10. Select three of the propositions you formulated for question 3. Assume that you are a negative debater and work out legitimate *substitute plans* for each. Be prepared to defend your plans as bona fide alternate proposals.

RECOMMENDED READINGS

BEARDSLEY, MONROE C. *Thinking Straight: Principles of Reasoning for Readers and Writers.* Englewood Cliffs, N.J.: Prentice-Hall, Inc., 1956.

BETTINGHAUS, ERWIN P. *The Nature of Proof.* Indianapolis: The Bobbs-Merrill Co., Inc., 1972.

EHNINGER, DOUGLAS, and WAYNE BROCKRIEDE. *Decision by Debate.* New York: Dodd, Mead & Co., Inc., 1963.

EISENBERG, ABNE, and JOSEPH A. ILARDO. *Argument: An Alternative to Violence.* Englewood Cliffs, N.J.: Prentice-Hall, Inc., 1972.

EWBANK, HENRY L., and J. JEFFERY AUER. *Discussion and Debate.* New York: Appleton-Century-Crofts, 1951, chaps. 23, 24, 25, 26, 27, and 28.

FREELEY, AUSTIN J. *Argumentation and Debate,* 3rd ed. San Francisco: Wadsworth Publishing Co., Inc., 1971.

HUBER, ROBERT B. *Influencing Through Argument.* New York: David McKay Co., Inc., 1969.

KRUGER, ARTHUR N. *Modern Debate: Its Logic and Strategy.* New York: McGraw-Hill Book Company, 1960.

NEWMAN, ROBERT P., and DALE R. NEWMAN. *Evidence.* Boston: Houghton Mifflin Company, 1969.

SMITH, CRAIG R., and DAVID M. HUNSAKER. *The Bases of Argument: Ideas in Conflict.* Indianapolis: The Bobbs-Merrill Co., Inc., 1972.

THOMPSON, WAYNE N. *Modern Argumentation and Debate: Principles and Practices.* New York: Harper & Row, Publishers, Inc., 1971.

WINDES, RUSSEL R., and ARTHUR HASTINGS. *Argumentation and Advocacy.* New York: Random House, Inc., 1965.

Chapter 14

Stage Fright

> Every artist . . . ja . . . *every* artist feels sick
> before *every* performance. The one that does
> not feel sick, that one is no artist! Remember
> that.
>
> MADAME SCHUMANN-HEINK

Harry P. Harrison, as a young agent for the Lyceum and tent Chautauqua, was assigned to a season's tour with Mme. Ernestine Schumann-Heink, a world-renowned contralto. Just before her first concert, as a huge crowd was gathering, she announced to her distressed agent in her heavy Teutonic accent that she was too sick to sing. Then as Harrison, himself reduced to illness by her words, tried to compose his apology to the local committee, a knock signaled the start of the show and with little hesitation the great singer marched to the stage and performed brilliantly. Later she joined Harrison for a hearty meal. The next two performances were nearly identical, prompting young Harrison to ask about her preperformance malady. Her answer and his own observation of countless lecturers in Chautauqua, including William Jennings Bryan, led Harrison to conclude that the speaker "who did not meet each new audience with a hollow feeling in his stomach was . . . at best a second-rater."[1]

Madame Schumann-Heink's ailment, common to most professional performers on stage, radio, television, or the public platform, afflicted Cicero, the classical orator, who admitted turning pale at the outset of a speech. And John Sirica, the celebrated judge in the Watergate trial, suffered from butterflies when he looked out at the large crowds at the hearings.[2] Even Winston Churchill described the occasional discomfort he felt as "a nine-inch square block of ice in the pit of his stomach." Fortunately, in most instances the ice melts away as the performance begins and exhilaration replaces the initial state of discomfort. Yet students seem frighteningly concerned with methods of thawing the ice, and when questioned at the start of a semester about their reasons for taking a course in public speaking, often place the elimination of stage fright as first on the list.

[1] Harry P. Harrison, *Culture Under Canvas: The Story of Tent Chautauqua*, ed. Karl Detzer (New York: Hastings House, 1958), pp. 113–114, 163.

[2] *Time*, January 7, 1974, p. 12.

THE NATURE OF STAGE FRIGHT

Actually the much-used term *stage fright* is a misnomer or incorrect label; the sensation might more accurately be described as anxiety, intense stimulation, or emotional tension. Few of us are really frightened by an audience. If we were, the inevitable would more frequently take place: flight would follow fright, and we would run away. Nearly all of us desperately crave an audience, and the pain of an undelivered speech can be well-nigh unbearable—far worse than any discomfort we may experience during the event. Rather than being frightened, we are more truly stimulated by an audience and the thought of having to face one. A bit of apprehension engendered by respect for an audience is generally good, especially for the audience.

We may be excited and nervous, and somewhat concerned about our performance. But these elements do not of themselves constitute fear. To be sure, what happens to us physically and mentally when we are stimulated by an audience includes changes we also experience when afraid. A *fearlike* element is undoubtedly present. But the same element is present when we are experiencing pleasurable excitement and when we anticipate good things. We are not afraid when we watch a well-played basketball or baseball game, and we are not afraid while waiting for the seconds to tick away before the time for our big date. We are intensely stimulated and we are excited. This is normal. Why, then, the confusion with fear or fright?

Physical symptoms

We confuse intense stimulation with fear because parts of the picture are the same. The physical symptoms of fear may include rapid pulse, strong heartbeat (palpitation), excessive perspiration, dryness of the mouth, trembling of the limbs (hands and legs), and disturbances of secretion and excretion. All of these physical symptoms need not be present to cause the reaction known as fear, but usually two or more are present. In stage fright the overt manifestations may include trembling of the arms and legs, quavering of the voice, random movements, and a general lack of controlled and poised appearance. In general, the performer feels unstable; occasionally he looks unstable.

Intellectual changes

In addition to the physical symptoms, fear includes an outstanding mental change. A person afraid is suffering from *intellectual disorganization*. A person afraid is one whose thinking has gone astray. Not knowing how to think, he does not know *what to do*. A person who is experiencing true fear either does nothing, or behaves in ways that are inappropriate. Fear may cause a child to run into the path of an oncoming automobile. A mother, observing the behavior of her child, may experience an intense, *fearlike* feeling. This feeling will not, however, prevent her from snatching the child out of the path of danger. In fact, the physical changes she experiences enable her to act more vigorously and quickly in the accomplishment of her task. In stage fright, the performer may be blocked in his thinking and so find himself unable to go on with what he had planned to say or do. His internal behavior may be basic to the overt expressions of his inability to mobilize and integrate his inner forces. In extreme stage fright, as in an extreme state of emotion such as fear, the individual is suffering temporarily from the dynamics of disintegration.

Heightened feeling

The difference between the behavior of the child and the behavior of the mother is the difference between fear and heightened feeling. The child suffered from fear because he did not know what to do. His mother experienced heightened (fearlike) feeling because *she did know what to do.* Heightened feeling prepares the body for vigorous emergency activity. The feeling results mostly from an increase in the amount of adrenalin supplied to the blood stream. The athlete preparing for a contest has such a feeling. So do we as speakers when we anticipate appearing before an audience. It is not only good but necessary for us to have some feeling about facing an audience. It makes us more alert and alive. We sound and act interested in our job of speaking.

Perhaps we can approach the matter of stage fright as one of *degree* rather than of kind. We may then accept the term *stage fright* to mean any notable degree of psychological and physiological arousal experienced by a performer before an audience. Mild arousal may be stimulating and helpful. A severe amount of arousal may be disrupting and disorganizing and impair rather than improve a performance.

RESEARCH ON STAGE FRIGHT

Despite an abundance of research on the nature, causes, and cures for stage fright, we still possess few absolute, positive answers. Yet some of the generalized findings will prove valuable to students in their search for ways of coping with and using the emotional tension they feel when facing a speech communication experience, be it public speaking, group discussion, or the interview. Only rarely do we experience severe tension during social conversation.[3]

1. All speakers, the novice and the expert alike, undergo some degree of psychological and physiological arousal before or during their speaking efforts.

---

[3] See J. Eisenson, J. J. Auer, and J. V. Irwin, *The Psychology of Communication* (New York: Appleton-Century-Crofts, 1963), chap. 18, for a review of the literature on the subject of stage fright.

2. Happily the listeners' perceived awareness of emotional tension or disruption is less than the speaker believes is taking place.
3. No significant or apparent relationship exists between stage fright and reasoning ability, or the level of intelligence.
4. There is no significant relationship between personality traits, or aspects of personality, at least as these components are measured or are measurable by standard personality inventories.
5. Stage fright is no respecter of sex. Both men and women experience similar kinds of stress, but men are more likely to show overt and obvious manifestations of this state of feeling or emotion than are women.
6. Task performance seems to improve under conditions of mild stress.[4]
7. The disruptive influences of stage fright diminish with improved speaking ability, increased experience, and with age. These factors may, of course, be interrelated.

CAUSES OF STAGE FRIGHT

An approach-avoidance conflict[5]

Many of us accept commitments for future responsibilities and then do whatever we can to avoid the deed and the day of reckoning. Most of these situations contain both desirable and undesirable features. We like being asked, but shrink from the more painful effort of preparation. A day at the beach sounds marvelous, but we can't face the arduous trip. Attending an athletic event may prove highly enjoyable, but not the necessary effort to get to and from the stadium. If the event is far enough away, our wishes to participate may dominate our behavior, and so we make a positive commitment. But as the time for the event approaches, so too do our counterinclinations. Avoidance behavior increases, we seek a means of escape, and panic may set in.

We believe a tenable analogy exists between approach-avoidance behavior in general and reactions to speech communication situations in particular. Many persons who have a choice in accepting or refusing speaking engagements are likely to accept them if the time is not too near. The wish to speak—to perform and to impress—dominates the drives and determines the immediate behavior—acceptance of an engagement. As the day of the speech draws closer, the avoidance drives mount. Theoretically, if a performer arrives at the time for the execution of his responsibilities with approach and avoidance equal in strength, he reaches a state of impasse.

[4] See a discussion of Yerkes-Dodson law in C. N. Cofer and M. H. Appley, *Motivation: Theory and Research* (New York: Wiley, 1964), pp. 521–525.

[5] See Charles N. Cofer, *Motivation and Emotion* (Glenview, Ill.: Scott, Foresman, 1972), pp. 136–138.

Inadequate preparation

Unfortunately conflicting drives may block preparation for the speech event, thus strengthening the avoidance drive. If circumstances, conscience, or a sense of responsibility result in strengthening the approach, we may meet the commitment, but without adequate preparation and with shaky confidence. The result may be more avoidance on the next occasion and possibly more conflict, and with this state an increased likelihood for a severe case of stage fright.

The unprepared speaker has reason—good reason—to be afraid. Not having researched his subject, organized his thoughts, or rehearsed the phrasing in advance, any speaker, especially the inexperienced speaker, becomes suddenly aware of his inadequacies. Fear arises when we feel ourselves inadequate to meet a situation.

Faulty evaluation

Even if you prepare thoroughly, true fear of an audience may develop out of the heightened feeling if you fail to evaluate accurately the physical changes occurring within you. You may suddenly become aware of a palpitating heart or a dry mouth. You may also, consciously or unconsciously, recall that these symptoms were also present when you were actually frightened. If you fail to recognize that the cause of the old fear is nonexistent in the present situation, you may indeed give way to fear. You are in essence responding to two elements—palpitating heart and dry mouth—as you did originally in a totally different situation. The other fear symptoms such as trembling and excessive perspiration may also appear. If you then become overwhelmed by the physical changes taking place within you, you may succumb to actual fear. Random talking and random, disorganized movement may take the place of organized thoughts and gestures. True fear—stage fright in a real sense—has set in.

HOW TO PREVENT STAGE FRIGHT

Appraisal of the situations

The first suggestion for overcoming the effects of stage fright is to evaluate accurately what we are experiencing. In all probability it is heightened feeling, and not fear. The physical changes in heightened feeling—though, as we have indicated, often resemble the change in fear or fright—serve a useful purpose in supplying extra energy and muscle tonus necessary for an effective performance. Moreover, the symptoms are common and shared by public performers of all degrees of ability and practice.

We should also go beyond recognizing the changes when they occur, anticipating their occurrence so that the element of surprise is not present. To be able to say "Oh, yes, that's what I expected would happen" is much less disconcerting than to ask "What's happening to me?" when the knees begin to tremble. An athlete expects the heart to beat fast while engaged in a contest and is not caught by surprise at the anticipated changes. The speaker, similarly fortified by expectation, would not mistake feeling and physiological changes for fear. Fear is the response to the unknown. The familiar for which we can prepare should command respect rather than fear.

Preparation

Preparation, in all respects and with thoroughness, is your most potent weapon to combat stage fright. Preparation includes appropriate dress, perceptive audience analysis, and complete familiarity with your speech material, including the sound of the words, the turn of the phrase, and the meaning of every utterance. An early start will help preclude the approach-avoidance conflict, build confidence, and aid the memory.

Notes, if used, should be easy to read and designed to promote ready recall of ideas. In other chapters (see pages 379–382) we have covered in more detail the process of outlining and the use of notes in discussion, debate, and public speaking. Your instructor may also want to vary your assignments, prescribing the type and extent of notes used in each situation. Such exercises will help you determine how much written assistance, if any, is best for you. As you gain experience and confidence, you will probably use fewer notes and rely more on your memory. Even though you may gain confidence in the knowledge that notes are available, your ultimate aim should be preparation so complete as to promote a maximum of direct contact with your audience, free from the distractions of either notes or outward evidence of stage fright.

Confidence in subject matter

If your preparation is complete, you will have confidence in your facts and adequate support for your opinions. The careful selection of a subject that interests you keenly and is within your present intellectual range will add to your feeling of confidence. Of course, the more we research a subject, the more painfully aware we may become of the vastness or complexity of our chosen topic. We can probably never completely conquer this conflict. But as we gain confidence in our material, we also build inner confidence in ourselves, a necessary prerequisite designed to relieve stage fright.

Interest in subject

Search for a subject that moves you emotionally, one that you want to share with others. A strong *desire to communicate* must be present for communication to be effective. Further, the speaker who has an urge to share an idea and who has confidence in his idea will have little reason to have fear of fear. On the other hand, the speaker who lacks interest in what he is saying is probably correct in assuming that his audience will lack interest in listening to him.

Shifting focus of attention

As a speaker who is vitally interested in the subject you will usually want to share your ideas with your audience. You will, therefore, be more concerned with the reactions of your listeners than with your own feelings. If you assume a mental attitude and set of talking to and with your listeners and actively engage in communicating, you will find less time and opportunity for excessive introspection and reaction to your own internal reactions. While you are wondering what the members of an audience think about you, remember that they are also wondering what you think about them. By shifting your attention to your subject and audience, you will gain confidence from the realization that your listeners are indeed listening and responding to your ideas. With such confidence, intensification of feeling will serve to stimulate rather than to produce disintegration and true stage fright.

Movement

Muscular tensions usually accompany heightened feeling. If not released, they may immobilize a speaker. Moreover, the rigid, tense, unmoving speaker will likely produce empathic tensions in the audience. The language of the body in this instance disturbs both the speaker and the listener. Fortunately these muscular tensions can be effectively used and drained off through movement. As speakers we hope that our body language coincides with and reinforces the verbal message. Under stress we may resort to unmotivated, self-directed gestures such as fumbling with our clothing, or hair, rocking on our toes, or simply walking for the sake of walking. This random activity, unrelated to the message, should be replaced by controlled gestures that punctuate and reinforce the speaker's ideas. However, for every speaker, particularly one experiencing emotional tension, the cardinal principle is this: *almost any movement is better than no movement.* If you feel tense and not intellectually equal to the task of using a meaningful gesture, then move for the sake of movement. With the draining off of tension and the regaining of intellectual composure, you will find yourself better able to employ appropriate action.

Practice

Happily we know that stage fright decreases with age and experience. For almost every public performer—actor, teacher, or public speaker—a first performance is likely to be something of an ordeal. Repeated performances reduce the severity of the ordeal, and thus the best advice for the beginner is to seek out every possible opportunity for practice.

"If anyone is ever fool enough to ask you to speak," one teacher of public speaking advised, "be fool enough to do it." And if you have really experienced stage fright, follow the practice of the skier who has taken a rough spill or the aviator who has made a poor landing. Find another occasion to speak just as soon as you can.

SUMMARY

True stage fright—fear in a speech situation—is a rare phenomenon. Heightened feeling, which shares physical symptoms in common with fear, is what most speakers experience while facing an audience. Fear is disruptive; heightened feeling is useful in speaking.

The speaker can avoid having heightened feeling become fear by following several suggestions. These include (1) evaluating the speaking situation; (2) anticipating the physical changes that accompany heightened feeling; (3) preparing thoroughly; (4) using notes; (5) speaking only on subjects on which he is qualified to speak; (6) being interested in his topic; (7) using action to drain off tension; and (8) shifting focus of attention from himself to his listeners.

QUESTIONS AND EXERCISES

1. Interview several speakers, perhaps your minister or a favorite professor, who impress you as particularly poised and self-confident. Ask them about any early experiences they might have had with stage fright and methods they found successful in overcoming their fears. Prepare a two-to-three-minute speech in which you report your findings and conclusions.

2. What is the value of knowing the nature of the physical and mental changes in the prevention of stage fright? This question might constitute part of your speech above.

3. How can you overcome the effect of stage fright? Try to answer in your speech.

4. Prepare a two-minute talk on the relationship of muscle tensions to stage fright. In your talk prepare to use movement to demonstrate its usefulness in "draining off tension."

5. Prepare a two-minute talk on one of the following topics or on a topic of your own choosing. Outline your talk. Commit the opening and closing sentence to memory.
    (a) When I Graduate Will I Be Educated?
    (b) Fear—and Its Usefulness
    (c) One of Life's Anxious Moments
    (d) A Television Personality I Can Do Without
    (e) A Relative I Would Like to Disown

RECOMMENDED READINGS

BAKER, ELDON E. "An Experimental Study of Speech Disturbance for the Measurement of Stage Fright in the Basic Speech Course." *Southern Speech Journal,* 29 (1964), 232–243.

BRANDES, PAUL D. "A Semantic Reaction to the Measurement of Stage Fright." *Journal of Communication,* 17 (1967), 142–146.

EISENSON, J., J. J. AUER, and J. V. IRWIN. *The Psychology of Communication.* New York: Appleton-Century-Crofts, 1963, chap. 18.

McCROSKEY, JAMES C. "The Effect of the Basic Speech Course on Students' Attitudes." *Speech Teacher,* 16 (1967), 115–117.

OLIVER, R. T., and R. L. CORTRIGHT. *Effective Speech,* 5th ed. New York: Holt, Rinehart and Winston, Inc., 1970, pp. 51–57.

ROBINSON, E. R. "What Can the Speech Teacher Do About Students' Stage Fright?" *The Speech Teacher,* 8 (1959), 8–14.

WATKINS, D. E., and M. K. HARRISON. *Stage Fright and What to Do About It.* Boston: Expression Co., 1940.

Chapter 15

$Speaking$
in $Public$

> The dumbness in the eyes of animals is more
> touching than the speech of men; but the
> dumbness in the speech of men is more agoniz-
> ing than the dumbness in the eyes of animals.
>
> HINDU PROVERB

Why speak in public? Many students, both liberal and conservative, during the late 1960s and early 1970s asked that question repeatedly. Their bitter, cynical answer was to turn away from verbal dissent toward the rhetoric of violence. Free expression, many of them argued, was an exercise in futility, useful only to powerfully entrenched interests but impotent to improve the condition of minorities or to turn a nation from war to peace. The dissenters questioned our faith in the spoken word and moved instead to the streets where the "body rhetoric" of sit-ins and marches largely supplanted verbal persuasion.

For the student of public speaking the contentions of the violent dissidents demand serious attention. Their claims are not easy to answer. Just as the conditions that often produce violence are complex and illusive, so too are the reasons supporting the ultimate superiority of verbal eloquence. The roots reach deep into the history of dissent and of man's continuing struggle to relieve the oppressed, cope with conflict, and establish community and world standards of justice and morality.

When we embrace violence we not only betray the lessons learned through the long history of dissent but we admit as well our own personal failure to learn and to use speech communication effectively. Fists fly and bombs explode when inarticulate spokesmen abandon rationality and reason. Yet the Word, the Idea, endures and ultimately conquers. It was the philosophers of the Enlightenment, the abolitionists and antislavery spokesmen, rather than the guillotine or northern cannon, that established the concept of human equality and brotherhood. Words are still as potent as ever, and Lord Keynes wrote wisely when he declared, "It is ideas, not vested interests, which are dangerous for good or evil." Above all, as students of public speaking we dare not despair of spoken discourse before we have at least mastered it.

Unfortunately a large number of those persons mounting the public platform have failed to achieve a mastery of the art of speaking. As one cynical observer put it, "If you never go to hear a speech, you'll miss a lot of poor ones." Yet most ineffective speakers are capable of developing satisfactory speech habits. A person with normal intelligence, an idea worth communicating, and a knowledge of the basic principles of public speaking can become an effective speaker if he is willing to prepare and practice. While some of us enjoy greater intelligence, a wider background of experience, a more flexible, sensitive speech mechanism, and a commanding physique, anyone, through study and training, should be able to share an idea with a group of listeners. The need is not for more public speaking, but for improved public speaking. The only substitute for poor speaking is better speaking.

Effective, responsible public speaking is difficult but challenging. Unlike the popular magazine advertisement, we cannot promise immediate success through any "magical formula" that will "make people listen the moment you start to talk" and continue their listening for a significant time thereafter. We know of no way to succeed "without really trying" in business or public speaking. Excellent public address demands time, thought, effort, and sensitivity. Harry Emerson Fosdick, long-time pastor of Riverside Church in New York City, made it a rule of thumb to spend one hour in the study for every minute in the pulpit, and Mark Twain observed slyly that it usually took him three weeks to prepare a good impromptu speech. Winston Churchill, still the acknowledged master of the apparently informal and nonoratorical style of public speaking, was nevertheless painstaking in his preparation. He admitted that his efforts to achieve informality were produced by careful rehearsing and dependence on notes while pretending with more or less success to be making it up during the actual presentation.

Ideally, the world of listeners and speakers would be spared much mutual suffering if everyone held his tongue until inspired by noble thoughts. Such a perfect state is clearly unattainable. The listener, however, should enjoy certain inalienable rights. Among these are speakers of character, opportunities to hear worthwhile messages, and speakers capable of sustaining audience attention. The candidate unwilling to submit to a regimen of concentrated study, planning, and practice should avoid inflicting his speeches on audiences that may be too polite to accord him the reception he deserves.

Yet the citizens of a democracy dare not shirk the responsibility of developing completely their full potential as public speakers. Free government depends on free speech, and if our form of self-rule is to survive we must learn to speak and to listen. When rocks fly and bombs explode, one of the first casualties is likely to be freedom of expression and the right to dissent. Furthermore, the frustrations we suffer because of slow evolutionary changes in democratic society, sometimes imperceptible to the naked eye, might be speeded considerably by an articulate electorate.

The communication failures that plague the world of politics and government likewise afflict society in general, including the realms of business and industry, religion and education. Thanks to modern technology with its satellites, computers, laser beams, and ever-expanding assemblies of electronic mass-media hardware, our whole society endures a deafening roar of oral-visual communication. A moment of silence, welcome though it might be, seems virtually beyond our grasp. Where we once received letters or memos, we now get calls; news and editorial opinions penetrate both the ear and the eye. In the business world the average white-collar worker spends seven out of every ten minutes of a normal day attempting to communicate through speaking, writing, or reading. Conservative estimates indicate that at least 75 per cent of those communication experiences occur on the oral level—in speaking or listening.[1] While most of these communication encounters would hardly fall in the category of speaking in public, many of the skills and techniques of the public speaker are readily transferable to the small-group or one-to-one setting.

The study of public speaking represents one of the oldest, yet in some respects the newest, of man's intellectual endeavors. Firmly tied to the liberal arts and sciences, public speaking embraces the humanistic tradition in its fundamental concern for the human condition. The theories, principles, and practice of public address reach even beyond the classical Greek and Roman periods, but the present-day demand for its use and the imminent need for its improvement are as new as the latest political campaign, congressional investigation, television commercial, sermon, professorial lecture, sales conference, or session of the student government on campus.

The Greeks in the fifth century B.C., the first to enjoy the fruits of democracy, understood the indispensable tie—the linking of effective public address with free self-government. As in our world today, theirs was also divided between Western democracy and Eastern autocracy. Yet, in the midst of a life-and-death struggle and with the enemy advancing to the gates of Athens, free speech remained unrestricted and final authority rested on the Assembly where every Athenian citizen enjoyed the privilege of free speech. It is hardly surprising then that we look to the Greeks for our first systematic treatment of the art of public address. Indeed, the principles of public speaking formulated by Corax, Isocrates, Plato, and Aristotle, later restated and amplified for the Roman World by Cicero, Quintilian, and St. Augustine, form the basic foundation for modern speech theory.

1 See Carl H. Weaver, *Human Listening: Process and Behavior* (Indianapolis: Bobbs-Merrill, 1972), pp. 12–13; also Ralph G. Nichols, "Do We Know How to Listen? Practical Helps in a Modern Age," *The Speech Teacher,* 10 (March 1961), 118.

Greek and Roman rhetoricians established five canons of rhetoric, essential skills every public speaker must master:

1. *Inventio* (the discovery of logical, emotional, and ethical proofs).
2. *Dispositio* (analysis, synthesis, organization, and outlining the proofs).
3. *Elocutio* (words, phrases, language—clothing the proofs with an appropriate style).
4. *Memoria* (the treasure-house of ideas).
5. *Pronuntiatio* (delivery—proper management of the voice and body).

The classical canons furnish the substance for seven fundamental questions every speaker faces. The completeness and accuracy of his answers will determine the quality of the delivered speech.

1. What *responses* do I want from the audience?
2. What *proposition* will best express these responses?
3. How will this particular *audience* on this specific *occasion* affect my choice and treatment of the proposition?
4. What *supporting materials* (logical and psychological, ethical and emotional proofs) will motivate the desired responses?
5. What plan of *organization* will promote the desired responses?
6. What *style* (words, phrases, figurative language) will stimulate the audience to make the appropriate responses?
7. What mode of *delivery* (extempore, manuscript, memorized) will most effectively produce the selected response?

GENERAL AND SPECIFIC PURPOSES

Every successful speech takes accurate aim at securing an appropriate audience response precisely attuned to the speaker's *general* and *specific purposes.* Frequently the principal cause for ineffective public address is our failure to determine or to analyze accurately our own motivations for speaking. Too many speakers suffer the same affliction as the artist in *Don Quixote.* When asked what exactly he was painting, he declared, "That is as it may turn out." If the listeners ever wonder where the speaker is heading, the chances are he and they are on their way to nowhere. The speaker who would increase our knowledge, add to our enjoyment, rekindle our faith, strengthen our courage, or change our beliefs must possess a complete comprehension of the precise purpose for speaking.

Usually the general and even the specific purpose lies in part beyond the speaker's control. Selection is dictated by the times, the topic, and the particular audience the speaker is addressing. The same limiting conditions also prevail in the so-called practice or classroom situation. In many cases your instructor will determine the *general purpose,* leaving you free to select your own *specific purpose*. During the course you may be asked to speak to a number of general and specific purposes, just as the lawyer, teacher, or businessman faces a similar task in appearances before the same audience. Even for the individual who speaks only occasionally, the conditions of the invitation often dictate the direction toward one goal—one *general purpose*. Within the framework of external or self-imposed limits the speaker is then free to become a creative artist, molding and shaping the specific message.

INTERMIXTURE OF GENERAL PURPOSES

The *general purposes* for the speech are not rigid or mutually exclusive. While every speech contains *one* general purpose, it may also contain subsidiary aims as long as they tend to support and promote the one goal. The speaker who favors the adoption of a city income tax has as his general purpose *to convince*. The *specific purpose* is to win votes for the new tax measure, and his proposition, thesis, or purpose sentence may be stated: "All citizens should support the income tax to provide improved police and fire protection, better streets, and needed recreational facilities." To accomplish his *general purpose, to convince*, he must likewise sustain audience attention, perhaps through his ability *to entertain*. With most audiences he must also deliver a speech *to inform*, supplying the listeners with the facts, rationalizations, and inferences necessary to promote their acceptance of an additional tax burden. Finally, he must arouse popular enthusiasm and enlist the support of those who agree with his proposal through a speech *to stimulate*.

Clearly, whether our tax proponent fuses all these *purposes* into one speech or concentrates on one purpose, the general aim is *persuasion*. He hopes the listeners will accept and understand the ideas, perhaps enjoy his wit, renew their faith in the cause, and respond favorably. For convenience and greater clarity, however, it is helpful to subdivide the speech purposes,[2] which in turn furnish convenient names for the possible types of speeches. Authorities use a large variety of names to designate the possible general purposes, including speeches to interest, entertain, inform, inquire, persuade, convince, actuate, stimulate, impress, arouse, instruct, explore, and even confuse.

With the exception of the speech to confuse, an element that a speaker may accidentally or deliberately inject into any address, we would consider all the other types as legitimate. We are not here concerned with the speaker who intentionally and demagogically muddies the stream in an effort to befuddle his audience into making illogical decisions based

---

[2] Cicero's threefold aim for every speech, namely, *docere, delectare, movere* (instruct, win, move) received a new interpretation through the centuries, particularly by George Campbell, who considered the *ends* in terms of the *audience response*, thereby paving the way for modern classifications.

on lies, a studied distortion of the evidence, and appeals to hatred and bigotry. While we consider this attempt to pervert public address highly unethical, we also share Aristotle's belief in the inherent superiority of truth. When error prevails, the blame rests mainly on the unpersuasive speaking of the advocates of truth. We likewise share Quintilian's faith in the good judgment of the jury and in its ability to detect a charlatan. We also recognize that all truth is rarely found on one side of a question. Both the advocates and the opponents of a proposal for a city income tax may have a legitimate cause and case. The audience must base its decision on the action it deems as *probably* the best in the light of immediate or ultimate interests.

Although the speaker may select any of a dozen general ends for the address, we feel that for greatest clarity four *general purposes* are sufficient. Those four purposes, in turn, supply convenient names for the types of speeches, namely *to entertain, to inform, to stimulate,* and *to convince.* Beyond emphasizing the flexibility of speech purposes, we would stress the audience role in determining the actual objective of the speech. Even in the same audience, an address designed *to stimulate* one listener may constitute a speech *to convince* for another. The after-dinner speaker whose primary aim is *to entertain* may also *stimulate* his audience to increased devotion to home, church, or state.

THE SPEECH TO ENTERTAIN

Some authorities consider the speech to entertain the least difficult to prepare and rank the speech purposes in order of increasing difficulty from entertainment through conviction. Such an analysis may be misleading. It is also probably erroneous to consider humor as an indispensable and necessary component of a speech to entertain. The listener may hold his sides or smile faintly or not at all. Speeches to entertain are often quite properly soberly serious.

The entertaining speech is sometimes less complex in structure than the speech to convince, but it is not necessarily easier to prepare or deliver. Indeed, if you decide to employ humor, you will wisely heed the advice of many professional comedians who will usually testify to the effect that "being funny is no laughing matter."

Speakers who find it relatively easy to develop the speech to inform or convince often succeed merely in impaling themselves on their own wit when they attempt to entertain. A mayor of Chicago once introduced Chauncey Depew, a long-time member of Congress, perhaps more famous for his after-dinner speaking than his political addresses, as an automatic machine. "You put in a dinner and up comes a speech." In his response, Depew noted the difference between his after-dinner speaking and the mayor's: "He puts in a speech and up comes your dinner."

It is likewise misleading to equate the speech to entertain with the holding of audience interest or attention. Every successful speech sustains audience attention. The superior speech to entertain holds attention through those subtle, elusive substances of wit, repartee, and all the histrionic elements that have held men spellbound in the theater and music hall. The excellent entertaining speaker becomes one with the master storyteller. While he may not increase the world's storehouse of knowledge or move men to momentous decisions, he helps reduce tensions, offers keen insights into human and national problems, often unmasks pompous sophistry, and certainly adds immensely to the sheer enjoyment of living. While individual television performers supply a large percentage of the speeches to entertain, this general purpose forms the staple diet for many social and service organizations. Entertainment may actually constitute the aim of the speaker offering his listeners an account of his travels to a foreign country or even explaining a new process developed by his company. It is apparent that the nature of the audience and the occasion as well as the speaker's intent determines the actual speech purpose.

THE SPEECH TO INFORM

Much of our speaking in public hall and school, in business office and factory, in church and home requires the precise, accurate transmission of information. Costly, tragic breakdowns in government, industry, and society result from our continual failures to exchange information understandably. The speech to inform is often more complex than the speech to entertain; it is almost always more precise in its aim to impart useful information. While a speech on the habits of the headhunters in South America might contain novel, interesting information, this speech for most mixed audiences serves largely as entertainment. If, on the other hand, the listeners are planning a scientific expedition to the Ecuadorean Amazon where survival depends on an accurate knowledge of the headhunter's tactics, the speaker's purpose transcends mere entertainment to the imparting of vital information. What may be entertainment for one listener is lifesaving instruction for another. The truly informative speech answers the *who, what, why, when, where,* and *how* questions vital to the listener's needs in any area.

Speeches to entertain and to inform deal mainly with expository materials. A responsible radio or television newscaster presumably attempts to give us *information* through an attempt at an unbiased selection and a factual account of the day's occurrences. Information as the primary purpose stops when the newscaster interprets the material or forecasts the probable consequences of the events, e.g., the ecological implications of laying an oil pipeline from Prudhoe Bay to Valdez in Alaska. The commentator might also consider the threat to the environment as compared to the intense need for energy, particularly oil. The commercial following the news "sounds" factually instructive and usually strives hard to "entertain," but its real objective is to increase sales by creating favorable attitudes toward one product and sometimes hostile reactions toward all rivals. The editorial comment and the commercial fall in the classification of the speech whose central intent is persuasive rather than expository, whose purpose is to change the attitudes, beliefs, and the behavior of listeners.

THE SPEECH TO STIMULATE

The distinctively persuasive speech usually falls into one of two classes. It is either directed toward those actively opposed to a proposition or to those who through apathy or human frailty respond at best with something less than genuine enthusiasm. In the speech to stimulate, the speaker is not attempting to change beliefs or attitudes, but tries instead to promote increased exertion for a cause. He seeks to win from those who are already convinced a devotion that goes beyond mere lip service. For many the spirit is willing but the flesh is weak. Some walk the high road and a few the low, while most are content to remain on the misty flats where action is indefinitely deferred. All too frequently the "convinced" behave in the manner of the congressman who assured an inquiring reporter for a college newspaper: "Yes, I often change my mind as a result of debate on the floor of the house. But as for my vote, son, almost never."

The so-called *speech to impress*[3] is a type of speech to stimulate, which lifts up the accomplishments of a hero or the significance of an event or concept in a way designed to inspire the listener to an appreciation of his heritage. The implications of such a speech are obvious. Often the speaker in the speech to stimulate appeals directly for increased devotion to the church, the party, or the fraternity.

Most individuals accept certain ethical principles, believe that honesty is the best policy, the life they save may be their own, that a stitch in time saves nine. Most persons also require periodic reminders and stimulation through speech, drama, religion, and various art forms to help them raise their everyday performance to more acceptable levels. The ministers in almost all faiths seek to strengthen beliefs rather than to convert their listeners. The vast majority are already convinced, believing, and acting with various degrees of enthusiasm. Even sermons whose primary purpose seems doctrinal, expository, or devotional usually carry overtones, implications, or direct appeals for greater personal dedication and more active stewardship. The preacher often furnishes the rational foundation for emotionally held personal convictions.

[3] See W. E. Gilman, Bower Aly, and Hollis White, *The Fundamentals of Speaking,* 2nd ed. (New York: Macmillan, Inc., 1964), chap. 10.

In the introduction to his address on "The Fragility of Freedom," Chief Justice Warren E. Burger, speaking in St. John's Cathedral in Jacksonville, Florida, outlined clearly the rationale for the speech to stimulate.

> What I have to say today . . . will be quite simple and I will tread no unfamiliar ground. We are in a house of worship where it is common practice to deal in a simple way with old truths; people gather here regularly to repeat old creeds, old prayers, psalms and songs from times long past. As we restate a creed or recite the 23rd Psalm to draw fresh inspiration and new strength, so we can turn to old truths learned by countless generations before us at great cost over many centuries.[4]

During times of crisis and national emergency, leaders frequently rise to articulate a message the ordinary man feels but cannot express. In World War II, when Churchill growled out his matchless prose to a frightened, isolated beleaguered Britain, the most timid soul on the island took heart, determined to join his comrades in their finest hour.

Historically the national political conventions—often boring, amusing, or aggravating to the independent voter—were designed in part to inspire and impress the party faithful. The hoopala, the planned "spontaneous" demonstrations, and the emotionally charged oratory represent rhetorical attempts to stimulate the loyal but weary party patron to redouble his partisan efforts. Party infighting at the convention over platform planks, credentials, and even the selection of candidates, fade away during the keynote address, the nominating speeches, and the standard bearer's acceptance message. With the virtues of their own party and the vices of the opposition still ringing in their ears, the faithful leave the convention hall, arms locked together as they march to "certain" victory in November.

With the innovation of radio in the twenties and television in the fifties the potential convention purposes have necessarily shifted. No longer are ward healers, precinct committeemen, and party hacks the main audience. The whole nation attends and watches, often with a mixture of amusement and horror at this seeming perversion of democracy. Political leaders of both parties have thus far coped unsuccessfully with the highly complex intermixture of convention purposes, failing thereby to meet either the needs of the party loyalists or the unconvinced. In 1972 the McGovern forces attempted to turn the convention into a more representative body, less like the political caucus of old, but they failed to hold a significant segment of the party leadership and almost completely underestimated the necessity of coordinating the demands of television with their convention schedule. McGovern's accep-

[4] *Vital Speeches,* June 15, 1973, p. 514.

tance speech delivered in the early morning hours reached few of either the committed or the uncommitted. The subsequent 1972 campaign demonstrated for a variety of reasons the imperative for managerial, rhetorical, and moral reforms in the total election process.

Every speaker, irrespective of political persuasion, will testify to the annoyingly difficult problem he faces in his task of inspiring the listeners to increase their devotion to legitimate and worthwhile causes. The already committed listener is sometimes ashamed of his less-than-satisfactory achievement. Yet the speech to stimulate may impress him as the "same old stuff," a dull recital of clichés and pious pronouncements. Perhaps more dangerous, the speaker in his effort to inspire may provoke an argument, thus driving the already convinced into the position of defending an opposing position. How often in our penchant to serve as "devil's advocate" do we end up embracing the evil we previously had deplored? The so-called nagging wife rarely needs to convince her erring spouse that his performance is unsatisfactory, that he ought to clean up the yard, take a more active interest in the PTA, or spend more time with the children. Her task, never an easy one, is to stimulate him toward activities he is already admittedly convinced he should undertake.

THE SPEECH TO CONVINCE

The most complex, though not necessarily the most difficult, speech attempts to change attitudes, shift opinion, or promote overt behavioral changes in the listeners. The speaker may want the audience to accept his point of view or he may seek more overt changes of behavior—a contribution, a favorable vote, or another vocal supporter. A change of mind is as much an action as a change of vote. The particular audience and occasion will determine in large measure the type of response the speaker may legitimately seek. It requires a delicate intermixture of all four general purposes. Obviously the speaker must sustain attention (the basic ingredient in the speech to entertain) throughout the entire address. Indeed, early schools of psychology considered attention a causative persuasive element, and William James' famous dictum, "What holds attention determines action,"[5] inspired one of the first of the modern authorities on speech communication, James Winans, to shape his philosophy of persuasion around the concept of attention. "Persuasion," wrote Winans, "is the process of inducing others to give fair, favorable, or undivided attention to propositions."[6] Although attention is a necessary first step and the common denominator in all speeches, it is not, in itself, the motivating element in persuasion. The speech to convince

[5] Williams James, *Psychology—Briefer Course* (New York: Holt, Rinehart and Winston, 1892), p. 449.

[6] James A. Winans, *Public Speaking* (New York: Appleton-Century-Crofts, 1917), p. 194.

demands a precise application of logical, emotional, and ethical proofs, which we will cover in more detail in Chapter 16 (see pages 348–352).

Increasingly listeners demand evidence (the speech to inform) before they will accept a speaker's proposition that asks for a change in attitude or behavior. The television advertisers' use of animated drawings supposedly revealing what happens to our sinus cavities, dentures, or digestive tracts after using their pills, sprays, or elixir—often an insult to our intelligence—is nevertheless a way of satisfying the popular demand for "proof." For college assemblies a speaker's most effective emotional weapon is often his expressed intention of employing logical proofs for an audience that makes or believes it makes its decisions on the basis of facts and evidence. Even the hardest-headed logician rarely behaves logically in all situations. Most of us are like the dowager in the cartoon who in the midst of an argument with her spouse shouted across the room, "It's going to take more than facts to convince me!"

The speaker who would convince must begin by appealing to attitudes the audience possesses at the outset. He stimulates previously accepted responses and may wait until late in his speech to move into areas of disagreement. As much as possible he attempts to associate the acceptance of his proposition with the fulfillment of previously held attitudes and beliefs. Thus, the speech to convince becomes a careful blending of speeches to entertain, to inform, and to stimulate.

THE BLENDING OF PURPOSES

In nearly every listening situation involving a controversial topic are some individuals who already accept the speaker's proposition. For them the speech is one to stimulate. For the unenlightened the speech may constitute one to inform. For those on the fence and for the actively opposed, the speaker seeks to convince. Thus, for most audiences we must blend the speech purposes of entertaining, information, and stimulation if we hope to accomplish the primary objective of conviction.

Moreover, a speaker using a given subject will necessarily blend and use different amounts of entertainment, information, stimulation, and conviction as determined by the background of the audience and their attitudes toward the topic. For example, a speech supporting or opposing "school bussing" will demand a different blending of general purposes if delivered to the NAACP, a university education class, a White Citizens Council, or a PTA in the suburbs. A speaker facing this wide a variety of audiences will be forced to use a different blending of speech purposes on each occasion. Indeed, it might be virtually impossible to receive a fair hearing before any of these audiences if the group realizes the speaker's position in advance.

Table 15–1 illustrates the possible blending of speech purposes which

Table 15–1   Blending of Speech Purposes

Audience	Topic or speaker	Entertain	Inform	Stimulate	Convince
PTA	New methods of teaching reading	+++	+++++		
Teachers' convention	The best method of teaching reading			+	+++
Rotary Club	Travel talk on Africa	+	++	++	+++
College YMCA	Join Peace Corps	+++++	+++	+++	
College YMCA	World religions	+	+++		+
Kiwanis Club	Highlights of Kiwanis International	+++	+++++++		
White Citizen's Council	Pro-Bussing	+	+++	++	+++
NAACP	Pro-Bussing	+	+++	++++++	
Am. Medical Association	New treatment for diabetes	+	+++++	++	+
Am. Medical Association	Pro-Socialized Medicine	+	+	+	++++++
Lions Club	New treatment for diabetes	+++	+++++		
TV audience	Bob Hope	+++++++			
TV audience	Jack Benny	+++++++			

might occur in speeches delivered before the particular audiences listed. The relative weights given to entertainment, information, stimulation, or conviction would, of course, vary with individual speakers and the specific purposes they selected.

ETHICAL IMPLICATIONS OF AUDIENCE ADAPTATION

The blending of speech purposes (see Table 15–1) represents another way of discussing a basic principle of speech persuasion usually called *audience adaptation*. Because each audience holds particular attitudes, beliefs, and desires, the message—even on the same theme—must be tailor-made for the specific occasion. Audience adaptation assumes crucial proportions when we face a highly controversial, emotion-laden issue fraught with moral and ethical judgments. If the audience is friendly and favorable, we can probably move with vigor to the speech to stimulate, but if the listeners are unconvinced or hostile, we must decide how to approach and adapt to this group and still remain faithful to our own convictions.

Many candidates for public office repeatedly meet and address audiences with widely divergent economic, social, and moral views. Often the candidates abandon moral principles for easy expediency and fail to maintain a consistent position during their campaign. They twist, bend, and blur the message in an attempt to be all things to all people, to offend none, and to appease all. Even if immediately successful, the ultimate result for the erring individual and for the nation at large is catastrophic and morally demeaning. The history of public scandal in our own nation, from Grant to Tea Pot Dome to Watergate, underscores the tragedy of trusts betrayed and commitments to false ideals.

The late Supreme Court Justice Hugo Black, staunch defender of free speech and civil rights, almost lost his chance to serve on the Court because of his brief membership in the Ku Klux Klan in the early days of his political career. His forthright radio speech of apology for his youthful error, a demonstration of ability for audience adaptation, helped to swing the Senate's confirmation vote and paved the way for his outstanding service on the Court. Stephen A. Douglas, in his celebrated debate with Lincoln, accused the rail-splitter, with some justification, of delivering "jet black" speeches in northern Illinois, "decent mulatto" in the center of the state, and "almost white" addresses in the southern part. To be sure Lincoln's racial views by contemporary criteria may have been reactionary. In 1858 they were liberal if not radical.[7]

[7] Allen Nevins, *The Emergence of Lincoln,* Vol. I (New York: Scribners, 1950), p. 386.

Facing every speaker are perplexing ethical questions related to audience adaptation, questions that are never easy to answer. Shall I give the listeners what they *want* to hear or what they *ought* to hear? Can I combine both elements in the same speech? How can I present the "truth" even when unpalatable and still retain favorable rapport with that audience?

Even such a time-tested rhetorical device for audience adaptation as the illustration or anecdote has its ethical overtones. A critical anlysis of an issue may well receive a less enthusiastic audience reception than a story or witty epigram, so we drop the more difficult task and forthwith pepper our speeches with anecdotes and epigrams. Certainly there is nothing wrong with the use of this essential device, as we shall observe in later chapters, but as Glen Frank, once president of the University of Wisconsin, observed, it is always tempting for any speaker to allow his mind to become "a weathercock, nervously sensitive to the automatic applause of flattered prejudice."

Throughout your study of the various forms of speech communication —casual conversation, public address, discussion and debate—you will want to keep uppermost in your thinking the ethical responsibilities you bear both as a speaker and as a listener.[8] The answers to ethical questions are rarely if ever certain and never easy or simple, thus making your venture in public speaking an exciting and challenging experience. As you select and develop the general and specific purposes, attempting to adapt them to particular audiences, some of the following guidelines may prove valuable in setting the ethical standards.

1. Although I recognize that truth in most propositions is seldom, if ever, absolute, have I nevertheless exercised diligence and careful judgment in selecting and evaluating the evidence that led me to this position?

2. In adapting this proposition to a particular audience, have I steadfastly adhered to the basic premises undergirding my position?

3. Have I searched my own conscience to determine whether my self-interest is tempered by a long-range concern for the improvement and welfare of others and of society at large. A century ago James Russell Lowell expressed the ideal poetically: "They are slaves who fear to speak for the fallen and the weak. . . . They are slaves who dare not be in the right with two or three."

4. Finally, we should recognize that it is virtually impossible to adapt every message without antagonizing some listeners. If to please a particular audience, we must compromise or conceal our moral convictions, then antagonize we must. But when we antagonize,

[8] See Richard L. Johannesen, *Ethics and Persuasion: Selected Readings* (New York: Random House, 1967).

we also reveal our failures to find the right words, the proper expression, the appropriate facts, the apt illustration, the precise motivation that might otherwise have won that particular group.

SUCCESS OR FAILURE

As students of public address we try to discover the elements that promoted the success or failure of a speech. Favorable audience response, however, can serve only as a partial guide. We must also consider the obstacles the speaker encountered as well as any resultant shift in audience attitudes or behavior. Under hostile conditions, for example, the speech may be successful even if it merely prompts the listener to say "I'm still opposed, but now I can see the other point of view."

We must further recognize that circumstances, seemingly beyond the speaker's control, may render a technically superior speech powerless. It may fail to achieve its intended goal because of insuperable obstacles, while a less ambitious effort may win over meager opposition.

Contemporary judgment of excellence in speech-making is tenuous at best. In situations where one speaker has failed, another facing the same obstacles may succeed through a more skillful aproach to the subject and the listeners. Moreover, we can never assume that audience behavior immediately following a speech is in fact a direct product of that speech.

In determining the degrees of success or failure, we must likewise consider the long-range as well as the immediate effects of the speech. Probably no speaker ever aimed his rhetorical shafts solely toward future generations. Those who fail on the contemporary scene sometimes attempt to console themselves with the thought that future generations will somehow appreciate them. Who would not say, for example, that Woodrow Wilson's heartbreaking attempt to win United States support for his League of Nations, even though it failed, did not pave the way a quarter of a century later for a more mature and chastened public to embrace the United Nations?

Every speaker also faces the question: "Shall I fix my goal at an easy, attainable level or set my speech purpose on a higher plane, thereby risking possible failure?" We offer no easy answer. Every speaker must make his own choice. This decision, however, will reflect in large measure his traits of character and that elusive, but highly persuasive quality the Greeks called *ethos*[9]—that proof which springs directly from the speaker. Certainly, after setting his goal, no speaker ever dares succumb to the easy temptation of blaming his rhetorical failures on the stupidity of the crowd. Even Wilson, grand though his rhetoric was, might have

[9] See the next chapter, page 352, for a discussion of *ethos*, ethical proof.

won more "willful men" to walk the pathway toward world order if he had been as astute a student of persuasion as he was of style.

DELIVERY (BODILY ACTION)

As we indicated earlier in this chapter, the fifth canon of rhetoric concerned the actual presentation of the speech. Yet this skill, which the Greeks seemed to place at the end of the preparation process, is of immediate concern to the beginning speaker. The learning process forces us to step before an audience well before we have had an opportunity to study or master the other skills (invention, organization, and style). Thus, it seems appropriate at this point to include a discussion of delivery, answering in particular some of the questions concerning the use of gesture. The student may also wish to review Chapter 4, "Nonverbal Communication," pages 50–59, and may perhaps want to look ahead to Chapter 16 for a discussion of the vocal and physical forms of support (see pages 358–360).

Gestures in public speaking

Although gestures are an integral part of all our speech behavior, we generally are more aware of gestures when engaged in public speaking or in listening to a public speaker. We begin to become aware that some speakers look timid or afraid and tell us so before even making a sound; others appear defiant or aggressive; some look relaxed and friendly. There are speakers who distract us through the use of meaningless movements. We may begin to feel more concerned about whether a speaker's buttons will stand the strain of his frequent handling, or about what he may pull out of his pockets, than we do about what the speaker is trying to tell us through his words.

The gestures of the public speaker are not so highly conventionalized as the articulated movements of organized gesture language. For the most part, the speaker's gestures reveal attitudes, consciously or unconsciously entertained, and belong to the expressive aspect of speech. For example, an attitude of friendliness is expressed when a public speaker steps toward the audience; one of abhorrence (usually for the idea being presented) when the speaker steps back or away from the audience.

Although hand gestures are generally more conventionalized than movement involving the body as a whole, speakers are tending toward less formual use of the hands when using gestures. Some examples of the traditional use of the hands include the open-hand, *palm-up* gestures to signify *agreement* or acceptance of an idea. It may also mean friendship or willingness to join in a friendly relationship. A *palm-down* gesture, on the other hand, signifies *negation*. Even more emphatic negation is the *thumb-down*. The pointed index finger is used to help point out an object or to single out an idea. Strong feeling and unity of purpose are revealed through the *clenched fist*.

Two gestures of the head are highly conventionalized. A nod of the head means approval; a lateral shake of the head means disapproval.

Facial expressions, that is, facial gestures, can be used with great effectiveness to reveal degrees of feeling. The speaker may smile with pleasant approval, or sneer in scornful or contemptuous rejection; his eyes may open wide in surprise or wonder, or half close in anger or hate; he may knit his brows to show concern or concentration, or smooth his brows to reveal relaxation.

Empathic responses

At this point we might pause to consider a basic principle of expressive behavior that will help us to appreciate why action is so important in public speaking. Any performer who can succeed in having an observer do and feel in a manner in accord with his purposes increases the likelihood that he will succeed in his objective. If the doing and feeling can take place on an unconscious basis, the speaker further increases the chance of success. If we identify with athletes we are observing in competition, we tend, as far as we are physically able, to imitate the behavior of those being observed. So, we may tense our muscles and "jump and roll over" while watching a high jumper; we buck the line with our favorite ball carrier at a football game; sometimes we actually kick the person in the stand immediately below us while watching a kick-off or field goal attempt. The underlying principle of this projective behavior is *empathy*. In essence, empathy is sympathetic, kinetic response. The speaker who succeeds in evoking empathic responses from his listeners almost literally has his listeners acting with him. To the degree that the actions are expressive of states of feeling, listeners feel as the speaker feels and, we hope, as he wishes them to feel according to the intentions of his speech.

The importance for the speaker to control his movements so that he may direct the empathic responses of his observers should be apparent. If the speaker is himself poorly controlled, if his actions are directed to no purpose but a manifestation of his own state of discomfort, his observers, while they continue to observe, will feel uncomfortable. Members of an audience may cease to look as well as to listen, to avoid this state. Once a negative reaction is evoked, the speaker may lose his audience and from that point on speak to no purpose. Fortunately most members of an audience are sympathetic as well as empathic and so may make allowance for initial fidgetiness or random movement. But a speaker should not count on sympathy to be indefinitely maintained. Listeners in a public speaking situation should not be taxed beyond easy endurance. If a speaker is deserving of an audience, the members of an audience are deserving of a controlled speaker who can quickly get on with his job of doing and saying what the occasion requires.

Extent of action

The term *extent* shall be used in two ways: (1) to indicate how much action is appropriate in a public speaking situation, and (2) how broad, how much sweep, should any action be. Hamlet's advice to the players may well serve as a guide for the public speaker. He may recall that Hamlet advised a group of actors to be sure to "suit the action to the word, the word to the action," with this special observance, "that you o'erstep not the modesty of nature." How much action is appropriate depends, of course, on the time, the place, the occasion, and the performer.

The amount of action, how much obvious gesture is employed, is determined by the nature of the occasion and the specific nature of the speech. A member of Congress, when called upon to give a commencement address at a college or university, should endeavor to sound more like a statesman than a politician. As a statesman he would be more restrained though not inhibited in his use of gestures than he would at a political rally. We would hope, also, that his choice of topic would be one that would not be impaired by a modest use of gestures devoid of pulpit-pounding and pointing to give significance to platitudes. The member of Congress speaking at a political rally may let himself go. The audience members expect action and will be disappointed if it is not produced and evoked. By and large, older persons expect more restraint in the use of gestures than do younger persons. Should the older persons attend a ceremony where relative abandon rather than control is the mode, as they might at a college reunion, then gestures might be used more freely.

Most audiences, particularly student audiences, are quick to detect artificiality in a speaker's use of gesture. And as we observed in Chapter 4, when the nonverbal cues contradict the verbal message the audience tends to accept the language of action.

The size of the room, as well as the size of the audience, should determine the sweep of the gestures as well as the amount of gesture used. A small group in a small room calls for speaking in a conversational mode and so for gestures that are essentially those used in conversational situations. A larger audience, a scattered audience in a large room, or an audience at a distance from the speaker in a moderately large room would dictate the use of gestures with a broader sweep than those in conversation. In general, we may follow the principle that gestures should be readily visible to the members of an audience at the greatest physical distance from the speaker. If the gesture cannot be discerned, it may serve as an expressive movement for the speaker, but it will not help materially in communicating the speech content to the listener-observers.

Suitability

We have already anticipated one aspect of suitability in our discussion of the speech occasion. The other aspect of suitability to be considered is directly related to the specific speech content—the suiting of the action to the word. Gestures, we have indicated, are used to convey meaning. As such they either reinforce oral words or are substitutes for words when they are insufficient to communicate the speaker's thoughts or feelings. If gestures are not used for either of these purposes, they must at least serve to release speaker and audience tension. This objective is sometimes necessary when either speaker or listeners have become tense and need release from tension to avoid physical discomfort.

Gestures used to convey meanings are usually used to emphasize a point. The point should be worthy of emphasis. If this is not the case, then the speaker is in effect misleading his listeners and so getting in the way of his own communicative effort. Too much emphasis may easily become equivalent to no emphasis. Random movements suggest random thinking. Controlled movement, in general, and controlled gestures, in particular, suggest selection. Such movements constitute a speaker's non-oral way of highlighting the thoughts he wishes most to be remembered.

Timing

The timing of gestures, as we have indicated, should be related to the overall content of the speech and "distributed" so that main thoughts are reinforced. There is another aspect or principle of timing that we shall consider briefly. A specific gesture should be timed to *precede the words* to be reinforced. In a sense, a speaker's gesture serves to "point" to the idea about to be presented in words. Beyond this, of course, the gestures give emphasis to the words. When a speaker moves or leans toward the audience, it should be to bring the listener closer to the thought to come because it is a particularly important thought. If a speaker wishes to indicate a transition in thought or a major division of his speech, he may accomplish this by a vocal pause and by moving during the pause from one part of the platform to another. If this is not possible because the speaker is "mike bound" or "podium bound," this purpose may be served by a shift in position. Movement of this sort is the approximate equivalent of the use of punctuation and division of a page into paragraphs and sections in written communication.

Emphatic gestures should also precede the words to be highlighted. Thus, the movement of an arm, the use of a pointed finger or an extended arm, the closed-hand gesture, should precede the words worthy of such emphatic behavior.

An exception to the general principle that the gesture precedes the words is the one used to replace words. The gesture then should terminate the thought and be followed by a pause so that there is no confusion that action did not suit the word. Thus, if a speaker wishes to act out rather than say "oh well, what can one do" by shrugging his shoulders, a pause should follow the gesture before oral speech is resumed.

Practices in the use of gesture

We shall conclude our consideration of the language of action for the public speaker by suggesting some guides for the execution of movements and gestures with maximum effectiveness.

1. *Gestures begin with every movement that brings you as the speaker to the platform, as well as with movements while you are on the platform.* This includes the way the speaker sits while waiting to be introduced, the way you walk to the part of the platform where you will "take your stand" for your engagement, and whatever you do beyond that point. So, don't slouch while sitting and waiting or while standing or moving. Sit easily but upright and walk with ease and alertness to your first position. If you slouch it should be to suggest a slouchy idea to your listeners. If you become hypertense, it should also be to suggest a feeling or meaning that calls for hypertension.

2. *Permit your movements to be natural and free of inhibitions.* If the gestures you employ are an extension of those you would be inclined, unconsciously, to use in conversation, they are likely to be both natural and appropriate. Once a gesture is initiated, do not inhibit it. Inhibition will produce jerky movements and will evoke feelings of discomfort in the observers. Few beginning speakers are likely to "o'erstep the modesty of nature," so let yourself go.

3. *When you execute a gesture, as you "let yourself go" be sure that all of you is involved and coordinated in the going.* A gesture of the hand should involve the whole arm, and the arm in turn be part of the movement of the body as a whole. If your gesture is one of offering something to your audience with outstretched hands, the offering should involve the entire body. If it does, it will be a free and generous giving and likely to be well received. Every gesture should be, or at least suggest, a complete movement unless there is an intention to suggest inhibition or incompletion.

4. *Use variety in gestures as you use in words.* An effective speaker who wishes to maintain attention avoids the use of repeated phrases or of sentences all cast in the same pattern. Do not use the same gesture in such close sequence that the listener-viewers obtain the impression that your "vocabulary of gestures" is limited and inadequate for the ideas you are trying to communicate.

5. *Avoid self-conscious movements and random behavior.* Do not

"play" with any object unless you are using it for illustrative purposes. If you are not certain about your hands, just let them hang by the arms at your side. They will then be readily available for use when a hand-arm gesture is needed. By all means keep your hands out of your pockets unless you are really trying to extract something to show to your audience. Avoid any repetitive or ticlike action such as scratching part of your face or arranging and rearranging part of your attire. Come dressed for the occasion and assume that you will continue to be so dressed throughout your performance.

6. *Establish contact with the members of your audience by looking directly at them.* If your audience is large and the members spread out, shift your glance from time to time so that none will feel ignored. Do not, however, shift with rhythmic regularity. This is not an effective or appropriate way to sway your listeners.

7. *Bear in mind that every movement has a meaning and make certain that it is the meaning you wish to convey.*

SUMMARY

In a world still bent on settling issues by force rather than by forensics, where failures to communicate exact a frightful toll in science, business, society, industry, and government, an alert citizenry must learn to speak and listen effectively, intelligently, and responsibly. Essential to the development of effective public speaking is a mastery of the classical elements in speech preparation, namely (1) *invention,* (2) *organization,* (3) *style,* (4) *memory,* and (5) *delivery.*

The speaker's specialized treatment of these five essential skills will depend in large measure on the selection of the *general* and *specific purposes* of the speech. The purpose itself is directly correlated with the type of response or responses the speaker seeks from the audience. The objective of all effective public speaking is an appropriate response, either physical (vote or contribution) or mental (change of attitude or belief). The responses in turn furnish us with convenient names for the different kinds of speeches, usually classified under four headings:

Speech to Inform ⎰ Expository
Speech to Entertain ⎱

Speech to Stimulate ⎰ Persuasive
Speech to Convince ⎱

The visible elements of delivery, particularly the speaker's ability to employ gestures meaningfully, will determine in part the audience response.

QUESTIONS AND EXERCISES

1. Following the plan of Table 15–1, which shows the blending of speech purposes, set up a similar chart for the topics listed below. Select a potential audience for each topic.

  (a) Ban Private Gifts for Political Campaigns
  (b) The Pill
  (c) Anti-Abortion Amendment
  (d) Ban the Handgun
  (e) Energy Needs over the Environment
  (f) Anti-Foreign Military Aid
  (g) Coed Dorms
  (h) The English Educational System
  (i) Anti-Intercollegiate Athletics

2. Attend a public lecture and analyze the speech for the following:

  (a) The speaker's *general purpose*. How much blending of general purposes occurred?
  (b) The speaker's *specific purpose*. State this purpose in one sentence. If you find it impossible to state the specific purpose, can you decide why?
  (c) Did the speaker accomplish the specific purpose? Why? Why not?

3. Prepare a two-to-three-minute speech *to entertain* using an autobiographical approach.

4. What factors determine the success or failure of a public speech? Construct a four-minute manuscript speech to defend your point of view.

5. Choose a subject and then phrase four *purpose sentences* or *propositions,* one for each of the four general purposes—i.e., entertain, inform, stimulate, and convince.

6. Distinguish between the speech to inform and the speech to convince. Prepare a three-minute talk explaining the differences. Use at least three possible speech topics or subjects as illustrative supporting material for your talk.

7. Prepare a two- or three-minute speech to inform on a topic of your own choice to be delivered to your class. Using the same topic, construct and deliver a speech to convince.

8. In a three-minute speech to inform, explain the essential differences in the potential general purpose and response in social conversation as contrasted and compared with public speaking.

9. Study an address from *Vital Speeches* and after you have determined the speaker's purpose rewrite the introduction, keeping the same topic but radically changing the general purpose.

RECOMMENDED READINGS

ARNOLD, CARROLL C., DOUGLAS EHNINGER, AND J. C. GERBER. *The Speaker's Resource Book,* Glenview, Ill.: Scott, Foresman and Company, 1961, part I.

BRIGANCE, WILLIAM N. *Speech: Its Techniques and Disciplines in a Free Society.* New York: Appleton-Century-Crofts, 1961, chap. 9.

BRYANT, DONALD C., and KARL R. WALLACE. *Fundamentals of Public Speaking,* 4th ed. New York: Appleton-Century-Crofts, 1969, part I.

GRAY, GILES WILKESON, and WALDO W. BRADEN. *Public Speaking: Principles and Practice.* New York: Harper & Row, Publishers, Inc., 1963, parts I and V.

HILDEBRANDT, HERBERT. *Issues of Our Time,* New York: Macmillan Publishing Co., Inc., 1963.

MARTIN, HOWARD H., and C. WILLIAM COLBURN. *Communication and Consensus: An Introduction to Rhetorical Discourse.* New York: Harcourt Brace Jovanovitch, 1972.

McBURNEY, JAMES H., and ERNEST J. WRAGE. *The Art of Good Speech.* Englewood Cliffs, N. J.: Prentice-Hall, 1953, chap. VI.

MONROE, A. H., and DOUGLAS EHNINGHER. *Principles and Types of Speech,* 6th ed. Glenview, Ill.: Scott, Foresman and Company, 1967, chap. 3.

NADEAU, RAY E. *A Modern Rhetoric of Speech Communication.* Reading, Mass.: Addison-Wesley Publishing Co., Inc., 1972, part 1.

OLIVER R. T., and R. L. CORTRIGHT. *Effective Speech,* 5th ed. New York: Holt, Rinehart and Winston, Inc., 1970, chap. 13.

SMITH, DONALD K. *Man Speaking: A Rhetoric of Public Speech.* New York: Dodd, Mead Co., Inc., 1969.

Chapter 16

Finding & Fortifying the Proposition

> For it is precept upon precept, precept upon precept,
> line upon line, line upon line,
> here a little, there a little.
>
> ISAIAH 28:10

Where can I find a good speech topic? Few more perplexing, yet exciting, ventures ever face us as prospective speakers than the search for the "right" subjects for a "special" audience, supported by the "proper" precepts. As we experience the initial mind-probing frustrations, we can at least derive some comfort from the knowledge that this struggle for a relevant topic is a nearly universal condition, even among those who prepare frequent, even weekly, public addresses. While the more experienced speakers may possess a deeper reservoir of knowledge, a wider background of experience, less fear of the platform, and greater verbal facility, all speakers—the novice and the seasoned alike—must follow the same general process of selection, analysis, and preparation.

Good speech topics rarely flash into the speaker's mind spontaneously or easily. They come only after conscientious prompting and as a result of systematic techniques. Happily, as we develop correct research practices, we often discover more topics than we can find audiences. And just as beginners may find it difficult to "keep talking" for two minutes during the first speech, so they may later find it painful to stop at the end of ten or more minutes.

ANALYZING THE AUDIENCE AND OCCASION

Our first step in finding a topic is to determine the kind of response we can legitimately seek from a particular audience at the precise moment we speak to them. In the previous chapter we discussed the *general* and *specific purposes*, and our task now is to determine the suitability of the purposes for potential audiences. A primary cause of failure in public speaking, perhaps the major cause, is the speaker's inaccurate appraisal of the tenor and temper of the audience and the occasion. The speech,

341

we say, would have succeeded if the speaker had only addressed the National Association of Manufacturers instead of the AFL–CIO.

Even members of the same audience, if it were possible to duplicate an audience, might behave and react in one way during a message on Sunday morning and in a quite different manner at a Wednesdy noon luncheon. The subject matter of the speech should reveal the speaker's awareness of the time, place, and prospective listeners as well as the content *per se*. Thus, a talk on a subject such as "The Energy Crisis" or "The Impact of Fuel Shortages on the Environment" will probably vary widely in style, organization, and delivery, depending on whether we are addressing a high school audience, the National Press Club, the Chamber of Commerce, a college seminar in sociology, or the local Rotary or Lion's Clubs. Additional elements influencing our topic selection and its treatment will stem from the limitations imposed by the time of day and the events (other speakers, business meetings, songs, and ritual) immediately preceding or following our remarks. The formality or informality of the occasion, the physical conditions of the room, and the time allotted to our speech are all items to consider.

An appraisal of your audience may prompt you to shift subjects completely and use one other than "The Energy Crisis." But, if your invitation specifically requested "The Energy Crisis," then you are under an obligation to make this complex topic clear, provocative, and relevant to that group. Clearly the same speech will seldom be equally appropriate for the farm bureau, a high school assembly, and a college seminar.

Our analytic exercise is further complicated by the heterogeneous complexity of most audiences. They often include smatterings of widely divergent social, economic, and political groups, diverse elements making it virtually impossible to satisfy every person. In one address Adlai Stevenson, with his characteristic flair for self-directed humor, pictured the familiar dilemma always plaguing the commencement speaker. Like other June orators, Stevenson confessed, he could never decide whether to direct his remarks to the graduates or to their parents and teachers. The accepted formula of aiming somewhere in between would, he feared, only assure him a perfect miss.[1]

Your speech class provides an excellent opportunity for analysis of the audience and the occasion. Unless your instructor designs an assignment geared to some imaginary audience, you should avoid any temptation to consider the classroom setting as anything other than what it actually is. Any seasoned instructor will tell you that not all classes are alike, even in multisectioned courses with students drawn from the same level and discipline. Your task will be to assess the particular interests, motivations, and backgrounds of your colleagues and then try to adapt your speeches to the specific classroom situation. Further, if you meet at 8:00 A.M. and

[1] Commencement Address at Oberlin College, June 15, 1955.

you are the first speaker, your task will be somewhat different than if you meet at 10:00 and you are the third or fourth speaker. The time of the meeting and the stimuli the listeners have heard before you speak are only two of many variables that will necessarily influence the listener's reception of your ideas.

While recognizing the impossibility of achieving perfect audience adaptation, the wise speaker will nevertheless strive to discover the probable answers to these questions:

1. What is the educational, social, and cultural background of the audience?
2. Is this a predominantly professional, social, or religious group?
3. What professional and occupational groups are represented?
4. What is the general economic level of the audience?
5. What age group, if any, predominates?
6. Is the audience composed of men, women, or both?
7. What is the general political orientation of its members?
8. Is race or creed a significant factor?
9. Will the hour for the meeting affect audience reception?
10. Do the size of the audience and the physical arrangements present special problems?

After you have selected your specific proposition, you must investigate the potential attitude of your audience toward your subject. Will they be likely to have an apathetic, friendly, open-minded, or hostile attitude toward your proposition? In the *speech to inform* we must give particular attention to the background knowledge of our potential audience. We dare not bore them with the "same old stuff." Neither can we risk confusing them with technical material beyond their comprehension. In the *speech to convince* we must base our arguments on premises they are willing to accept and draw our inferences from evidence they can understand. No matter how important, vital, or interesting we may consider the topic, it must, first and foremost, contain materials within the comprehension and the frame of reference of the particular audience we are addressing. Specifically we must ask ourselves:

1. What kinds of background information does the audience possess which is directly and indirectly related to the proposition?
2. What basic attitudes does this audience hold toward the subject under consideration?

SELF-ANALYSIS AND SOURCE CREDIBILITY

Your selection, as well as your treatment of your topic, will depend to some degree on the audience's attitude toward you as the speaker. Source credibility is closely related to that form of support known as ethical proof, a topic we shall discuss more fully later in this chapter. At this point it is sufficient to ask ourselves:

1. Because of my background, training, or experience do the listeners anticipate a particular kind of speech? You may in some instances wish to deliver a radically different kind of speech from the one they expect. But you should project and be aware of their potential reactions.
2. Will the audience accept me as an authority in this area? A negative answer will not necessarily rule out a topic, but you may be forced to use more documentation or employ special forms of proof.

FINDING THE SPECIFIC TOPIC

Subjects often spring directly from self-analysis or from the audience and the occasion. The groups and the situations themselves create the stimuli and provide the atmosphere, but the speaker must still find the precise topic and phrase the specific proposition. This is the problem every student speaker faces after the instructor has assigned a speech to inform. The student has a better than average opportunity to analyze the audience and appraise the occasion. Yet in complete desperation we often tell the instructor or our roommate, "I can't find a topic; I have nothing worth saying." At that moment we are completely honest, if inaccurate. Usually a cursory investigation of three or four areas turns up more likely topics than we can immediately use.

1. LOOK TO YOURSELF. At first glance it would seem that there is no other place to begin. Unfortunately we are so close to our own experiences that they often strike us as too commonplace. Subjects from faraway lands and highly technical topics for which we have little background often hold a fatal attraction. No one should be discouraged from doing research on esoteric topics, but the student must recognize that unless he has some initial background knowledge, he will probably succeed in merely confusing himself and his audience. The beginning speaker will do well to look to his own *interests, hobbies, past experiences, travels,* and *work experiences* for speeches to inform. A subject on which you have some basic knowledge, either through firsthand experience or through course work makes the best starting point. From there you move into intensive research, increasing and enriching your original fund of knowledge.

2. LOOK AROUND. When one student turned in a fairly good outline for a speech on the slums of New York City, her instructor asked if she had ever examined the housing conditions in their own small Middle Western town. Her natural response was, "What is there to investigate?" Yet within easy walking distance of her dormitory were slumlike conditions (unknown to the average student) nearly paralleling on a smaller

scale the worst of New York or Chicago. After a visit to this area that student prepared a pertinent, dynamic speech, far more vital to her audience than any she might have developed on the housing conditions in New York City. Unfortunately only a handful of college students heard her speech. The more influential speakers in the community who had larger audiences remained silent on the subject of slums until a tragic fire swept a bedroom hovel, too small for even one child, and snuffed out the lives of seven of the nine children sleeping there. After the tragedy, everyone, on and off campus, had a speech ready to deliver at the mushrooming public indignation meetings. Every campus and community is filled with available subjects. But we need the insight and imagination to spot them.

3. LOOK TO COURSES. Students are constantly engaged in research, but they are not always sensitive to the latent speech topics within an economics, history, foreign language, or zoology assignment. From a psychology course one student developed an interest in cybernetics, pursued the topic with additional research, and ultimately developed an excellent speech on the implications of cybernetics to modern psychology. Another student discovered a topic in geology, and gave his speech on "Our Water Supply in the Future." In history and government classes we are exposed to a multitude of problems bearing directly on all our lives. The alert student continually jots down topics and tentative outlines, which through further research and study might become vibrant, meaningful speeches. A word of caution is also in order. Often student speakers attempt to cover all of Economics 101 in an eight-minute speech, resulting in a discussion so thin it fails to say anything new, or else one so entangled in economic theory that it only confuses the listeners.

TESTING THE TOPIC

From the moment you begin to search for a topic and start the investigation, you will want to put your topic to a rigorous examination. Some of the tests will apply to all topics; other parts bear directly on the particular speech under consideration. During your preparation for any speech you will want to ask yourself the following questions:

1. *Is the topic one in which I am vitally interested?* While the *sine qua non* of an excellent choice is always the speaker's enthusiasm, many potentially good subjects are cast aside before the speaker has realistically examined them. Seemingly drab topics, upon careful investigation, take on genuine luster. On the other hand, many subjects lose some of their initial glamor after close examination. Thus, we often need to refreshen and revitalize our enthusiasm. Above all, it is essential to maintain the feeling that our topic is important and necessary for the audience.

2. *Is the topic timely or timeless?* Other factors being equal, the timely topic is preferable to one that is "timeless." As long as man puts other men to death, the subject of capital punishment will remain as a timeless topic. When the Supreme Court hands down a decision (as it did in 1973) radically reinterpreting the constitutionality of the death sentence, this age-old topic takes on new, "timely" significance. Most timely topics spring out of ancient controversies, but every good "old" subject must be brought up to date.

3. *Is my topic relevant for my audience?* If the listeners ask themselves during the speaker's remarks just why they are receiving a talk on this particular topic, the chances are the speaker has overestimated its relevance. A denunciation of fraternities on a campus where they are already forbidden and where no sentiment prevails for their establishment will probably strike a student audience as totally irrelevant. The speaker is in effect attacking a "straw man" and developing a speech around an artificial issue.

4. *Is the topic suitable for oral discourse?* A skillful speaker can adapt most subjects to the platform. Complications often arise, however, when we attempt to treat a highly technical topic. Some subjects require several thousand words to be understood when written for a reader. Such topics, even if they can be presented for listeners, are likely to require longer rather than shorter treatment than they would for readers. The speaker who undertakes to present a complex topic in too few words and with an insufficient number of concrete illustrations is inviting inevitable failure. We likewise risk disaster, if we assume a background of information the audience does not possess. Even an audience with some college background in mathematics would probably find itself at sea during a discussion of "Geometrical Algebra."

A few topics, depending on audience makeup, may fall into the classification of taboo subjects. The list seems to have shrunk over the years, and subjects once discussed in "closed" sessions are now freely discussed in mixed groups. However, if as speakers we are merely hoping to shock our listeners or attempting to demonstrate our freedom from puritan shackles, we are likely to fail in both objectives. Few speakers ever increase their forcefulness or credibility by using four-letter words on the public platform. More often they merely impress the listeners with their poverty of ideas and vocabulary. Before venturing into taboo areas, we need to analyze the audience and our own capabilities.

POSSIBLE TOPICS

While the topics below are listed under two general headings, *Expository* and *Persuasive*, they can serve almost any speech purpose, depending on the specialized treatment given to them. Each speaker must *narrow* and phrase his or her own *specific proposition*.

EXPOSITORY (*Entertain and inform*)	PERSUASIVE (*Stimulate and convince*)
1. Beyond the Moon	1. Censorship
2. Energy Conservation	2. Clean the Environment
3. Summer Jobs	3. Union and Collective Bargaining
4. Procrastination	4. Pornography
5. Extrasensory Perception	5. Foreign Aid
6. Poetry, or "How Much Verse Can It Be?"	6. Gun Control
7. History of (our town, baseball, the UN, etc.)	7. Liberty—Justice
8. A Biography (an unforgettable character)	8. Violence and Reform
9. Me and the Weather (see Mark Twain's speech, pages 427–428)	9. Affirmative Action
10. Beards and Hair	10. Responsibility and Freedom of Speech
11. My Affair with Lady Nicotine	11. School Bussing
12. Watching My Weight	12. Urban Housing (Slum)
13. Music Lessons	13. Abortion, Right or Wrong
14. Pay Cable Television	14. College Athletic Programs
15. Thermal Energy	15. The Population Explosion
16. The Naked Ape	16. Right of Dissent
17. The Dean's List	17. Medicare
18. Rock Music Festivals	18. FBI
19. Back to Bicycles	19. Watergate
20. A Ring on the Hand Is Worth Two on the Tub or Phone?	20. Support the Heart Fund, Cancer Association, etc.
21. UFOs on the Rise?	21. The Road to Peace
22. The Establishment	22. World Government
23. Silence	23. Euthanasia (Right to Die?)
24. Natural Gas	24. Wounded Knee (Indian Rights)
25. Cable TV	25. Women's Liberation
26. Twenty-four Hours with . . .	26. Mass Transit

FORTIFYING THE PROPOSITION

Whether the speech is designed to inform, entertain, stimulate, or convince, the speaker's major obligation is to secure sufficient supporting evidence to promote the desired inferences and responses from the audience. The general techniques of research differ little from those of the debater or the discussant.[2] To establish the proposition and win the desired audi-

[2] See Chapter 12, pages 258–259, and Chapter 13, pages 292–297.

ence response, the speaker is wise to employ as wide a variety of supporting forms and materials as possible. Moreover, the steps in finding supporting materials closely approximate the steps used in finding a suitable topic. The best starting place is the speaker's own fund of knowledge. Even after we have apparently drained our own resources, we often find to our surprise that if we started preparation early, we continue to receive a flow of seemingly new ideas. Even during the actual presentation, the precise illustration we need may suddenly occur to us. While no one should rely on last-minute inspirations, they occur most frequently and successfully to speakers who are thoroughly prepared.

After you have formulated a tentative outline based on your own background resources, you then move beyond the narrow borders of your own experience. Excellent speakers never neglect, neither do they depend solely on, their personal storehouses of information, but look to the well-known indices to periodical literature for articles, to the reference books for factual support, and to the varied sources catalogued in the library card file. If individuals near at hand possess special knowledge on the subject, they search them out for interviews. To the traditional forms of support—*logical, emotional,* and *ethical*—they seek *expository* and *stylistic* methods of rendering the final product clear and vivid as well as persuasive. As we shall presently observe, no dividing line separates the various forms of support; they overlap at many points, and ultimately the speaker blends them into a unified speech which, if artistically designed, moves toward the establishment of the proposition. Finally, we place our evidence before the audience in a form best suited to the listeners and the specific occasion.

Logical forms

Basically, we employ two logical patterns to support the proposition—the *inductive* and the *deductive*. Although we sometimes consider these two as separate approaches, they are in reality inextricably interwoven and wholly dependent on each other. The scientific method proceeds inductively, moving from specific items of evidence toward a general truth. The police inspector follows the inductive process when he finds a cigarette that bears lipstick traces, a mink stole, and a lady's perfumed handkerchief in the same room with a murdered man. From these specific clues he may conclude, rightly or wrongly, that some female was mixed up with the homicide. Another inspector may attack the case deductively. When he receives the call at headquarters that a man has been murdered, he may remark, "No doubt a woman in the case. There always is!" He begins with the general premise that all murder cases include a woman. In deductive reasoning, then, we move from the general to the particular. From the general premise "Back of every successful man there stands a woman," we might conclude, rightly or wrongly, that the successful Mr. Smythe must have received his inspiration from his wife, mother, or another woman. But this particular Smythe may have been a woman-hater.

Clearly the most precarious, least reliable form of logical proof is probably the deductive. Since it begins with the generalization or a so-called "universal truth," the speaker must be sure he has established the validity of his premise. Books on public speaking and debate often spend much time examining the structure of deductive logic, i.e., the syllogism and enthymeme.[3] It is probably important to understand the various tests for the syllogism, cause-and-effect relationships, and the analogy. It is even more important to make sure the premises (generalizations) are substantiated by the facts. If all syllogisms were as infallible as the logicians' favorite concerning the mortal nature of man in general and of Socrates in particular, we would experience little difficulty.[4] But our major premises are seldom based on so universal a truth. As best we can usually establish only a probability of truth for our premises and thus for our conclusions. "All apples contain seeds," we say basing our generalization on rather widespread inductive evidence. The trouble is that it is not universally true. Seedless apples as well as grapes, grapefruit, oranges, and even watermelon do exist. At one time, no doubt, a generally accepted universal truth was: "All grapes contain seeds."

H. L. Mencken branded this kind of deductive logic, "sillygisms" listing some of the following among his favorites:

That Anglo-Saxons are a superior race.

That Americans are God's chosen people with a divine mission in the world.

That progress must be always upward and onward.

That obedience to constituted authority is the prime requisite of good citizenship.[5]

We do not mean to imply that speakers should avoid premises and inferences. They must use this form of support; they have no other choice. Indeed, the proposition is the fundamental deductive premise in the speech. It is the primary assertion or generalization we attempt to establish through specific facts, instances, and testimony. From these facts (induction), we draw further generalizations, point to causes and effects, construct analogies, and hope through this mixture of specific instances (induction) and general conclusions (deduction) to establish the validity

---

[3] The enthymeme is often called the rhetorical syllogism. Aristotle explained that since audiences were too impatient to follow the complete syllogism, the orator, shortened and omitted certain steps. The enthymeme might best be explained as a maxim, a general truth the audience will accept as valid.

[4] All men are mortal. (*Major premise*)
Socrates is a man. (*Minor premise*)
Therefore, Socrates is mortal. (*Conclusion*)

[5] C. Merton Babcock, "H. L. Mencken: Of Horse-Laughs and Syllogisms," *ETC: A Review of General Semantics*, **19** (February 1963), 430–431.

of our major proposition. But the excellent speaker tests every fact and every tentative generalization, recognizing the assertions and inferences (even the so-called facts) for what they are, namely possible truths.

Every four years, with the arrival of a new student generation, some magazine writer attempts to generalize, codify, and classify the present college crop. In one quadrennium they are "Beat," in another, "Lost," and in the next, "Concerned," and most recently they were branded as "The McLuhan Generation," a group whose minds have been shaped more by the electronic mass media than by print media. To test the validity of these premises (inferences) that "College students are 'beat,' 'lost,' 'concerned'[6] or 'McLuhanized,'[7] we need to ask some questions to discover the facts that led to these conclusions:

1. Are the alleged facts gleaned through testimony, statistics, and examples sufficiently abundant (how many colleges, students) to warrant a probable inference, generalization, premise, or contention?
2. Are the instances representative? (Ivy League, state schools, denominational schools?)
3. Does a direct relationship exist between the facts and the conclusions? In cause-and-effect relationships is the cause sufficient to produce the effect? (Progressive education, life adjustment courses may have produced a generation of mental midgets.)
4. Are our facts substantiated by a wide variety of sources? Do the witnesses (books, magazines, TV and radio reports, personal interviews, personal experience) tend to agree on the facts?
5. Were the facts (statistics, instances, examples) gathered by a responsible agency and can they be verified and supported by other sources?

Emotional forms

No clear-cut line separates logical from emotional proof. Just as inductive and deductive logic support each other, so the emotional strands of an argument interlace the logical, thus making it difficult, if not impossible, for even the trained rhetorical critic to identify and isolate the elements. The amount of emotion in any logical appeal depends on the treatment (word choice, phrasing, delivery) the speaker gives the facts and illustrations. The coldest statistic on a ticker tape may inspire some to wild, emotional responses and others to suicidal depression. George Whitefield's vocal control was such that he could supposedly bring tears to the eyes of his listeners with the mere repetition of the word "Mesopotamia."

[6] See Harold Taylor, "Portrait of a New Generation," *Saturday Review* December 8, 1962, pp. 10–12.

[7] Fred M. Hechlinger, "What Happened to the Best and Brightest?" *Saturday Review World*, February 9, 1974, p. 65.

When the chairman of the Federal Communications Commission, Newton Minow, delivered his famous TV "Wasteland" speech, he stirred up one kind of emotional response in his immediate audience, the National Association of Broadcasters. He appealed to another kind of motive and received a radically different reaction from the television viewers who read his remarks. Many in his immediate audience took offense and were deeply hurt and resentful, while 98 per cent of the reading public enthusiastically supported him. Certainly in the following passage from Minow's speech, we have trouble separating the logical and the emotional appeals. "When television is good, nothing . . . is better. But when television is bad, nothing is worse." We could state these generalizations syllogistically. They constitute some of the premises, maxims, and enthymemes fundamental to Minow's speech. To establish the validity of his assertion that TV was bad, indeed a "vast wasteland," he pictured a typical TV day, citing the following emotionally loaded specific instances (induction). "You will see a procession of game shows, violence, audience participation shows, formula comedies about totally unbelievable families, blood and thunder, mayhem, violence, sadism, murder, western badmen, western good men, private eyes, gangsters, more violence, and cartoons. And, endlessly, commercials—many screaming, cajoling, and offending. And most of all, boredom."[8]

Usually when people complain about an emotional address, they really mean that the speaker's appeals (premises) failed to coincide with their particular wants or drives. We need to recognize that emotional appeals are as logical or illogical, as sound or as specious, as the entire argument. Moreover, it is wholly inaccurate to consider emotion as synonymous with fallacious argument. Man is an emotional as well as a reasoning being. These two elements are not mutually exclusive, but complementary features of our total character. And the speaker who would persuade through language must make appeals through both logic and emotion. Indeed, any appeal to reason that runs counter to emotionally held attitudes will rarely if ever succeed.

Even so, we do not consider all emotional appeals as legitimate or ethical. We cannot condone or promote the demagogue and the huckster in their use of emotion and specious argument as smoke screens to blind the eye of reason and promote irrational decisions. Appeals to class hatred, the big lie, the half-truth, noisy repetition, name-calling, and the suppression of evidence lie outside the realm of ethical persuasion. The end, however noble, never justifies the use of these means. And truly noble goals do not require underhanded means for their promotion, nor are they enhanced by shoddy techniques.

On the other hand, we do not consider all appeals based on emotion

---

[8] For an analysis of Minow's speech, see Paul H. Boase, "The T.V. Wasteland: A Rhetorical Analysis," *Ohio Speech Journal*, 4 (1966), 46–55.

as unethical. Man's wants and drives range from his narrowest selfish concern to his noblest aspiration for the liberation of all peoples. Keeping in mind our earlier contention that it is virtually impossible to separate logical appeals from emotional appeals, we would still caution the speaker to ask himself one fundamental, soul-searching question: "Should my audience accept this proposition solely on the basis of the best logical proof available?" If the answer is affirmative, the speaker may then seek the *ethical motivation* that will promote audience acceptance of the proposition. In Chapter 18 we shall examine in greater detail the potential appeals.

Ethical proof

This form of proof—ethical proof—Aristotle considered as "almost" the most "potent of all the means to persuasion." It contains an illusive mixture, many so subtle that they defy analysis. This proof which comes from the speaker includes more than "goodness" and "sincerity." Many honest, upright men have failed utterly to develop ethical proof. It seems to include personality, appearance, reputation, character, nuances of delivery, word choice, vocal quality, and a host of intangibles. "Image" is perhaps the popular term for ethical proof, particularly when used with a favorable connotation.

Every speaker hopes his ethical appeal is high and usually strives, consciously or subconsciously, to increase his stature. Student speakers often wonder what they, relative unknowns, can do in the classroom situation to develop this illusive quality, one that is seemingly reserved for persons with wider experience. While the development of this quality is frequently the task of a lifetime, most observers recognize the presence of varying degrees of ethical proof in student speakers. We can isolate some of the reasons:

1. By demonstrating a complete command of the subject each time you appear before the class.
2. A thoroughly prepared speech, including a mastery of ideas, organization, style, and delivery.
3. Absolute fairness in treating the evidence and in drawing your inferences.
4. The use of recognized authority to support matters of opinion.
5. A manner free on one hand from negative suggestion and unnecessary apology and on the other from a "know it all" attitude.
6. A friendly, relaxed poised presentation.
7. Dress and bearing suitable to the subject, audience, and occasion.
8. A strong sense of communication with the audience and a willingness to respond to cues you receive from the audience.
9. In summary, the speaker strives to develop those qualities that prompted Quintilian to describe the perfect orator as a "good man skilled in speaking."

Expository and stylistic forms

A common lament of the speaker to the listener who misunderstands or fails to grasp an idea is the oft-repeated excuse, "But I said it." And equally distressing to both the speaker and the listener is the recorded proof. The speaker did say "It." In hurt tones the speaker then complains, "People just don't listen." And again the speaker is right. Many people listen with only half an ear and with an efficiency rating of 50 per cent or less.[9] And unless they hear essentially the same message at least three times the percentage may drop even lower. In the area of organization they often need an initial summary, an expanded discussion, and a final summary. See Chapter 17, pages 363–387.

The supporting material throughout the speech also needs *amplification* through restatement, explanation, concreteness, figurative imagery, and all the stylistic devices that add vividness to our speaking and a clear sense of understanding for our listeners. If necessary, a reader may reread a passage. An idea stated once may suffice for him. The listener, on the other hand, may need to hear the same message repeated—the more complex the material, the greater the need for amplification and restatement.

RESTATEMENT. Repetition is probably our most important single device for reinforcing an impression. The opening quotation for this chapter demonstrates the Old Testament Prophet Isaiah's keen understanding of this communication concept. For most of us, Madison Avenue learned this lesson too well, but irritating though the noisy, repetitious radio and television commercial may be, it attracts our attention, making it difficult to forget the name of a particular product when we stop by the corner drugstore.

We hope that speakers will avoid a commercial-like repetition, but we likewise emphasize the necessity for generous amplification through restatement—not through mere repetition. The idea is subtly restated in fresh phraseology, insulting neither the most sophisticated listener nor losing the ear of the least perceptive. Notice how Adlai Stevenson, for example, amplifies the concept of democracy through apt restatement.

> And I suppose that most of us, if we were asked to name the most profound issues at stake in the world to- day, would say the issues of freedom and democracy. We would say that the Western World, for all its errors and shortcomings, has for centuries tried to evolve a society in which the individual has enough legal, social, and po- litical elbow room to be not the puppet of the commu- nity, but his own autonomous self.[10]

[9] Carl H. Weaver, *Human Listening: Processes and Behavior* (Indianapolis: Bobbs-Merrill, 1972), pp. 21–22.

[10] *Vital Speeches,* March 1, 1963, p. 306.

EXPLANATION. Another form of amplification is explanation. Clearly most speeches contain a generous intermixture of repetition, restatement, and explanation. In a speech on the same general theme as Stevenson's, Chief Justice Warren E. Burger examined "The Fragility of Freedom" and explained the need for dissent within the constraints of law.

> Very often social explosions are brought on by rigid and unreasoning resistance to change. Long ago Disraeli said, "We must choose to be managers of change, or we will be victims of change." Mature, reasoning people elect to be the managers, and, being mature, they know that change must be orderly to preserve continuity with the past. The rule of law permits us to be the managers of change and to maintain our links with the experience of the past.[11]

CONCRETENESS. Only a small fraction of the population can think in abstractions. No one can speak clearly to another in abstract terms. And when two or more do talk with each other in the abstract, neither can ever be sure that he understands precisely what the other is talking about. If they speak of "truth" and "justice," these concepts evoke widely different sensory images in each person. When Disraeli said in a speech, "Justice is truth in action," he made them somewhat more concrete. When John Galsworthy compared justice to "a machine that when some one has once given it the starting push, rolls on of itself," we see more clearly. Then if we can wrap these abstractions in human personalities and specific illustrations, they take on a vivid accurateness.

STATISTICS. The best as well as the poorest parts of a speech are often those fortified with statistics. Capable of lending concrete liveliness, they can also assume the deadly and confusing inhuman visage of the most foreboding mathematical equation. Yet the dullest figures, when classified, compared, and integrated with the proposition, can take on real color. Bob Hope demonstrated how specific data given the human touch can be highly entertaining:

> Today my heart beat 103,389 times, my blood traveled 168,000,000 miles, I breathed 23,040 times, I inhaled 438 cubic feet of air, I spoke 4,800 words, moved 750 major muscles, and I exercised 7,000,000 brain cells. I'm tired.[12]

By using the exact figures (inaccurate though they were) Hope managed to heighten the humor. The speaker is often puzzled over the ques-

---

[11] *Vital Speeches,* June 15, 1973, p. 515.
[12] From "Quotable Quotes," *Reader's Digest* (January 1949), 131.

tion of whether to use the complete statistic or round off the figures. In the serious speech, absolute accuracy is necessary and yet the complete statistic may only confuse. For situations where exactness is important, the speaker must avoid overwhelming the listener. We can sometimes accomplish this by using the round number in association with the exact numbers. An additional restatement in *percentages* may further amplify the concept.

In all instances the raw figures must be put in terms the audience can comprehend. When a speaker announces with vigor the astronomical figures in the national debt, most listeners, whose checkbooks rarely carry a balance beyond three figures, have no frame of reference in which to place these billions. The naive listener may be impressed, but the serious student will resent the confusion resulting from the speaker's failure to interpret the statistics. On the other hand, a commonly used device of putting the debt on a "per person" basis increases the understanding of all listeners.

Speaking on "The Bounds of Earth: One Last Try," Arthur H. Doerr, vice president of the University of West Florida, employed a vivid technique for translating the complex statistics of the population explosion and the energy crisis into understandable terms for his audience. Pointing to the figures for 1974 he noted that 3,800,000,000 persons live in our world. He then reduced the size so that members of the audience could understand more clearly their own positions in the world struggle for food, resources, and survival.

> Suppose world population was compressed into a single city of 1000 people. In this imaginary city 55 of the 1000 people would be American citizens, and 945 would represent all other nations. Of this 945 people, 215 would be citizens of the People's Republic of China. The 55 United States citizens would receive more than 40 percent of the town's income. These 55 people, representing 5½ percent of the population would consume almost 15 percent of the town's food supply; use, on a per capita basis, 10 times as much oil, 40 times as much steel and 40 times as much general equipment.
>
> Among the 1000 people in the town, less than 300 would be Christian, and more than 700 would have some other religion or no religion at all. Of the population about 300 would be white and 700 non-white. The 55 Americans and their European counterparts would have a life expectancy of 70 years compared to 45 years for the other citizens of the town.
>
> And, although most of the citizens of the world have accepted their lot, this has ceased to be so. This has be-

come an era of rising expectations of the world's peoples. Everyone seeks his share of the 'good life.'[13]

In presenting figures and statistical data it is essential that they be authoritative and that the listener be so impressed. He will not get such an impression if statistical data are introduced with a vague and evasive statement such as, "Records show that . . ." or "Statistics prove that. . . ." Instead, the precise source of the data should be presented in such a way that any listener may check their authenticity should he so desire.

FIGURATIVE IMAGERY. "Man is a creature who lives not upon bread alone," wrote Robert Louis Stevenson, "but principally by catchwords." We would add to this—figurative phraseology. President Kennedy packed his Inaugural Address with vivid imagery, as a writer in *The New Yorker* on February 4, 1961 pointed out.

> The oration is so rich in figures of speech—the many metaphors include a torch, a beachhead, jungles, a trumpet, a tiger—that we can imagine students of the future studying it for examples of antithesis ("If a free society cannot help the many who are poor, it cannot save the few who are rich"), personification (". . . the hand of mankind's final war"), and anaphora ("Not as a call to bear arms, though arms we need; not as a call to battle, though embattled we are . . ."). "Battle" and "embattled" —an excellent example of paronomasia.[14]

A word of caution may be necessary in the use of stylistic devices. Excellent oral style should be *clear, appropriate,* and *vivid.* We must also recognize that style appropriate for the Kennedy Inauguration would be out of keeping in an after-dinner address or a lecture on the federal budget. Moreover, style that calls attention to itself usually needs reworking. Adjectives and adverbs, metaphors and similes, through overuse, turn into clichés. As G. L. Mehta, Indian Ambassador to the United States, in an editorial entitled "Spare That Adjective," points out: "Times are always 'critical,' sessions of conferences 'momentous,' and tests 'acid' . . . policies have to be 'firm' and 'enduring' but statesmanship (of opponents) is usually 'bankrupt.' "[15] All of us too easily adopt the once vivid figures of the past, turning them into the clichés of the present. For example: *Each* and *every* one of us *views with alarm* the perilous state of our nation, but *point with pride* to the accomplishments of the Fathers as they guided the *grand old ship of state* through treacherous waters to

[13] *Vital Speeches,* February 1, 1974, p. 229.
[14] Reprinted by permission; © 1961 The New Yorker Magazine, Inc.
[15] *Saturday Review,* August 10, 1957, p. 18.

havens of safety. Even in our final hour (another cliché) we are not permitted to die, but must fall asleep, be cut down by the grim reaper, cash in our chips, or fly to our eternal reward.

Nearly as frightful as cliché mongering is the common tendency to mix our images. Even Shakespeare was guilty when he had Hamlet "take arms against a sea of troubles." One student speaker, urging the audience to speak and act in support of a meritorious cause, said, "Open your mouths and throw yourself into it!" An English orator, carried away by the grandeur of Empire, extolled the virtuosity of the British Lion, which he maintained would cross the jungles of Africa and climb the trees of India, but would never pull in its horns or shrink into its shell.

As a student speaker you will want to concentrate on improving your language style. Some of the following guidelines will help:

1. Recognize that some triteness and a few clichés mark every speaker's style. Try to strike a happy balance between the old and the new.
2. Search for the vivid personal noun, the active "hairy-chested" verb. Avoid overuse of passive voice. Keep your word choice specific and follow abstractions with illustrations. If possible, tape-record some of your practice sessions, listening for clichés, and then devise more concrete, exciting language for the same concepts.
3. In your manuscript speeches write and rewrite, polish and edit your ideas, searching for the apt, appropriate, and vivid words, phrases, and images.
4. Study figurative language (metaphor, simile, oxymoron, personification, alliteration, epithet, analogy), the speaker's primary means of achieving stylistic vividness.
5. Analyze the speeches of historical and contemporary figures, seeking to discover and identify their uses of figurative imagery. See Chapter 19, pages 425–428, for examples of auditory, gustatory, olfactory, tactile, visual, and motor imagery.

AUDIOVISUAL SUPPORT

Certain types of speeches, particularly those designed to inform, are often improved by the skillful use of audiovisual aids—by charts, graphs, pictures, enlarged models, filmstrips, movies, tape recordings, and records. Modern projectors now permit the use of audiovisual presentations, once possible only in a small room with a blackboard. Overhead viewers can enlarge the speaker's pictures, charts, graphs, and writing and place them within easy viewing for an almost unlimited audience. The speaker does not break contact by turning away from the audience as required by use of the blackboard or easel. The energy invested in preparing slides and securing the projector and screen frequently pays rich dividends in audience interest and comprehension. But whether using conventional means or electronic assistance, the speaker needs to consider these suggestions:

1. If you decide to use an audio or visual aid, it is important to plan its use carefully. A visual aid can easily degenerate into a frustrating block. Few practices are more annoying than to bring an aid too small to be seen in row one or to wave a chart or picture in front of the audience so rapidly that none can see it.
2. Keep the aids clear and simple. They need not to be artistic unless you are demonstrating your own or another's pencil sketching or oil.
3. Omit all unnecessary detail and complicated sets of figures. Round off statistics and where possible use percentages.
4. Remove the aid when you have finished using it; otherwise the listener may continue studying it rather than listening to you. This situation may also prevail if you pass a visual aid around the audience.
5. Make sure that your aid will actually promote the purpose of your speech.

VOCAL AND PHYSICAL FORMS. The answer to the oft-asked question, "Shall I use gestures?"[16] is that you cannot avoid using them. No action (if that is possible for a speaker) constitutes a vivid, meaningful gesture. It is probably incongruous if not ludicrous, contradicting rather than reinforcing the speaker's message. But just as you cannot deliver a speech without voice (we would direct your attention to the first part of the text again for assistance in pronunciation, articulation, and vocal control), so the public speech is incomplete until the speaker achieves the proper management of the body.

The appropriateness and effectiveness of a speaker's physical presentation are determined by the *empathic reactions* it touches off in the audience. We may define *empathy* as our muscular, emotional, and mental reactions to the audible and visible stimuli we receive from a speaker. For example, while listening to a person with a husky voice, our own throats tend to become scratchy. The fidgety speaker, all "tied up in knots," makes the audience nervous and ill at ease. On the other hand, the person who is relaxed and in command places the audience at ease and in a receptive state to respond to the appeals. The question is, "How does the speaker achieve a satisfactory empathic relationship with the listeners?"

We do not propose to enter the age-old controversy between the natural and artificial schools over the best methods of improving the physical aspects of delivery. The so-called artificial school lays heavy emphasis on the study and practice of gesture. The other school places less emphasis on the actual gesture, maintaining that if the speaker understands his ideas and truly feels the emotion at the moment of speaking, he will natu-

---

[16] See pages 333–338 for additional help on the use of gestures.

rally employ the "right" action. Both groups devoutly hope to produce an artist with no trace of artifice in the final production.

Taking a position somewhere between these two extremes, we would suggest the following premises:

1. The *idea, organization,* and *style* must form the basic structure for any study of delivery. No amount of training in gesture will ever enable a speaker to present empty thoughts effectively. An empty bag will not stand upright; it also needs more than hot air. *We can never divorce the teaching of speech delivery from speech content.*

2. All bodily action, facial expression, and movement must start from within, receiving their motivations from the speaker's thought and feeling.

3. Speech preparation is an active, vigorous process, never an enterprise carried on exclusively in the seclusion of the closet. You will need moments of quiet meditation and research, but the final stages call for vigorous vocalizations. You may even prepare much of the speech on your feet, pacing the floor, employing uninhibited gesture. As you rehearse your speech orally, before facing the audience, your gestures will become less random and self-directed; ideally they should always reinforce and clarify the idea.

4. Public speaking calls for a total reaction of the entire body toward the reinforcement of the thought and feeling of the speaker.

5. During the actual speaking experience, the *idea* and the *desire* to communicate with the audience take precedence over any subsidiary thoughts about gesture or action. A basic rule is to avoid "holding back." If the rehearsal and preparation have been thorough, many of the gestures will come forth quite naturally. And as you become more accustomed to using gestures, they will come more spontaneously.

6. Every speaker needs criticism from the audience. If you are sensitive, you will receive unmistakable feedback. But unhappily the gods denied us the power to see ourselves as others see us—even when we look in a mirror or see ourselves on video tape. Thus, your instructor and classmates will serve as corrective influences, pointing out the virtues and shortcomings in your ideas, your organizational pattern, the language and imagery you employed, and your vocal and physical presentation.

After you have rehearsed your speech several times, you may feel that some ideas and phrases that struck you as fresh and lively when you first discovered them have lost some of their original luster. In all probability your audience, hearing them for the first time, will respond as you did initially unless you "go stale" during your delivery. The good actor always creates the "illusion of the first time," and you as a speaker must never lose that sense of the value and importance of your ideas, thus making the words seem to fall "hot from your lips."

SUMMARY

Appropriate topics for speeches usually spring directly from the speaker's personal experiences and vital interests. They also arise from the specific occasion and are in all instances governed by the audience and the setting for the speech. In testing a potential topic the speaker must always make an evaluation according to the *timeliness*, the *relevance* for a specific audience and occasion, and the *suitability* for oral presentation.

After selecting a topic and phrasing the proposition, you turn first to your own storehouse of knowledge. Your continuing research will lead to expert authority through the interview and library sources. Throughout this preparatory stage the speaker seeks the *logical, emotional,* and *ethical* forms of proof to strengthen the proposition and further fortifies the topic with *expository* and *stylistic* supports, thereby adding color and vividness to the topic. Additional forms of support include *restatement, explanation, concreteness, statistics, figurative imagery,* and *audiovisual aids.* We shall consider the speaker's special problems in organization in the next chapter. Finally, to bring the proposition to the listener, the speaker must select and practice appropriate and effective modes of delivery.

QUESTIONS AND EXERCISES

1. Rewrite the description of a typical day on television (read Newton Minow's indictment once more on page 351) as one of the television executives might have written it. Indicate the kind of audience he might be addressing. Be prepared to read your version to the class.

2. Prepare and present extemporaneously a two-to-three-minute speech to clarify the abstract. Your instructor will assign an abstract term (truth, freedom, beauty, democracy, love, etc.) as the general topic. Your job is to limit and illuminate the subject, avoiding clichés and empty generalities. Use at least three different forms of support.

3. Attend a public lecture and analyze the speaker for evidence of *ethical proof.* After listening to the speaker, write a two-minute talk to be read to the class on the elements that added or detracted from the speaker's *ethos.* You may want to discuss some of the following:

    (a) The effect of his appearance, dress, and general bearing,
    (b) His voice,
    (c) His pronunciation,
    (d) Direct or indirect references to his background, experience, or qualifications,
    (e) The use of supporting materials.

4. Bring to class five propositions that might serve as the major premise in a syllogism, e.g., "All men are prone to make mistakes." Try to find premises you believe are "Universal Truths." Be prepared to defend your selections in class.

5. Distinguish between restatement and repetition. Select a simple proposition and "restate" the idea in at least three ways without employing "repetition."

6. Listen for examples of mixed imagery in ordinary conversation or look for some in literature. Bring five examples to class.

7. Make a list of ten common clichés. How can you express the same concept just as clearly and vividly with fresh phraseology?

8. Prepare and present to the class a four-minute speech to inform, using visual aids. Make sure the aids are merely supplemental help and that the speech does not turn out to be merely a visual aid.

9. At the next athletic contest you attend, analyze the empathic responses of the audience to the game. Describe in a two-minute speech to the class the physical responses of the spectators to the tense game-situations.

10. Give a two-minute speech in which you employ statistics. With each statistical support you use, restate the statistics by means of a comparison. For example, Albert J. Nevins said in one speech: "If our military budget for a single year was spread back over this same period, we would have spent more than $40 a minute since the birth of Christ. We no longer measure bombs in pounds as we did in World War II, nor even in tons. Today we speak in megatons. One megaton equals 166,000 block busters of World War II. It would take 20,000 box cars to carry enough TNT to make a single megaton bomb." (*Vital Speeches,* December 1, 1962, p. 117.)

11. Take an editorial on a current issue and analyze it for the *proposition* and the *supporting* material. State the writer's proposition in one sentence and classify the supporting evidence.

RECOMMENDED READINGS

BAIRD, A. CRAIG, FRANKLIN H. KNOWER, and SAMUEL L. BECKER. *Essentials of General Communication.* New York: McGraw-Hill Book Company, 1973, chaps. 3 and 4.

BLANKENSHIP, JANE. *Public Speaking: A Rhetorical Perspective,* 2nd ed. Englewood Cliffs, N.J.: Prentice-Hall, Inc., 1972.

BRIGANCE, W. N. *Speech Composition.* New York: Appleton-Century-Crofts, 1953, chaps. II and VI.

CLEVENGER, THEODORE, JR. *Audience Analysis*. Indianapolis: The Bobbs-Merrill Co., Inc., 1966.

MILLS, GLEN E. *Putting a Message Together*, 2nd ed. Indianapolis: The Bobbs-Merrill Co., Inc., 1973, chaps. 1 and 2.

SARETT, LEW, W. T. FOSTER, and ALMA JOHNSON SARETT. *Basic Principles of Speech*. Boston: Houghton Mifflin Company, 1958, chaps. 12, 13, and 14.

WALTER, OTIS M., and ROBERT L. SCOTT. *Thinking and Speaking: A Guide to Intelligent Oral Communication*. New York: Macmillan Publishing Co., Inc., 1973, chaps. 2, 3, 6, 10, and 11.

WHITE, EUGENE E. *Practical Speech Fundamentals*. New York: Macmillan Publishing Co., Inc., 1960, chaps. 5, 10, and 11.

Chapter 17

Synthesis &
Organization

> But to avoid all display of art in itself requires
> consummate art.
>
> QUINTILIAN

Radio and television were exciting new discoveries for your parents and grandparents. Now, with the technological explosions of the 1960s and 1970s, a multitude of "new" subjects bombard us almost daily. Yet despite these startlingly new scientific achievements, the writer of Ecclesiastes was nearly accurate in his cynical observation that "there is nothing new under the sun." Many speech topics are old. A few members of your audience may recognize even the most obscure supporting material. But your *organization of your materials* and the *style* you employ must impress the audience as fresh and new, a *creation distinctively your own.* Above all, your development of the organizational pattern and your phrasing of the ideas will distinguish you from the *plagiarist* who has stolen another's speech. In a strict legal sense you cannot copyright an idea, but you *can copyright the expression* of that idea.

In the preparation process you first select your topic (proposition or purpose) and then collect the supporting materials (facts, illustrations, testimony). Next you face the highly personal task of synthesizing, discarding, limiting, subdividing, and finally ordering the usable evidence in a way designed to promote the desired audience responses. If you depend on one source for your facts, your organization, and even your style, you not only plagiarize but usually bore your listeners with an ill-digested, oversimplified analysis.

Even if you acknowledge, as you must, your reliance on one source and thereby avoid the stigma of plagiarism, your speech will likely degenerate into the "vanity" deplored in Ecclesiastes and a mere "striving after wind." The audience may be and often is familiar with that one source. From the speaker they deserve a study in depth and breadth, a mature analysis including the speaker's own individualistic interpretation, phrasing, and organizational pattern. A warmed-over summary of a *Reader's Digest* article may constitute a "report," but not a speech.

SPEECH ORGANIZATION

Ancient and modern writers agree on the necessity for larger divisions in the speech, but differ markedly on the number. Aristotle, perhaps in revolt against excessive subdivisions, stripped speech organization of all but its two essential parts: (1) the *proposition* and (2) the *proof*. Yet, he also recognized the practical necessity of additional parts, audiences being "what they are."[1] Thus, he recommends four parts: *Proem* (introduction), *Statement* (proposition, *Argument* (body), and *Epilogue* (conclusion). The Roman rhetoricians Cicero and Quintilian recommended five to seven divisions depending on the type of speech (forensic, deliberative, or ceremonial) and the circumstances under consideration.[2]

Modern authorities tend to favor Plato's three-divisional plan, which he described in his matchless analogy in the *Phaedrus*: "Every speech ought to be put together like a living creature with a body of its own, so as to be neither without head, nor without feet, but to have both a middle and extremities, described proportionately to each other and to the whole."[3] We recommend, then, that for greater clarity and convenience the speaker use three major divisions: *Introduction, Body*, and *Conclusion*. More important are the elements in each division and the various methods of developing each major part.

THE INTRODUCTION

Most speeches contain a rather clearly defined introduction. One possible exception is the humorous speech to entertain in which the speaker weaves together a series of loosely connected illustrations. A special type of introduction often accompanies the speech to convince in which the speaker examines all the available solutions for a problem, finally rejecting all except one. The plan here is sometimes called "this or nothing," or the method of "residues,"[4] and will be discussed later in this chapter.

---

[1] Lane Cooper, *The Rhetoric of Aristotle* (New York: Appleton-Century-Crofts, 1960), p. 224.

[2] The sevenfold classical Roman divisions included (1) exordium (introduction), (2) narration, (3) proposition, (4) partition (listing main points), (5) proof, (6) refutation, (7) peoration (conclusion). The ancients were particularly sensitive to the need for audience adaptation in the organization of the speech. Writing on the major divisions of the speech, Quintilian declared, "Let no one however demand from me a rigid code of rules," citing "the all-important gift for an orator . . . a wise adaptability since he is called upon to meet the most varied emergencies." Nevertheless, Quintilian proceeded to establish many rules. We would emphasize, however, that the student must understand the rules *before* he knows how to deviate from them. (*The Institutio Oratoria*, trans. by H. E. Butler, Bk. II, Chap. XIII.)

[3] *Plato . . .*, Lane Cooper (trans.) (New York: Oxford University Press, 1948), p. 51.

[4] See W. N. Brigance, *Speech Composition* (New York: Appleton-Century-Crofts, 1953), pp. 102–109; also W. E. Gillman, Bower Aly, and Hollis White, *The Fundamentals of Speaking*, 2nd ed. (New York: Macmillan, Inc., 1964), p. 98.

Irrespective of the speaker's general and specific purpose, the opening statements or introduction must accomplish the first four and usually all five of the following objectives:

1. Secure the *immediate attention* of the audience.
2. Impress the audience with the timeliness of the topic.
3. Promote *long-range, continuous* attention.
4. Establish a *favorable rapport* between the speaker and audience.
5. Provide the audience with a *forecast* of the specific purpose and the general direction of the speech.

The speaker must, of course, sustain the first three objectives throughout the speech. In the opening minutes they are crucial. Nearly all members of the audience are willing to attend during the first sentence or two; a few will hang on doggedly to the end, hoping even if in vain, for some new thought or inspiration. Most will decide during the introduction whether to listen or to amuse themselves with more pleasant pastimes. During the introduction, the speaker must earn the right to be heard. We do not imply that audiences bear no responsibility. Ideally, both the listener and the speaker should contribute a 100 per cent effort to maintain the dialogue essential to communication, regardless of the virtues or vices of the other party. But as the speaker, you occupy stage center, bear the major responsibility for initiating the message, and possess the potential to analyze your listeners and apply the appropriate measures to hold their attention.

The wise speaker avoids certain fatal temptations when developing the introduction. We have all heard persons handicap themselves during the opening moments by assuming the role of an *apologist,* the *humorless humorist,* an *abstractionist,* or the *cliché monger.*

THE APOLOGIST. While most listeners dislike the egotistical speaker and consider modesty a virtue, overt attempts to demonstrate a humble mien are often mere expressions of self-love. The subtle qualities of modesty are usually reserved for the truly great. A respected scholar, after a lifetime of research, may suggest to the audience that he or she possesses only a fraction of the available knowledge in the field. The average speaker who advertises an inadequate knowledge, incomplete state of preparation, lack of platform skill, or diseased larynx probably has no right to waste the listener's time. But even when you are thoroughly prepared, you may sometimes entertain some doubts about your adequacy. It is best to keep these self-doubts to yourself. By apologizing you will administer what may turn out to be a fatal dose of negative suggestion. You may succeed only in planting attitudes and concepts in the conscious or subconscious thinking of the audience that you least want them to accept. While negative suggestion is best avoided at all times, it is particularly detrimental during the introduction. The wise speaker prepares as thoroughly as possible and then presents the speech confidently, without excuses or apology.

THE HUMORLESS HUMORIST. Happily the erroneous assumption that a speaker should begin with a humorous story is no longer widely held. Indeed, any humor that does not contribute to one of the five previously mentioned objectives for the introduction or does not relate to the topic or the occasion has no legitimate place in any part of the speech. Humor is a powerful attention-catcher and used wisely can win the respect and attention of the audience. Ineptly employed, it can seriously damage the effect of the speech.

Self-directed humor in the introduction, while dangerously negative, is often effective in dispelling hostility toward a speaker whose reputation with a particular audience is less than attractive. When the chairman of the Federal Communications Commission, Newton Minow, addressed the National Association of Broadcasters for the first time, some members of his audience were suspicious of him and fearful of what he might say. As it turned out, their fears were not groundless. But before Minow branded television "a vast wasteland," he employed humor rather effectively to win the good will of his audience. In words adapted to the radio or TV industry, he said, "I seem to have detected a certain nervous apprehension about what I might say or do when I emerged from that locked office for this, my maiden station break." (laughter) He followed this with two more instances of self-directed humor, first, by denying the rumor that he regarded himself "as the fastest draw on the New Frontier" and, second, by suggesting that the FCC assume a name similar to a current TV crime serial: "I may even suggest that we change the name of the FCC to the Seven Untouchables!" (applause and laughter).[5]

THE ABSTRACTIONIST. In the world of art the abstractionist appeals to a small, esoteric coterie. And even then the experts often disagree among themselves as they attempt to explain the significance, meaning, or mood that the artist attempted to paint on the canvas. The abstractionist on the speaker's platform likewise gives the listener a less than sharp, clear-cut picture. The idea itself may be vividly implanted in the speaker's mind, but the image-bearing word for the listener has somehow miscarried. As one student explained to a friend when they left the auditorium, "I understood every word of the speaker and not a single sentence." The speaker had couched the message in abstraction and generalities, and his friend could only remark sardonically that the speech was indeed vague enough to be impressive.

The general or abstract word or phrase usually lends itself to a dozen or more interpretations and fine shades of meaning for the listener, none of which may have been in the mind of the speaker when he uttered the abstraction. Take, for example, the relatively "concrete abstraction," *car*. By making it specific we can put in color, speed, rattle, and contour with words like *bug, dart, mustang, tin lizzie, thunderbird,* and a host of

---

[5] A complete text of Minow's address is in *ETC: A Review of General Semantics,* **18,** (July 1961), 134–147. It also appears in the *Congressional Record,* 87th Congress, 1st session, and in *Vital Speeches,* June 15, 1961, pp. 533–537.

others. In all parts of the address, but particularly in the introduction (where attention is vital), a specific illustration or lively word or phrase must always follow hot on the heels of each abstraction. The listener lost through "Abstract Expressionism" in speech may never recover a sense of direction. The abstract word is a lazy word, used by a speaker unwilling to search for a vivid, lively, specific counterpart.

THE CLICHÉ MONGER. Every speech demands a particular introduction geared to the audience and the occasion, and it is sometimes appropriate to say "Thanks." But how to cross this barrier without joining the cliché mongers often puzzles the best speakers. C. Howard Hardesty, Jr., executive vice president of the Continental Oil Company, speaking on "The U.S. Energy Situation," accomplished the feat and probably achieved a degree of rapport with his audience. Notice how quickly he set forth the problem and gave his listeners the outline and direction for his remarks. If a compliment or a reference to the occasion is necessary, it is best kept brief and correlated, if possible, with the theme and purpose of the speech.

> I appreciate this opportunity of discussing with you the nation's number one problem—the energy situation. With each passing day and every new report of personal inconvenience and economic dislocation, the urgencies of the U.S. energy problem intensify. There is little doubt that energy matters, in all their many ramifications, will rank high on our list of national priorites and be prime determinants of our domestic and foreign policies for many years to come.
>
> Today, I would like to cover what might be called the "four C's" of the U.S. energy situation—conditions, causes, concerns and cures.[6]

Securing attention

While one of the main purposes of the introduction is the focusing of attention on the topic and the successful crossing of the interest barrier, a word of caution is necessary. The overly dramatic, bizarre opening, even though electrifying an audience, may defeat the speaker's long-range purpose. Every attention-catching effort must bear a direct relationship to the speaker's topic. The speaker who stepped to the platform, smashed a phonograph record and then exclaimed, "Our company has been breaking production records for years," strained the pun and misunderstood the purpose of the attention-getting device. A speaker who opens sensationally should be prepared to sustain an unusually high degree of vividness throughout. This is not an excuse for the many prosaically dull introductions, but following a foretaste of the exciting,

[6] *Vital Speeches,* January 15, 1974, p. 208.

the audience often demands as its price of attention nothing less than the extravagant.

The supporting materials used in the introduction to secure immediate and long-range attention are not markedly different from those employed throughout the speech. Some of the more effective methods of developing the introduction include the use of *illustrations,* the *vital,* an *apt quotation,* and the *novel.* Every speaker should recognize the necessity for a generous intermixture of these components.

THE ILLUSTRATION OR NARRATIVE. Everyone loves a good story. It is the basic ingredient of the speech to entertain. It is the seasoning element in every speech. Well-constructed, it contains the basic attention-catching elements—conflict, specific detail, and the unusual. It often dramatizes our vital concerns, and if the illustration is a personal one, the speaker and audience immediately identify with each other.

The most popular speech of the nineteenth and twentieth centuries, delivered over six thousand times and grossing over $1 million was unashamedly narrative from the beginning to the end. Russell Conwell's celebrated speech, "Acres of Diamonds," thrilled audiences here and abroad, and the proceeds helped to build one of our institutions of higher learning, Temple University. Conwell always opened his speech with the same exotic story of Ali Hafed, who sold his farm to search the world over for diamonds only to perish in wretched pennilessness at almost the same moment the Golconda diamond mine was discovered on the farm he deserted. Conwell's proposition that it was every man's moral duty to get rich may be hopelessly out of date, but the illustrative techniques he employed throughout the speech are still valid. Charles Grandison Finney, one of the truly great evangelists of his day, ridiculed preachers who thought illustrations destroyed their ministerial dignity. Said Finney in defending the sermon illustration, "You have Jesus Christ and common sense on your side!" The illustration, extended narrative, anecdote, and specific instance can serve as particularly apt instruments to focus attention on your proposition during the introduction.

THE VITAL COMPONENT. Every introduction, if it is to hold the audience and inspire continuous attention, must contain some references vital to the listeners' wants and desires. It may not always be wise or even possible to place an audience in a position of impending disaster or bliss. But the speaker with the imagination to develop an introduction touching the listeners' highest or lowest concerns will best hold interest. Prior to our entry into World War II, Robert Hutchins employed the vital component effectively in a nationwide radio address.

> I speak tonight because I believe that the American people are about to commit suicide. We are not planning to. We have no plan. We are drifting into suicide. Deafened

by martial music, fine language, and large appropria-
tions, we are drifting into war.[7]

APT QUOTATION. Even brilliant phrase-makers often find that someone
else has expressed a key idea better than they. The pithy epigram, the
provocative question, the line of poetry often serve to heighten the effect
of the introduction. Comptroller General of the United States Elmer B.
Staats, in his commencement address at the University of South Dakota,
successfully set the stage for his message "Idealism or Cynicism: Is Either
Wise in Today's World?" with a quotation from Bob Hope. Recalling his
own graduation thirty-eight years earlier he recalled his wish that the
speaker would be brief. Staats surmised that he and his classmates were
in a hurry because they hadn't heard Hope's words to a modern class of
college seniors—"My advice to those of you who are anxious to go out
into the world is—reconsider and don't."[8]

Arnaud de Borchgrave, senior editor of *Newsweek*, speaking before
the American International Club on "Middle Eastern Oil," opened with
a quotation from a current book.

> A little over a year ago, Herman Kahn, America's
> distinguished futurologist published a book entitled
> "Things To Come." Thinking about the 70s and 80s,
> Kahn listed 24 "sources of instability," eleven "relatively
> unlikely events but almost certainly turning points" and
> eleven "relatively possible events but less likely to be
> decisive."
>
> Not one of his scenarios mentioned oil, or the Persian
> Gulf, or the energy crisis, or the de-stabilizing effect on
> $40 to $50 billion a year in the hands of Arab oil produc-
> ers on the international monetary system.
>
> The conventional wisdom—at least in some circles—
> when Kahn wrote his book was that the Arabs couldn't
> drink their oil and, therefore, would have to go on selling
> it to the West. And that was all Kahn had to say about
> oil.[9]

The question, direct or rhetorical, is always provocative, and usually
serves as an effective attention-catcher. It can also provide the transitional sentence, bridging the gap between ideas. Even so, you need to
recognize the danger of destroying your effectiveness through the overuse

[7] *American Issues.* Vol. One: *The Social Record,* ed. Willard Thorp, Merle Curti, and
Carlos Baker (Philadelphia: Lippincott, 1944), p. 1031.

[8] *Vital Speeches,* July 1, 1973, p. 546.

[9] *Vital Speeches,* September 15, 1973, p. 716.

or misuse of the question. Opening a speech with an "Are you aware" question relating to a condition or an event on the level of Columbus' discovery will usually prompt an inaudible but sarcastic audience response.

THE UNUSUAL. The novel possesses limited attention value. Indeed we are incapable of attending to the absolutely new for more than a short period of time. On the other hand, the old soon bores us. But a judicious mixture of the familiar and the unusual with a twist of paradox can produce a lively provocative introduction. Richard J. Babcock, the president of the *Farm Journal*, in the introduction of his speech at Kansas City, Missouri, effectively intermixed the unusual with a paradoxical twist.

> When a Connecticut Yankee comes to Missouri to speak on the subject of agriculture, surely one must wonder if this isn't carrying coals to Newcastle. Perhaps not necessarily so. Way back in 1877 when a forward thinking man by the name of Wilmer Atkinson began to publish a little farm paper called the *Farm Journal* it was dedicated, as he said, "to serving the interests of farm families within a day's ride of Philadelphia."
>
> *Farm Journal* is still published for farm families who live within a day's ride of Philadelphia. Thanks to the jets, that day's ride now includes the 900-odd farm families who read *Farm Journal* in each of our two newest states, Alaska and Hawaii, as well as the 3,000,000 subscribing families who live in the 48 contiguous states.[10]

Favorable rapport

In his first State of the Union message, President Kennedy recognized the necessity of developing a working relationship with the Congress. Calling on his past experience in both Houses, he extended a genuine compliment to members of both parties.

> Mr. Vice-President, members of the Congress, it is a pleasure to return from whence I came. You are among my oldest friends in Washington and this House is my oldest home.
>
> It was here, more than fourteen years ago, that I first took the oath of Federal office. It was here, for fourteen years, that I gained both knowledge and inspiration from members of both parties in both houses—from your wise and generous leaders—and from the pronounce-

[10] *Vital Speeches,* February 15, 1961, p. 269.

ments which I can vividly recall, sitting where you now sit—including the programs of two great Presidents, the undimmed eloquence of Churchill, the soaring idealism of Nehru, the steadfast words of General de Gaulle. To speak from this same historic rostrum is a sobering experience. To be back among so many friends is a happy one.[11]

A year later, facing an even more hostile audience in the Sixty-sixth Congress of American Industry, President Kennedy attempted through self-directed humor and a gentle jibe at his listeners to reach common ground. His frank recognition of audience hostility and his direct appeal for cooperation between business and government "to advance the common interest" was an attempt to secure a fair hearing.

> Mr. President and gentleman. I understand that President McKinley and I are the only two Presidents of the United States to ever address such an occasion. I suppose that President McKinley and I are the only two that are regarded as fiscally sound enough to be qualified for admission to this organization. . . .
>
> I have not always considered the membership of the N.A.M. as among my strongest supporters. I'm not sure you have all approached the New Frontier with the greatest possible enthusiasm and I was, therefore, somewhat nervous about accepting this invitation until I did some history—studying of history of this organization.
>
> I learned that this organization had once denounced —on one occasion, our "swollen bureaucracy" as among the triumphs of Karl Marx, and decried on another occasion new governmental "paternalism and socialism."
>
> I was comforted when reading this very familiar language to note that I was in very good company. For the first attack I quoted was on Calvin Coolidge and the second on Herbert Hoover.
>
> I remind you of this only to indicate the happy failure of many of our most pessimistic predictions—and that is true of all of us.[12]

The forecast

Some speeches leave the listeners with that lost feeling of having just completed a harried expedition through an uncharted Sahara. They

[11] *Vital Speeches*, February 15, 1961, p. 258.
[12] *Vital Speeches*, January 1, 1962, p. 162.

realized simply that they were adrift on a sea of sand, totally devoid of directional markers. The speaker who is careful to state the proposition clearly and who subdivides the topic with an *initial summary* in the introduction takes an effective step in avoiding this "uncharted desert" effect. Moreover, if you can employ some stylistic subtlety in your forecast, you can even heighten the enthusiasm of the audience, creating genuine anticipation for the rest of the speech.

In a speech at Amherst College, Arthur R. Taylor, president of Columbia Broadcasting, used his first sentence to forecast the direction and outline of his speech and at the same time developed his own credibility as an authority.

> Within the framework of the theme of this Colloquium, "What's Worth Doing?," I propose to take a hard, critical look at the American corporation—its virtues and vices, its strengths and weaknesses, and most of all its future— and to consider whether or not the modern American corporation is a place worthy of investing one's life. I've worked closely with perhaps 25 major U.S. corporations —as an investment banker, as a financial advisor, and more recently as an employee. I'm convinced that, on balance, work for the corporation constitutes work worth doing. Let me try to say why.[13]

Any time you omit a statement of your purpose and a forecast of your major divisions, you should be sure that your reason is legitimate. When you face a sharply hostile audience, one you suspect might reject your proposition at the outset, you may want to state the proposition in question form or even omit it completely. Naturally, the development in the body of the speech must conform to the forecast. Few errors in organization are more confusing than to set up one order in the introduction and another in the body.

THE CONCLUSION

Getting off the platform gracefully constitutes a serious problem if the speaker fails to prepare adequately in advance. The feeble, negative, apologetic "thank you" gives the audience a less than satisfactory impression. If you have planned your speech carefully and completed your task successfully, the audience should thank you with their applause.

The conclusion ought to include one or more of the following:

1. A short but complete summary. This is essential in the speech to inform, if the speaker entertains a serious hope that the audience will carry away the factual material.

[13] *Vital Speeches,* June 1, 1973, p. 491.

2. An appeal for increased devotion to an ideal or an institution. The speech to stimulate usually concludes on such a note.
3. An appeal for a change of attitude, perhaps for a specific course of action. In the speech to convince, the speaker hopes to produce a change of belief.
4. A call to action. If you can also legitimately ask for an overt physical response (vote, write, protest, support), the audience response is more easily assessed and may even be more lasting.

The specific types of suporting material for the conclusion do not differ in kind from those used in the introduction. An appeal at this point is usually a more emotional part of the speech, and many speakers rely rather heavily on the epigramatic quotation, a verse, line of poetry, or a directly phrased question. Occasionally a speaker will conclude with an extended illustration whose implications the listener cannot ignore. Above all, the speaker must keep the conclusion as brief as possible. Nothing so exasperates an audience as the speaker who missed a good place to stop. Otherwise excellent speeches are sometimes marred with the anticlimactic "just one more thing," "finally," "and so in conclusion."

THE DISCUSSION OR BODY

The second major division, the discussion or body, contains the full development of the speaker's proposition. In this section you will expand, illustrate, amplify, and establish the validity of your proposition in the persuasive speech or clarify it in the expository speech. The process involves selecting and synthesizing the evidence and dividing and subdividing the supporting materials.

In your final step you will determine the best order for your main heads (major supporting arguments) and arrange each part (introduction, body, conclusion) to give proper balance to the whole speech.

Every good speech is essentially a *one-point speech*. The one point, as we have previously emphasized, is the proposition, thesis, purpose, aim, end, or objective. Occasionally a speaker states the proposition and completes the speech with an extended illustration.

You may also wish to employ the more indirect approach and by implication begin with the illustration and conclude with your proposition. Many speeches to stimulate use this formula. The popular safety slogan, "The Life You Save May Be Your Own" readily lends itself to a one-point development through a single illustration or a series of specific instances, followed with a restatement of the proposition and perhaps a direct appeal.

Main heads and subheads

Every successful speech consists of definite lines of argument (stated or implied) that converge to establish the truth of your one point, the proposition. Most speech propositions, including the one on safety, lend themselves to a major subdivision or two. If your proposition appears to contain more than two or four main heads, you should reexamine your proposition to determine the scope of your speech. Either the topic is too broad or a number of subheadings have erroneously assumed the stature of a main head.

Average listeners are able to retain about three or four of the ideas they hear in a speech. We hope they will remember the proposition and the main supporting ideas. If the major supporting heads for the proposition are phrased clearly and impellingly, listeners should remember these and may even recall some of the subpoints and illustrative materials. We can be sure that with any complex or simple subject where the divisions and transitions are obscure and where the relationships of idea to idea are cloudy, the listener will succeed in carrying home only confusion. The length of the speech in no way determines the number of major divisions. Longer speeches simply contain additional supporting illustrations and facts.

Kinds of arrangement

Probably no two speakers, even when facing the same audience and using the same proposition, will employ precisely the same plan of organization. Your personality, background, and the frame of reference in which you select and evaluate the lines of argument will lend a distinctiveness to your total speech. Still, your purpose, the proposition, and the response you seek from your audience must influence and guide the general overall organization. Moreover, you may even employ several types of organization (discussed below) in the same speech. But if your speech does seem to call for more than one type, you should carefully reexamine your topic to determine whether you are actually speaking to two propositions, rather than to one. Although some intermixing may occur, one of the following methods usually predominates:

Topical
A. Chronological
B. Spatial
C. Logical
   1. Problem-solution
   2. Cause and effect relationships
   3. This or nothing

TOPICAL. Broadly considered, every speech is organized topically. The *main heads*, whether expressing time sequence or spatial, logical, or psychological relationships, are stated as topics. The organizational pattern, frequently described as *topical*, will be discussed with the logical forms of arrangement.

CHRONOLOGICAL. The time-order or time-sequence is easily adapted to the historical subject or to any part of the speech calling for the developmental history of a product, an idea, or a movement. A speech on the customs of the Hopi Indians entitled "The Journey from Birth to Death" covered topically the practices and rites of the tribe and followed an overall chronological pattern: birth, childhood, adulthood, and death.

SPATIAL. As with the chronological method, the spatial is perhaps best suited to the expository (informative) type of speech. A talk on television might employ the time-order plan. A somewhat similar talk might be set up spatially as follows:

    I. Commercial television
    II. Educational television
    III. Pay television

We may also decide, after surveying commercial, educational, and pay television, that our original plan is too broad and decide to concentrate on one of the areas. Clearly any of the three lends itself to chronological development. The spatial order best fits geographical topics and subjects calling for a division of a large area into more comprehensible parts. It is the (1) first floor, (2) second floor, (3) third floor type of speech. Sometimes it is called the *simple list*, which may be misleading to those who fail to recognize that a meaningful spatial, chronological, or logical relationship must exist between the listed topics.

LOGICAL. Speakers often employ the chronological or spatial plans in developing the speech to stimulate or convince. Indeed, Franklin D. Roosevelt's message to Congress following the Japanese attack on Pearl Harbor and President Kennedy's demand for an arms' quarantine of Cuba[14] used chronological order with devastatingly persuasive force. In attempting to demonstrate the seriousness of the farm problem and the plight of the farmer, one speaker organized his speech spatially around three heads:

    I. The commercial farmer
    II. The subsistence farmer
    III. The migrant farmer

In most instances, however, the speaker will use the *logical* or *psychological* development for the speech to convince. Indeed, both forms may appear in the same speech. They are not distinctively different from each other or mutually exclusive. Logical and psychological more accurately describe the phrasing, the use of motive appeals, and the substantive matter contained in the topical heads.

When the speaker attempts to demonstrate the "Why's" of a course of action or attempts to discover the "causes" or the "effects," he or she looks for supporting *main heads* or *topical statements*. The main heads sometime follow a logical pattern and at other times a psychological one with appeals related directly to our wants and desires. Most speeches to con-

---

[14] *Vital Speeches*, November 15, 1962, pp. 66–68. (For the complete text of Roosevelt's Pearl Harbor address see the section "Bringing Print to Life," pages 411–412.)

vince and stimulate contain an intermixture of logical and psychological headings.

PROBLEM-SOLUTION. The logical organization often follows a pattern similar to those we outlined in the chapter on debate.[15] The speaker outlines the *problem* (need for a change) and then presents his *remedy*. Usually both the problem step and the solution are developed topically. For example, we face the problem of finding the kind of educational system that will best enable each child to achieve to the full extent of his capabilities. We may set up the problem as follows:

I. Unusual children both bright and dull, face problems the conventional school cannot meet.
   A. Bright children do not work up to capacity.
      1. They soon get bored and lose interest.
      2. They may develop intellectual sluggishness.
   B. Dull children are forced to work beyond their capacity.
      1. They become frustrated and insecure.
      2. They cease to try for fear of failure.

CAUSE-AND-EFFECT RELATIONSHIPS. Cause-and-effect relationships also furnish the speaker with the main topical heads, the lines of argument for the persuasive speech. Again, we would warn you of the dangers involved in your use of cause-to-effect and effect-to-cause reasoning, urging you to examine carefully the alleged relationships you attempt to establish. It is easy to draw unwarranted inferences from the facts and to conclude hastily that because two events occurred simultaneously or in close sequence, they are joined causally.[16]

When the stock market declined sharply in 1962, laymen and experts alike searched for the probable causes. Since the "crash" came close on the heels of President Kennedy's stinging rebuke of the steel companies' announced price increase, some immediately placed the blame directly and solely on the President's shoulders. A dozen years later, in 1973 and 1974, when the market took a series of dives, the causes cited included the Middle East War, the Arab embargo on oil, the Watergate affair, the lack of confidence in the dollar, and a multitude of others. Rarely is any occurrence, particularly one as complex as a decline in the economy, the result of a single cause.

Unhappily political parties seem to thrive on the oversimplified causal relationship. Following "Cleveland's Panic," for example, the Democrats were labeled as the party that "causes" depressions, until 1929 when the Republicans assumed that unenviable role. Even though three major wars in the twentieth century occurred during Democratic administrations, it is hardly logical, as is often done in the heat of a political campaign, to

[15] See pages 286–289 for a review of the material as related to debate techniques.

[16] Check again the pertinent materials in the section "Debate," pages 294–295, and the section "Finding and Fortifying the Proposition," pages 348–350.

blame the wars on the Democrats. Nor were the Democrats fair in their post-1929 oratory in linking the Republicans causally to depressions.

If we understand the limitations and hazards of causal reasoning, we can employ three types in setting up the organization in expository and persuasive speeches: *effect to cause, cause to effect,* and *effect to effect.*

1. Effect to cause. If you attempt to analyze the stock market decline, you may construct your topical headings and organizational pattern with an *effect-to-cause* structure. The *effect* (Dow-Jones decline) is the *known* element, and you are seeking the possible or probable *causes* (the unknown). Your approach is historical. You are searching for past behavior and events that might have caused present delight or distress.

2. Cause to effect. As you work toward the conslusion of your speech on the stock market, your reasoning may shift. As you present the solution for the bear market, your proposed remedy (the known cause) will lead you to predict improved economic health (the effect). When President Nixon announced wage and price controls, he considered that act a *cause* that would slow down inflation (the effect). The cause in this case (wage and price controls) did not live up to Nixon's expectations due perhaps to other causes that canceled out wage and price controls. In cause-to-effect reasoning you look toward the future, you peer into your crystal ball.

3. Effect to effect. The third approach, known as *effect-to-effect, is a* combination of the first two. The rat has cancer (effect) caused by the application of nicotine tars. Reasoning from this situation, we conclude that nicotine tars will cause cancer in human beings. The *effect-to-effect* relationship then appears as follows: rat cancer (effect) to nicotine tar (cause) leads us to the assumption that nicotine tar (cause) will lead to human cancer (effect). Effect-to-effect reasoning is similar to reasoning by analogy. In urging Bill to attend college, his counselor may have cited the income statistics of recent graduates, inferring that after Bill has attended college, he will enjoy similar pecuniary rewards. In causal terms the outline looks like this: Alumni income (effect) is due to their college training (cause), and if Bill will go to our college (cause), he too will enjoy an income like our alumni (effect).

By setting up a series of cause-and-effect relationships we can construct a chain of circumstances seemingly triggered by a single cause. The familiar nursery rhyme that joins causally the lost kingdom with the need for a horseshoe nail employs a series of effect-to-cause relationships.[17] But we need to remember that such reasoning is no stronger than

[17] For want of a nail, the shoe was lost,
   For want of a shoe, the horse was lost,
   For want of a horse, the rider was lost,
   For want of a rider, the battle was lost,
   For want of a battle, the kingdom was lost,
   And all for the want of a horseshoe nail.

its weakest causal link. The argument falls if a cause is insufficient to produce the desired or alleged effect.

THIS OR NOTHING. The speaker employing this method examines in an expository manner all the possible solutions for a problem. If the listeners accept the speaker's analysis, they are finally left with no alternative other than to accept "This" (remedy) or "Nothing" (the impossible or inadequate solutions). During his campaign for governor of Indiana, Clifford Townsend used this method successfully with college audiences in defending a recently enacted gross income tax law, branded by its opponents as a "gross injustice." Using the manner of an economics professor, Townsend gave every impression of delivering a speech to inform, talking about the general state tax structure and the various methods of increasing state revenues. He examined each potential and actual tax, and by the time he reached the conclusion his listeners suddenly realized they had been placed in a position where they were virtually compelled to accept the tax, despite their opinion that it was grossly unjust.

The primary advantage of this plan is that it provokes no argument but stays on common ground with the audience throughout. The disadvantage includes the danger of missing a possible solution. The audience may also stubbornly reject "this" as worse than "nothing." "Convinced against their will, they hold the same opinion still."

Primacy or recency (anticlimactic or climactic plans)

As you develop your major headings that support your proposition (never more than five for a particular speech), you will want to give careful attention to the *order* in which you marshal these arguments or ideas. The same will hold true for the subpoints supporting each major head.

For centuries classical scholars have puzzled over this intriguing question of where within the speech framework to place the strongest arguments, the essential information, the most potent appeal. Are first expressions or parting comments best remembered or most persuasive? In recent years research scholars, employing controlled experimental studies, have attempted, with only limited success, to solve this ancient riddle. Generally, the ancient authorities took what seemed to be a commonsense approach, advising the speaker to put the weakest argument in the center and close with the strongest.

Modern scholars are not sure. Communication and psychological research up to this point has been inconclusive in furnishing definitive answers, in part because of the difficulty of controlling the many variables inherent in any speaker-audience situation. Where one study will support primacy, another finds recency preferable. Our experience (supported by some research studies) in judging speeches and organizing debate cases would lead us to give a slight edge to primacy over recency in both the persuasive and the informative speeches. In the speech to stimulate, the speaker may wish to build the speech climactically, reserving the strongest appeal for the closing portion. Presumably the audience is "with" the speaker throughout and may even have anticipated the ideas in advance, thereby generating their own enthusiasm for a favorable reception of the strongest appeal. In the informative speech, we probably should present the vital information early in the major units of the speech and in the subunits or supporting units. As you organize your speeches you will want to try various organizational plans, always keeping uppermost in your thinking the particular response you seek from that particular audience.[18]

OUTLINING THE SPEECH

The outline is the speakers' blueprint. No end in itself, its principal purpose is to assist the speaker in constructing an orderly address. Without it, your speech is likely to degenerate into a hodgepodge of unrelated, disjointed ideas. With it, you can determine in advance whether your platform effort will meet the essential rhetorical tests of unity, coherence, and emphasis, and whether you have structured the proposition logically and psychologically for maximum persuasive effect.

Most experienced speakers find it desirable to write out their outlines in rather complete form, making it easier to examine and alter their plans as the situation demands. Through practice and experience, speakers develop those habits of preparation which work best for them. We dare not, however, deceive ourselves with the thought that if we are "full of the subject," little outlining in preparation of the speech is necessary. Exactly the opposite holds true. Indeed, the more information the speaker possesses, the greater the necessity for careful outlining to ensure the transmission of the maximum quantity of information during the allotted time. No matter how astute an authority we may be, we always face the exacting task of ordering our thoughts on paper in outline form. A few rare geniuses may construct and carry outlines in their heads. More often we witness the depressing spectacle of the famous authority, apparently unwilling to take time from research to organize a storehouse of information. The expert often succeeds only in boring and confusing the listeners.

[18] For a summary of research on primacy and recency, see Ralph L. Rosnow, "Whatever Happened to the 'Law of Primacy'?" *The Journal of Communication* 16 (March 1966), 10–13.

A research project on organization conducted at Ohio University by Richard F. Whitman and John H. Timmis has confirmed the importance of message organization in the retention and utilization of information in receivers. These researchers demonstrated that organization is a function of the use to which receivers will be required to put the information—that some organizational strategies are better adapted to certain kinds of tasks required of receivers than other forms of structure. In short, the speaker should carefully consider what he wishes his audience to do with the information he presents before he makes organizational decisions. One form of structure might be more efficacious if a more complex learning outcome is desired for receivers.

Novice and experienced speakers alike usually find it helpful to incorporate most of the following features in their outlines. Your instructor will probably indicate a preference for the inclusion of specific elements. We do not insist on one type of outline as the only correct form. But we would caution that deviation from the following format should occur only after mature consideration.

BEGIN WITH THE TITLE. Although the completed outline and the speech itself begin with the title, the speaker may actually discover the "right" phrasing for the title at any point in his preparation. During the research period it is wise to jot down appropriate wording that will set forth the topic *briefly, relevantly,* and in a way designed to excite the *expectations* of the listeners. Too often the selection of a title is a last-minute affair, resulting in a mere cliché—"The Challenge of Our Age" or "The Hope of the Future." Best titles usually strike a happy medium somewhere between the flamboyantly novel and the prosaically dull.

STATE THE PURPOSE. The necessity of stating in one clear declarative sentence the purpose of the speech may prevent the selection of a subject too broad for adequate treatment. If the purpose is to stimulate or convince, we should phrase the purpose in terms of the specific audience responses we seek. For example,

Speech to Stimulate: "Give generously to the United Appeal." The assumption is that the audience accepts the proposition.

Speech to Convince: "To save your money and your lungs stop smoking now."

In the speech to inform and entertain, the audience response is no less important, but the purpose is often expressed as follows:

Speech to Inform: "To explain the origin, the aims, and the future outlook for UNESCO."

Speech to Entertain: "To amuse the audience with some ways of fooling the faculty and passing any course without cracking the text."

USE INDENTATION AND UNIFORM SYMBOLS. Be consistent throughout. This will help you maintain the logical and normal sequence and will serve as a check on the logical relationships between your main heads and the evidence and reasoning you have used as supporting material. A generally acceptable plan is as follows:

I. Main Head
    A. First supporting division of the main head
        1. Logical subdivision under (A)
        2. Second subdivision of (A)
            (a) First supporting division under (2)
            (b) Second supporting division of (2)
    B. Second supporting division of the main head
        1. Supporting evidence for (B)

> (a) First supporting item under (1)
> (b) Second supporting point under (1)
> 2. Second supporting division under (B)
> II. Second Main Head

The major divisions of the speech—that is, *introduction, body,* and *conclusion*—should follow this general plan, each beginning with Roman numeral I. The actual number of main heads and supporting subpoints will vary from speech to speech, depending on the nature of the subject. It is often wise to include *transitional sentences* between major divisions.

USE COMPLETE SENTENCES. Words and phrases as supporting subpoints are often vague. A full-content outline will enable your instructor to criticize your style and transitional phrasing as well as your overall plan of organization. Experienced speakers may later depend on less than the full-content outline. Many continue to find the discipline of the complete outline a rewarding experience.

EMPLOY DIRECT PHRASING. The outline should contain an oral sentence structure similar to the actual language of the speech. Instead of "Explain Joe's situation at the plant," support for the main head should appear as follows:

> I. Many employees at the Reed Company have fared well.
> A. Let's look, for example, at the case of Joe Moore.
> 1. He has worked for the company for fifty years.
> (a) For the first three years he worked as a stock boy in the lowest paid job in the corporation.
> (b) He was then promoted to the machine shop.
> (c) Three years later he was made foreman over ten men.
> (d) For the past twenty years he has served as the plant superintendent.
> 2. Joe now looks forward to the "Golden Years."
> (a) He owns his home.
> (b) The company will grant him an ample pension when he retires.
> (c) In addition he and his wife will receive social security payments from the government.
> B. (The second supporting subpoint under I.)

ONE ITEM PER SYMBOL. Include only one item in each main head or supporting subpoint. Notice the problem in the following student outline:

> I. Television offers wide opportunities in the future.
> A. It enables Presidents to meet the public in a more personal way than in the radio speech; it has given the nation a better means of securing information; and it has been used as a tremendous aid to teaching.

Obviously subpoint A needs to be broken down into three parts. And probably for an effective speech, each of the "opportunities" needs additional support.

SUPPORT EACH HEADING ADEQUATELY. One of the virtues of the outline is that it enables the speaker to see clearly how much supporting material is included under each heading. If we are dividing a main head, it is obvious that the minimum number of subpoints is two. Even if we are simply supporting with evidence or an illustration, one supporting instance is rarely sufficient. Additional testimony, facts, and illustrations are nearly always necessary to give strength and substance to the speech.

Full-content outline

If you have followed the previously stated instructions, you will have developed a full-content outline and included all of the major and supporting divisions, the evidence, and illustrations. A word of caution, however, about the uses of the full-content outline may be necessary.

1. The full-content outline is *not a manuscript* of your complete speech broken down by symbols and indentation.

2. It should contain the main heads and supporting evidence, but is *not a verbatim report*. Without additional amplification and restatement your speech will sound stiff and will lack life and vigor.

3. Under *no* circumstances should the full-content outline serve as your "speaker's notes."

4. If you need notes, construct a *key word outline,* based on the complete form. Place long quotations and statistics, too complex for memorization, on research cards.[19] This advice on the use of notes, when your instructor permits them, is particularly pertinent for the beginning speaker who should develop an *extempore mode of delivery,* i.e., a thoroughly prepared and practiced speech, delivered with the aid of a few notes, perhaps, but *not memorized.*

The following student outline illustrates many of the foregoing principles. This outline was designed for a five-to-six-minute speech given with the help of visual aid drawings of the phonetic symbols. The speech contains three main heads: (1) Shaw's dream of a new alphabet, (2) a description of the Shaw-Read alphabet, and (3) an evaluation of the new system.

THE ABC's OF SHAW-READ[20]

General Purpose: To inform.
Specific Purpose: To describe and evaluate the new Shaw-Read phonetic alphabet.

[19] See pages 295–297 for a sample research card and suggestions for recording evidence.

[20] Outline prepared by Jayne Ann Richards for Speech 1 at Oberlin College, January 29, 1963.

INTRODUCTION

I. These written symbols [visual aid] you've seen popping up in coded messages on campus this week are not the work of some misguided Greek or Hebrew student.

   A. They stand for the famous George Bernard Shaw quotation—"The more you study, the less you know. Why study?" written in the new Shaw-Read phonetic alphabet.

   B. A study of the essential features of this new alphabet may prove valuable.

      1. We will constantly encounter, as in the past, various proposals for simplified spelling.

         (a) Benjamin Franklin tried to reform our spelling.

         (b) Teddy Roosevelt attempted to force a new spelling system for governmental publications, including Presidential messages.

         (c) *The Chicago Tribune* attempted to promote a more simplified spelling of some words like "thru" and "nite."

      2. As students of speech we are concerned with new methods of improving pronunciation and spelling.

      3. If you take phonetics next year, you can get the jump on the class.

      4. As finals draw to a close you can join your friends in this pleasant form of artistic procrastination.

Transition: What then are the ABC's of the Shaw-Read phonetic alphabet?

DISCUSSION

I. The new alphabet is the realization of a Shavian dream.

   A. In his play, *Pygmalion* and its familiar musical counterpart, *My Fair Lady*, the action centers around a dialectician who could record in his own phonetic system any vowel or consonant sound.

   B. With the trust fund Shaw set up in his will, he provided the finances for the establishment of a new phonetic alphabet.

   C. In his plan for the new alphabet, Shaw characteristically suggested that we scrap our present system and begin from scratch.

      1. The new alphabet was to have 48 symbols, including 24 separate vowel sounds.

      2. Each symbol was to represent a separate sound, pronounced the same way no matter where it appeared in a word.

      3. Shaw asked that the new alphabet be easy to write.

   D. English phonetist Kingsley Read set out to devise the new alphabet.

      1. Read based his work on the Shavian stipulations, corresponding with Shaw before his death concerning the proposed alphabet.

      2. After 15 years, he produced the first sample last November in the form of a transliteration of Shaw's "Androcles and the Lion" with the famous play written in "Old" English on one side of the page and the Shaw-Read version on the other.

Transition: Now, that we've seen Shaw's dream, the plan and the originator, let's take a closer look at the actual changes and the structure of the new alphabet.

II. The Shaw-Read alphabet, following Shaw's stipulations, does start afresh with new symbols and the required 48 characters.

   A. Its "letters"—the most common English sounds—come in several matching-size categories [visual aid].

      1. For example, the voiced consonants—such as "b," "d," "g," "v," and "z"—are known as "deeps."

2. Their voiceless counterparts are called "talls," or "deeps" turned upside down.

B. The most commonly used words in English, "the," "of," "and," and "to" are represented economically by one-symbol forms.

C. It is now theoretically possible to write every word in English just as it is pronounced.

   1. Now, as Shaw hoped, the phonetic vagaries of our language can be eliminated.

   2. It is also possible to do away with Shaw's own favorite example of the phonetic madness of our language.

     (a) He pointed out that "ghoti" spells "fish," pronouncing the "gh" as in "cough" the "o" as in "women," and the "ti" as in "nation."

     (b) Thanks to the new Shaw-Read, "fish" is clearly "fish" and "ghoti" is written "g-hoti."

Transition: Although it appears to be a step in the right direction phonetically, we might look at some of the shortcomings.

III. The Shaw-Read phonetic system seems to have at least four drawbacks.

A. It is virtually impossible to duplicate every sound variation as Shaw recognized when he stated in his will: "I desire my Trustee to bear in mind that the Proposed British Alphabet does not pretend to be exhaustive as it contains only [24] vowels, whereas by infinitesimal movements of the tongue countless different vowels can be produced, all of them in use among speakers of English who utter the same vowels no oftener than they make the same fingerprints."

B. This statement by implication indicates another pronounced difficulty—(pardon the pun) the fact that it is a British phonetic alphabet.

   1. There are obvious differences between British and American pronunciations.

   2. The dialects in our own country pose a barrier.

     (a) A Southerner writing about the "floors" in a house might confuse a Northerner who thought the word being used was "flaws."

     (b) A native of New Jersey might be hard to understand in another part of the country since he might write the name of his state phonetically as "Noo Joisey."

   3. The "old" English alphabet presents words in forms familiar to everyone in spite of local accent.

C. Our friend from New Jersey or "Joisey" would also have trouble transcribing the new alphabet.

   1. As indicated earlier, Shaw wanted to make the system easy to write.

   2. With the Shaw-Read system, however, the writer must lift his pencil after each character of a word, rather than writing them in a flowing script.

D. Several phonetic alphabets already exist, making Shaw-Read just one more system.

Transition: To all the criticisms Shaw would undoubtedly have answered: This standardized alphabet would eventually standardize spelling and pronunciation faster than our present system.

Conclusion

I. Be all this as it may, the Shaw-Read alphabet with its advantages and its shortcomings is a noteworthy addition to our language.

A. Time alone will measure its value.

B. And, anyway, *Androcles and the Lion* makes interesting reading, whether written phonetically or in the "old-fashioned" English.

SOURCES

Fuller, J. G. "Trade Winds," *Saturday Review* (October 13, 1962), p. 14.
Knowles, Melita. "New Alphabet Makes Debut," *The Christian Science Monitor* (September 23, 1962), p. 1.
Read, Kingsley, and Shaw, George Bernard. *Androcles and the Lion.* London: Penguin Books, 1962.
"Oh Pshaw!" *Time* (December 7, 1962), p. 96.

SUMMARY

After you have selected your general and specific purposes and have found the supporting materials (illustrations, facts, testimony) to amplify and illuminate your proposition, you must then turn to the creative tasks of synthesizing and organizing the raw materials. Usually the speech is organized around three major divisions or parts: *introduction, body, conclusion.*

The speaker then must phrase the main headings (two to five in number) that explain or promote the proposition. These topical headings and their subheadings are usually set forth in one of the following arrangemental plans, or a combination of them: chronological, spatial, logical (problem-solution, cause and effect, and this or nothing).

The construction of the outline is an important, vital preparation step. The precise type of outline selected will depend primarily on the subject, occasion, purpose. The *full-content outline,* including the use of complete sentences, direct phrasing, appropriate and consistent symbols, and indentation, serves as the best form for preparation. If the speaker plans to use notes, the *key-word* outline is most satisfactory for the extemporaneous mode of delivery.

QUESTIONS AND EXERCISES

1. How does the quotation by Quintilian at the head of this chapter apply to the study of speech organization?

2. Come to class prepared to read or present a one-minute *extempore* introduction to a speech. Be sure the introduction contains:

   (a) An attention-catcher.
   (b) Direct adaptation to the audience—the answer to the question "Why bring us this subject?"
   (c) A forecast of the general or specific direction of the speech.
   (d) The proposition or purpose sentence. This may appear at a point in the introduction you deem most appropriate. Be prepared to defend your introduction.

3. Select three introductions from speeches in current issues of *Vital Speeches* and, after considering the specific purpose, the audience, and the occasion, determine the answers to the following questions:

(a) Did the speaker cross the cliché barrier? Indicate which phrases were in need of reworking.

(b) Did the speaker omit any of the four elements listed under question 2 above? Was he justified in this omission?

(c) What changes would you have made in the introduction if you had been in the speaker's shoes?

4. Examine the conclusions to the three speeches you previously studied for the structure of the introduction. What type of conclusions did the speakers employ? Summary, appeal, overt action? What changes would you have made in the conclusions?

5. Write three different conclusions to the speech for which you constructed the introduction in exercise 2.

(a) Make the first conclusion largely a summary.

(b) Include in the second an appeal for direct action.

(c) In the third, employ one of the following forms of support: *illustration, rhetorical question, quotation, line of poetry.*

6. Prepare a two-minute, *one-point* speech, using *one* extended illustration as supporting evidence.

7. Work out three possible *titles* for speeches on the following topics. In each case indicate what the *specific purpose, audience,* and *occasion* for the speech is:

(a) Freedom of Speech

(b) Fraternities on the College Campus

(c) The Energy Crisis

(d) Federal Health Insurance

(e) Procrastination

8. Select two speeches from *Vital Speeches* or from a collection of speeches, e.g., Ernest J. Wrage and Barnet Baskerville, *Contemporary Forum: American Speeches on Twentieth-Century Issues* (New York: Harper & Row, 1962). Outline the main speech structure and answer the following questions:

(a) Is the speech organized chronologically, spatially, logically, or psychologically? Is there an intermixture of types?

(b) How would you have changed the order if you had delivered this speech?

9. Attend a public lecture and make as detailed a key-word outline as possible during the address. At your room make a more complete outline, including a critical evaluation of the speaker's organization:

(a) Did the speech have clearly stated *main topical headings?*
(b) Were the *transitional sentences* adequate to bridge the gaps between the main heads?
(c) Was the *supporting material* for the main heads arranged in an orderly way?
(d) If you found it difficult or impossible to outline the speech, how might the speaker have arranged his materials for greater clarity?

10. Select a general topic and then formulate five propositions or purpose sentences which call for at least three different kinds of organizational patterns. Write a paragraph in defense of the plan you selected in each case.

11. Bring to class two examples of *cause-to-effect, effect-to-cause,* and *effect-to-effect* reasoning. Be prepared to defend or question the validity of the causal relationships in each case.

12. In the outline in the text of the "ABC's of Shaw-Read" (pages 382–385), what changes or additions would you make in the introduction and conclusion? Why? For which of the *general speech purposes* is the conclusion best suited? Why?

RECOMMENDED READINGS

BLANKENSHIP, JANE. *Public Speaking: A Rhetorical Perspective,* 2nd ed. Englewood Cliffs, N.J.: Prentice-Hall, Inc., 1972, chap. 5.

BUEHLER E. C., and WILMER A. LINKUGEL. *Speech: A First Course.* New York: Harper & Row, Publishers, Inc., 1962, chaps. 8 and 9.

GIBSON, JAMES W. *Speech Organization: A Programmed Approach.* New York: Holt, Rinehart and Winston, Inc., 1971.

GILMAN, WILBUR, E., BOWER ALY, and HOLLIS WHITE. *The Fundamentals of Speaking,* 2nd ed. New York: Macmillan Publishing Co., Inc., 1964, chaps. 2, 4, and 5.

LOMAS, CHARLES W., and RALPH RICHARDSON. *Speech: Idea and Delivery.* Boston: Houghton Mifflin Company, 1956, chap. 5.

MILLS, GLEN E. *Putting a Message Together.* Indianapolis: The Bobbs-Merrill Co., Inc., 1973, chap. 3.

WILSON, JOHN F., and CARROLL C. ARNOLD. *Public Speaking as a Liberal Art,* 3rd ed. Boston: Allyn & Bacon, Inc., 1973, chaps. 8 and 9.

WISEMAN, GORDON, and LARRY BARKER. *Speech—Interpersonal Communication.* San Francisco: Chandler Publishing Co., Inc., 1974, chap. 5.

Chapter 18

Securing the Appropriate Response

> To study persuasion intensively is to study
> human nature minutely.
>
> CHARLES H. WOOLBERT

Nearly everything we have written up to this point applies directly or indirectly to the securing of an appropriate response from the listener. Most of our speaking during casual conversation, in discussion or debate, and from the public platform has for its basic, underlying purpose the implied or direct intent to persuade. Even in the speech to entertain, we hope to hold the attention of our listeners, to persuade them to relax and to escape, momentarily at least, from their everyday concerns. The *sine qua non* of all human communication is *dialogue,* which must include *feedback.* Thus, in the total communication process the forces of persuasion are in constant operation.

ETHICS OF PERSUASION

As the persuader or as the object of persuasion, we inhabit many different worlds—personal, social, religious, economic, national, and international. In each of these spheres, regardless of whether we relish, despise, or master the theories and practices of persuasion, we find ourselves under the dominion of an inexorable law which says, in effect, "persuade or perish." The voices and appeals are often blatant and crude on the one hand and subtle and sophisticated on the other. At one moment they speak to our noblest stirrings and highest aspirations and in the next they may plumb the depths of greed and malice. While the demagogic madman Hitler preached a doctrine of racial and religious hatred, inspiring his nation to commit genocide, two world statesmen, Franklin Roosevelt and Winston Churchill, drew up the Atlantic Charter, boldly proclaiming "that all the men in all the lands may live out their lives in freedom from fear and want."

In nearly all of our worlds we witness this curious paradox of persuasive perversity and contrasting utility. Our democratic government, dependent for its very existence on persuasive speech, seems to rely on

388

elections, won or lost with half-truths, catchwords, and slogans. Yet through the centuries man has also developed a higher concept of persuasion in the courts, where all men are considered equal and where a man is presumed innocent until he is proved guilty. And while men under the guise of religious persuasion have sometimes put other men to the rack, they have also developed a tradition based on brotherhood, a reverence for human life, and a profound respect for the human personality.

When Captain Robert A. Lewis dropped the atom bomb on Hiroshima, his only words were, "My God!" And following that awesome event came the conviction that the military weapons of international persuasion made any future world war unthinkable, thereby forcing nations to rely on subtler methods of force and on verbal, rather than violent, persuasion. Despite a spate of nasty local skirmishes, including our own direct involvement in Southeast Asia, nations of the world may be grasping, slowly and painfully (often under duress), the inevitable truth that they must talk out rather than shoot out their differences. Robert M. Hutchins wisely observed in "The Civilization of the Dialogue" that "We have reached a point . . . when force cannot unit the world; it can merely destroy it."[1] Even if the United Nations were only a debating society, as some erroneously imply, the concept of a world parliament of men ruled by verbal rather than violent persuasion would in itself justify the UN's existence.

Yet the persuasive techniques and motives, the appeals and devices both brutal and sublime, often become so intermixed and confused that we nearly despair of the persuader and the process. Such dismay is neither modern nor the product of this century. Through the ages men have echoed a Platonic lament, condemning the persuader and the teachers of persuasion as diabolical prophets who make the true appear false and the false seem true. As we have indicated earlier we do not consider every technique and device of persuasion legitimate or ethical (see pages 330–332). At the same time the difficulty of formulating valid generalizations in the realm of ethical persuasion continues to plague the best minds. Most of the persuasive techniques and devices are amoral, unfeeling, subject to the whim of the persuader. The axe can build or destroy the dwelling. Further complicating the process is the utter impossibility of determining absolute "truth."

Our best safeguard against the unscrupulous demagogue is the open and free discussion of all questions. While the courts have imposed limits in cases of slander, "fighting words," and invasion of privacy, a few explosive situations may justify the silencing of a rabble-rouser, but we can, in general, hold that "error" may take the stand as long as "truth"

---

[1] Floyd W. Matson and Ashley Montagu, *The Human Dialogue: Perspectives on Communication* (New York: Macmillan, Inc., 1967), p. v.

is granted equal time. Freedom of speech calls the citizen to an increased responsibility as a critical listener. It should also furnish additional stimulation for those who feel they posses some degree of truth, to arm themselves with skills in persuasion that transcend mere "righteous indignation."

In previous chapters, we have discussed the role of the scientific method and logical proof in decision-making and persuasion. We reiterate our faith in reason. We also indicated the virtual impossibility of separating logical from emotional proof (see pages 350–351). In this chapter we propose to consider those aspects of proof, sometimes considered nonlogical or pathetic, the wants and desires, the motivations which profoundly influence our decisions. When the emotional is blended with the logical, the speaker probably develops the strongest appeal, emotion serving as the catalytic agent, energizing and stimulating us *to want* to make the decision that logically we ought to make. We will consider then the motivating forces in persuasion and their relationship to attention and suggestion.

NATURE OF ATTENTION

In a previous chapter we indicated that attention once occupied a central position in the study of persuasion (see pages 327–328) and was considered by earlier authorities as the actual instrument of persuasion. All will agree that persuasion is impossible without attention, but it is no longer considered the motivating force. More accurately, attention furnishes the atmosphere, the climate, the environment in which persuasion may occur. The securing of attention does, however, constitute the necessary first step in the process. As speakers who would gain acceptance for our ideas we must first capture and then sustain the attention of the audience.

Unless we have established unfortunate reputations for dullness, we may assume at the outset a maximum of listener attention. Some will pay initial attention out of sheer curiosity. All listeners need special treatment if the speaker expects to hold their attention throughout the speech. Thus, an examination of the nature of attention is the first step toward securing the appropriate response.

INCREASED AWARENESS. An object, a figure, a sound, or a movement catches our attention when it stands out in contrast with all background stimuli. Attention in this situation serves functionally to make clear—to make one idea or group of ideas stand out vividly at the expense of all competing ideas.

A SPECIAL BODILY SET. The runners waiting for the shot of the starter's gun illustrate both the bodily set and the purpose of this physical state during periods of attention. The stance enables the runners to respond as quickly as possible. While they are waiting for the shot, their responses to surrounding situations are considerably reduced. They become only dimly aware of other sounds or actions and are only marginally aware of persons nearby who may be talking or moving about. But they are keenly aware of the starter whose every sound and gesture become clear and significant.

Because it is important to the runners to attend, they pay strict attention to the starter. The greater their desire to win, the more closely they are likely to attend. We are not, as public speakers, concerned with winning a race. We are concerned, however, with winning a clear right-of-way to the minds of our listeners. In a sense, the speaker is to the audience what the starter is to the runner. We must somehow make our listeners want to attend because it is to their best interests to attend. To do this, we must overcome the effects of all competing elements in the surroundings and become, in effect, the main source of stimulation. How can this be done? A review of highlights in studies of the psychology of attention will give us part of the answer.

PSYCHOLOGY OF ATTENTION

Attention span

How long can we pay continuous and unwavering attention to a situation? Experimental evidence indicates that the duration of a single act of attention varies in length from as little as three to as long as twenty-four seconds. Most of us attend continuously to a situation for from five to eight seconds. We pay attention in spurts. Between spurts we experience both physical and intellectual lapses. We may blink our eyes and shift position, but are still probably able to get some meaning out of the material under discussion. During the lapses we are also more susceptible to competing stimuli, either external or self-generated. We may suddenly remember the examination we are taking the next hour or decide to start making plans for the next weekend. Moreover, experimental studies indicate that we are capable of absorbing material when delivered to us two or three times faster than any person is capable of speaking. Thus, during every minute of a speech, we enjoy several hundred extra words of thinking time.[2]

The trouble is that members of an audience all too rarely use these "spare" moments for constructive listening. Instead, they pick a gap as a moment to pursue some subject other than the speaker's, and if their own thoughts prove interesting, they may never return to the speaker. The audience is always paying attention to something. We hope that at the conclusion of each ten-second interval the listeners will return to us

[2] Ralph G. Nichols, "Do We Know How To Listen? Practical Helps in a Modern Age," *The Speech Teacher*, 10 (March 1961), 123. See Carl H. Weaver, Human Listening: Process and Behavior (Indianapolis: Bobbs-Merrill, 1972), p. 96.

rather than succumb to more attractive stimuli. We must also remember that the "length" of an expressed thought is still circumscribed by the short attention span of a few seconds. This is true in spite of our rapid potential listening speed. As speakers, we need, therefore, to keep our spoken thought units short, breaking up longer units through appropriate phrasing.

What is ordinarily thought of as continuous attention is in reality the cumulative effect of brief and successive periods of attending. Since attention is not steady but comes in spurts, the speaker must consider the best means of sustaining or renewing the listener's attention. A knowledge of the *factors of attention* should help.

Change or variety

Probably the best method of securing and sustaining attention is through the use of ever-changing stimuli. This change includes variety in *idea, language, voice,* and *action.* Sameness of idea or phrasing and a monotone or static delivery will eventually destroy even the most eager listener's will to attend. The ideas of the speaker, especially the ones he restates for emphasis, should usually contain variety in wording and phraseology.

Vocal variety

Fortunately the speaker can employ changes in pitch, quality, and loudness to sustain attention as well as to clarify meanings and promote emotional responses. He can always attract attention, with a marked or sudden change in voice. But he may also defeat his purpose of sustaining long-range attention unless the vocal variety coincides with the emotional and intellectual significance of what he is saying.

Animation

Each change of bodily position and each gesture serves as an attention-catcher. Our primary concern is that they not only promote attention but also reinforce and amplify the idea and feeling we are attempting to project. Change, not necessarily the movement itself, is the actual attention-catcher. The extremely active speaker, for example, may secure attention by suddenly stopping all action—just as the teacher often catches attention by a lengthened pause in speech.

Repetition

It is difficult to ignore a situation if it is repeated several times at unpredictable intervals. A word or phrase spoken once may not attract attention. The same word or phrase repeated is difficult to ignore. Too frequent repetition, however, may result in irritation, and unless the speaker wishes to irritate his listeners with a particular thought, he should employ repetition in moderation. The reiteration of a word or phrase, accompanied by a change in vocal pattern and reinforced with bodily action, serves both to hold attention and add emphasis.

The speaker then who would gain and hold attention must offer his listener constantly changing stimuli—visual and auditory cues—of differing intensity, animation, and quality. A word of caution, however, may be necessary. Any device used deliberately to secure attention must conform with the customs of the groups and the circumstances of the occasion. Above all, it must tend to promote the general and specific puposes of the speech. The whistle, while appropriate to the basketball court, is probably out of place in the banquet hall.

INTEREST

The factors just considered are largely methods of delivery we use to attract and to maintain attention. Equally important is the public speaker's treatment of the content and the use of supporting materials (see pages 353–357) that will make his listeners *want* to pay continuous attention. All of the previously mentioned factors of attention will remain impotent and short-lived if the content fails to attract and interest.

While content that holds one person may bore another, certain *natural values,* despite individual differences, will tend to stimulate attention in most listeners. We refer to the *factors of interest,* including *vitalness, suspense, conflict, familiarity, novelty, concreteness,* and *humor.* We have already discussed most of these elements (see pages 367–370) but we would emphasize again that unless the speaker can sustain attention both through delivery and content treatment, nothing else really matters. If as speakers we can accomplish this feat, we may then link our proposition to the motivating forces inherent to the theme, and present in the audience. Indeed, as we turn to a discussion of motivation, we shall observe how closely it is related to attention.

THE NATURE OF MOTIVATION

Most human action is based on desire. Much of our so-called reasoning is merely self-justification (rationalization), the finding of good reasons (not necessarily the real reasons) for believing or acting in a particular way. When our thinking and our actions enjoy social approval, are sanctioned by authorities we respect, and are phrased as convenient slogans or in stereotyped words and phrases, we find it easier to justify a course of action or a belief. On the other hand, we find it difficult to carry out an action that lacks social approval. Persons with a strong conscience and keen social awareness may abandon contemplated actions when they fail to secure appropriate social or group approval. Housewives, the advertisers discovered, sometimes hesitate to purchase kitchen labor-saving devices and cooking short-cuts because they feel guilty in their neglect of their culinary responsibilities. By showing the lady of the house how the new method would enable her to spend more time with her family (a legitimate desire), the advertisers managed to soothe the feminine conscience and to win wider acceptance for the product.

The concept of cognitive dissonance set forth by the psychologist Leon Festinger also helps explain the attraction of the housewife's helpers. According to this theory we experience the discomfort of "cognitive dissonance" when we sense a contradiction between our attitudes or beliefs and our actions. When, for example, we fail to practice what we preach, we search for some means to restore a right relationship with ourselves—to relieve the dissonance we feel. Emerson was probably right in branding a "foolish consistency" the "hobgoblin of little minds," but the persuader whose message helps us to rationalize our inconsistencies often gives us the necessary motivational nudge to change our behavior.[3]

We would not want to give the impression that people are motivated solely by desire or that desire establishes credibility regardless of how incredible the situation may be. As Minnick[4] has shown, desire influences belief and action most strikingly when the means for establishing proof are unsure, vague, and uncertain. Where little or no empirical evidence exists, we tend to follow our desires. But even where the situation is uncertain, desire may exert little influence in rendering extreme statements believable. If a particular belief is highly important to us, we tend to look for facts to conform or deny our position. The degree to which wants and desires influence belief will, quite naturally, vary from person to person. We do not deny the strength of belief, but we would caution the persuader that he cannot expect his statements to receive acceptance simply because they are associated with the wants and beliefs of his audience. We must seek as wide a variety of methods and forms of proof as possible to establish the validity of our proposition.

Even so, one of our tasks as public speakers, if we are to persuade, is to align the mode of action or the pattern of behavior we seek to promote in our listeners with the motivating forces that will meet with approval. The approval must come from the listeners and from those persons with whom the listeners will have contact. To accomplish this we must first understand the nature of the fundamental drives that motivate and help to determine human conduct.

FUNDAMENTAL DRIVES

As normal persons, we share many wants, interests, and attitudes. We may or may not recognize their presence or their potency, but nevertheless strive continually for their fulfillment. Some of the basic drives,

[3] See Judson Mills, ed., *Experimental Social Psychology* (New York: Macmillan, Inc., 1969), pp. 213–221.

[4] See Wayne C. Minnick, *The Art of Persuasion* (Boston: Houghton Mifflin, 1957), pp. 198–202.

necessary to our biological existence, include the desire for self-preservation, the relief of hunger, thirst, and fatigue, the need for sexual expression, and the elimination of wastes. We eat and fight illness to keep alive and to perpetuate life. In some instances our strivings are immediate and impelling; at other times they are ultimate and long-range. For example, we save money to buy food, to educate our children, to secure insurance for the accident we hope won't occur, or to devise a scheme for our early retirement with a comfortable income. Of course, our present and future objectives often conflict, and then we face the alternative choices of an early marriage or a career, an immediate position or graduate school.

From the biological drives, we could probably glean a nearly endless list of our specific physiological, psychological, and sociological wants. Vance Packard, in *The Hidden Persuaders,*[5] indicated that the motivation research practitioners attempt to discover all the unconscious cravings and hidden desires that prompt us to smoke, buy big cars (before the energy crisis), and patronize the supermarket. We doubt that the speaker need pursue the subject quite as intensively as the depth psychologists who decided that air conditioning satisfied our unconscious desire to return to the controlled climate of the womb. We even suspect that our purchase of a unit might be the obvious desire to keep cool during hot weather. Still, the speaker needs to study his proposition and its relationship to such widely divergent needs as ego satisfaction, health concerns, reputation, esthetic enjoyment, power, security, ownership, freedom from restraint, and any of a multitude of other wants and value patterns present in the listeners. Most of these fall under one of several categories we shall briefly discuss.

1. PHYSICAL HEALTH AND WELL-BEING. A native speaker from the Far East, addressing an affluent, Western audience, observed pointedly that those listeners who had never gone to bed hungry could not possibly understand the motivations of his people who never have enough to eat and go to bed each night with empty stomachs. Thus, political appeals that appear shabby and destructive to the Westerner may seem bright and attractive to hungry listeners, particularly if the appeals are associated with the improvement of their physical well-being.

At regular intervals, day and night, radio and television commercials seem to proclaim endlessly the efficacy of some product designed to save our teeth, aid our digestion, or soothe our aching heads and muscles. Our relatively recent ecological concerns, designed to eliminate various kinds of pollution, were perhaps even more closely related to saving our bodies and lungs than to preserving the environment.

The twin drives, of course, are not antithetical. We tend to avoid, as much as possible, those situations that endanger our lives or produce pain, hunger, or physical deprivation. As the TV commercial repeats

[5] Vance Packard, *The Hidden Persuaders* (New York: McKay, 1957).

endlessly, "When you've got your health, you've got just about everything." The speaker who can tie the proposition closely to the improvement of our physical well-being or to our desire for economic security and the ability to earn a livelihood has used a powerful appeal.

2. ALTRUISM. Man does not, however, live by bread alone. Deep within each of us is the strong desire to serve others. Sometimes branded as "enlightened selfishness," we actually derive more genuine pleasure from helping others than we receive from the purely selfish desire to "get" for ourselves. The biblical injunctions—"He that loses his life (in service to others) shall save it" and "It is more blessed to give than to receive"— still ring true and carry a powerful message. The appeal to "adopt" or help to feed, clothe, and educate a deprived child here or abroad, the enthusiastic response to the Peace Corps, and our annual drives for the United Appeal are clear evidence of the strong motivation to serve others.

3. MENTAL HEALTH. A series of popular best sellers over the past several decades have attempted to put our minds at ease or assure us that we're all O.K. This eternal search for peace of mind, also clearly allied to our desire for physical security and freedom from worry and fear, bears a close relationship to the theory of cognitive dissonance, discussed earlier.

4. GREGARIOUSNESS. We are by nature "joiners," striving to belong and to be wanted. If possible, we also seek the respect and admiration of our associates. Usually this includes identification with a group enjoying status in the community. Persons in business belong if they are accepted by respectable business or professional organizations. So we have local, state, and national chambers of commerce, medical associations, scientific societies, and service clubs such as Kiwanis, Rotary, Elks, and Lions.

On some college campuses, for a student to belong he or she must receive an invitation to join a fraternity or sorority. On other campuses, it may be the drama club, debating society, or student government that are the marks of status. Children constantly form clubs. If not accepted, they may join gangs. The need to join, *to belong,* is exceedingly important and as a motivating drive can scarcely be overemphasized.

5. SEX. It hardly seems necessary to point to the overworked use of the sex drive to promote TV and print advertising of everything from toothpaste and mouthwash to farm tractors and bulldozers. The use of the sex drive can rarely be employed in platform address as openly as in TV or print advertising, in part because the dramatic, onstage feature is absent in the usual public speaking or discussion setting. Some persons apparently respond favorably to television commercials like the ones picturing the singularly unattractive male who splashes himself with a particular after shave lotion and is suddenly beseiged by a bevy of lovelies. In the more literal surroundings of debate or discussion, the appeals to sex must be more subtle and less blatant.

6. LOVE. Closely allied to the sex drive, love also includes the feeling of patriotism, which may in part be explained as a combination of *love* and *wishing to belong*. The gregarious drive to belong is also coupled with our desire to be loved by someone we love. In a sense, being loved fulfills our desires to belong. It is a need fulfilled in an intimate, personal way. To be scorned by those we love, to feel not wanted, constitutes a cruel punishment. Psychiatrists tell us that the child who feels unwanted, who is not loved, becomes a problem child and a difficult adult.

7. ZESTFUL LIVING. Most of us strive not only to live in peace and security, to be well physically and mentally, but also to live zestfully. Each political party tries to outdo the opposition in promises of "Peace and Prosperity." In one generation it's a "chicken in every pot" and in another it's "two cars in every garage." When we face oil and meat shortages, colder homes, and unemployment, the party in power faces nearly insuperable odds. We not only want clothes, but the latest styles as well, even if blue jeans at the moment happen to represent mod attire. We need shelter, but also want to travel and leave our shelter, even on a go-now, pay-later basis—as long as the payments are easy and we can always return home. In short, we strive for a life that has sufficient novelty to be interesting, that combines safety and security with occasional new experiences.

MOTIVATION IN PUBLIC SPEAKING

Persuasion may occur on an individual or group level, and although there may be no such thing as a "group mind," individuals do behave differently when they are in groups. We need to consider some of the characteristics of the audience, and the way individuals behave when members of an audience.

Conformity of behavior

As we assume a position as the member of an audience, our behavior and our thinking tend to take on the coloring of the group. When we are aware that others are observing our behavior, we are inclined to conform to the standards we think are expected of us. We become less individualistic and more conforming in our thinking and acting. To a speaker's humorous remark we are likely to laugh only as heartily as our neighbors. On the occasions when we miss the speaker's point, we will still laugh a little if everyone around us is laughing. Indeed, in the midst of our laughter, we often turn to our neighbor and ask him to repeat the speaker's humorous quip.

Several psychological studies indicate that we are more inclined to accept the opinion of the majority or the group in preference to the opinion of an expert. Marple found that students on the high school and college levels as well as adults were more strongly influenced by group opinion than by expert opinion.[6] Unfortunately one expert in the "right" does not seem to constitute a majority for the group. We should bear in mind, however, that the older adults in Marple's study were less influenced by the group. Other studies found some evidence to support the stronger prestige of the expert,[7] and while we can draw general conclusions about the nature of the group, we never dare lose sight of the deviants. Group opinion probably plays the strongest role in influencing attitudes and beliefs in most situations, but a particular subject presented by a highly credible expert may very well prove stronger than the group.[8]

Psychology of group behavior

In terms of the psychology of group behavior, we can understand this usual tendency of individuals to conform to the "mode of behavior" of the audience. Students of public speaking, discussion, and social psychology continue to study the behavior of people in groups, and some of their conclusions are especially relevant to persuasion.[9]

1. *People in groups think less logically than individuals alone.* We rationalize, tend to allow desire to predominate, respond more readily to personal appeals, and generally accept specious argument even more easily than we do as individuals.
2. *Persons in groups avoid extremes in judgment.* Unconsciously we tend to moderate our judgments to conform to group standards. At the same time an individual member of an uncontrolled mob may commit extreme acts under the influence and sanction of the crowd that he would not consider committing as an individual.
3. *The conformity of persons increases with group homogeneity.* The more nearly persons are alike in occupation, earning power, and social, political, and religious beliefs, the more readily they will conform as members of the group.

There are, of course, exceptions to these generalizations. Persons disinclined to conform on any grounds would probably continue as nonconformists when in a group. Highly intelligent and well-educated persons are less likely to conform, in part, perhaps, because

---

[6] Clare H. Marple, "The Comparative Susceptibility of Three Age Levels to the Suggestion of Group *vs.* Expert Opinion," *Journal of Social Psychology,* 4 (May 1933), 176–186.

[7] See D. H. Kulp, "Prestige, as Measured by Single-Experience Changes and Their Permanency," *Journal of Educational Research,* 27 (1934), 663–672; also I. Lorge, "Prestige, Suggestion, and Attitudes," *Journal of Social Psychology,* 7 (1936), 386–402.

[8] Jon Eisenson, J. Jeffery Auer, and John V. Irwin, *The Psychology of Communication* (New York: Appleton-Century-Crofts, 1963), p. 234.

[9] See David Krech, Richard S. Crutchfield, and Egerton L. Ballachey, *Individual in Society: A Textbook of Social Psychology* (New York: McGraw-Hill, 1962), pp. 215–273, 383–530, for an excellent discussion of groups and individual behavior in group situations.

they are constantly urged to "think for themselves." Persons inclined to be negativistic might very well maintain and exercise their negativism even when in a group.

One of the tasks of the persuader, then, is to select the motivating drives that are especially applicable to the constituents of a given audience. The previous discussion on analyzing the audience (pages 341–343) should prove useful in directing the speaker in his selection of motive appeals. In analysis of audiences in general the speaker will also discover that the individual in a group is usually more susceptible to the use of suggestion.

SUGGESTION

We can define suggestion as the uncritical acceptance of an opinion as the basis of belief or action. The speaker evokes thoughts in the listener largely through a process of association. The listeners may or may not be aware of the precise process of suggestion that prompted their appropriate response to the speaker's stimuli. Advertising is often pure, direct suggestion; most is largely suggestion intermixed with a dash of the pseudological to "prove" the value of some product to satisfy our needs or whet our desires. After a supposedly scientific demonstration or dramatic skit, the TV huckster proudly announces, "This proves that Ozone Mist restores free breathing in seconds!" Or some confident, but naive, shopper proclaims it the Mist most doctors recommend. Nearly all of the slogans consist of total suggestion, and the best ones prove quite durable, such as "Good to the Last Drop." In the commercial world the huckster's "purpose," as *Time* expressed it, "is to condition customers —recalling Pavlov's dogs which salivated at the sound of the dinner bell—so that they will drool at the sight or sound of a selling gimmick with the symbolism that appeals to the unconscious. M[otivation] R[esearch] practitioners are convinced that most shoppers buy irrationally to satisfy unconscious cravings."[10] Moreover, the concept of *operant conditioning* holds that we can produce behavioral changes by rewarding and reinforcing desired activity.[11] Thus, the speaker who senses favorable audience responses to his suggestions may reinforce that behavior and thereby achieve message acceptance where logic proved ineffective.

Conditioning and motivation research add two additional facets to our understanding of suggestion. First, when listeners respond to suggestion, they do so unwittingly, arriving at the conclusion the speaker had in mind. The second is the close relationship of motivations, inner drives, latent attitudes, and beliefs. For suggestion to operate successfully, the

[10] *Time,* May 13, 1957, p. 51.

[11] Robert S. Woodworth and Harold Schlosberg, *Experimental Psychology* (New York: Holt, Rinehart and Winston, 1960), p. 547.

idea, belief, hidden craving must be present. Suggestion has little or no effect in *changing* beliefs or attitudes. It merely uses already existing motives to promote the course of action the speaker desires. Some guidelines for employing suggestion successfully include:

1. SPONTANEITY. Suggestion gains strength if it appears to originate spontaneously with the listener. "Those are my sentiments, exactly!" spoken by a listener probably means the speaker has applied suggestion successfully. The so-called "hidden" persuasion, popularized by Vance Packard, reveals Madison Avenue's effort to discover the motivational drives mentioned earlier and to associate a product with this drive through subtle suggestion. Sex is probably the most frequently employed appeal, with products designed to make us kissable and generally irresistable to the opposite sex. For example, the advertisement pictures a rugged, virile mountain climber, a deep-sea diver, or racing driver pursuing his dangerous, exciting hobby and then lighting up his favorite cigarette—or better still is surrounded by lovely ladies, one of whom gives him a light.

The more blatant advertisements suggest directly that after using a particular cologne or perfume, it will be virtually impossible to fend off all the ardent pursuers. In the subtler approach, the huckster never says, "You too can be a he-man, popular and successful if you use our brand of shaving cream or liquid beverage." Instead, the concept is wholly *implied* that we too would share something in common with the great athlete or movie star were we to shave with his brand of razor or smoke his brand of cigarettes. If the listener, particularly the sophisticated member of the audience, recognizes the appeal as pure suggestion, its motivational force is decreased considerably.

2. A CREDIBLE SOURCE. It was during the Presidency of John F. Kennedy that the word "charisma" was popularly associated with one of our leaders. That is not to say that many others did not possess that special quality (ethos, credibility, personality, character) that gave them increased power as persuasive speakers. The potency of a suggestion is directly related to the *prestige* of the source. It pleases most of us to know that a prominent industrialist, politician, athlete, or actor holds the same point of view as we do. Moreover, we tend to accept suggestions more readily from persons we admire and respect. We would hope that students of persuasion, at least, would demand that the prominent person be recognized as an authority in the field of thinking which encompasses his testimony. A famous scientist may possess no more than a layman's knowledge in theology, and what a movie star says about the alleged health value of a cigarette is probably less important than the testimony of a physician. Jane Fonda may be a competent actress, but her skills on stage and personal popularity do not in themselves qualify her as an expert in international politics. The opinions of a noted physicist, such as

Hans Bethe of Cornell, on the implications of nuclear energy and fall-out shelters should hold greater significance than those of the manager of a major league baseball team. We often have difficulty, however, when the opinions of the natural or physical scientist come into conflict with those of the political scientist on such matters as nuclear testing and fall-out hazards. As listeners, we need to review the tests for authority. And as persuaders, we can still recognize and employ the prestige of authority without committing the obvious practices of the hucksters. Certainly we must understand and appreciate that better educated audiences are less likely to confuse popularity with authority.

An intriguing concept, long associated with the persuasive impact of "source credibility," has been the so-called *Sleeper Effect*. According to this theory, widely accepted and allegedly verified experimentally, a message sent out by a speaker low in credibility might somehow generate greater impact on the listener after some time delay. We hear a person whose ideas or suggestions we question at the moment, perhaps because we doubt the credibility of the source. Later, for some strange reason, the message takes on for the listener increased significance and persuasive power. In 1974 two psychologists reported their extensive and completely unsuccessful attempts to verify through replication any of the results of previous experimenters. They finally concluded that "if the sleeper effect is alive, we do not know where it is living."[12] In sum, a speaker of low credibility can entertain little hope that his message or suggestions will improve with age.

3. POSITIVE APPROACH. In our discussion of the introduction to the speech (see pages 365–367) we warned about the dangers of negative suggestion. While it may be impossible, as this sentence and the previous one demonstrate, to keep all suggestions positive, persuasion operates most effectively in a positive atmosphere. As much as possible we need to keep the desired course of action uppermost rather than the undesired, lest our listeners perversely decide to taste the forbidden fruit. The parent who warns junior not to put beans up his nose is probably asking for trouble, and the student who says to the Dean of Women, "Of course, you wouldn't be in favor of liberalizing the social rules on campus," is not necessarily right, but to her sorrow may get the answer she demanded. "I didn't do very well on this one," the student says as he hands his blue book to the teacher, thereby implanting a negative suggestion, the one idea he least wants his teacher to accept. The advertiser who declares his product "less fattening" or "less irritating" is in a positively negative fashion suggesting that his product will indeed increase your weight and does contain an irritant.

[12] Paulette M. Gillig and Anthony G. Greenwald, "Is It Time to Lay the Sleeper Effect to Rest?" *Journal of Personality and Social Psychology*, 29 (January 1974), 132–139.

Habits and attitudes

In using suggestion we should avoid violating the lifelong habits or fixed moral feelings of our listeners. Indeed, a suggestion running counter to the listener's deep-seated prejudices or values will have little desired effect. Religious toleration, for example, was brought about in the United States, not by suggesting the "legitimacy" of all religious persuasions or the "shortcomings" of any particular sect, but by convincing each group that a part of his true religion included the concept of tolerance for others. When the notion of tolerance is reinforced with the more selfish wish to preserve one's own right to worship, vote, or speak without undue restriction, the likelihood of establishing tolerance is increased. We need a realistic view, however, and an understanding that the changing of long-standing attitudes or ways of behaving, however socially desirable, is seldom a single-speech accomplishment. We can cite numerous studies to show that attitudes can be modified by a single speech, but more often the way is long and the process slow.

The language of suggestion

What is the most effective way to phrase a suggestion? The difference between the right word and any word, as Mark Twain observed, is the difference between lightning and the lightning bug. The more vividly the suggestion is offered, the more powerful the suggestion. But we need also to consider another factor that on the surface may seem to contradict this idea. In general, a wording the listeners will not interpret as a command will be more effective than a direct wording. Direct commands are likely to meet with opposition. An indirect wording usually includes the speaker as well as the listeners in the recommended action. The speaker who says, "I urge you to join me in signing this petition . . ." will create less resistance and is likely to obtain more signatures than one who informs his audience that "petitions are available—sign them."

Occasionally a directly worded suggestion may be effective. If the speaker is a person who commands great respect and is accepted as a leader by the audience, if the listeners have assembled to hear directions and to follow them, then directly worded suggestions are likely to be effective. In such circumstances the tactful "Let us . . ." approach may be changed to the "Here is what we ought to do" order. A speaker may then conclude the address with a directly worded statement along the lines of "Sign the petition before you leave the hall," or "Do not leave this hall without signing the petition."

Whether the suggested action is directly or indirectly stated, the actual wording should be as specific as possible. If a letter is to be written to a congressman, the name and address of the congressman should be given. If the audience is one not given to the writing of letters, a sample letter may be read or actually given to the listeners. In short, the sugestion should be one readily understood and easily executed.

MOTIVATION AND SUGGESTION

We have considered attention, motivation, and suggestion as three essential and interrelated components for the initiation and direction of the activities of the listener. When, as speakers, we succeed in holding the attention of the listeners and motivating them to act on our suggestions, we have succeeded in persuasion. We may define persuasion then as a process of initiating certain action patterns in our listeners and of blocking off others which might interfere with our securing the appropriate audience response.

Previously we have treated the factor of *ethical proof*—ethos—(see pages 351–352). We need at this point to emphasize once again the potent force in persuasion that is found in source credibility and in the personality of the speaker. When we can, through voice, language, and behavior, succeed in making our listeners comfortable, we have taken the first step toward securing acceptance for the proposition. Attitudes of enthusiasm, combined with sincerity and confidence, if devoid of any trace of cockiness, communicate themselves to listeners. If we can add to these the speaker's reputation for wisdom and truthfulness, listeners will be predisposed to agreement.

Listeners are not usually conscious of their impressions of the speaker's personality. Neither are they generally aware of a predisposition to the acceptance of a point of view because it is associated with a speaker. If nothing is done to disturb this favorable listener state of mind, the speaker will have made effective, even if unwitting, use of "personality" as a factor in persuasion.

DEVELOPING THE PERSUASIVE SPEECH

As we have indicated earlier (see pages 374–379), the speech to convince or persuade may be organized topically according to a logical (problem-solution or cause-and-effect) plan. The speech may also follow a psychological pattern, using a "this or nothing" approach or a greater reliance on blending the emotional with the logical when setting up the main topical heads. In this chapter we have concerned ourselves primarily with the psychological approach and the discovery of the motivational appeals. We would emphasize again the inevitable intermixture of the logical and the emotional and of the necessity and importance of a strong logical foundation for the speech.

By way of review, we would remind the speaker intent on persuasion to keep the following steps uppermost in the planning and developing of his proposition.

1. Secure immediate and sustain long-range attention.
2. Establish audience rapport, seeking a common ground of understanding.
3. Find those main supporting heads that will in themselves touch off the desired response. Support your arguments with evidence, established fact, and authoritative opinion.
4. Make sure the foundation of the speech is logically sound.
5. Seek the motivations (wants and desires) present in the audience that will promote the desired response.
6. Use as wide a variety of appeals (logical, emotional, and ethical) as are appropriate for the subject, audience, and occasion.
7. Use the language of persuasion.
8. Reinforce ideas with appropriate delivery (language, voice, bodily action).

SUMMARY

Our most frequent purpose in public speaking is to effect a change of action or thought in our listeners. While this change appears to be the result of many forces—logical, emotional, and ethical—it is perhaps best accomplished through an appeal to the listener in terms of fundamental human drives. These drives are directed toward the satisfaction of our biological, psychological, and sociological needs and wants. They include (1) physical well-being, (2) altruism, (3) mental well-being, (4) belonging, (5) sex, (6) love, and (7) zestful living.

Persuasion operates in an atmosphere where the listener's attention is focused on the speaker's proposition. Since attention is of short duration, it must be constantly renewed by using the natural *factors of attention*: (1) change or variety, (2) animation, (3) repetition, and through the *factors of interest*: (1) vitalness, (2) suspense, (3) conflict, (4) familiarity, (5) novelty, (6) concreteness, (7) humor.

Intermixed with attention and motivation is the third factor in the persuasion process—*suggestion*. We may define suggestion as the uncritical acceptance of an opinion as the basis for belief or action. A suggestion gains strength when (1) it appears to be of spontaneous origin with the listener, (2) it is associated with a high credibility source, (3) it is presented positively, (4) it does not violate the listener's lifelong habits or fixed moral feelings.

Persuasion is a process, operating through attention, of initiating certain action patterns in our listeners and blocking off others that might interfere with our objectives. Motivating techniques and suggestion, fortified by the speaker's personality, are primary forces in the securing of an appropriate response from the listener.

QUESTIONS AND EXERCISES

1. Prepare a two-to-three-minute speech announcing a forthcoming event on campus. Include several of the *factors of interest* and *attention* discussed in the chapter.

2. Select an advertisement from one of the "slick" magazines such as *Fortune* or *Harper's* and from a "pulp" magazine. Compare the two for the following:
    (a) Basic motivating appeals,
    (b) Appropriateness of the advertisements for the probable reading audience,
    (c) Methods each used to catch attention.

3. Select a speech topic, e.g., School Bussing, Disarmament, United Nations, or Legalized Gambling. Phrase a proposition designed to establish a point of view. In a three-minute speech give the names of three persons you might employ as authorities to back your point of view. Evaluate your three authorities, indicating why their opinions would be persuasive. With what kind of audiences would each witness carry the *greatest* impact? the *least*?

4. During the next round of speeches in class, construct a list of the annoying mannerisms that distracted your attention from the speakers. Make another list of techniques or devices, either in content or delivery, that recaptured your attention.

5. Select a speech designed to change the listener's attitudes that appears in a current issue of *Vital Speeches* and analyze for
    (a) the speaker's use of negative suggestion,
    (b) the speaker's use of positive suggestion,
    (c) instances of direct suggestion.

6. What kind of advertising appeals are most likely to influence you to buy a product? Why? What appeals do you generally object to? Why?

7. Bring to class two advertisements, one illustrating predominantly nonlogical, emotional appeals and the other mainly logical forms of support.

8. Look through a recent issue of *Vital Speeches* for a speech with which you are in complete disagreement. After reading the speech were you more strongly opposed? Less strongly opposed? About the same? Can you account for any shift in your attitude? Did you consider the speaker's general approach to be ethical?

9. Develop a five-minute talk in which you indicate the three main reasons why you decided to go on to college. Analyze each reason for logic and emotion.

10. During the past year you have probably changed your attitude toward different subjects. Think of an instance when a speaker helped to promote this change. How much influence did the speaker's personality play in bringing about this change? In what other ways do you account for your shift in opinion?

11. Analyze five radio or television "commercials" that annoy you. Indicate specifically why. Reword the commercials so that they become more acceptable to you.

RECOMMENDED READINGS

ANDERSON, KENNETH E. *Persuasion: Theory and Practice*. Boston: Allyn & Bacon, Inc., 1971.

BETTINGHAUS, ERVIN P. *Persuasive Communication*. New York: Holt, Rinehart and Winston, 1968.

BREMBECK, WINSTON L., and WILLIAM S. HOWELL. *Persuasion: A Means of Social Control*. Englewood Cliffs, N.J.: Prentice-Hall, Inc., 1952.

BRIGANCE, WILLIAM N. *Speech Composition*. New York: Appleton-Century-Crofts, 1953, chap. V.

EISENSON, J., J. JEFFERY AUER, and J. V. IRWIN. *The Psychology of Communication*. New York: Appleton-Century-Crofts, 1963.

EWBANK, H. L., and J. JEFFERY AUER. *Discussion and Debate*. New York: Appleton-Century-Crofts, 1951, chap. 14.

FOTHERINGHAM, WALLACE C. *Perspectives on Persuasion*. Boston: Allyn & Bacon, Inc., 1966.

HOVLAND, CARL I., IRVING L. JANIS, and HAROLD H. KELLEY. *Communication and Persuasion*. New Haven: Yale University Press, 1953.

MILLER, GERALD R., and MICHAEL BURGOON. *New Techniques of Persuasion*. New York: Harper & Row, Publishers, Inc., 1973.

MINNICK, WAYNE C. *The Art of Persuasion*, Boston: Houghton Mifflin Company, 1957.

OLIVER, ROBERT T. *Psychology of Persuasive Speech*. New York: David McKay Co., Inc., 1957.

REID, LOREN. *First Principles of Public Speaking*. Columbia: Artcraft Press, 1962, chaps. 17 and 18.

Chapter 19

Reading to the Listeners

Bringing Print to Life

> Read, mark, learn and inwardly digest.
>
> BOOK OF COMMON PRAYER

When you read silently, the black marks on the white paper represent one kind of communication. If you add the dimension of human sound and reinforce these symbols with physical action, you will alter substantially the nature of that message. As an oral reader, you may speak your own words or attempt to translate someone else's written thoughts into appropriate vocal and visible symbols. No matter who places the black marks on the paper, reading effectively to others constitutes a highly complex process, a blending of thought, feeling, and technique. It is never solely or even primarily an action of lungs, larynx, and articulators.

To convert the printed word into a meaningful, persuasive, interesting, and perhaps even an aesthetic experience, is the fascinating and practical art nearly everyone at some time attempts in a multitude of ways and in widely different places. For ministers, teachers, lawyers, actors, radio and television personalities, reading aloud is an almost daily part of their professions. Even in the home, we can derive and receive special pleasure from reading good literature to children and to the adult members of the family.

WHY READ ALOUD?

Apart from pure pleasure and the insight into our own lives and those around us, reading aloud is a necessary, integral part of many communication experiences. As a student of public speaking, debate, and group discussion, you will, of course, strive to improve your extemporaneous, conversational mode of delivery, but you will also find it necessary, sometimes preferable, to read from a book or manuscript. In nearly every prepared speech, and even in impromptu situations, you will want to include direct quotations (memorized or read) from prose or poetry that amplify, support, and make vivid your ideas and contentions. In this chapter we shall examine more particularly the techniques of oral reading as they apply to the public speaker, debater, or discussant, rather than to the stage or artistic interpreter, while still recognizing that many of the principles are equally applicable to all forms of oral communication. Those students whose primary interest is in the mass media, radio or television, will wish to give special attention to developing the skills of reading aloud.

Special thoughts and precise words

We often read aloud because another person has written a better story, essay, or poem than we. Or, a distinctively fresh idea couched in epigramatic language strikes us as appropriate and, rather than paraphrase, we read it because the exact words carry the essence and the meaning better than the approximate words. By memorizing the precise phraseology, a practice sometimes used by public speakers as well as actors, we are usually better equipped to tell the story, interpret the poem, or deliver the aphorism. Nevertheless, we are still reading: we are reading from memory—words other than our own. Under these circumstances the speaker approaches the art of the actor or impersonator. Indeed, a study of the greatest speakers of the past often reveals their successful blending of the arts of rhetoric and poetic.

We read not only because we wish to convey the exact *words* or *precise thoughts* of the writer, but also because we wish to make clear our agreement with or our opposition to the writer's opinion. You may embrace his idea or take strong exception to his point of view and then go on to explain, in your own words, why you agree or disagree. To avoid any possible misunderstanding, it is necessary to quote accurately.

Unusual circumstances

On many occasions speakers are justified in using a manuscript; special situations sometimes demand it. Most radio and television talks are read directly from a script, a teleprompter, or both. Rigid time limits and the necessity for some degree of "content control" prompt most stations or sponsors to request a complete script. In times of national emergency where exactness of language is essential, the speaker may ensure accuracy through the use of a carefully prepared manuscript. Presidential addresses in times of national crises call for precise, careful phraseology. In their peace overtures to the North Vietnamese, both Presidents Johnson and Nixon used carefully prepared texts in their public statements. During the Cuban missile crisis in 1962, President Kennedy's nationwide television address marked an occasion when the wrong word or an ill-turned phrase could have ushered in a nuclear holocaust. Reading to a tense world, John F. Kennedy closed his speech with these words:

Seventh, and finally, I call upon Chairman Khrushchev to halt and eliminate this clandestine, reckless and provocative threat to world peace and to stable relations between our two nations.

I call upon him further to abandon this course of world domination and to join in an historic effort to end the perilous arms race and to transform the history of man.

He has an opportunity now to move the world back from the abyss of destruction by returning to his Government's own words that it had no need to station missiles outside its own territory, and withdrawing these weapons from Cuba, by refraining from any action which will widen or deepen the present crisis, and then by participating in a search for peaceful and permanent solutions.

This nation is prepared to present its case against the Soviet threat to peace and our own proposals for a peaceful world at any time and in any forum—in the O.A.S., in the United Nations, or in any other meeting that could be useful without limiting our freedom of action.

We have, in the past, made strenuous efforts to limit the spread of nuclear weapons. We have proposed the elimination of all arms, and military bases in a fair and effective disarmament treaty. We are prepared to discuss new proposals for the removal of tensions on both sides including the possibilities of a genuinely independent Cuba free to determine its own destiny.

We have no wish to war with the Soviet Union for we are a peaceful people who desire to live in peace with all other peoples.

But it is difficult to settle or even discuss these problems in an atmosphere of intimidation.

That is why this latest Soviet threat or any other threat which is made either independently or in response to our actions this week must and will be met with determination.

Any hostile move anywhere in the world against the safety and freedom of peoples to whom we are committed including in particular the brave people of West Berlin will be met by whatever action is needed.

Finally, I want to say a few words to the captive people of Cuba to whom this speech is being directly carried by special radio facilities.

I speak to you as a friend, as one who knows of your deep attachment to your fatherland, as one who shares your aspirations for liberty and justice for all.

And I have watched and the American people have watched with deep sorrow how your nationalist revolution was betrayed and how your fatherland fell under foreign domination.

Now your leaders are no longer Cuban leaders inspired by Cuban ideals. They are puppets and agents of an international conspiracy which has turned Cuba against your friends and neighbors in the Americas and turned it into the first Latin-American country to become a target for nuclear war, the first Latin-American country to have these weapons on its soil.

These new weapons are not in your interests. They contribute nothing to your peace and well being; they can only undermine it.

But this country has no wish to cause you to suffer or to impose any system upon you. We know that your lives and land are being used as pawns by those who deny your freedom. Many times in the past the Cuban people have risen to throw out tyrants who destroyed their liberty.

And I have no doubt that most Cubans today look forward to the time when they will be truly free, free from foreign domination, free to choose their own leaders, free to select their own system, free to own their own land, free to speak and write and worship without fear or degradation.

And then shall Cuba be welcomed back to the society of free nations and to the associations of this hemisphere.

My fellow citizens, let no one doubt that this is a difficult and dangerous effort on which we have set out. No one can foresee precisely what course it will take, or what course or casualties will be incurred.

Many months of sacrifice and self-discipline lie ahead, months in which both our patience and our will will be tested. Months in which many threats and enunciations will keep us aware of our dangers. But the greatest danger of all would be to do nothing.

The path we have chosen for the present is full of hazards, as all paths are. But it is the one most consistent with our character and courage as a nation and our commitments around the world.

The cost of freedom is always high, but Americans have always paid it. And one path we shall never choose, and that is the path of surrender, or submission.

Our goal is not the victory of might, but the vindication of right; not peace at the expense of freedom, but both peace and freedom here in this hemisphere, and, we hope around the world.

God willing, that goal will be achieved.[1]

President Roosevelt's war message to Congress on December 8, 1941, came at a time when democratic civilization faced its severest test:

Yesterday, December 7, 1941—a date which will live in infamy—the United States of America was suddenly and deliberately attacked by naval and air forces of the Empire of Japan.

The United States was at peace with that nation and, at the solicitation of Japan, was still in conversation with its Government and its Emperor looking toward the maintenance of peace in the Pacific.

Indeed, one hour after Japanese air squadrons had commenced bombing Oahu, the Japanese Ambassador to the United States and his colleagues delivered to the Secretary of State a formal reply to a recent American message. While this reply stated that it seemed useless to continue the existing diplomatic negotiations, it contained no threat or hint of war or armed attack.

It will be recorded that the distance of Hawaii from Japan makes it obvious that the attack was deliberately planned many days or even weeks ago. During the intervening time, the Japanese Government had deliberately sought to deceive the United States Government by false statements and expressions of hope for continued peace.

The attack yesterday on the Hawaiian Islands has caused severe damage to American naval and military forces. Very many American lives have been lost. In addition, American ships have been reported torpedoed on the high seas between San Francisco and Honolulu.

Yesterday the Japanese Government also launched an attack against Malaya.

Last night Japanese forces attacked Hong Kong.

Last night Japanese forces attacked Guam.

Last night Japanese forces attacked the Philippine Islands.

[1] The conclusion to President Kennedy's speech and other long excerpts in this chapter are included with the thought that in addition to their illustrative value, they may also be used as practice reading material. Some of the selections in Chapter 7 "Improving Your Voice" may be used for the same purpose. The complete text of President Kennedy's address is in *Vital Speeches*, November 15, 1962, pp. 66–68.

Last night the Japanese attacked Wake Island.

This morning the Japanese attacked Midway Island.

Japan has, therefore, undertaken a surprise offensive extending throughout the Pacific area. The facts of yesterday speak for themselves. The people of the United States have already formed their opinions and well understand the implications to the very life and safety of our nation.

As Commander-in-Chief of the Army and Navy I have directed that all measures be taken for our defense.

Always will we remember the character of the onslaught against us.

No matter how long it may take us to overcome this premeditated invasion, the American people in their righteous might will win through to absolute victory.

I believe I interpret the will of the Congress and of the people when I assert that we will not only defend ourselves to the uttermost but will make very certain that this form of treachery shall never endanger us again.

Hostilities exist. There is no blinking at the fact that our people, our territory and our interests are in grave danger.

With confidence in our armed forces—with the unbounding determination of our people—we will gain the inevitable triumph—so help us God.

I ask that the Congress declare that since the unprovoked and dastardly attack by Japan on Sunday, December 7, a state of war has existed between the United States and the Japanese Empire.

ADVANTAGES OF READING

Accuracy

The manuscript speech has certain advantages over the purely extemporaneous address. The speaker need not worry about immediate word choice, forgetting, or the unintended remark. He can polish his style, avoid grammatical errors, and escape the faux pas or the "slip of the tongue." "Thoughts unexpressed," Will Carleton once observed, "may sometimes fall back dead; But God himself can't kill them when they're said." Jeremy Bentham likewise reminds us that "the turn of a sentence has decided the fate of many a friendship and, for aught that we know, the fate of many a kingdom." No one could gauge the number of votes Thomas E. Dewey lost in Wisconsin when he delivered a speech from the steps of the State Capitol in Madison and inadvertently expressed his appreciation for the opportunity to speak "from the steps of your courthouse." And when President Nixon ran unsuccessfully in 1960, he could never quite escape President Eisenhower's reply to one question: when a reporter asked Eisenhower to mention some state decisions in which his Vice-President played a direct part, replied: "If you give me a week maybe I can think of one." Senator George McGovern's remark during the 1972 campaign that he supported Tom Eagleton 1000 per cent just before requesting the vice-presidential candidate's resignation plagued the Democratic nominee right down to the election. Off-hand remarks with racial or ethnic overtones, like the one that occurred during the Watergate hearings when a lawyer referred disparagingly to Senator Daniel Inouye's Japanese ancestry, do irreparable damage to the credibility of the speaker.

The apt quotation

Oral reading also furnishes the extemporaneous speaker with a more authoritative method of presenting short items, including statistical and factual data. The wise speaker, as we have indicated earlier, should fill his mind with the prose and poetry of the ages as well as with the works of modern authors. Such a practice will help the speaker enrich his own style and will also furnish him with the direct quotations, usually best read verbatim. Occasionally a speaker will quote a point of view he opposes. Such quotations are better read than presented from memory. To read a quotation or to cite statistics directly ensures accuracy and creates a favorable impression (not a false one we trust) of a speaker who has made every effort to present the exact position of a supporter or an opponent. Many listeners, perhaps to their own misfortune, are inclined to accept the published word as the authoritative word.

Lord Halifax, as British Ambassador to the United States, cleverly employed the technique of direct quotation to refute the Nazi point of view and establish his own.

> I take at random a few examples from recent broadcasts. The German radio told you one evening:
> "The British determine Washington's policy. Churchill requests, Roosevelt obeys."
> But a week later the same radio was saying to us:
> "The strategic directions are dictated solely by Washington; Washington orders, Churchill obeys."
> Or there was this:
> "It certainly never entered Churchill's calculations that old England would become a colony of the United States." But a little later Goebbels was saying to you:
> "It must be frightful for Mr. Average American in these days not to be quite sure whether his own nationality is actually Yank or British."

Then you are told that:

"So long as the mothers of the United States are so willing, England will fight to the last drop of Iowa blood." And a few days later we are told:

"Churchill has not yet realized that the United States has resolved to fight to the last Tommy."

Well, if we are going to fight to the last drop of Iowa blood and you are going to fight to the last Tommy, it looks like being a hard war—for Hitler.[2]

DISADVANTAGES OF READING

Lack of spontaneity

If any one of us is suddenly confronted with a deeply moving issue in a public meeting and rise to speak impromptu, our words and phrasing, unless we are overwhelmed by stage fright, will probably sound natural and spontaneous. But if we are suddenly stopped and asked to write out and read our message, we would, in all probability, lose much of the color, vigor, and spontaneity that marked the impromptu effort. Ministers who are highly skilled extemporaneous speakers often falter when they read the Bible, or lose all sense of communication when they insert a written quotation in their sermons. Frequently our own words, when we attempt to read them, sound dull and lifeless, as if they belonged to someone else, and few talks are deadlier or more surely designed to promote inattention than the obviously "read" speech.

Lack of audience adaptation

Sensing boredom in their audiences, extemporaneous speakers, unfettered by a manuscript, can modify their remarks. After receiving the unfavorable audience feedback, they can restate (using different phraseology) or perhaps amplify, employing another illustration. Readers enjoy less latitude. If the words are another's, they may feel compelled to continue regardless of the effect. Excellent manuscript speakers, however, give themselves wide degrees of freedom and flexibility in departing from their manuscripts for extemporaneous or even impromptu remarks. Wendell Phillips, the celebrated nineteenth-century antislavery orator, skillfully developed the techniques of inserting or removing memorized material so that his auditors could not distinguish the memorized from the extemporaneous portions. Franklin D. Roosevelt, a masterful reader, developed the conversational flavor of the "fireside chat" for which he was justly famous. One investigator found that FDR frequently added or

---

[2] From an address delivered at a dinner under the auspices of the Association of the Chamber of Commerce, Baltimore, 1942.

deleted words and phrases from his manuscript during the actual delivery.[3]

Doubt of authorship

The manuscript speaker usually suffers a loss of credibility if the listeners suspect that someone else conceived the ideas and phrased the speech. Ghost writers belong to one of the "oldest" professions, deplored by many under any circumstances, but sanctioned by others for busy executives and persons in high offices whose time demands seem to make speech assistance at least legitimate. For the student such a practice is not only morally indefensible but self-defeating as well. While drawing from and consulting with as many sources as possible, the student must transform the supporting material into his or her own stylistic creation. Your final manuscript in concept, organization, and style must be your own, bearing your own personal mark.

Barrier of notes

Unfortunately the written material, yours or anothers, may get between you and your listeners. Even notes or a key word outline may form a similar barrier for the extemporaneous speaker who risks a break in audience contact each time he refers to his material. The good reader, recognizing the potential dangers, will consistently strive to sustain or reestablish good listener relationships. If the quotation is worth reading, it's worth reading well. All too often the debater or public speaker flings off a quotation, reading it with little consideration for its content or meaning for the audience.

While reading, except for special occasions, may not constitute the best means of communication, it can be made effective if the reader is willing to master the techniques and minimize its inherent disadvantages. Fortunately reading aloud is not without its virtues. We all derive much information and pleasure from manuscript public addresses and frequently need to use written materials for communication. Our concern now is to make the most of these occasions, to communicate meanings, to express feelings, and to use the written page to full advantage.

HOW TO IMPROVE READING

Basic considerations

As we turn our attention to the techniques of oral reading, we need to consider some of the fundamental problems and principles influencing an effective performance.

---

[3] See Earnest Brandenburg, "The Preparation of Franklin D. Roosevelt's Speeches," *The Quarterly Journal of Speech*, 35 (April 1949), 214–221.

1. FEW PERSONS HAVE MASTERED THE SKILLS OF ORAL READING. A few years ago Rudolph Flesch shocked the educational world by telling the experts *Why Johnny Can't Read*. Mortimer J. Adler of the University of Chicago had already discovered our deficiencies, pointing out that even college students and their teachers did not know how to read or, at least, read well below their intellectual capacity. His shocking conclusion was that adults read no better than youngsters just out of grammar school. New techniques for teaching reading may have raised levels slightly, but the important question for us is the relationship, if any, that exists between silent and oral reading skills.

2. LITTLE CORRELATION SEEMS TO EXIST BETWEEN SKILL (SPEED AND COMPREHENSION) IN SILENT READING AND SATISFACTORY ACHIEVEMENT IN ORAL READING. For a number of years all students enrolled in oral interpretation classes at Oberlin College took a silent reading test at the beginning of the semester. A comparison of their scores with their grades at the end of the semester revealed little apparent relationship between silent reading skills and performance in oral interpretation. While this cursory investigation could lay no claim to scientific accuracy, it may point to the fact that these two methods of reading demand widely different skills. Indeed, after we pass the initial reading stages we are systematically discouraged from practicing any form of oral reading. Silent, rapid scanning with no perceptible movement of the lips or tongue is considered ideal for students who must cover vast reading assignments in short periods of time. Correct though this method is for silent reading, the practice may significantly retard the skill of oral reading.

3. THE MATERIAL SELECTED DETERMINES THE MODE OF READING. A cardinal principal of all oral reading requires the performer to adjust his technique to the meaning and mood of the material. The personality of the reader must match as nearly as possible the language and thought of the writer. As a student you will want to select the best in rhetorical and poetical literature, using a wide variety of samples to expand your potential as an oral reader. By testing yourself with all kinds of material, you can determine your strengths and weaknesses in using different types of literature.

4. EFFECTIVE READING, ORAL OR SILENT, DEMANDS A COMPLETE UNDERSTANDING OF THE MATERIAL. Mere pronunciation of the words never represents reading. And just as we have all "read" several pages silently without comprehending a word, so oral readers sometimes "say" the words, but the essential meaning and feeling are neither understood by the readers nor communicated to the listeners.

5. WE READ WITH OUR PERCEPTIONS. Unless our eyes behold the visual image and unless our bodies respond to the auditory, gustatory, motor, olfactory, and tactile sensations that envelop the written symbol, we have failed to catch the meaning or experience the emotion. While perhaps less true for highly objective material than for passages rich in feeling,

we read all materials through our past perceptual experiences. A mathematical equation may leave some cold and others highly stimulated.

6. EFFECTIVE ORAL READING DEMANDS A TOTAL REACTION, A COMPLETE RESPONSE. The reaction, as we indicated in (4) above, must occur at the moment of utterance and requires the precise coordination of body and voice. Reading is an *active process,* demanding complete intellectual and emotional responses to the printed or memorized word.

7. ORAL READING DEMANDS THE SAME SKILLS IN BODILY ACTION AND VOICE AS PUBLIC SPEAKING. Not all written materials, of course, should be read in a conversational, direct manner appropriate for factual, objective sources. Some highly dramatic literature and introspective poetry, for example, might sound ludicrous if so delivered. But in all situations involving oral communication, the same basic skills are employed. The reader, like the speaker, must achieve that high degree of *control, flexibility,* and *responsiveness* in which the audible and visible cues convey accurately the precise meaning and feeling contained in the selection.

8. WE ARE NOT HERE CONCERNED WITH IMPERSONATION OR ACTING. Even though the stage demands the use of memorized material, we are considering primarily the person who reads his own message or incorporates memorized or manuscript materials in a speech. The content may be drawn in part from poetry or prose and many of the finest speakers in history developed a rhetorical style, closely akin to the poetical in the majestic sweep of its tropes and figures, the rhythm and meter of its structure. Lincoln, Robert Ingersoll, William Jennings Bryan, Martin Luther King, Jr., and John F. Kennedy, to name only a few, possessed this quality, and on occasion their oratory touched the sublime as rhetoric and poetic seemed to blend into one. The student of public speaking should search for current and historic literary masterpieces of all types for future use in public address.

Analysis of the written material

Obviously the first step in achieving excellence as a reader is a complete understanding of the written material. Wtih this comprehension should also come a wide discernment of differences, even within the same selection, making it virtually impossible to read all material in the same manner. Naturally, we would not expect to apply the same methods to the reading of prose as we would apply to poetry. Moreover, a prose quotation from Winston Churchill would differ in some respects from one by Harry Truman or Dwight Eisenhower. Even in reading our own material, we must decide what kind of writing we have attempted—its meaning, purpose, and the occasion for which it is intended. Every selection then demands its own specialized analysis and treatment, requiring the reader to go beyond the form itself to an examination of the *logical* and *emotional* foundations.

The logical structure

Fundamental to our understanding of any selection is a complete comprehension of the logical structure and the author's motivations. While recognizing that logical and emotional meanings nearly always overlap, we need at the outset to discover the rationale for the material. We need to ask ourselves these questions:

1. WHAT WAS THE AUTHOR'S PURPOSE? What was the writer trying to accomplish? The general purposes we discussed in our chapter on public speaking (see pages 321–330) furnish a good starting place. Did the author write to entertain? If so, was the topic merely amusing or did we become so engrossed in the material that we forgot the physical world around us? Or perhaps the author wanted to teach, either to impart information or to inspire and convince us to change our way of thinking or behaving.

2. WHAT WERE THE AUTHOR'S MOTIVATIONS? A writer never produces literary work in a vacuum. He or she is often quite literally driven to the desk, drawing the substance from bitter or sweet life experiences, from the stress and pull of the environment. If we can discover the circumstances that motivated the writing, if we know the milieu and ferment, the mental and emotional struggle, we often gain a fresh view of the final literary product. For example, Teddy Roosevelt's best remembered speech, "The Man with the Muck-Rake," delivered in 1906, has never lost its timeliness and will continue to speak to us as long as we endure "mudslinging" politicians, "yellow" journalists, and the selfish, grasping power of the wealthy at the expense of the poor. But to appreciate the motivation that prompted the "Trust-Buster" to tackle this particular subject requires an understanding of the tightrope he was walking between the conservative elements in his own party and the social reformers whose crusades he championed. Roosevelt's analysis in the following excerpt pointed to the twin evils he felt were threatening society.[4]

> At the risk of repetition let me say again that my plea is not for immunity to, but for the most unsparing exposure of, the politician who betrays his trust, of the big business man who makes or spends his fortune in illegitimate or corrupt ways. There should be a resolute effort to hunt every such man out of the position he has disgraced. Expose the crime, and hunt down the criminal; but remember that even in the case of crime, if it is attacked in sensational, lurid, and untruthful fashion, the

[4] For a complete discussion of the logical motivations for this speech, see Stephen E. Lucas, "Theodore Roosevelt's 'The Man With the Muck-Rake': A Reinterpretation," *The Quarterly Journal of Speech,* **59** (December 1973), 452–462.

attack may do more damage to the public mind than the crime itself.

It is because I feel that there should be no rest in the endless war against the forces of evil that I ask the war be conducted with sanity as well as with resolution.

The men with the muck rakes are often indispensable to the well being of society; but only if they know when to stop raking the muck, and to look upward to the celestial crown above them, to the crown of worthy endeavor. There are beautiful things above and round about them; and if they gradually grow to feel that the whole world is nothing but muck, their power of usefulness is gone.

Unless we understand the life-philosophy of the author, we are likely to miss the point of much that he has written. An outstanding example of a reformer whose writings we might misunderstand (and he has been misunderstood) is Jonathan Swift. He wrote his *Gulliver's Travels* to ridicule and reform British society of the eighteenth century, only to have his story become a children's classic. Swift wrote *A Modest Proposal* in an attempt to improve living conditions in Ireland. Unfortunately many persons took him literally and thought Swift to be mad. Said Swift:

I have been assured by a very knowing American of my acquaintance in London, that a young healthy child well nursed is at a year old, a most delicious, nourishing, and wholesome food, whether served stewed, roasted, baked, or boiled; and I make no doubt that it will equally serve in a fricassee or a ragout.

I grant this food will be somewhat dear, and therefore very proper for landlords, who, as they have already devoured most of the parents, seem to have the best title to the children.[5]

3. WHAT IS THE AUTHOR'S METHOD? Closely allied to the purpose and motivation is the method the author chooses to achieve his goal. Is the approach intellectual or emotional? Does the writer appeal to reason or to feeling? In many instances the two elements are so intertwined they seem to defy separation. But if the main appeal is to reason, the writing should contain objective data, cause-and-effect thinking, and assertions supported by facts and inferences. If, on the other hand, the appeal is to feeling, the language should be rich in imagery, a factor we will discuss more fully in the section on the emotional structure.

[5] Henry Craik (ed.), *Swift: Selections from His Works,* Vol. II (Oxford: Clarendon, 1893), pp. 147–148.

4. WHAT ARE THE WORD MEANINGS? Obviously, we can never judge the logical structure of a selection until we understand the meanings of all the words. The dictionary is helpful in giving us the denotative (literal) meanings, but in judging the logical structure, we may also need to understand these words in context and even sense their emotional connotations, and their affective meaning. We will discuss this element later in the chapter.

5. WHAT IS THE ORGANIZATIONAL PATTERN? Constructing an outline of the selection often helps reveal the logical relationships. If you encounter difficulty, it may be that the author's logical thinking was faulty or you may have failed to analyze the selection properly.

6. WHAT IS THE BASIC THEME? The five preceding steps should help the reader understand the author's theme. One of the best methods for discovering the central message is to construct a *precis*, which we may define as a condensation of the original selection to as few words as possible. The *precis* usually runs about one-fourth to one-third the length of the original but still retains its style and organization. The *precis* is probably most useful with prose and less helpful with poetry.

In some writings the dominant theme is presented at the outset. The first sentence may state the theme, and the remainder of the writing may develop it. The passage below is an example of this kind of writing:

> The United States is in sore need today of an aristocracy of intellect and service. Because such an aristocracy does not exist in the popular consciousness, we are bending the knee in worship to the golden calf of money. The form of monarchy and its pomp offer a valuable foil to the worship of money for its own sake. A democracy must provide itself with a foil of its own, and none is better or more effective than an aristocracy of intellect and service recruited from every part of our democratic life.[6]

Occasionally a piece of writing seems to open with the essential thought of the selection. Actually this may serve only as a transitional sentence leading to the dominant theme. Sometimes no one sentence states the major theme. The reader then must synthesize the theme from a number of related ideas found throughout the writing. The following selection from Benjamin Franklin illustrates this kind of writing:

> There are two ways of being happy; we may either diminish our wants or augment our means. Either will

[6] Nicholas Murray Butler, *True and False Democracy* (New York: Macmillan, Inc., 1907), pp. 14–15.

do, the result is the same. And it is for each man to
decide for himself, and do that which happens to be
the easiest. If you are idle or sick or poor, however hard
it may be for you to diminish your wants, it will be
harder to augment your means. If you are active and
prosperous or young or in good health, it may be easier
for you to augment your means than to diminish your
wants. But if you are wise, you will do both at the same
time, young or old, rich or poor, sick or well. And if you
are very wise, you will do both in such a way as to augment the general happiness of society.

Franklin seems to present the entire theme in the opening sentence,
but does not. We might abstract the essential idea in the following statement: "We may be happy either by reducing our wants or increasing our
ability to satisfy our wants. A wise man will do both. A very wise man,
in doing both, will also try to make society happy."

The emotional structure

Few selections are totally devoid of feeling. Even the minutes of a
meeting (wholly objective if they are properly written) carry emotional
connotations for those who attended. Usually the writer creates a mood, an
atmosphere, an attitude or a feeling. In poetry and dramatic literature
this is always true. It is likewise true for speeches to entertain, stimulate,
and convince. Only a most objective, scientific report may lack an emotional appeal—unless it is described as "dreary" for the uninformed. And
for those in the field, it may prove delightfully stimulating, even emotionally irritating.

Just as it was necessary to state the author's theme in as few words
as possible for the logical analysis, so in our search for the emotional
structure it is important to translate the *dominant mood* into a word or
a phrase. Possible terms might include *joy, sorrow, hate, eeriness, anger,
reverence, righteous indignation, respect, trust, "other-worldliness,"
humility, awe,* and any other words that express an emotional state. Sometimes the mood is directly expressed; for example, the author may say,
"It was an eerie night on the moor, a night fit for murder." More often
the writer will describe, suggest, and add detail until we are overwhelmed
with *terror* as we are when we read in Edgar Allan Poe's *The Tell-Tale
Heart:*

No doubt I now grew very pale; but I talked more
fluently and with a heightened voice. Yet the sound increased—and what could I do? It was a low, dull, quick
sound—much such a sound as a watch makes when en-
veloped in cotton. I gasped for breath—yet the officers

heard it not. I talked more quickly—more vehemently;
but the noise steadily increased. I arose and argued about
trifles, in a high key, and with violent gesticulations; but
the noise increased.

In some selections the dominant mood is presented at the outset, while
the theme is withheld until later. Such was the case when Harold Macmillan faced the television cameras immediately following the French
veto of British entry into the Common Market. The prime minister
immediately revealed his bitter disappointment and dismay over what he
and many of his listeners considered the arbitrary and unfair action of
General de Gaulle and the French government:

What has happened at Brussels yesterday was bad:
bad for us, bad for Europe, bad for the whole free world.
A great opportunity has been missed. Now, it is no good
trying to disguise or minimize that fact. What we and our
friends were trying to do at Brussels was something very
creative and imaginative—dramatic. We were trying to
strengthen the whole of Western Europe in a way which
would spread all over the free world.[7]

Robert G. Ingersoll, brilliant nineteenth-century lecturer, an avowed
agnostic, critic of the Bible and the religious tenets of his day, could still
speak to the eternal longings of the human spirit and appeal to the
emotions of his listeners through his compelling use of language rhythm.
Few orators, ancient or modern, were his equal in this respect. In his
"Oration at His Brother's Grave," the mood is set in part by the occasion
but is carried through more impellingly by his poignant combination of
images, which we shall examine more closely in the next section.

ORATION AT HIS BROTHER'S GRAVE

Delivered at the Funeral of His Brother,
Ebon C. Ingersoll,
in Washington, June 3d, 1879

Friends, I am going to do that which the dead oft
promised he would do for me.

The loved and loving brother, husband, father, friend
died, where manhood's morning almost touches noon,
and while the shadows still were falling toward the West.

He has not passed on life's highway the stone that

---

[7] *Vital Speeches*, March 15, 1963, p. 332.

marks the highest point, but, being weary for a moment, he lay down by the wayside, and, using his burden for a pillow, fell into that dreamless sleep that kisses down his eyelids still. While yet in love with life and raptured with the world, he passed to silence and pathetic dust.

Yet, after all, it may be best, just in the happiest, sunniest hour of all the voyage, while eager winds are kissing every sail to dash against the unseen rock, and in an instant hear the billows roar above a sunken ship. For, whether in mid sea or 'mong the breakers of the farther shore, a wreck at last must mark the end of each and all. And every life, no matter if its every hour is rich with love and every moment jeweled with a joy, will, at its close, become a tragedy as sad and deep and dark as can be woven of the warp and woof of mystery and death.

This brave and tender man in every storm of life was oak and rock, but in the sunshine he was vine and flower. He was the friend of all heroic souls. He climbed the heights and left all superstitions far below, while on his forehead fell the golden dawning of the grander day.

He loved the beautiful, and was with color, form, and music touched to tears. He sided with the weak, the poor, and wronged, and lovingly gave alms. With loyal heart, and with the purest hands, he faithfully discharged all public trusts.

He was a worshiper of liberty, a friend of the oppressed. A thousand times I have heard him quote these words: "For justice all place a temple, and all season, summer." He believed that happiness was the only good, reason the only torch, justice the only worship, humanity the only religion, and love the only priest. He added to the sum of human joy; and were every one to whom he did some loving service to bring a blossom to his grave, he would sleep to-night beneath a wilderness of flowers.

Life is a narrow vale between the cold and barren peaks of two eternities. We strive in vain to look beyond the heights. We cry aloud, and the only answer is the echo of our wailing cry. From the voiceless lips of the unreplying dead, there comes no word; but in the night of death hope sees a star, and listening love can hear the rustle of the wing.

He who sleeps here, when dying, mistaking the approach of death for the return of health, whispered with his latest breath: "I am better now." Let us believe, in spite of doubts and dogmas, of fears and tears, that these dear words are true of all the countless dead.

And now to you who have been chosen, from among the many men he loved, to do the last sad office for the dead, we give his sacred dust.

MASTERING DETAILS

After reading a selection and analyzing the author's purpose, background, and method and becoming aware of the dominant theme and mood of the selection, we are ready for the next step—mastering the details.

Word meanings and sensory images

We have already considered word meanings, at least those we can find in the dictionary. But the perceptive reader goes beyond the denotative definitions to look for the shades of meanings, the subtleties, the implications, and the innuendoes. These submeanings are found not only in the connotations of the words, but in the relationship of word to word, phrase to phrase, and sentence to sentence. They are found in the sensory images these words invoke in the reader. Unless we understand the full meaning of the written words and respond to the imagery, we are bound to fall short of knowing the full meaning of what we have read, and, obviously, if we do not understand or sense what we have read, we cannot possibly communicate the meaning and sensation to others. The study of details, then, begins with a study of words and images.

We have already emphasized the necessity for consulting the dictionary for unfamiliar words. We may also need dictionary assistance when familiar words puzzle us by the context in which they are used. But some word meanings go beyond any dictionary. Take the word, "fire," for example. The dictionary lists some ten or twelve meanings but it hardly hints at the terror this word inspires when shouted in a crowded theater.

The connotative meanings in public speeches are somewhat different from those of poetry, since the speaker is addressing a particular audience he hopes will be familiar with the allusions and implications of the words he uses. Joseph Cook, the popular nineteenth-century Boston orator who addressed overflow crowds each week in Tremont Temple and Old South Meeting House, thrilled them with his dramatic, epigram-filled analyses and oracular utterances. Yet a reader of those speeches today will need to examine the social, political, and economic ferment to understand the full meaning of his words. Massachusetts was in the midst of a wild political canvas, trying to choose between Benjamin F. Butler, the Greenbacker famous for his "bloody shirt" oratory during Johnson's impeachment trial, and a hard-money Republican candidate, Thomas Talbot. Dennis Kearney, the San Francisco sandlot demagogue had joined

Butler's forces. With this background information, Cook's opening words take on fresh symbolic and connotative meaning.

> Massachusetts is to give her opinion, before another sun goes down, concerning the hard-money political party, and a cheap-jack and burglar, greenback and greenhorn gang. [Applause.] The first skirmish in the presidential contest of 1880 will be fought in this not thoughtless Commonwealth to-morrow. An attempt is making to use the chair of Gov. Andrew as a block to aid a political adventurer into the saddle of the wild horse of inflation. Sitting Bull, travelling in Massachusetts under the assumed name of Dennis Kearney, appears in Faneuil Hall in his shirt-sleeves, and preaches a crusade of the poor against the rich. Massachusetts weighs him, and finds him first indecent, then blasphemous, then shallow [applause], and last, and chief of all, blood-thirsty.

Affective language

To some words we respond primarily with feeling rather than with thinking—if we can really separate the two responses. Further, we can speak almost any word in a way that makes its significance affective rather than intellectual. But with written language we must depend upon context and word selection to promote an emotional effect. Much of this sensation comes to us in that degree to which we are able to respond to the imagery the author's words are intended to produce.

Kinds of images

Modern psychologists have isolated and added to the traditional five senses. For our purposes, however, if we add *motor* imagery to *sound, taste, smell, touch,* and *sight,* we can probably describe adequately most of the literary images. As you read the following selections, try to discover what sensations you experience. If you feel no sensation at the moment of reading, you are perhaps (1) merely pronouncing the words, (2) unaware of the meaning, (3) unfamiliar with the experience, (4) failing to *react* to the imagery.

AUDITORY IMAGERY. Auditory images cover all the variations of sound, including pitch, quality, force, and duration, coupled with sweetest and sourest of musical notes or noises. Involved too are the onomatopoetic uses of words such as *hiss, buzz, whirr, whine, scratch, snarl, purr.* Re-read the selection by Poe (page 421) and you will notice, in spite of the combination of images, a strong auditory impulse. Or listen with General Douglas MacArthur as he delivered his farewell address at West Point on "Duty, Honor and Country."

. . . I listen then but with thirsty ear, for the witching melody of faint bugles blowing reveille, of far drums beating the long roll.

In my dream I hear again the crash of guns, the rattle of musketry, the strange, mournful murmur of the battle-field. But in the evening of my memory I come back to West Point. Always there echoes and re-echoes: Duty, honor, country.

GUSTATORY IMAGERY. The taste buds are capable of strong reactions, and words themselves can set the salivary glands into action as they encounter the bitter, sweet, sour, or salty. The lines following the first two in the stanza from John Keats' "The Eve of St. Agnes" are rich in gustatory imagery:

> And still she slept an azure-lidded sleep,
> In blanched linen, smooth, and lavender'd,
> While he from forth the closet brought a heap
>   of candied apple, quince, and plum, and gourd;
> With jellies soother than the creamy curd,
> And lucent syrups, tinct with cinnamon;
> Manna and dates, in argosy transferr'd
> From Fez; and spiced dainties, every one,
> From silken Samarcand to cedar'd Lebanon.

OLFACTORY IMAGERY. Many consider the sense of smell one of the most powerful in moving the emotions, perhaps because it is linked to taste as well. In *A Christmas Carol*, Charles Dickens put together a mixture of smells, at least some of which the reader needed to experience to enjoy the description:

> Hallo! A great deal of steam! The pudding was out of the copper. A smell like a washing day! That was the cloth. A smell like an eating-house and a pastry-cook's next door to each other, with a laundress's next door to that! That was the pudding!

TACTILE IMAGERY. *Contact, pressure, intensity,* and extent of *pressure, hardness, smoothness, roughness, softness, stickiness, sharpness, bluntness, clamminess, wetness.* These and countless other words describe our reactions to touch. If as a reader you are responding to the images, you will feel something of the sensations that Robert G. Ingersoll's audience felt during his lecture on "The Liberty of Man, Woman, and Child" as he described the tortures used to punish religious heretics.

I saw, too, what they called the Collar of Torture. Imagine a circle of iron, and on the inside a hundred points almost as sharp as needles. This argument was fastened about the throat of the sufferer. Then he could not walk, nor sit down, nor stir without the neck being punctured by these points. In a little while the throat would begin to swell, and suffocation would end the agonies of that man. This man, it may be, had committed the crime of saying, with tears upon his cheeks, "I do not believe that God, the father of us all, will damn to eternal perdition any of the children of men."

VISUAL IMAGERY. Probably the major element is color, but we also respond to brightness, shade, and line as well. Martin Luther King, Jr., in his speeches employed an abundance of imagery of all types, but one of his most effective was his use of the dark and the light. In his sermon "A Knock at Midnight," he effectively combined both auditory and visual imagery, and his conclusion was a particularly moving use of contrasting visual pictures.

This is our faith. The psalmist is right. Midnight may come, "weeping may tarry for a night, but joy cometh in the morning." With this faith we will be able to move out of the dark and desolate midnight into a beautiful daybreak. With this faith we will be able to adjourn the councils of despair and bring new light into the dark chambers of pessimism. With this faith we will be able to transform the jangling discords of our nation into a beautiful symphony of brotherhood. With this faith we will be able to transform dark yesterdays into bright tomorrows and speed up that day when "every valley shall be exalted and every hill and mountain should be made low; the rough places will be made plain and the crooked places straight, and the glory of the Lord shall be revealed and all of flesh shall see it together." And when this happens morning stars will sing together, and the sons of God will shout for joy.[8]

In a totally different manner Mark Twain employed visual imagery in his after-dinner lampoon on New England weather. In a mock-serious vein he pictured all the distressing features of Eastern weather only to conclude with a brilliant description of his favorite meteorological phenomenon.

[8] The complete sermon taken from a tape recording is in Paul H. Boase, *The Rhetoric of Christian Socialism* (New York: Random House, 1969), p. 171.

Mind, in this speech I have been trying merely to do honor to the New England weather; no language could do it justice. [*Laughter*] But after all, there are at least one or two things about that weather (or, if you please, effects produced by it) which we residents would not like to part with. [*Applause*] If we had not our bewitching autumn foliage, we should still have to credit the weather with one feature which compensates for all its bullying vagaries—the ice-storm—when a leafless tree is clothed with ice from the bottom to the top—ice that is bright and clear as crystal; every bough and twig is strung with ice—beads, frozen dew-drops, and the whole tree sparkles, cold and white, like the Shah of Persia's diamond plume. [*Applause*] Then the wind waves the branches, and the sun comes out and turns all of those myriads of beads and drops to prisms, that glow and hum and flash with all manner of colored fires, which change and change again, with inconceivable rapidity, from blue to red, from red to green, and green to gold; the tree becomes a sparkling fountain, a very explosion of dazzling jewels; and it stands there the acme, the climax, the supremest possibility in art or nature of bewildering, intoxicating, intolerable magnificence! One cannot make the words too strong. [*Long-continued applause*]

Month after month I lay up hate and grudge against the New England weather; but when the ice-storm comes at last, I say: "There, I forgive you now; the books are square between us; you don't owe me a cent; go and sin some more; your little faults and foibles count for nothing; you are the most enchanting weather in the world!" [*Applause and laughter*]

MOTOR IMAGERY. In "A Musical Instrument" by Elizabeth Barrett Browning appears a combination of auditory and motor images as the great God Pan "hack'd and hew'd as a great god can." The empathic muscle reactions we receive while watching an athletic contest shows the potency of this image. Amy Lowell in "A Winter Ride" catches the inspiration of motor impulses, and if we are sensitive to the selection, we experience the muscle sensation too.

Who shall decleare the joy of the running!
Who shall tell of the pleasures of flight!
Springing and spurning the tufts of wild heather,
Sweeping, wide-winged, through the blue dome of light.[9]

[9] From *A Dome of Many-Coloured Glass* by Amy Lowell. Reprinted by permission of Houghton Mifflin Company, Boston.

While reading any material, particularly poetry and drama, we must remain sensitive and alert to discover and to react to the images. Occasionally we may respond to words affectively even though the writer intended them as essentially informative words. Our faulty response is probably a result of the prejudices and stereotypes that are a part of our upbringing. Scientific writing frequently contains words used informatively which most of us use only for affective purposes. If you analyze your material and properly understand the method and purpose of the author, you will not confuse the affective word with the informative word merely because superficially they look alike.

PHRASING

The next basic step, closely related to determining word meaning and imagery, is the understanding of the phrasing. In written language, phrases are usually set off from one another by punctuation marks. But these marks are intended primarily for the silent reader, and the presence or absence of punctuation marks does not determine how we should read a sequence of words aloud. A phrase is a unit of thought. It may consist of a single word or a group of words so related as to comprise a thought unit. Unless we have a thought unit, we have no true phrase. If conventional punctuation is misleading with regard to the thought units, then the reader must establish a "decent disrespect" for punctuation.

The oral reader faces three problems in phrasing:

1. We must determine the units of meaning.
2. We must decide how long a phrase we can legitimately expect our listeners to follow.
3. We must discover how long a phrase we are physically able to sustain.

The reader may occasionally find it necessary to break up a long phrase into two or more subphrases for the practical purpose of presenting the unit of words (thought) without labored breathing. From the point of view of oral language, then, *a phrase may be defined as a group of related words normally uttered without interruption for breath.*

Relationship of ideas

Phrasing, however, includes more than the determination of thought units and appropriate length. The reader must also discern the relationship of unit to unit and to the material as a whole. At this point, then, the reader can decide how much emphasis each phrase should receive in terms of the whole selection. Of course, we must also analyze each phrase to determine which word presents the core meaning. The reader must give special emphasis to the word or words that carry the heart of the message.

Clearly the problem of phrasing is largely one of evaluation. The reader decides on the major units of meaning and the core of each unit. Having made these decisions, we next determine how to communicate the related meanings to the listeners. Unfortunately no absolute rules exist to guide us in our recognition of relative meanings, dominant thoughts, and subordinate thoughts. In general, however, we may assume that new ideas are more important than old ideas. A new idea when read aloud should, therefore, receive greater emphasis than an old idea. We may consider a "new idea" as one introduced for the first time; an "old idea" has already been presented in one form and is now being presented in a different or expanded form. This will become clear in an analysis of the following selection. The *"new ideas" are underlined;* the "old ideas" are printed without underlining.

When I Was One-and-Twenty[10]

When I was one-and-twenty
    I heard a wise man say,
'Give crowns and pounds and guineas
    But not your heart away;
Give pearls away and rubies
    But keep your fancy free.'
But I was one-and-twenty,
    No use to talk to me.

When I was one-and-twenty
    I heard him say again;
'The heart out of the bosom
    Was never given in vain;
'Tis paid with sighs a-plenty
    And sold for endless rue.'
And I am two-and-twenty,
    And, oh, 'tis true, 'tis true.

—A. E. HOUSMAN

Suppose we examine Housman's poem for phrasing. The first phrase, we find, is the entire first line, "When I was one-and-twenty." In preparing to read this selection aloud we might mark off the phrases by placing, tentatively, a vertical mark(|) at the end of each phrase. As we read the selection it becomes apparent rather quickly that all phrases are not of equal weight in their relationship to one another. Some phrases introduce "new ideas," others modify or expand "old ideas." Some phrases appear to be in direct contrast with others; their thoughts are not only "new" but different. In reading aloud to communicate thoughts to another, we may pause after each thought. In general, we pause longer when introducing a closely related idea. As a practical device we might add a second vertical line (|||) to indicate a longer pause before the reading of a new or different thought; the single verticle line (|) may be used to separate phrases that are closely related in thought. The poem with phrase markings and "new thoughts" indicated might be arranged as follows:

When I was one-and-twenty |
    I heard a wise man say, |
'Give crowns and pounds and guineas ||
    But not your heart away; ||
Give pearls away and rubies ||
    But keep your fancy free.' ||
But I was one-and-twenty, |
    No use to talk to me. ||

When I was one-and-twenty |
    I heard him say again, ||
'The heart out of the bosom |
    Was never given in vain; |
'Tis paid with sighs a-plenty |
    And sold for endless rue?' ||
And I am two-and-twenty ||
    And oh, | 'tis true, | 'tis true. ||

We are now ready to reread the selection to determine which words carry the main meanings. As we indicated earlier, these are the basic or core words of the selection. We must emphasize these words so clearly and precisely that the listener will recognize at once the meaning, mood, and image the author of the selection had in mind. We might begin by asking ourselves, "What is the general theme of the poem? What, above all else, does the poet mean by his two stanzas?" The answer might be summed up in two sentences: "At twenty-one the poet was advised that it is easier and less expensive to give material things away than to give his heart away. At twenty-two the poet realizes that he should have followed the advice given him at twenty-one."

Which words present this dominant meaning and which words present the shades, implications, and modifications of the dominant meaning? The important words are those underlined once. These should be emphasized. The key or basic words are underlined twice. Those should be given even greater emphasis so that the listener cannot help but remember them.

THE TECHNIQUES OF READING ALOUD

Thus far in this chapter we have been chiefly concerned with how the reader can make certain that he gets the meaning of what he is reading. Unless the reader understands what he has read, unless he appreciates the thinking and feeling of the author, he has only a small chance of getting the thoughts and feelings across to his listeners. But to have good understanding of what is read is not enough! The effective reader-speaker must know how to communicate his knowledge to his listeners. He must know the techniques of translating written symbols into audible symbols so that his audience can share ideas with him.

Communicative reading

Basic to all technique is the necessity for a clear, vivid portrayal of the author's intended meaning and mood to the listeners. This does not imply that the reader necessarily employ the "conversational mode," a "folksy literalness," or a highly "stylized" dramatic delivery. If we are delivering a speech, the chances are that we should try to keep our reading as close to excellent public speaking as possible. If our purpose in the speech is to entertain, we might assume a "folksy" manner of reading. The interpreter of Shakespeare will probably give the passage a decided dramatic flavor.

Communication is possible only if the reader is thoroughly familiar with the material. Indeed, we must so thoroughly master the word units and thought sequences that it will hardly matter if we lose the place on the written page. We can read from memory or substitute a word of our own for the word we can't find and still keep the proper ideas flowing. We can accomplish this feat only if we have become creative as well as re-creative artists. Taking the work of another, and while remaining as true to the original as is humanly possible, we have, at the same time, read it with the only equipment at hand—our own experience, our own background, our own evaluations of another person's written words.

Mastery of pronunciation

The reader not only should know what the words look like, but also should be certain of the sound of the words. All of us recognize at sight many words we have never attempted to pronounce. The first attempt at pronunciation should not take place before an audience interested in getting ideas. The one final way of preparing to read aloud is *to read aloud*. If doubt arises about the pronunciation of a word, we should consult the dictionary and then say the word aloud several times in the context of the material. An incorrectly pronounced word will distract or confuse listeners and will probably cause them to lose confidence in the reader.

Audience contact

Thorough familiarity with the written material makes it possible for the reader to keep in contact with the audience. The written page, we noted earlier, inevitably constitutes some degree of barrier between the speaker and his listeners. Each time the speaker takes his eyes away from the audience to look at the written material, direct eye contact with the audience is broken.[11] Contact may be maintained by the voice if the reader, knowing what comes next, continues to speak the phrase he remembers as next. Effective reading involves speaking what the eye has seen and the mind recalls. Your eye must jump ahead of your voice. The word *jump* is intended literally, because good reading takes place in jumps or sweeps of the eye. A number of words are scanned, the eye pauses, the mind absorbs and translates written symbols into meanings, and the eyes move onto the next group of words. In oral reading we can train ourselves to take in long phrases quickly without losing the place on the page. In direct, expository material the reader should look directly at the audience frequently and for proportionately as long a period of time as possible. With practice, a courageous reader can learn to spend 75 to 80 per cent of the time in direct eye contact with the listeners, and 25 per cent or less with the written page. But we can develop this skill only if we are familiar with the material, almost to the point of having memorized it.

Almost, but not quite to the point of memorization. Why not complete memorization? The answer is that complete memorization may result in a loss of spontaneity. Memorized reading, to sound conversational and spontaneous, takes more time than most readers can afford. Effective memorized reading must *not sound memorized*. It must avoid sounding automatic and stilted. To sound spontaneous and conversational in reading from memory, the reader must memorize words and inflections and pauses as well as accompanying gestures. Even hesitations should be memorized so that the reading will not sound memorized. This becomes the job of the actor rather than that of the reader or speaker.

Vocal variety

Good reading should be as close to good speaking as the situation permits. Good speaking calls for a speaker's voice that has variety. In an earlier chapter on the components of speech, we related voice variety

---

[11] We do not mean to imply here that every time the reader looks up from every kind of material, he must look directly into the eyes of some member of the audience. With highly introspective, emotional material, the speaker may even avoid eye contact, looking instead, like the actor, just over the heads of the audience.

to meaning and emphasis. This relationship is as important in reading as in public speaking or conversation. Pitch changes, for example, communicate both thought and feeling. In reading aloud, the range of pitch change is generally wider than in conversation. A large audience or a room separating the speaker from the listener calls for increases in any vocal changes the speaker employs.

Fundamentally, all vocal changes depend on the nature of the material and the meaning and mood of the selection. By way of review, we recall that high pitch and wide range are related to heightened emotion; low pitch and narrow range to depressive emotional states. Inflectional changes are used for intellectual implications and to indicate phrasing. A phrase that presents an incompleted thought will end with an upward, or rising, inflection; a phrase that presents a completed thought will end with a downward, or falling, inflection. Aside from phrasing, upward inflections imply doubt or uncertainty, deference, and occasionally weakness or cowardice. Downward inflections, on the other hand, imply completion, decision, certainty, and assurance. The following sentence illustrates the use of inflectional changes in phrasing.

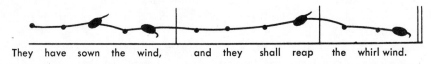

They have sown the wind, and they shall reap the whirl wind.

Of course, these principles are general and every reader must understand his material thoroughly, react totally and completely to the feeling and imagery. Without this total reaction any resort to planned vocal variety will probably produce merely a stilted and artificial sound.

Pitch change

We may give ideas emphasis through the use of *pitch variation*. An important word in a phrase may be emphasized by raising the pitch level of that word above the level of the other words. Occasionally we may emphasize a word by lowering rather than raising the pitch level. This kind of change is especially appropriate if the content is extremely serious or solemn. The essential point to remember is that change or variety attracts attention, and that which attracts attention will likely be remembered. Thus the job of the reader is to use vocal variety, in all its aspects, to emphasize the important content he wants his listeners to remember. The example used above also illustrates the use of pitch change for emphasis.

Rate

The *rate of speech* in reading, especially of prose, is generally slower than that of conversation. This is especially true of material that is read during the course of a speech. The very fact that the speaker has chosen to read something, rather than to present the material extemporaneously, implies that the material is important. Serious or profound matter calls for a slow rate of reading. Solemn content requires a very slow tempo. Content that is on the light side, the gay or trivial, calls for a comparatively rapid rate of reading. No selection of any length should be spoken at a uniform rate. If the general tempo of a selection is slow, the less important ideas will be spoken somewhat more rapidly than the more important ideas. Similarly, if a selection calls for a dominantly rapid rate, the words or phrases that are most significant should be spoken more slowly than the less significant words.

In reading a speech with or without poetry we may vary the rate in two ways. The more usual way is through varying the duration of utterance of the individual speech sounds, especially of the vowels, diphthongs, and voiced consonants. Sentences such as those below from Lincoln's "A House Divided" should be uttered slowly. The underlined words should be spoken at an especially slow rate.

> A house divided against itself cannot stand. I believe this government cannot endure, permanently half slave and half free. I do not expect the Union to be dissolved— I do not expect the house to fall—but I do expect it will cease to be divided. It will become all one thing, or all the other.

The second, and less usual, method of varying rate is through the *use of pause*. When we pause before a word we bring attention to the word that follows. In addition, a pause before a word produces a dramatic effect and creates a state of incompletion or suspense. The state of incompletion becomes satisfied by the word or phrase that follows the pause. In using pause for dramatic effect, the speaker should be certain that what he has to say is worthy of the preceding pause. To pause before the unimportant or the insignificant amounts to making too much out of too little. It reveals poor evaluation on the part of the reader and causes the listener to have a "let-down," disappointed feeling because he was led to expect more than he received.

Pause

To pause after a word or phrase is another method of creating emphasis. This device permits an idea to "sink in" into the listener's mind. Our minds tend to abhor emptiness. If, even for a moment, we hear nothing, we begin to recall the last item we heard. To pause after an item is equivalent to repeating the item, except that the listener rather than the speaker does the repeating.

In Shakespeare's *King Henry VIII,* as Cardinal Wolsey sees the "frown" of the king, hears the taunts of his enemies, and recognizes the incontrovertible proof of his malfeasance in office, he realizes that his personal and political fortunes are at an end. In Wolsey's poignant soliloquy that follows, the symbol (|||) will be inserted where such pauses may be effectively used.

> Farewell! (|||) a long farewell, to all my greatness! (|||)
> This is the state of man: (|||) today he puts forth
> The tender leaves of hopes (|) tomorrow blossoms,
> And bears his blushing honors thick upon him; (|||)
> The third day comes a frost, (|) a killing frost, (|)
> And, when he thinks, good easy man, full surely
> His greatness is a-ripening (|) nips his root,
> And then he falls, as I do. (|||) I have ventured
> Like little wanton boys that swim on bladders,
> This many summers in a sea of glory,
> But far beyond my depth: (|) my high-blown pride
> At length broke under me and now has left me,
> Weary and old with service, to the mercy
> Of a rude stream, that must for ever hide me. (|||)
> Vain pomp and glory of this world, I hate ye: (|||)
> I feel my heart new open'd. (|) O, how wretch'd
> Is that poor man that hangs on princes' favors! (|||)

Again, we would caution that no two readers will read the same passage in precisely the same way and that no particular way is necessarily "correct." Using the above passage, re-mark it to eliminate or add pauses without substantially changing the meaning. Or take the famous lines from George William Curtis' address "The Public Duty of Educated Men" and notice that the following lines may be read with a different inflectional and pause pattern and yet convey the essential meaning. The symbol (|) again denotes a pause.

> Public duty in this country (|) is not discharged, (|||) as
> is so often supposed, (|) by voting. (|||) A man may vote
> regularly and still fail essentially of his political duty. . . .

> Public Duty in this country (|||) is not discharged, as is
> so often supposed, (|) by voting. (|||) A man may vote-
> regularly (|) and still fail essentially of his political
> duty. . . .

When using your own or another's words you need to study the pauses to reinforce and emphasize through meaningful, planned silence.

Force

Changing force or loudness is usually the least subtle way of using voice variety for emphasis. The naive speaker increases the volume of his voice for the important things he has to say and decreases the volume for the less important. If there is no need to be subtle, if a straight story is being read or a simple announcement is being presented, emphasis through change in voice volume is in order.

Although we generally expect the emphasized idea to be spoken more loudly than the unimportant, there are exceptions to this rule. A marked decrease in volume will attract attention merely by the degree of change. If, for example, we read a sentence such as "Please dear, be still" with the last two words barely audible, the idea of stillness is impressed by the lack of force.

The well-trained speaker uses a change of force subtly and sophisticatedly. Deliberate, degree-by-degree change in volume, usually from low intensity to high intensity, may produce a dramatic effect. It is important that the changes in volume are made smoothly, and that the material read is worthy of the technique employed. The effect of a gradual increase in loudness is to point to a climax. The material, therefore, should be such that the final idea at the height of the crescendo is climactic. We occasionally find this kind of material in emotional speeches; more often it is found in drama or poetry.

John Gillespie Magee, Jr., the young poet-flier who was killed in action three days after Pearl Harbor while on duty with the Royal Canadian Air Force, gives us a poem rich in motor imagery. In "High Flight" the entire selection seems to build in intensity, requiring gradually increased vocal force until the reader reaches the last three lines.

High Flight[12]

Oh! I have slipped the surly bonds of Earth
    And danced the skies on laughter-silvered wings;
Sunward I've climbed, and joined the tumbling mirth
    Of sun-split clouds,—and done a hundred things
You have not dreamed of—wheeled and soared and swung
    High in the sunlit silence. Hov'ring there,
I've chased the shouting wind along, and flung
    My eager craft through footless halls of air. . . .

[12] In Hermann Hagedorn, *Sunward I've Climbed: The Story of John Magee, Poet and Soldier, 1922–1941* (New York: Macmillan Publishing Co., Inc., 1942), p. 7. Reprinted by permission of the poet's mother, Mrs. John G. Magee.

Up, up the long, delirious, burning blue
   I've topped the wind-swept heights with easy grace,
Where never lark, or even eagle flew—
   And, while with silent, lifting mind I've trod
   The high untrespassed sanctity of space,
Put out my hand and touched the face of God.

         —PILOT OFFICER JOHN GILLESPIE MAGEE, JR.

Quality

Emotional implications in reading, as in speaking, are projected through *changes in the tone quality* of the voice. The basic quality of the voice is subject to limited modification, and tone qualities are not readily taught. Like emotions, they are more easily caught. A specific tone quality such as we might associate with love, anger, fear, awe, or sorrow is attained through a combination of vocal factors. The combination includes muscle tension of the body as a whole, and the vocal folds in particular, plus resonance and force. The vocal quality suggestive of fear can best be produced when the muscle tensions and "set" of body are ones that are associated with a state of fear. The pitch will tend to be high, and the volume either very great or barely audible. Consider the following passage from Jonathan Edwards' celebrated sermon, "Sinners in the Hands of an Angry God." The empathic reactions of the listener will depend in large measure on the ability of the reader to create the mood through subtle changes of vocal quality.

> O sinner! Consider the fearful danger you are in: it is a great furnace of wrath, a wide and bottomless pit, full of the fire of wrath, that you are held over in the hand of that God, whose wrath is provoked and incensed as much against you, as against many of the damned in hell. You hang by a slender thread, with the flames of divine wrath flashing about it, and ready every moment to singe it, and burn it asunder; and you have no interest in any Mediator, and nothing to lay hold of to save yourself, nothing to keep off the flames of wrath, nothing of your own, nothing that you ever have done, nothing that you can do, to induce God to spare you one moment.—

The use of tone quality as a special device for emphasizing emotional meanings usually appears less frequently in informative speeches, and more often in artistic selections. However, any situations, including dramatic and imaginative prose or poetry and impassioned public speaking with content having affective rather than informative substance, will call for special use of vocal quality. You will want to study and practice the materials in Chapter 7, pages 108–138.

Action

Gesture and pantomime are added means of giving emphasis to thoughts when reading aloud to an audience. Our inclination in reading, unless we have memorized our material, is to use less bodily movement than in extemporaneous speaking. The need, however, is for more rather than less movement. More visible action is needed in order for the speaker to gain a feeling of freedom that is restrained by the need to "stick to the text." Written material, we recall, serves as a barrier between speaker and listener. The use of gesture and pantomime helps to overcome the effects of the barrier.

The ability to execute an appropriate gesture or to use movements of the body as a whole (pantomime) becomes an effective test of our capacity to understand what we have read. Actions are the outer manifestations of inner changes. If we know our material thoroughly, we have experienced thoughts and feelings that have produced inner responses. These need to be translated to outer responses so that the observant listener can react to them and so get meanings out of what is being presented.

SUMMARY

Translating the black marks and bringing print to life through an appropriate use of the audible and visible code provides a vital form of support for the public speaker, debater, and discussant. Occasionally the manuscript or the memorized materials assume a primary role in communication. To read aloud well, using our own or another's material, requires special techniques and energy no less rigorous than those demanded of the extemporaneous speaker.

Perhaps a word of caution is in order. The reader of another's words has an obligation to the author of factual, literal material never to modify intentionally the context or facts so that the reader's wishes rather than the writer's thoughts are presented. This is particularly true in quoting opinion or fact, and the speaker, debater, or discussant who misquotes or quotes an authority out of context is not only morally at fault but loses the respect of the knowledgeable listeners. In the reading of poetry or dramatic prose, where meanings and moods are harder to assess, the interpreter may be granted some degree of "poetic or dramatic license." In reading all materials it is, of course, true that we can interpret only in terms of our own background of experience.

In reading aloud we succeed only insofar as we can react mentally and physically to the logical and emotional impact of the message. Understanding the motivations, purposes, and methods of the author and responding totally to the imagery of the language therefore provide the best guide to accomplishing a safe and honest delivery.

QUESTIONS AND EXERCISES

1. Select a famous American orator of the nineteenth century—e.g., Susan B. Anthony, Lucy Stone, Lincoln, Bryan, Ingersoll, Webster, Clay, or Calhoun—and write a five-minute radio speech on one phase of his or her speech-making. Prepare to read your speech to the class or if a tape recorder is available, your speech may be recorded in advance and played back to the class. Use quotations from the speeches.

2. Find two poems in which the basic mood of the one contrasts with that of the other. Prepare to read them in a manner designed to project the mood of each selection. Be ready to defend your method and explain to the class your techniques.

3. Select a short essay, requiring about five minutes for oral reading, and prepare to read it to the class. As a part of your preparation, prepare the following:

     (a) a *precis,*
     (b) a statement of the author's purpose in writing the essay,
     (c) a list of words whose meanings (denotative) were unknown or not quite clear.

4. Find six selections in either speeches current and historical, or poetry to illustrate each of the kinds of imagery (motor, sound, taste, smell, touch, or sight) and prepare to read them to the class.

5. Cite three works of literature (speeches or poetry) that could not be properly understood without a knowledge of the author's life. Prepare to read one of these selections aloud to the class.

6. Work out a short story in pantomime. Using no words, set up a short scene (two or three minutes) and try to convey the meaning solely through facial expression, gesture, and bodily action. The class may attempt to discover what "idea" or "situation" you are portraying.

7. Write out and read to the class a description (with or without dialogue) of the story or event you acted out in pantomime. How much of the physical activity of the pantomime carried over to the oral reading?

8. Watch a television news reporter read the news. Write a short critique including the following judgments:

     (a) his freedom or lack of freedom from the manuscript,
     (b) his use of phrasing,
     (c) the transmission of meanings.

9. Analyze a speech for the use of *affective language.* Compare the affective meaning the author has given the words with the literal meaning or meanings.

10. Prepare to read a literary essay from the works of a prominent nineteenth-century essayist. For your preparation, determine the author's purpose, his method, and the central theme of the essay. Write his theme in a brief sentence.

RECOMMENDED READINGS

AGGERTT, OTIS J., and ELBERT R. BOWEN. *Communicative Reading,* 3rd ed. New York: Macmillan Publishing Co., Inc., 1972.

BELOOF, ROBERT. *The Performing Voice in Literature.* Boston: Little, Brown and Company, 1966.

COBIN, MARTIN. *Theory and Technique of Interpretation.* Englewood Cliffs, N.J.: Prentice-Hall, Inc., 1959.

GRIMES, WILMA H., and ALETHEA S. MATTINGLY. *Interpretation.* San Francisco: Wadsworth Publishing Co., Inc., 1961, chap. 4.

LEE, CHARLOTTE I. *Oral Interpretation,* 4th ed. Boston: Houghton Mifflin Company, 1971, chaps. 6, 7, and 8.

LOWERY, SARA, and GERTRUDE JOHNSON. *Interpretative Reading.* New York: Appleton-Century-Crofts, 1953.

MACLAY, JOANNA H., and THOMAS O. SLOAN. *Interpretation: An Approach to the Study of Literature.* New York: Random House, Inc., 1972, chap. 2.

PALMER, RICHARD E. *Hermeneutics.* Evanston, Ill.: Northwestern University Press, 1969, chap. 2.

PARRISH, WAYLAND MAXFIELD. *Reading Aloud.* New York: The Ronald Press Company, 1953.

WOOLBERT, CHARLES H., and SEVERINA E. NELSON. *The Art of Interpretative Speech.* New York: Appleton-Century-Crofts, 1956.

Index